PAUL'S TRUE RHETORIC

Emory Studies in Early Christianity

The cover design introduces an environment for disciplined creativity. The seven squares superimposed over one another represent multiple arenas for programmatic research, analysis, and interpretation. The area in the center, common to all the arena, is like the area that provides the unity for a volume in the series. The small square in the center of the squares denotes a paragraph, page, or other unit of text. The two lines that extend out from the small square, perpendicular to one another, create an opening to territory not covered by any of the multiple squares. These lines have the potential to create yet another square of the same or different size that would be a new arena for research, analysis, and interpretation.

Emory Studies in Early Christianity

Volumes in this series investigate early Christian literature in the context of Mediterranean literature, religion, society, and culture. The authors use interdisciplinary methods informed by social, rhetorical, literary, and anthropological approaches to move beyond limits within traditional literary-historical investigations. The studies presuppose that Christianity began as a Jewish movement in various geographical, political, economic, and social locations in the Greco-Roman world.

*The second and third volumes were published by and are available from Peter Lang Publishing, Inc., 275 Seventh Avenue, 28th Floor, New York, NY 10001-6708; (212) 647-7700; FAX (212) 647-7707; customer service (800) 770-5264, (212) 647-7706.

All other volumes are available through Trinity Press International.

PAUL'S TRUE RHETORIC

RHETORIC

Ambiguity, Cunning, and Deception
in Greece and Rome

Mark D. Given

TRINITY PRESS INTERNATIONAL

Trinity Press International, P.O. Box 1321, Harrisburg, PA 17105

Trinity Press International is a division of the Morehouse Group.

Cover design: Laurie Westhafer

Library of Congress Cataloging-in-Publication Data

Given, Mark Douglas
    Paul's true rhetoric: ambiguity, cunning, and deception in Greece and Rome / Mark D. Given
        p. cm.
    Includes bibliographical references and index.
    ISBN 1-56338-341-1 (alk. paper)
    1. Bible. N.T. Epistles of Paul–Language, style. 2. Bible. N.T. Acts XVII–Criticism, interpretation, etc. 3. Rhetoric in the Bible. 4. Rhetoric, Ancient. 5. Sophists (Greek philosophy). I. Title.

BS2655.L3 G58 2001
227.'066–dc21

2001027485

Printed in the United States of America

01   02   03   04   05   06   10   9   8   7   6   5   4   3   2   1

To my wife, Janet,
my mom, Lola,
and in memory of my dad, James Bruce

...he is accounted most skilled in this art
who speaks in a manner worthy of his subject
and yet is able to discover in it
topics which are nowise the same as those used by others.
—Isocrates (*Against the Sophists*, 12)

For what makes you so special?
And what do you have that you did not receive?
and if indeed you received it,
why boast as if you did not receive it?
—Paul (1 Cor 4:7)

Contents

Recognitions

This text is a revised version of my doctoral dissertation for the University of North Carolina at Chapel Hill, and I wish to begin by thanking the readers who served on my dissertation committee: Tom Cohen, Bart Ehrman, Richard Hays, Dale Martin, and Paul Meyer. Each in his own unique way contributed not only to strengthening this project, but also to my development as a scholar by being an exemplary teacher, researcher, and writer. Above all, I wish to thank my advisor, Bart, who faithfully guided me through all the stages of my graduate work at Chapel Hill. My debts to Bart are too many to list. While I was working on this project, he encouraged when I was frustrated and criticized when I was content. In short, he was and is the ideal *Doctorvater*. Nor will I try to express my fondness and respect for each of these scholars. Suffice it to say, all have saved me from some egregious mistakes, but all have allowed me the freedom to persist in my own errors. They are in no way responsible for any remaining "deceptions."

I want to thank Vernon Robbins, who served as my mentor when I received an SBL Regional Scholar Award in 1996, and who encouraged me to submit this study for inclusion in *Emory Studies in Early Christianity*. His excitement about publishing my work made the task of revising and polishing the manuscript more bearable. And here I should also thank my editors at TPI, Henry Carrigan and Laura Hudson, for patiently and competently guiding a novice writer through his first major publishing experience.

I also want to thank all the members of the Department of Religious Studies at Southwest Missouri State University, and all the rest of our new friends in Springfield, Missouri, for their friendship and support. Special thanks go to Jim Moyer (department head), Charlie Hedrick, Victor Matthews, and Russ McCutcheon, all of whom know how to shepherd junior faculty members. Thanks also to the Rev. George Latimer and our entire South Street Christian Church (Disciples of Christ) family, who quickly embraced me as their new organist and my wife Janet as their new associate minister.

Finally, and most importantly, thanks to those whose names appear in the dedication. More than those I have named and others I could have named — you know who you are — they made this work possible.

Abbreviations

AB	Anchor Bible
ABD	*Anchor Bible Dictionary.* Edited by D. N. Freeman. 6 vols. New York, 1992.
ABR	*Australian Biblical Review*
AnBib	Analecta biblica
ANRW	*Aufstieg und Niedergang der römischen Welt: Geschichte und Kultur Roms im Spiegel der neueren Forschung*
ASNU	Acta seminarii neotestamentici upsaliensis
BAGD	Bauer, W., W. F. Arndt, F. W. Gingrich, and F. W. Danker. *Greek-English Lexicon of the New Testament and Other Early Christian Literature.* 2d ed. Chicago, 1979.
BDB	Brown, F., S. R. Driver, and C. A. Briggs. *A Hebrew and English Lexicon of the Old Testament.* Oxford, 1907.
BHT	Beiträge zur historischen Theologie
BJRL	*Bulletin of the John Rylands University Library of Manchester*
Bib	*Biblica*
BibInt	*Biblical Interpretation*
BNTC	Black's New Testament Commentaries
BTB	*Biblical Theology Bulletin*
BZ	*Biblische Zeitschrift*
CBET	Contributions to Biblical Exegesis and Theology
CBQ	*Catholic Biblical Quarterly*
CRBR	*Critical Review of Books*
CTM	*Concordia Theological Monthly*
DSS	Dead Sea Scrolls
ESCJ	Etudes sur le christianisme et le judaïsme
ESEC	Emory Studies in Early Christianity
EDNT	*Exegetical Dictionary of the New Testament.* Edited by H. Balz, G. Schneider. English Translation. Grand Rapids, 1990–1993.

ExpTim	*Expository Times*
FF	Foundations and Facets
FRLANT	Forschungen zur Religion und Literatur des Alten und Neuen Testaments
HBC	*Harper's Bible Commentary.* Edited by J. L. Mays et al. San Francisco, 1988.
HNTC	Harper's New Testament Commentaries
HTR	*Harvard Theological Review*
HUT	Hermeneutische Untersuchungen zur Theologie
IBC	Interpretation: A Bible Commentary for Teaching and Preaching
ICC	International Critical Commentary
Int	*Interpretation*
JAAR	*Journal of the American Academy of Religion*
JAC	Jahrbuch für Antike und Christentum
JBL	*Journal of Biblical Literature*
JETS	*Journal of the Evangelical Theological Society*
JRH	*Journal of Religious History*
JSNT	*Journal for the Study of the New Testament*
JSNTSup	Journal for the Study of the New Testament: Supplement Series
JSOT	*Journal for the Study of the Old Testament*
KJV	King James Version
LCL	Loeb Classical Library
LSJ	Liddell, H. G., R. Scott, H. S. Jones, *A Greek-English Lexicon.* 9th ed. with revised supplement. Oxford, 1996.
LXX	Septuagint
MT	Masoretic Text
NAC	New American Commentary
NASB	New American Standard Bible
NEB	New English Bible
NICNT	New International Commentary on the New Testament
NIV	New International Version
NKJV	New King James Version

NovT	*Novum Testamentum*
NovTSup	Novum Testamentum Supplements
NRSV	New Revised Standard Version
NTS	*New Testament Studies*
OCD	*Oxford Classical Dictionary.* Edited by N. G. L. Hammond and H. H. Scullard. 2d ed. Oxford, 1970.
RSV	Revised Standard Version
SBLDS	Society of Biblical Literature Dissertation Series
SBLSP	*Society of Biblical Literature Seminar Papers*
SBLSS	Society of Biblical Literature Symposium Series
SBT	Studies in Biblical Theology
SD	Studies and Documents
SNTSMS	Society for New Testament Studies Monograph Series
SP	Sacra Pagina
ST	*Studia theologica*
SUNT	Studien zur Umwelt des Neuen Testaments
TDNT	*Theological Dictionary of the New Testament.* Edited by G. Kittel and G. Friedrich. Translated by B. W. Bromiley. 10 vols. Grand Rapids, 1964–79.
ThH	Théologie historique
TZ	*Theologische Zeitschrift*
VC	*Vigiliae christianae*
WBC	Word Biblical Commentary
WUNT	Wissenschaftliche Untersuchungen zum Neuen Testament
ZNW	*Zeitschrift für die neutestamentliche Wissenschaft und die Kunde der älteren Kirche*
ZTK	*Zeitschrift für Theologie und Kirche*

Pre-texts

...there are also good reasons for thinking that [Plato's] diatribe against writing is not aimed first and foremost at the sophists. On the contrary: sometimes it seems to proceed *from* them. Isn't the stricture that one should exercise one's memory rather than entrust traces to an outside agency the imperious and classical recommendation of the sophists? Plato would thus be appropriating here, once again, as he so often does, one of the sophists' argumentations. And here again, he will use it against them. And later on, after the royal judgment, Socrates' whole discourse, which we will take apart stitch by stitch, is woven out of schemes and concepts that issue from sophistics.   — Jacques Derrida ("Plato's Pharmacy," 108)

Paul frequently denounces his opponents as sophists in the most pejorative sense, and in the same connection vehemently dissociates himself from their methods. Paradoxically, all of Paul's protests about not having professional qualifications or using the accepted methods of persuasion imply the opposite. They make it clear for one thing that he was himself attacked on the same charges that he brought against his competitors. In the case of his claim not to have accepted maintenance from his audience, it can be shown that he only refused it to make a point, that he always insisted on his right to support, and did in fact accept it in the normal way where it was not an issue. His catalogues of personal hardships and indignities prove not that he was an insignificant person, but that he was sufficiently important for his misfortunes to afford a valuable lesson in humility. Lastly his direct renunciations of sophistry are explicitly made in order to cast the opprobrium of professionalism on to his opponents, and lead not to the claim that he was incompetent, but, ultra-sophistically, to the claim that his skill was by special endowment and, therefore, in fact superior to theirs.
                                        — E. A. Judge

I

True Rhetoric

1. Incision

While it was once typical to limit Greco-Roman rhetorical influence on Paul to encounters with ubiquitous Stoic-Cynic street preachers, the current flood of formal rhetorical analyses of the undisputed Pauline epistles leaves little room for doubting that he had at least a rudimentary rhetorical education.[1] Similar analyses of the disputed epistles demonstrate that rhetorical polish was an ongoing concern in the Pauline school or schools.[2] Indeed, the trend is to suspect that Paul himself knew quite a lot about such matters, and that his letters attest to a combination of a fair amount of formal training with undeniable natural gifts.[3]

1. For a brief but decisive argument for why we should acknowledge that Paul had some rhetorical training see Dale B. Martin, "The Rhetoric of the Body Politic," in *The Corinthian Body* (New Haven, Yale University Press, 1995), 38–68. Rhetorical criticism is a large and diverse growth industry in NT criticism. A recent overview is provided by Dennis L. Stamps, "Rhetorical Criticism of the New Testament: Ancient and Modern Evaluation of Argumentation," in *Approaches to New Testament Study* (ed. Stanley E. Porter and David Tombs; JSNTSup 120; Sheffield: Sheffield Academic Press, 1995), 77–128. A fine brief introduction is provided by Burton Mack's *Rhetoric and the New Testament* (Minneapolis: Fortress, 1990). The work of Betz and Kennedy is fundamental. Betz's commentary on Galatians was the landmark study in the recognition of Paul's rhetorical competence (Hans Dieter Betz, *Galatians* [Hermeneia; Philadelphia: Fortress, 1979]). George A. Kennedy's *New Testament Interpretation Through Rhetorical Criticism* (Chapel Hill: The University of North Carolina Press, 1984) has inspired several formal rhetorical analyses of Pauline texts. See also his *Classical Rhetoric and Its Christian and Secular Tradition from Ancient to Modern Times* (Chapel Hill: The University of North Carolina Press, 1980). Significant methodological refinement in formal rhetorical analysis of Pauline texts is evidenced in the impressive work of Betz's student, Margaret M. Mitchell, *Paul and the Rhetoric of Reconciliation: An Exegetical Investigation of the Language and Composition of 1 Corinthians* (Louisville: Westminster John Knox, 1993). For a description of a postmodern rhetorical biblical criticism, see "Rhetorical Criticism" in The Bible and Culture Collective, *The Postmodern Bible* (New Haven: Yale University Press, 1995) 149–86. To a great extent, my work fits this description, as does that of Vernon K. Robbins (see especially *The Tapestry of Early Christian Discourse: Rhetoric, Society, and Ideology* [London and New York: Routledge, 1996]). For recent arguments against classical rhetorical approaches to Paul, see R. Dean Anderson, Jr., *Ancient Rhetorical Theory and Paul* (CBET 18; Kampen: Kok Pharos, 1996), and Philip Kern, *Rhetoric and Galatians: Assessing an Approach to Paul's Epistle* (SNTSMS 101; Cambridge: Cambridge University Press, 1998.)

2. Kennedy's comment on a Deutero-Pauline epistle is apt: "If Ephesians is not by Paul, it is by someone of considerable rhetorical skill who was determined to produce a letter which Paul could have written" (*New Testament*, 156).

3. The possibility that his declamatory skills approached his epistolary gifts can neither be proved nor disproved. I do not think we can learn much about Paul's bodily presence from his

1

Widespread recognition of Paul's self-conscious employment of established rhetorical techniques and *topoi* naturally raises the question of the
range of impressions he was likely to make on his epistolary audiences from
the standpoint of rhetorical strategy. Here I refer not to formalistic debates
about whether this or that letter or portion of a letter is forensic, deliberative,
or epideictic, but to the broader question of where in "the Greco-Roman humanistic tradition" his rhetorical strategies tend to locate him. In the wake
of Betz's outstanding study, most New Testament rhetorical criticism would
appear to presume and perpetuate two perspectives on this question.[4] The
first is that Paul's rhetoric has far more in common with the philosophic
than the sophistic rhetorical tradition.[5] The second, and closely related, perspective is that Paul employs recognized rhetorical techniques in a variety of
situations to make his discourse as unambiguous and truthful as possible.
Kennedy gives voice to this perspective when he says that "Like Socrates,

---

cryptic remarks about the Galatians' willingness to tear their eyes out for him, or his thorn in
the flesh (*contra* Martin, *The Corinthian Body,* 53–55). In any case, it seems unlikely that, as
Martin suggests, Paul's "weakness of the flesh" that *occasioned* his preaching to the Galatians
was some permanent disfigurement that always kept him from making a favorable impression
(Gal 4:13–14). Surely he would have spoken of it more often had this been the case. And even
if we were to assume that Paul did not measure up to the Greco-Roman upper class physical
ideal, we know of highly successful sophists who also did not (see Maud W. Gleason, *Making
Men: Sophists and Self-Presentation in Ancient Rome* [Princeton: Princeton University Press,
1995]). Aelius Aristides was a notorious hypochondriac, and the wildly popular Favorinus,
a eunuch, was virtually the opposite of the upper class ideal (Gleason, *Making Men,* 3–20).
Given the at least modest success of his ministry combined with the rhetorically astute and
occasionally poetic qualities of the letters, I suspect that though Paul may not have been a
golden-tongued Dio, neither was he likely the proverbial stammering Moses.

4. Hans Dieter Betz, *Der Apostel Paulus und die socratische Tradition: Eine exegetische
Untersuchung zu seiner "Apologie" 2 Korinther 10–13* (BHT 45; Tübingen: J. C. B. Mohr,
1972).

5. This perspective is undoubtedly reinforced by the long tradition of comparing and
contrasting Paul and Paulinism with various Hellenistic popular philosophers and philoso-
phies. See, e.g., Rudolph Bultmann, *Der Stil der paulinischen Predigt und die kynisch-stoische
Diatribe* (FRLANT 13; Göttingen: Vandenhoeck & Ruprecht, 1910); Norman Wentworth De-
Witt, *St. Paul and Epicurus* (Minneapolis: University of Minnesota Press, 1954); Max Pohlenz,
Paulus und die Stoa (Reihe Libelli 101; Darmstadt: Wissenschaftliche Buchgesellschaft, 1964);
Stanley Stowers, *The Diatribe and Paul's Letter to the Romans* (SBLDS 57; Chico, Calif.:
Scholars Press, 1981); Benjamin Fiore, *The Function of Personal Example in the Socratic and
Pastoral Epistles* (AnBib 105; Rome: Biblical Institute Press, 1986); Abraham J. Malherbe, *Paul
and the Popular Philosophers* (Minneapolis: Augsburg Fortress, 1989); Clarence E. Glad, *Paul
and Philodemus: Adaptability in Epicurean and Early Christian Psychagogy* (NovTSup 81;
Leiden, New York, Cologne: E. J. Brill, 1995); Troels Engberg-Pedersen, ed., *Paul in His Hellenistic Context* (Minneapolis: Fortress, 1995); idem, *Paul and the Stoics* (Edinburgh: T. & T.
Clark, 2000). For an overview see Abraham J. Malherbe, "Greco-Roman Religion and Philosophy and the New Testament," in *The New Testament and its Modern Interpreters* (The Bible
and its Modern Interpreters; ed. E. J. Epp and G. W. McRae; Atlanta: Scholars, 1989), 3–26.
Interestingly, after expressing his skepticism about the possibility that Paul was as influenced
by the philosophical tradition as Betz's study required, the classicist John Dillon stated, "That
is not to say that he does not know Greek, or indeed that he has not perfected a certain Greek
style — a style, indeed, which has much in common with contemporary and later Greek sophistic" (quoted in Hans Dieter Betz, "Paul's Apology: II Corinthians 10–13 and the Socratic
Tradition" [Colloquy 2; Berkeley: Center for Hermeneutical Studies, 1975], 17).

Paul regarded some kinds of rhetorical appeal as unacceptable: anything that departed from the truth as he understood it or from his duty to preach the gospel."[6] Both of these perspectives are questionable. The contrasting perspective of this study, to be supported by fresh readings of a number of relevant Pauline texts, is rather that *Paul's rhetorical strategies, both according to the historical novel called Acts and his own epistles, display such a degree of intentional ambiguity, cunning, and deception as to make him justifiably vulnerable to the polemical charge of perpetrating sophistries.*[7]

This perspective takes two increasingly accepted conclusions very seriously. First, as already mentioned, Paul's methods of argumentation demonstrate considerable rhetorical self-consciousness. Second, Paul was accused by enemies both inside and outside his own congregations of speaking and acting in a veiled, opportunistic, and not completely trustworthy manner.[8] I want to take seriously the concurrence of these conclusions. I am quite sympathetic with Paul,[9] but I am also sympathetic with Paul's critics

---

6. *New Testament*, 138. This view of Paul is not shared by more radical Pauline critics such as some feminist interpreters and others who practice various kinds of cultural and ideological criticism. Even more problematic, however, is the highly traditional and naïve assumptions about Socrates' rhetoric of truth implied by Kennedy's remark. As I will demonstrate later, although the great classicist Gregory Vlastos undoubtedly shared this same attitude toward Socrates, his own careful reading of certain dialogues thoroughly undermines it.

7. The mention of "intentional ambiguity" reminds us that attention to intentions, both writers' and readers,' is unavoidable when interpreting highly rhetorical texts like those found in the NT. As one who would claim to be practicing a postmodern rhetorical criticism, I would suggest that anyone who mistakenly thinks that all forms of postmodernism/poststructuralism require the exclusion of authorial intentions from interpretation, or that interpretation is possible at all without positing intentions, should read Jacques Derrida, *Limited Inc* (Evanston: Northwestern University Press, 1988), 146–47, and Stanley Fish, *Doing What Comes Naturally* (Durham and London: Duke University Press, 1989), 96–100, 294–96; idem, *There's No Such Thing as Free Speech and It's a Good Thing, Too* (New York and Oxford: Oxford University Press, 1994), 299–300. Considerable confusion exists among biblical poststructuralists on this issue. Stephen Moore, e.g., while complaining of historical criticism's failure to "defamiliarize most of its seminal methodological assumptions," asks us to "witness the persistence, even in current biblical studies, of such problematic notions as . . . *the recoverability of authorial intentions*, and so on" (*Poststructuralism and the New Testament* [Philadelphia: Fortress, 1994], 117, italics mine). Yet earlier in the same work he states "that deconstruction, in particular, can enable us to read against the grain of the biblical authors' intentions in ways that affirm women" (52). How does one read against the grain of intentions that cannot be recovered? The real issue is not the recoverability of intentions, but what one means by intentions (e.g., are they metaphysical presences or material constructs, monological or dialogical, unified or diffuse, univocal or equivocal?).

8. E.g., with regard to 2 Corinthians, "Throughout, Paul's fundamental aim, in the face of suspicions of his double-dealing, is to assert his utter transparency and openness and his single-minded commitment to his vocation" (Frances Young and David F. Ford, *Meaning and Truth in 2 Corinthians* [London: SPCK, 1987], 15). See also pp. 17–18, 20. Similar observations and further references can be found in Peter Marshall, *Enmity in Corinth: Social Conventions in Paul's Relations with the Corinthians* (WUNT 2.23; Tübingen: J. C. B. Mohr [Paul Siebeck] 1987), 317–25, and Glad, *Paul and Philodemus*, 312.

9. See Robbins' comments on "The Interpreter's Location and Ideology," *Tapestry*, 24–27. In this study I make little effort to still the "personal voice." The importance of the "personal voice" that has long been recognized in feminist and poststructuralist writing generally is beginning to be felt in classical scholarship as well. See Judith P. Hallett and Thomas Van Nortwick,

and enemies who were found among Jews, pagans, non-Pauline Christians, and even Pauline Christians who deigned to disagree with their "father" (1 Cor 4:14–15). My attitude is not simply to be equated with that of a radical anti-Paulinist hermeneutics of suspicion — though I would hardly deny that it is hermeneutically suspicious. I see little justification for the notion that Paul was an insincere, power hungry, clandestinely self-seeking opportunist.[10] Paradoxically, however, *my thesis is that Paul's sincere conviction that he knew the Truth and had a divine mandate to promote it in an apocalyptic world filled with deception is an important key for explaining the perennial and entirely justified suspicion that his rhetorical strategies are not always irreproachable when judged by philosophical rhetorical ideals.* To anticipate, one might say, fully cognizant of the irony, that Paul is more Socratic, and thus more sophistic, than most interpreters realize.[11]

Although much of the Pauline corpus and some of Acts will come into play in this study, I have chosen to focus primarily on three examples. Chapter two, "Ambiguity in Athens," deals primarily with the Lukan Paul's famous Areopagus speech — surely a fictional tale to some extent. Estimates of the degree of creativity range from essential accuracy to total fabrication.[12] Neither extreme is warranted, but even if we were to lean toward

---

eds., *Compromising Traditions: The Personal Voice in Classical Scholarship* (London and New York: Routledge, 1997). Can there be any doubt of its importance for the ideologically charged arena of biblical scholarship?

10. The most persuasive statement of this position is perhaps found in Graham Shaw, *The Cost of Authority: Manipulation and Freedom in the New Testament* (Philadelphia: Fortress, 1983).

11. See the "pre-texts" above, p. xix. For the most part in this work, the Socrates I compare and contrast with Paul might simply be called Plato's Socrates. Scholarly distinctions between the Socrates of the earlier, middle, and later dialogues, and other issues related to the "Socratic problem (or question)" are not critical for what I am doing here. Two recent and invaluable resources for the Socratic problem are James W. Hulse, *The Reputations of Socrates: The Afterlife of a Gadfly* (New York: Peter Lang, 1995), and Mario Montuori, *The Socratic Problem: The History — The Solutions* (Amsterdam: J. C. Gieben, 1992).

12. One's overall impression of "Luke" as a historian will inevitably play a role in one's estimation of the historical value of individual episodes. Consider Lüdemann's perspective: "The letters are [to be] supplemented by the Acts of the Apostles; while this work was not written by an eyewitness, it is based on numerous old and reliable traditions which have to be extracted carefully from the text of Acts and then can be cautiously used in a description. It can be taken as a rule of thumb that the chronological framework of Acts is usually incorrect and has to be corrected by the letters of Paul, whereas the individual reports may be accurate, where they do not betray a clear Lukan bias.... Moreover the theology attributed to him in the speeches — with some significant exceptions — has little to do with the Paul of the authentic letters" (Gerd Lüdemann, *Heretics: The Other Side of Early Christianity* [Louisville: Westminster John Knox, 1996], 61–62). Lüdemann correctly observes that Acts must be used and that authentic traditions can be detected throughout. But the last statement, while granting some value to the speeches, does not seem quite fair. I see little evidence that Luke invents Pauline theology. Rather, he emphasizes some aspects more strongly than the letters and nearly ignores others (e.g., justification by faith). In short, Luke is an interpreter of Paul and operates no differently than most other interpreters in the history of Paulinism, including modern mainline Protestants who would, e.g., like to ignore the fact that Paul claims for himself the same spiritual "excesses" — miracles, revelations, tongues, etc. — as the super-apostles (witness the

the latter opinion, the evidence of how at least a second-generation Pauline Christian imagined Paul's rhetorical strategy for introducing himself to a sophisticated Athenian audience is worthy of our attention, especially if it can be shown on the basis of Paul's own writing that this strategy bears some resemblance to the way he introduced himself to strangers elsewhere. Chapter four, "Deception in Rome," deals with just that. I will attempt to show that several perplexing features of Romans can be illuminated by paying attention to the sophistical qualities and strategies of Pauline rhetoric.[13] I trust that my earlier remarks against interpreting Paul as a self-serving opportunist will lead the reader to suspect that I use "deception" in a rather sophisticated fashion. Later in this chapter I will begin to develop the concept as it will be utilized in this study. Suffice it to say for now that I believe that deception (ἀπάτη) is of great importance for understanding Paul's apocalyptic epistemology and rhetorical strategies, and it leads us into deep and sometimes disturbing aspects of his theology, Christology, soteriology, anthropology, missiology, and ecclesiology.[14] The intervening chapter, "Cunning in Corinth," will focus on three selections from the Corinthian correspondence (1 Cor 1–4, 1 Cor 9:19–23, 2 Cor 2:14–4:6) which suggest that Paul's sophistic weapons were aimed not only at non-Christians as in Acts, and not only at non-Pauline Christians as in Romans, but also at his own "children." A theme that will be introduced later in the present chapter, that of similarities in Socrates and Paul's skeptical attitudes toward knowledge and language, both written and oral, will also be more fully explored in chapter three. The final brief chapter, a customary peroration

---

strong dichotomy Betz sets up between Paul and his opponents [below, pp. 12–13]). We can hardly ignore the fact that Paul can describe himself in ways reminiscent of the Paul of Acts (e.g., "signs, wonders, and mighty works" in 2 Cor 12:12b; cf. Rom 15:19). Nor can we easily dismiss the possibility that the author briefly travelled with Paul and knew firsthand that signs, wonders, and resurrection-centered preaching were characteristic of Paul's missionary activities. Such brief contact would neither guarantee a profound understanding of Paul's theology nor accurate details about Paul's entire career. Indeed, if he were writing fifteen or twenty years afterward, it would not guarantee accuracy for the time he spent with Paul. The possibility of traditional Lukan authorship remains an open question for me.

13. For a similar perspective on Paul's Roman rhetoric, see Johan S. Vos, "To Make the Weaker Argument Defeat the Stronger: Sophistical Argumentation in Paul's Letter to the Romans," in *Rhetorical Argumentation in Biblical Texts* (ed. Thomas Olbricht, Walter Übelacker, and Anders Eriksson; Harrisburg, Pa.: Trinity Press International, forthcoming).

14. In a methodologically rich investigation combining, among others, psychological, existential, and structuralist narratological insights, Dan Via has also stressed in his own way the importance of deception in Pauline anthropology and theology (*Self-Deception and Wholeness in Paul and Matthew* [Minneapolis: Fortress, 1990]). Loyal D. Rue argues in an original work that "Western culture has feared nothing quite so much as it has feared deception. This concern over deception has played a fundamental role — I believe a *directive* role — in the formulation of our doctrines of sin and salvation, our definitions of philosophical problems, our conceptions of mental health, and even our justifications of the scientific enterprise. It would not be excessive to claim that in the Western tradition deception has commanded as much aversion as death itself" (*By the Grace of Guile: The Role of Deception in Natural History and Human Affairs* [Oxford: Oxford University Press, 1994]).

called "Reel Paul," will summarize my findings and briefly reflect on possible hermeneutical and theological implications.

Seeing Acts 17 and 1 Cor 9 together in my outline is reminiscent of older investigations of Paul's missionary strategy, but the decisive differences should already be clear. I do not approach Acts as an unproblematic historical source from which to distill accurate information about the *ipsissima verba et acta Pauli*, even if it were written by an occasional travelling companion of Paul.[15] On this point I mostly agree with the perspective of Günther Bornkamm's famous essay, "The Missionary Stance of Paul in I Corinthians 9 and in Acts."[16] All but the most conservative interpreters now admit that the speeches of Acts are to a considerable degree compositions original to Luke.[17] And the presence of both chronological incongruities and factual errors related to Paul is highly likely, though not incontestable due to the nature of the evidence.[18] This is not to say, as some do rashly, that Acts

---

15. The desire that it could be such an unproblematic source still lives on in conservative scholarship. Near the end of his impressive survey of Roman imprisonment as it pertains to Paul in Acts, Rapske remarks that "An eye to the ancient context helpfully furnishes the modern reader with a 1st century A.D.-based appreciation of the events. This moves toward the resolution of a number of alleged difficulties in the direction of a greater confidence in the historical trustworthiness of the Lukan record" (Brian Rapske, *Paul in Roman Custody* [vol. 3 of *The Book of Acts in Its First Century Setting*; ed. B. W. Winter; Grand Rapids and Carlisle: Eerdmans and Paternoster, 1994], 429). In this and similar comments, Rapske perpetuates the old error of assuming that the more accurately Acts reflects a first-century setting, in this case that of Roman legal and prison culture, the more likely it is that the words and deeds of its main character are mostly factual. Actually it does nothing more than prove that Acts is a fine early example of a historical novel, a vivid blend of fact and fantasy (see Richard I. Pervo, *Profit with Delight: The Literary Genre of the Acts of the Apostles* [Philadelphia: Fortress, 1987]). A far more glaring example of this error is found in Bruce W. Winter's "Official Proceedings and the Forensic Speeches in Acts 24–26," in *Ancient Literary Setting* (vol. 1 of *The Book of Acts in Its First Century Setting*; ed. Bruce W. Winter and Andrew D. Clarke; Grand Rapids: Eerdmans, 1994), 305–36. After arguing that these speeches could well be based on official court transcripts, Winter does not appear to recognize the irony of his conclusion that "The forensic speeches in Acts are then useful to the ancient historians [i.e., modern historians of antiquity] in the same way that the second century novel of Apuleius, *Metamorphoses* or *The Golden Ass* has proved to be a valuable source for ancient historians who are interested in understanding forensic activities in Corinth and the East in general" (335–36). Apuleius is writing pure fiction, but he is a master of mimesis. The setting has loads of verisimilitude, but the events are, as Lucian might have put it, "a true story."

16. Günther Bornkamm, "The Missionary Stance of Paul in I Corinthians 9 and in Acts," in *Studies in Luke-Acts* (ed. Leander E. Keck and J. Louis Martyn; Nashville and New York: Abingdon, 1966), 194–207.

17. Even interpreters who argue for the essential faithfulness of a narrative account to the rhetorical action portrayed are likely to grant that "Ancient historians, in their recording speeches in their works, were giving records of events rather than transcripts of words" (Conrad Gempf, "Public Speaking and Published Accounts," in *Ancient Literary Setting*. [vol. 1 of *The Book of Acts in Its First Century Setting*; ed. B. W. Winter], 259).

18. For a description of the evidence and the variety of scholarly attitudes toward it see David Wenham, "Acts and the Pauline Corpus II. The Evidence of Parallels," in *Ancient Literary Setting* (vol. 1 of *The Book of Acts in Its First Century Setting*; ed. Bruce W. Winter), 215–58. See also the somewhat polemical yet informative survey by W. Ward Gasque, *A History of the Interpretation of the Acts of the Apostles*, 2d ed. (Peabody, Mass.: Hendrickson, 1989).

is worthless as a historical source in general, even one for Paul in particular. Indeed, the paradox of Acts is the peculiar combination of how much the author appears to get right and wrong, what he seems (to want?) to know and not know. But in light of the radical metamorphoses implied by 1 Cor 9:19–23, what interests me about Acts, especially Acts 17, is the possibility of a similar willingness on the part of the Lukan Paul and the "real" Paul of the epistles to employ ambiguity, cunning, and deception to achieve a rhetorical goal.[19] Even Bornkamm found one example of the disconcerting adaptability of Paul in Acts to be historically plausible in light of 1 Cor 9:19–23.[20] He clearly accepts that vv. 19–23 mean that Paul "played different roles in different places," conduct that his adversaries "misunderstood and denounced . . . as ambiguity, conformism, opportunism, and unprincipled vacillation."[21] But what I hope to show here is not the controversial idea that we should take the speeches and narrative of Acts more seriously as precise descriptions of particular events, but rather that an image of Paul as a shifty, sophistic persuader/debater survived into the second-generation of Pauline Christianity in circles that based this image not on an interpretation of his writings, but on popular traditions. This would provide independent attestation that 1 Cor 9:19–23 and other texts that tend to suggest Paul's rhetorical strategies were questionable are to be taken seriously and that the suspicions of Paul's critics and enemies were not merely baseless polemic.

In the remainder of this chapter I will do several things. First, in "A Philosophic Paul," I will survey some important Pauline social and rhetorical criticism that has, in various ways, and in differing degrees, explored similarities between Paul and the philosophers, especially those of the Socratic tradition. We will see that, for the most part, when Pauline scholars relate Paul to this tradition and its rhetorical ideals, they tend to perpetuate a false dichotomy between philosophic and sophistic rhetoric, Socrates and the Sophists. This false dichotomy will be discussed at the beginning of "Like Socrates, Paul . . . " and will lead into a discussion of the Platonic Socrates' vision of a True rhetoric, a rhetoric that actually reflects and relies upon sophistic traits such as ambiguity, cunning, and deception. The possibility that Paul's rhetoric has the characteristics of such a True rhetoric will be suggested. Next, in "Ambiguity," and in "Cunning and Deception," I will discuss these terms as they will be employed in this study. My discussion of deception (ἀπάτη) is especially important because it attempts to add more philosophical and, indeed, theological depth into the subject of Paul's rhetoric than has been typical of such discussion. Because of the formalistic

---

19. One might say that I am interested in the essential accuracy of Luke's "characterization" of Paul. In this respect my interests are similar to those of John A. Darr in his *On Character Building: The Reader and the Rhetoric of Characterization in Luke-Acts* (Louisville: Westminster John Knox, 1992).

20. Bornkamm, "Missionary Stance," 204–5.

21. Ibid., 197.

tendencies of much of New Testament rhetorical criticism, one might get the impression that deciding whether or not one might reasonably consider Paul to be in some sense sophistic is simply a matter of observing his attitude toward epideictic and the "grand style," or perhaps of counting up the number of times he uses Gorgianic figures, as if the difference between "rhetoric" and "sophistic" could be determined by a statistical analysis. Determining Paul's level of debt to the philosophical or sophistical rhetorical traditions is not simply or primarily a matter of style since the differences between these traditions are themselves not simply or primarily stylistic. In the course of this discussion, I will begin to observe important similarities between Socrates' and Paul's attitudes toward the world and language. Finally, in "A Truly Socratic Paul," I will argue that Paul's epistemology, especially as illustrated by his Christology and theology, did not discourage but rather encouraged the use of an ambiguous, cunning, and deceptive rhetoric of both body and voice. This last section will serve as an appropriate bridge into chapter two, for I contend that the earliest extant interpretation of Paul presents him in much the same way through a narrative presentation in Acts 17 and elsewhere.

2. A Philosophic Paul

From the time of Plato, Greek, and later Roman, philosophers in the Socratic tradition sought to distinguish between their own philosophic rhetoric, one of truth and reality, and sophistic rhetoric, one of falsehood and mere appearance.[22] Indeed, Plato himself barely allowed the possibility that dialectic, which he considered the true philosophical discourse, could be called rhetoric at all, leaving Aristotle to describe a philosophic rhetoric that could be distinguished from a sophistic one. But the influence of Plato's more extreme division was by no means limited to the classical and Hellenistic periods. The polemical dispute between philosophy and rhetoric continued in earnest well into the eighteenth century when rhetoric ceased to be the crowning glory of a liberal education, and is still perpetuated in less conspicuous ways even into the present. According to Vickers,

> While Plato's hostility towards rhetoric, expressed over a thirty-year period, was idiosyncratic and extreme, the rivalry between the two disciplines persisted just as long as rhetoric was a living force. It flared up in the second century B.C.; again in the first century A.D., in the movement known as the 'second Sophistic'; in the Middle Ages it formed part of the recurring 'Battles of the Liberal Arts'; in the Renaissance it was largely found in the humanists' attack on scholastic philosophy; while in later periods it has been the work of individuals rather than coherent groups.[23]

22. A fundamental text is Plato's *Gorgias*, especially 449a–465e. See discussion in Kennedy, *Classical Rhetoric*, 45–52.

23. Brian Vickers, *In Defence of Rhetoric* (Oxford: Clarendon, 1988), 148.

The deceptive nature of this debate has received a fair amount of attention from classicists in recent years and I will return to this subject in the next section. For now, I will briefly survey some important Pauline social and rhetorical criticism that has operated within the terms of the debate as classically formulated.

Upon seeing the title of the present study, a reader familiar with the recent history of Pauline interpretation may already have thought of the work of E. A. Judge. After all, did not Judge call Paul a sophist pure and simple? This classification, however, was not nearly so radical as it might appear on the surface since Judge's use of the term sophist left much to be desired.

> Our object is to place St. Paul in his correct social class in terms of the impression his activities must have given to the contemporary observer. The term "sophist" has been chosen for lack of a better, and is meant to include many scholars (quite apart from St. Paul!) who would have hotly rejected it.[24]

Judge, in effect, defines a sophist as any Greco-Roman itinerant teacher. This is a dubious procedure. Can it be wise to designate a rather diverse group of individuals by a single title many despised, a name that many of them considered to represent the opposite of what they stood for? In fact, a better term can be chosen for the scholars which Paul most resembled, the name most of Judge's examples wore with pride, that of "philosopher." In the years since Judge's article it has become customary to call them "popular philosophers." Such philosophers tended to be eclectic even though they often associated themselves with some particular well-established tradition such as Platonism, Stoicism, Epicureanism, or Pythagoreanism. In this light one must have real reservations about placing Paul even in this category without considerable qualification. Abraham J. Malherbe carefully notes both debts and differences.

> During the last hundred years, New Testament scholars have shown that many aspects of Paul's life and letters are illuminated when they are examined in the light of Greco-Roman culture. There can no longer be any doubt that Paul was thoroughly familiar with the teaching, methods of operation, and style of argumentation of the philosophers of the period, all of which he adopted and adapted to his own purposes. This is not to argue that he was a technical philosopher; neither were his philosophical contemporaries.[25]

Malherbe's essay "Paul: Hellenistic Philosopher or Christian Pastor?" shows that he is more comfortable with calling Paul philosophic than a philosopher, and rightly so.

What Judge was really trying to say by locating Paul among the sophists was that his social class was much higher than most people think. This

---

24. E. A. Judge, "The Early Christians as a Scholastic Community: Part II," *JRH* 1.3 (1961): 125.

25. Malherbe, *Paul and the Popular Philosophers,* 68.

insight has been confirmed by subsequent socio-historical research.[26] Even here, however, Judge's procedure is flawed. In the first place, what dò we really learn by placing Paul within a proposed catch-all social class that includes everyone from the opulent Herodes Atticus down to lowly vagabond Cynic preachers? Here again we see the effects of Judge's nebulous definition of a sophist. The Eleatic Stranger declares that the tribe of sophists is not the easiest thing to catch and define,[27] but vagabond Cynic preachers were hardly sophists in any but the most pejorative sense. Neither, for that matter, were itinerant apostles who took great pride in claiming not to charge for their services — however problematic this claim may have been. Even though an underlying theme of this chapter is the difficulty of distinguishing between philosophy and sophistry, dialectic and sophistic (a very real difficulty that quite concerned Plato, and one that only increased as time went on), social-historical descriptions of sophists from the classical through the imperial periods are certainly possible. Most basic definitions will immediately reveal the folly of calling Paul a sophist. For example,

> This was the profession of itinerant teachers who went from city to city giving instruction for a fee. The subjects of instruction varied somewhat in content, but always had a relation to the art of getting on, or of success in life.... Under the Roman Empire, particularly from the second century onwards, the word acquired a more specialized meaning and became restricted to teachers and practitioners of rhetoric, which by this time was tending to become a purely literary exercise practised for its own sake.[28]

But just as we have seen that Malherbe considers Paul, especially in terms of his *modus operandi*,[29] philosophic in the popular sense, though not technically a philosopher, I consider him sophistic in various ways, though not technically a Sophist.

Secondly, Judge supported his image of Paul the sophist with an uncritical acceptance of the evidence of Acts, the deutero-Pauline, and the Pastoral epistles. There is indeed ample evidence in Acts that "St. Paul provided himself with a secure social position, consciously or unconsciously, by adopting

---

26. See Wayne Meeks, *The First Urban Christians: The Social World of the Apostle Paul* (New Haven: Yale University Press, 1983), 51–73. The consensus would appear to be that "the most active and prominent members of Paul's circle (including Paul himself) are people of high status inconsistency (low status crystallization). They are upwardly mobile; their achieved status is higher than their attributed status" (73).

27. "But now you and I must investigate in common, beginning first, it seems to me, with the sophist, and must search out and make plain by argument what he is. For as yet you and I have nothing in common about him but the name; but as to the thing to which we give the name, we may perhaps each have a conception of it in our own minds; however, we ought always in every instance to come to agreement about the thing itself by argument rather than about the mere name without argument. *But the tribe which we now intend to search for, the sophist, is not the easiest thing in the world to catch and define...*" (Plato, *The Sophist* 218C, italics mine).

28. *OCD* (2d ed.), 1000.

29. See *Paul and the Popular Philosophers*, 76–77.

the conventions of the sophistic profession,"[30] but one must be very careful how one employs the evidence of Acts. I will be more interested in it as evidence for a later popular image of Paul than as a reliable account of the man as he was. But, to reiterate, if that popular image suggests a Paul given to sophisms (σοφισμάτα), and his handling of rhetorical situations in Corinth and Rome does likewise, then the persistence of such an image of Paul is not historically insignificant.

The question of whether Paul's argumentative strategies are sophistic raises a final criticism of Judge's inclusion of Paul among the sophists. Judge did not closely analyze Paul's rhetorical strategies — surely an indispensable line of inquiry if one wants to associate an individual with sophists in any way. Yet there are signs that he had reflected on this matter enough to form a rather radical opinion, as the quotation on the title page of this present chapter attests. But if his subsequent failure to develop this insight is any indication, Judge would appear to have changed his mind or to have been indulging in loose hyperbole when he spoke of Paul behaving "ultra-sophistically." Perhaps Judge would now agree with his student Bruce W. Winter that Paul was "among the sophists" yet "for the most fundamental of theological reasons...could [n]ever be one of them."[31]

An attempt to locate Paul's rhetoric squarely in the Socratic philosophical heritage, in explicit and conscious opposition to the sophistic, was made by Hans Dieter Betz in his groundbreaking study, *Der Apostel Paulus und die socratische Tradition: Eine exegetische Untersuchung zu seiner "Apologie" 2 Korinther 10–13*. Betz contends that Paul sides with philosophy in its great struggle with rhetoric/sophistry.

> Windisch rightly acknowledged the anti-sophistic tendency of Pauline argumentation. In what follows we will seek to show that in this way Paul stands squarely in a tradition associated with Socrates.[32]

And later,

> As "imitator of Christ," Paul thus positions himself in the tradition of Greek humanism and understands himself situated with this tradition in the struggle against the program of the "Sophists."[33]

Betz saw strong confirmation of this view in the form of 2 Corinthians 10–13. The well known "form-critical problem" is that while these chapters

---

30. Judge, "The Early Christians as a Scholastic Community: Part II," 126.

31. Bruce W. Winter, *Philo and Paul among the Sophists* (SNTSMS 96; Cambridge: Cambridge University Press, 1997), 244.

32. "Windisch erkennt richtig die antisophistische Tendenz der paulinischen Argumentation. Im folgenden werden wir zu zeigen versuchen, daß Paulus hiermit in einer bis auf Socrates zurückgehenden Tradition steht" (Betz, *Der Apostel Paulus*, 14). All translations of *Der Apostel Paulus* are my own.

33. "Als 'μιμητής τοῦ Χριστοῦ' stellt [Paulus] sich also hinein in die Tradition des griechischen Humanismus und versteht sich mit dieser Tradition im Kampfe befindlich gegen das Programm der 'Sophisten'" (ibid., 146).

appear to be an "apology," near the end Paul explicitly denies that he has been offering one (12:19).[34] Betz's solution to this strange state of affairs is to locate Paul's discourse in a tradition dating back to Socrates in which it was considered improper for the philosopher to defend himself because to do so would be to play the sophist.[35] Betz compares Paul's *Sitz im Leben* in 2 Cor 10–13 with that of other fairly contemporary figures who offered apologies which very clearly rely on the true philosopher vs. false philosopher (or sophist) topos (e.g., Apollonius of Tyana, Apuleius of Madaura, and Josephus).[36] After examining accusations against Paul having to do with his apostolic "image" (σχῆμα),[37] his supposedly contemptible "speech" (λόγος), his "weakness," his refusal of patronage, and his refusal to legitimize himself through self-comparison with other apostles,[38] Betz concludes that both the formulation of the accusations and the nature of Paul's response to them suggest that within the Christian movement he is consciously taking the position of a Greek humanistic philosopher in opposition to the Corinthian sophists.[39] The latter are in effect advocating "a new, Christian variation of the old sophistic program."[40] At various points in his concluding chapter Betz suggests that Paul's "dialogue" with the Corinthian community should become a dialogue with the Church today which is increasingly tempted to follow another gospel, one that emphasizes "wonders," "power," and "deification."

> This theology is diametrically opposed to the Pauline conception of the "reign of Christ." Paul is, therefore, fundamentally in the right when he sees another

---

34. Ibid., 14.

35. Ibid., 15–19.

36. Ibid., 19–26. The use of terminology like "form-critical problem," and *"Sitz im Leben"* reminds us that this study marks an early stage in the growth of NT rhetorical criticism as it developed within historical criticism. Betz's *Galatians* marked another stage in its maturation. Whether rhetorical criticism should remain a sub-discipline of historical criticism as in Mitchell's *Paul and the Rhetoric of Reconciliation* (6–8) or become its replacement — or at least an alternative to historical criticism's hegemony as in Robbins' *Tapestry* (235–36) — is currently subject to debate. J. David Hester Amador argues that neither Robbins nor other pioneers of "the (new) rhetorical criticism(s)" of the NT — including Mack, Wire, and Schüssler-Fiorenza — have really challenged the fundamental assumptions of historical criticism: "There is also a tension between pursuing the full implications and ramifications of a rhetorical approach to interpretation and the habits of inquiry firmly entrenched in their methods, the latter of which so thoroughly permeate their analyses that none of them ultimately questions the legitimacy of historical-critical reconstruction or sees the interpretive closure and ideological distortions of power it exerts upon their work" (*Academic Constraints in Rhetorical Criticism of the New Testament: An Introduction to a Rhetoric of Power* [JSNTSup 174; Sheffield: Sheffield Academic Press, 1999], 273).

37. Although σχῆμα as used in this sense is most often translated "appearance," the various positive and negative connotations of "image" in modern English come closer to capturing the word's ambiguity.

38. Betz, *Der Apostel Paulus*, 44–57, 57–69, 70–100, 100–17, 118–37, respectively.

39. Ibid., 138–48.

40. "...eine neue, christliche Variation des alten sophistischen Programms" (ibid., 140). Winter, *Philo and Paul*, 170–230, more fully develops a similar view of the Corinthian sophists.

Jesus, another Spirit, and another Gospel proclaimed in the opposing theology (2 Cor 11:4).[41]

Some aspects of Betz's study were received better than others.[42] The issues have often revolved around whether or not Paul consciously employed various Hellenistic philosophical ideas and rhetorical topoi. The possibilities that he was conscious of the importance of one's "image" (σχῆμα), and that he knowingly employed the standard *topos* of feigned rhetorical incompetence are now taken seriously. But other claims, such as Paul's conscious borrowing and agreement with various aspects of "the Delphic religion," tend to meet with skepticism. Furthermore, on strictly exegetical grounds, the notion that Paul simply parodies heavenly ascents and miraculous healings in 2 Cor 12:1–10 is very difficult to accept.[43]

Abraham Malherbe has further advanced the position that Paul consciously aligns his discourse with that of popular moral philosophers as opposed to sophists. In his article, "Gentle as a Nurse: The Cynic Background to I Thess ii," Malherbe first concentrates on the ways Dio Chrysostom "distinguishes himself on the one hand from the sophists and rhetoricians, and on the other hand from the so-called Cynics."[44] Although Dio distinguishes between various kinds of weak or disreputable characters — private and lecture-hall "philosophers," as well as "Cynics," both coarse and cultivated — he also appears to lump them all together as "flatterers, frauds, and sophists" (κολάκων καὶ γοήτων καὶ σοφιστῶν).[45] Malherbe's striking discovery is the close verbal parallels between Paul's description of his ministry in 1 Thess 2 and Dio's description of true philosophers in contrast to "sophists." I have arranged Malherbe's important comparative conclusions in Table 1 on the following page.[46]

---

41. "Dieser Theologie ist die paulinische Auffassung vom 'Christusereignis' diametral entgegengesetzt. Paulus ist darum grundsätzlich im Recht, wenn er in der gegnerischen Theologie einen anderen Jesus, einen anderen Geist und ein anderes Evangelium verkündigt sieht (2 Cor 11,4)" (ibid., 140). This dichotomy may be less tenable in light of recent presentations of a mystical-apocalyptic Paul who thinks of himself as being progressively metamorphosized into a son of God (see James D. Tabor, *Things Unutterable: Paul's Ascent to Paradise in its Greco-Roman, Judaic, and Early Christian Contexts* [Lanham, New York, and London: University Press of America, 1986], and Alan F. Segal, *Paul the Convert: The Apostolate and Apostasy of Saul the Pharisee* [New Haven and London: Yale University Press, 1990]).

42. In retrospect it is clear that some resistance was due to ignorance, both of classical scholarship about Pauline scholarship, and, to a lesser extent perhaps, vice-versa. The seminar responses and discussion included in "Paul's Apology" (17–30) betray assumptions stemming from the then still dominant notion that there was a great divide between Jewish and Hellenistic culture, even in the Diaspora.

43. Ibid., 89–100.

44. Malherbe, *Paul and the Popular Philosophers*, 37.

45. *Orat.* 32.11. The LCL offers the delightful translation, "toadies, mountebanks, and sophists." This polemical lumping together of sophists with more clearly disreputable characters was common. Quoting Burkert's study of ΓΟΗΣ, a word whose possible definitions include "liar," "deceiver," "imposter," and "charlatan," Betz lists as synonyms "ψεύστης," "ἀπατεών," "ἀλαζών," "μάγος," "φέναξ," and "σοφιστής" (*Der Apostel Paulus*, 33).

46. Malherbe, *Paul and the Popular Philosophers*, 216–17.

TABLE 1
Dio and Paul

Dio	Paul
Dio says that some Cynics fear the *hybris* of the crowd and will not become involved in the *agōn* of life. The speech of some of them can be described as *kenos*. The true philosopher, on the contrary, faces the crowd with *parrēsia* because God gives him the courage.	Paul says that although he had suffered and experienced violence (*hybristhentes*) in Philippi, his sojourn in Thessalonica was not empty *(kenē)*, but that he spoke boldly in God (*eparrēseasametha en tō theō*) in a great struggle *(en pollō agōni)* (vv. 1,2).
Dio says the charlatans deceive *(apatōsin)* their hearers and lead them in error (*planē.*)	Paul says he did not preach out of error (*ouk ek planēs*) (v. 3).
Dio says the ideal philosopher must speak with purity of mind (*katharōs*) and without guile (*adolōs.*)	Paul says he was not motivated by uncleanness (*ouk ex akatharsias*), nor did he speak with guile (*oude en dolō*) (v. 4).
Dio says that the true philosopher will not preach for the sake of glory (*mēte doxēs charin*), nor for personal gain (*mēt' ep' argyriō*), nor as a flatterer (*kolakōn*).	Paul claims that he did not use a cloak for greed (*oute en prophasei pleonexias*), nor did he seek glory from men (*oute zētountes ex anthrōpōn doxan*), or flatter them (*oute... en logō kolakeias*) (vv. 5, 6).
Dio claims that he was divinely directed to speak.	So does Paul (v. 4).
Dio emphasizes that the philosopher, in spite of personal danger, seeks to benefit his hearers by adapting his message to their situation, and being kinder to them individually than even a father. He represents the view that the philosopher should not consistently be harsh (*barys*), but should on occasion be gentle (*ēpios*) as a nurse.	Paul says that he was prepared to lay down his life for his converts (v. 8), that, like a father with his children, he worked with each one individually (*hena hekaston hymōn*, v. 10), and that, although as an apostle of Christ he could have been demanding of them, he was gentle as a nurse (*dynamenoi en barei... alla egenēthēmen ēpioi en mesō hymōn, hōs ean trophos thalpē ta heautēs tekna*, vv. 6–7).

The sheer number of verbal and conceptual parallels found by Malherbe in such a short passage proves beyond any reasonable doubt that Paul was fully aware of Hellenistic standards of philosophical and rhetorical respectability, and that he was at pains to show where he stands in relation to them, that is, in the best of the Greek humanistic tradition, as Betz would say. For Dio, the true philosopher is "a man who in plain terms and without guile speaks his mind with frankness, and neither for the sake of reputation nor for gain makes false pretensions, but out of good will and concern for his fellow-men stands ready, if need be, to submit to ridicule and to the disorder and the uproar of the mob."[47] This sounds like an echo of Plato's

47. *Orat.* 32.11.

descriptions of the ideal philosophical orator.[48] But in the eyes of "the mob," hard and fast Platonic distinctions between philosophers and sophists were ambiguous at best. In fact, it is the widely recognized resemblance between, and popular confusion of, philosophers and sophists, rather than any actual accusations, which probably necessitated both Dio's and Paul's apologetic tone in these particular examples. This problematic resemblance was recognized long before it was accepted by some that philosophers could also be rhetors and/or sophists, and vice-versa, as in Philostratus' *Lives of the Sophists*.[49] And, as we will see, the similarity is often hardly superficial.

3. "Like Socrates, Paul . . . "[50]

Indeed, the question to ask is whether Luke, without coming right out and saying it, wants to commend Paul as the "new Socrates."[51]

The deceptive nature of the dispute between philosophy and rhetoric has received a fair amount of attention from classicists in recent years.[52] As even so traditional a classicist as George Kennedy observes,

Some modern readers sympathize with philosophy in its dispute with rhetoric. In the former discipline they see devotion to truth, intellectual honesty, depth of perception, consistency, and sincerity; in the later [sic], verbal dexterity, empty pomposity, triviality, moral ambivalence, and a desire to achieve self-interest by any means. *The picture is not quite so clear cut.*[53]

Indeed, the greatest stumbling block to maintaining a clear cut binary opposition between philosophy and rhetoric is that opposition's very foundation — Plato's Socrates. Consider these remarks by prominent classicists, concatenated by Gregory Vlastos in his recent authoritative treatment of the historical Socrates

E. R. Dodds: "It looks rather as if Plato was content at this stage to let Socrates repay the Sophists in their own coin, as no doubt Socrates often did." Paul Friedländer: Socrates believes that to educate deluded persons "he must resort to dialectical tricks"; and he "knows how to deceive better than all the

---

48. See discussion of the Platonic concept of philosophical rhetoric in Kennedy, *Classical Rhetoric,* 41–60.

49. With reference to the Imperial period, Bowersock observes that "It was, in fact, possible for the professions of philosopher and rhetor to be conflated and confused. They had many tasks in common, and both were obliged to use the spoken and written word. Accordingly, as Philostratus recognized, eloquent philosophers might be numbered among the sophists" (G. W. Bowersock, *Greek Sophists in the Roman Empire* [Oxford: Oxford University Press, 1969], 11).

50. Kennedy, *New Testament,* 138.

51. "Es ist tatsächlich die Frage zu stellen, ob Lukas nicht Paulus, ohne es frei heraus zu sagen, als den "neuen Sokrates" empfehlen will" (Betz, *Der Apostel Paulus,* 39).

52. The work of Derrida played a decisive role in spurring such investigations. See especially "Plato's Pharmacy," 61–172.

53. George A. Kennedy, *A New History of Classical Rhetoric* (Princeton: Princeton University Press, 1994), 9, italics mine.

sophists." W. K. C. Guthrie: "Plato lets Socrates make a wickedly sophistical use of ambiguity when he likes." Charles Kahn: Socrates uses "dialectical trickery" to win his argument against Polus in *G.* 474c–475c.[54]

These quotations stand at the beginning of a chapter titled "Does Socrates Cheat?" By no means does Vlastos himself want to endorse such opinions, and at times it sounds as if he is writing yet another apology for Socrates.[55] Nevertheless, his own strategy for refuting the charge that Socrates was cunning and deceptive strongly confirms that, in a certain way, the charge is justified. According to Vlastos,

> What creates the problem is the Socrates of Plato's earlier dialogues — complicated, devious, cunning, and not averse to playing pranks on his interlocutors upon occasion. Does *he* remain always free of resort to deceit? I want to argue that he always does *when arguing seriously:* this is the all important qualification.[56]

And how can we know when Socrates is serious? "...*when Socrates is searching for the right way to live, in circumstances in which it is reasonable for him to think of the search as obedience to divine command,* his argument cannot involve wilful untruth."[57] How comforting it would have been for the often thoroughly duped interlocutors of Socrates to have known this, for instance, those involved in the *Protagoras,* a veritable war of words between Socrates and the great sophist named in the title. In Vlastos's own words, Socrates enters into this contest with complete prognostication of Vince Lombardi's famous sporting logion, "Winning isn't everything; it's the only thing." This is a fatal admission for Vlastos's defense of Socrates, for it is precisely this attitude for which Socrates condemns the sophists and

---

54. Gregory Vlastos, *Socrates: Ironist and Moral Philosopher* (Ithaca: Cornell University Press, 1991), 132.

55. I am not alone in this opinion: "This reader, however, is left unsatisfied that the overall strangeness of Socrates has been accounted for, at least in a way that allows one to share Vlastos's apparently unwavering admiration for the man, an admiration he seems to slip into unconsciously as he explicates Socrates' unique views. A serious question to be answered by readers is whether Vlastos's regard for the thought of Socrates has inappropriately slipped into veneration. Has Vlastos given us an old-fashioned portrait of Saint Socrates?" (G. Rickert, *Bryn Mawr Classical Review* 3.3.20 [1992]: 12 pars. 6 Jan. 2001. Online: http://ccat.sas.upenn.edu/bmcr/1992/03.03.20.html). The same could be said for old-fashioned portraits of Saint Paul that do not account for his overall strangeness. See, e.g., Romano Penna, *Paul the Apostle* (2 vols.; Collegeville, Minn.: Liturgical Press, 1996), in many ways a model theological and exegetical study of Paul that, nonetheless, hardly ever finds anything truly "critical" to say about Paul or his theology whatsoever, i.e., it never goes beyond what Derrida has termed "doubling commentary." Although she does not use this terminology, Schüssler-Fiorenza is describing the same phenomenon within Pauline scholarship on 1 Corinthians when she observes that a wide variety of interpretations "all follow Paul's rhetorical strategy without questioning it or evaluating it" (Elisabeth Schüssler-Fiorenza, "Rhetorical Situation and Historical Reconstruction in 1 Corinthians" *NTS* 33 [1987] 390).

56. Vlastos, *Socrates,* 133–34, italics his.

57. Ibid., 134, italics his.

rhetoric generally in the *Gorgias*, and to which he counterposes his argument that it is better to suffer wrong than to do it.

The contest in the *Protagoras* begins with an oration by the great name-sake of the dialogue, a masterful exhibition, featuring, among other things, some brilliant interpretations of Simonidean poetry. The speech is greeted with loud applause and Socrates feels like he has received a knock-out blow. Then, as Vlastos explains,

> To recover from the set-back [Socrates] tries a brazen maneuver and succeeds in pulling it off: he has the effrontery to claim that when the poet says "it is hard to be good" he is using "hard" (χαλεπόν) to mean "bad" — a willful travesty of the poet's meaning, for which he nonetheless manages to win support by wheedling endorsement for it from a distinguished member of the company, Prodicus, master of the "correct use of words."[58]

Vlastos goes on to note Socrates' thoroughly tongue-in-cheek representation of the anti-intellectual Sparta as "doing more than any other Greek state to foster philosophy."[59] Vlastos concludes that "It can hardly be disputed that throughout this performance Socrates is pulling the wool over his hearers' eyes. What is his game? Irony, certainly, but irony put to a very special use: mockery elaborately played out in sly concealment of its mocking intent."[60] But Vlastos sees a great divide between the impression Socrates' performance made on outsiders as opposed to insiders. Thus,

> ...when Alcibiades [one of Socrates' companions] hears Socrates say poker-faced that it is bad to be good he knows that someone's leg is being pulled. But others in the company who are not in the know would be easily fooled. No signal of irony would come across to them from the wild constructions Socrates puts on Simonides' verse. Nor would they have any way of knowing that the tale about the Spartans was a spoof. Only at the end of his long speech does Socrates give away the information from which his hearers, if they had the wit, could figure out that he had been putting on an act.[61]

All of these frank admissions of Socrates' devious dialectical stratagems lead me to conclude that Vlastos, at least, was certainly not a sophist. Would you wish to be defended in an Athenian court by someone who would seriously argue that charges that you are ambiguous, cunning, and deceptive are true except when you are being serious?

Vlastos ultimately tries to absolve the historical Socrates from accusations of sophistry by transferring the guilt to Plato so that the most offensive examples of the famous Socratic irony become instead Platonic irony. And so I will now shift the spotlight from the star of Platonic drama to the playwright. The theatrical analogy is apt. In James A. Arieti's words,

---

58. Ibid., 135.
59. Ibid., 136.
60. Ibid.
61. Ibid., 137.

I would venture to say that as Herodotus's boldness and genius lay partly in his adaptation of epic to prose, so Plato's lay partly in his adaptation of *drama* to prose. Tragedy and comedy are the genres that most resemble the Platonic dialogue.... [62]

The philosophical implications of this seemingly innocuous stylistic observation should not be overlooked.[63] In the *Sophist,* the Eleatic Stranger goes on a "hunt" for the "tribe" known as the Sophists. Derrida succinctly summarizes one of the hunt's findings.

> As a "wizard and imitator," the Sophist is capable of "producing" "likenesses and homonyms" of everything that exists (234*b*–235*a*). The Sophist mimes the poetic, which nevertheless itself comprises the mimetic; he produces production's double.[64]

Can we fail to see that Plato himself, by writing dramatic dialogues, mimes the poetic, even the dramatic, "producing production's double"?[65] As Stanley Rosen puts it, "A dialogue is a production, and more sharply stated, an image of images."[66] Is it not predictable, then, that the often uncritical acceptance of the — deceptively — clear Platonic dichotomy between dialectic and sophistic throughout much of the history of Western philosophy was combined with the avoidance of any real interest in the dramatic, or to put it more plainly, the theatrical aspects of the dialogues?[67]

Once one acknowledges the staged quality of Plato's productions, however, it will come as no surprise that the hunt for the sophist doubles back on itself, so to speak. At the beginning of the *Sophist,* after the appearance of the Stranger, Socrates remarks that real philosophers appear in all sorts of shapes, including those of the politician and the sophist.[68] He then enjoins the Stranger to discuss and define each of the three. When asked what method he prefers, long uninterrupted speeches or dialogue, the Stranger chooses the former, though not without some shame (217 D). The reason for the shame is significant. A preference for long speeches is a stereotype attached to sophists in the dialogues. But this is not the only surprise. The

---

62. James A. Arieti, *Interpreting Plato: The Dialogues as Drama* (Savage, Md.: Rowman & Littlefield, 1991), 3.

63. Arieti himself does not appear to see them.

64. Jacques Derrida, "The First Session," in *Acts of Literature* (ed. Derek Attridge; New York: Routledge, 1992), 134.

65. "To begin with, it is plain that Plato himself violates the restrictions on imitation at all periods of his development, including that of the *Sophist*" (Stanley Rosen, *Plato's Sophist: The Drama of Original and Image* [New Haven: Yale University Press, 1983], 19).

66. Ibid., 15.

67. Arieti further observes that while in the twentieth century many commentators, e.g., Jaeger, Friedländer, Strauss, and Guthrie, "see the dialogues as *dramatic,* they fail to see them as *dramas*" (Arieti, *Interpreting Plato,* 3). The close relationship between the sophistic movement and Greek tragedy is well known. See H. D. Rankin, "Sophistry and Tragedy," in *Sophists, Socratics, and Cynics* (Totowa, N.J.: Barnes & Noble, 1983), 122–34.

68. *Sophist,* 216A–D. This scene will receive more attention in the following chapter. See the excerpt below, p. 40.

Stranger thinks of his search for a definition as "hunting," as an attempt to "catch" the sophist (218 C). Hunting metaphors pervade the whole investigation. But after proposing that the argument proceed by analogy from the lesser to the greater, to what lesser thing does the Stranger propose to compare the sophist? A fisherman, the type of hunter most celebrated for his cunning in Greek and subsequent Greco-Roman culture.[69] So our search for the sophist is being conducted by a Stranger who prefers long speeches to dialogue, and has an affinity for hunting. Have we then found the sophist? Has he in fact been introduced in the first sentence of the *Sophist,* deceptively cloaked in his companions' claim that he is a "real philosopher" (μάλα δὲ ἄνδρα φιλόσοφον)? And what are we to make of the fact that in this dialogue the Stranger plays the starring role usually reserved for Socrates? While commenting on "Scene One" of *The Sophist,* Rosen remarks,

> It should also be noted that in the diaeresis section, the Stranger will identify refutation as the art of the noble sophist, a person of ambiguous nature whose description will remind us of Socrates. By raising the prospect that the Stranger is a refuting god, Socrates so to speak defends himself in advance, or places the same charge of noble sophistry against the stranger.[70]

Certainly from the preceding exposition we can conclude that the dramatic elements of the dialogue's opening are designed to dramatize the main theme, the great difficulty in distinguishing between original and image, genuine and fake, philosopher and sophist, an enigma Socrates himself embodies.[71] Is he a genuine philosopher, a noble sophist, or both? Is there a difference? Is a genuine philosopher a fake sophist?

We can begin to unravel this enigma by considering a recent reformulation of the relationship between philosophy and sophistry, Plato and rhetoric, found in Thomas Cole's *The Origins of Rhetoric in Ancient Greece.*[72] While Brian Vickers portrays Plato as an intellectual Odysseus, stealthily stealing the rhetorical arsenal of the sophists and using it to discredit them and subjugate the masses,[73] Cole argues that Plato, the reputed arch-enemy of rhetoric, is, along with Aristotle, its co-inventor. To some extent, this is simply a matter of taking Plato at his word when he sets forth his vision of what rhetoric ought to be in opposition to what he claims it is in the hands of the sophists.

---

69. Marcel Detienne and Jean-Pierre Vernant, *Cunning Intelligence in Greek Culture and Society* (Chicago: The University of Chicago Press, 1991), 28–34, 41–46.

70. Rosen, *Plato's Sophist,* 64.

71. Here we should remember that in the opinion of many of his contemporaries, Socrates was just another sophist, one of the most notorious in fact (see discussion in G. B. Kerford, *The Sophistic Movement* [Cambridge: Cambridge University Press, 1981], 55–57).

72. Thomas Cole, *The Origins of Rhetoric in Ancient Greece* (Baltimore: Johns Hopkins, 1991).

73. "In the later dialogues Plato's whole system has become rigidly authoritarian. The rulers of his city are given total control over the citizen, including the power to use lies and propaganda.... *We might say, then, that Plato first degraded rhetoric and then made use of it for degrading others*" (Vickers, *In Defence of Rhetoric,* 141, italics mine).

More original, however, is Cole's explication of Plato's definition, and his analysis of its philosophical foundations. Cole contends that full-fledged rhetoric, as opposed to either mere eloquence or Odyssean lying (sophistry in the most negative and polemical sense), requires "conviction" that knowledge of the true is possible. Such epistemological confidence deriving from "a morphology of the real" was the missing ingredient in the Sophistic movement.[74] Plato, on the other hand, understood that "The more thorough and exact a speaker's understanding of the way things are, the greater his ability to capitalize on those resemblances which allow an audience to be deceived into mistaking one thing for another (*Phaedrus* 261e6–62d6)."[75] Consequently, "Here as elsewhere in Plato (*Hipp. Min.* 366e-67a5), a thorough knowledge of the truth produces the most reluctant liars, but also the most successful ones."[76]

The crucial ingredient in Cole's description of Platonic rhetoric, or what I refer to somewhat playfully as "True rhetoric," is identified in the following remarks:

> Saying something other than what one means is not rhetorical when it merely seeks to conceal meaning from one possible audience (the uneducated, for example, or the uninitiated, or the wielders of political censorship) without any corresponding enhancement in the way meaning is received by the audience for whom it is intended. Nor is the simple conveying of a message known to be false (lying) or an argument known to be fallacious (sophistry) rhetorical per se, however often rhetoric may be used to make lies seem like truth or introduce sophistry in such a way that its fallaciousness passes unnoticed.[77]

The first sentence of this quotation implies that polyvalence is an essential ingredient in rhetorical discourse. Discourse is not truly rhetorical unless it both conceals and reveals meaning simultaneously. Not surprisingly, Cole will later link the advent of allegorical interpretation to the development

---

74. Cole, *Origins*, 141–43. Cole sells the sophists short on this point by failing to take into account recent scholarship that recognizes them as philosophers in their own right (see Kerford, *Sophistic Movement*, in toto; Rankin, *Sophists*, especially his treatment of Protagoras, Gorgias, and Prodicus, 30–52.) A morphology of the real, i.e., a metaphysically underpinned epistemology, was not simply a missing ingredient, but rather one carefully sampled and reasonably rejected by sophists like Protagoras and Gorgias.

75. Cole, *Origins*, 9.

76. Ibid., 10. In *Der Apostel Paulus*, p. 62, Betz quotes Friedländer's similar observations concerning the notion of rhetoric found in the *Hippias Minor,* and concerning its Socrates who "apparently tricked his opponents like a sophist" ("scheinbar als Sophist seinen Gegner 'täuscht' "). But Betz was mainly interested in associating one particular Socratic "deceptive maneuver" or "trick play" ("Täuschungsmanöver") with Paul, that of ironically pretending to be rhetorically incompetent. Although he quotes Friedländer's observation that "Socrates is the master of all the sophistic arts with the goal of 'the Good,' the deceitful teacher with an eye on the true end" ("Sokrates ist der Beherrscher aller sophistischen Mittel mit dem Ziel des 'Guten,' der mit dem Blick auf das rechte Ziel täuschende Erzieher"), he clearly assumes that Paul's pilfering of the sophistic arsenal could not be so thorough.

77. Cole, *Origins,* 14.

of rhetoric.[78] Discourse is truly rhetorical when at least two audiences are simultaneously in view corresponding to at least two levels of meaning. On the one hand, there is an unworthy audience that is kept in the dark either intentionally or simply because it lacks essential hermeneutical assets such as intelligence and training. On the other, there is the intended audience made up of those who are capable of detecting what the speaker really means. These observations should sound familiar. Cole's description of true rhetoric is strikingly similar to Vlastos's description of the sly concealments characteristic of Socratic/Platonic irony discussed earlier.

But Cole probably goes too far in limiting what counts as rhetoric only to discourse deriving from an epistemological confidence of Platonic proportions. One hardly needed the unchanging realm of the forms in order to have some semblance of epistemological assurance in ancient Greece. The leading sophists, though relativists at heart, still believed there were better and worse "arguments" (λόγοι), even "right arguments" (ὀρθοὶ λόγοι).[79] Surely this level of confidence was sufficient to lead to the construction of the sort of polyvalent discourse Cole would apparently limit to Plato. In fact, failure to recognize the type of multivalent discourse that Vlastos calls "Platonic irony" (or is it sophistic irony?) in the extant writings of the sophists probably leads commentators to misinterpret them from time to time, taking at face value statements that should be considered ironic in light of other statements.[80] Or is it that I am duped? Here we encounter a crucial perspective for all that will follow in this study: *Once one suspects that someone, for example, Gorgias, Socrates, Plato . . . or Paul, is a double dealer in this sense, someone who is sometimes addressing an audience within an audience, interpretation is severely complicated by the task of trying to decide which level of meaning is meant for this or that outsider and this or that insider.*[81] In this reader-response nightmare, the interpreter must always be

---

78. Ibid., 55–68.

79. See Kerford, "Sophistic Relativism," in *The Sophistic Movement*, 83–110; see also 72–73. Let us remember that one does not have to be an Idealist to have "ideals."

80. E.g., in *On Nature*, Gorgias sets forth arguments about the relationship of logos to external reality that render impossible the attainment of Truth or Knowledge, arguments that suggest that all logos is inherently deceptive. Yet in the *Encomium of Helen*, Gorgias intends to do nothing but "reveal the truth," and in his *Defense of Palamedes*, Palamedes declares his "intention of expounding what is true and of avoiding deceit in the process" (Kerford, *Sophistic Movement*, 81). Kerford tries to solve this contradiction by suggesting that Gorgias believes that the indication of truth or reality itself "can only be done by applying some kind of process of reasoning to the logos in question" (ibid.). But surely a process of reasoning is just more logos, more deception! Perhaps a better solution is to suppose that Gorgias is being Truly rhetorical in the *Encomium* and the *Defense*. Those who know how Gorgias really feels about the possibility of "telling the truth while avoiding deception" can relish their superiority over the *hoi polloi* who are ignorant enough to take such statements at face value.

81. To get a sense of just how complicated the situation can become, see Shadi Bartsch, *Actors in the Audience: Theatricality and Doublespeak from Nero to Hadrian* (Cambridge: Harvard University Press, 1994). In this brilliant analysis of both theater and prose in the early empire, Bartsch looks at cases where writers use intentionally ambiguous utterances to send

asking herself, "Am I being too clever, or not clever enough with regard to a given text?"

Perhaps the original audience of Paul's first letter to the Corinthians felt like they were trapped in just such a nightmare.

> Paul's mixing of praise and blame in 1 Corinthians as well as veiled arguments and covert allusions and ironical tone exacerbated the misunderstanding between Paul and the Corinthians. In Paul's polyphonic approach he appeared as a leader like [Philo's] Joseph, drawn in different directions, showing that his speech, mind, and action were not in harmony, and as such was no legitimate wielder of παρρησία [straight talk]. Such accusations conform to standard accusations against a Socratic type of philosopher who, instead of being direct and open in his approach, is indirect and oblique. Paul is like a "simple" friend, but has, like the Epicurean psychagogues, used a "varied and good method" of exhortation. Paul's audience has understood him as a Socratic type of philosopher and charged him with concealment. The charge of indirection hit home and Paul is at pains rectifying the image. Paul's language of openness is a response to charges of concealment and ambiguity.[82]

Some of the "language of openness" Glad refers to is Paul's protestations in 2 Cor 1 that he acts with "candor and godly sincerity," that he does not make plans in a worldly manner, and that he writes nothing other than what the Corinthians can read and understand.[83] Quite possibly some had charged that his gospel was "veiled" (3:12–4:6).[84] What might all this apologetic rhetoric imply?

According to Betz, and surely most would agree, it could not imply that Paul actually used "sophistic arts" in defending, commending, and propagating his gospel.

> The "Truth" around which his proclamation revolves is naturally the Christian message. But it is precisely Truth which cannot be defended with the arts of rhetoric — just as little as it is permitted to "commend" and "propagate"

---

politically subversive messages while simultaneously protecting themselves from censorship; cases where an actor or lector creates subversive double meanings with lines that were not intended to be so, simply by their interpretive performance of them; and cases where the audience itself creates such meanings by responses such as spontaneous laughter, knowing glances, etc., thereby becoming "actors in the audience." One comes away from this study with a deeper appreciation of what it means to say that the early empire marked a rebirth of rhetoric. Such doublespeak, which strongly resembles the definitions of Platonic rhetoric or Socratic irony discussed above, was the common coin of the realm in Paul's day, and I do not think he escaped this rhetorical economy.

82. Glad, *Paul and Philodemus,* 313–14. I do not agree, however, that the Corinthians' impression of Paul can be accounted for as a misunderstanding created by his "simple" but "varied and good" Epicurean-like psychagogy. As discussed in chapter three, from time to time Glad's study exhibits a Pauline apologetic quality. See, e.g., his rather abrupt and convoluted rejection of Dale Martin's view of 1 Cor 9:19–23 (327).

83. As Marshall notes, Chadwick called 2 Cor 1:13–24 "the locus classicus for the attacks on Paul for his versatility" (Marshall, *Enmity,* 317).

84. Glad, *Paul and Philodemus,* 313; H. Chadwick, " 'All Things to All Men' (I Cor. IX.22)," *NTS* 1 (1955): 271.

Truth with these arts. Aside from the inner content of the concept "Truth," Paul thus agrees entirely with the Socratic tradition.[85]

In the list of verses Betz provides to support this view, 2 Cor 4:2 stands out because of its clear relevance to the matter of rhetorical strategy. Here Paul maintains that "We have given up disgraceful concealments, not practicing cunning nor disguising the word of God, but rather by a manifestation of the truth we commend ourselves to everyone's conscience before God." What could be clearer? Paul is adamant that he would never further his cause by misrepresenting himself or his gospel. But as so often when Paul makes an unambiguous statement, he spoils it with a further remark that confuses it or implies/allows just the opposite.[86] In this case the unsettling comment comes immediately: "But even if our gospel is veiled, it is veiled only to those who are perishing. In their case the god of this world has blinded the minds of the unbelievers, to keep them from seeing the light of the gospel of the glory of Christ, who is the image of God" (4:3–4). Unbelievers are, in effect, kept in a state of ignorance by the god of this world. But Paul does not settle for simply saying that the eyes of their minds have been blinded. Rather, he allows the possibility that, for them, the gospel itself really is veiled. Is this merely a slip of the tongue/pen, an unfortunate choice of words that leaves open the possibility that the gospel both conceals and reveals at the same time, or that there is something about the way he propagates, commends, and defends his gospel that both conceals and reveals at the same time, helping it to become simultaneously "to one a stench from death to death, to the other a fragrance from life to life" (2 Cor 2:16; cf. 1 Cor 1:18)?[87] In short, is his gospel a True rhetoric?[88]

The readings presented in the following chapters will suggest that it is. I am persuaded that Paul mastered and deployed the sophistic arts in fuller

---

85. "Die 'Wahrheit,' um die es in seiner Verkündigung geht, ist natürlich die christliche Botschaft, aber es ist eben die Wahrheit, die sich nicht mit den Mitteln der Rhetorik verteidigen läßt — ebensowenig, wie sie sich mit diesen Mitteln 'empfehlen' und 'propagieren' läßt. Abgesehen von der inhaltlichen Füllung des Begriffes 'Wahrheit' stimmt also Paulus ganz der socratischen Tradition zu" (Betz, *Der Apostel Paulus*, 18).

86. This happens often in Romans, especially with regard to Jews and Judaism. For example, "Then what advantage has the Jew? Or what is the value of circumcision? Much in every way" (Rom 3:1–2a). But only a little later he is saying "What then? Are we Jews any better off? No, not at all..." (3:9). Now (theo)logically considered, in a certain way, this is not contradictory. But I cannot help but think it significant that Paul often expresses himself by saying both "yes" and "no" to an issue, especially a controversial one. Chadwick spoke of Paul's "giving with one hand what he takes away with the other" (Chadwick, "All Things," 271). This is a major rhetorical feature of Romans. See especially Vos, "To Make the Weaker Argument Defeat the Stronger."

87. This "veiled language" will be discussed in greater depth in chapter three, especially as it relates to the preceding verses and Paul's casting of himself as an anti-Moses.

88. Another interesting question would be, Is Paul's gospel Paul's pharmacy? See Martin's discussion of the logic of the *pharmakon* in 1 Cor 11:17–34 (*The Corinthian Body*, 190–97).

ways than Betz and most other scholars allow.[89] We cannot naïvely take Saint Paul at his word in this matter any more than we can Saint Socrates. I think that they both knew quite a lot about veils, or perhaps we should say "screens,"[90] and that Paul actually went beyond Socrates in clothing himself with "weapons of righteousness for the right hand and for the left" (2 Cor 6:7).[91] In what follows I will discuss aspects of some of the more controversial weapons of True rhetoric: ambiguity, cunning, and deception. This is by no means a comprehensive treatment. As the notes will attest, major studies have been written on each of these subjects and the reader is encouraged to consult these studies. Rather, I want to set the stage for the following chapters by focusing on some particular aspects of ambiguity, cunning, and deception that I find especially relevant to Pauline discourse. Since there is considerable semantic overlap in this unholy "sophistic" trinity, in the following chapters we will find considerable cunning and deception combined with the "Ambiguity in Athens," ambiguity and deception combined with "Cunning in Corinth," and ambiguity and cunning combined in "Deception in Rome."

4. Ambiguity

But since in the eyes of some people it is more profitable to seem to be wise than to be wise without seeming to be so (for the sophistic art consists in apparent and not real wisdom, and the sophist is one who makes money from apparent and not real wisdom), it is clear that for these people it is essential to seem to perform the function of a wise man rather than actually to perform it without seeming to do so. *To take a single point of comparison, it is the task of the man who has knowledge of a particular subject himself to refrain from fallacious arguments about the subjects of his knowledge and to be able to expose him who uses them.*[92]

In the first place, then, just as we say that we ought sometimes deliberately to argue plausibly rather than truthfully, so too we ought sometimes to solve questions plausibly rather than according to truth. . . . One must, therefore,

---

89. Betz knows that "Philosophers say they don't use rhetoric but of course they do" (Betz, "Paul's Apology," 27), but the underlying assumption is that there is a line separating the philosopher's rhetoric from sophistic that Paul could not possibly have crossed. Paul uses "Philosopher's rhetoric — not κατὰ σάρκα" (28).

90. See Plato, *Protagoras* 316c–317c.

91. See the long footnote 72 in Detienne and Vernant, *Cunning Intelligence*, 98–99, concerning the *topos* of the ambidextrous or "double" warrior. The implication is that the complete warrior or athlete uses every weapon or skill available. The final paragraph contains much that I find suggestive for 2 Cor 6:7 and 1 Cor 9:19–23: "Georges Dumézil . . . was well aware of these aspects of warrior magic which confers upon warrior gods all the weapons of *maya*, ranging from cunning to a plurality of forms and the gift of transformation over and above their bodily strength. He writes: 'The warrior must be able to be beyond laws, not only moral but even cosmic and physical ones; to defend order he must be in a position to pass beyond it, to step outside it — at the risk sometimes of yielding to the temptation of attacking it' " (99).

92. Aristotle, *On Sophistical Refutations*, 165a.20–28, italics mine.

beware not of being refuted but of appearing to be so, since the asking of ambiguities and questions involving equivocation and all similar fraudulent artifices mask even a genuine refutation and make it uncertain who is refuted and who is not. . . . *As we said, then, since there are some seeming refutations which are not really refutations, in like manner also there are some seeming solutions which are not really solutions. These we say that we ought sometimes to bring forward in preference to true refutations in competitive argument and in meeting ambiguity.*[93]

There is a great lesson to be learned about "rhetorical situations" from *On Sophistical Refutations,* especially competitive, agonistic ones similar to those Paul often faced. It is a lesson also found in the *Rhetoric* where Aristotle summarizes it rather aphoristically: *"Sophistry is not a matter of ability, but of intention"* (ὁ γὰρ σοφιστικὸς οὐκ ἐν τῇ δυνάμει ἀλλ᾽ ἐν τῇ προαιρέσει).[94]

This important principle is sometimes overlooked. Consider this description of *On Sophistical Refutations* provided by the Loeb translator, D. J. Furley.

Just as Aristotle treats of the demonstrative and the dialectical syllogism in the *Posterior Analytics* and the *Topica,* respectively, so in this treatise, which forms a kind of appendix to the *Topica,* he deals with the sophistical syllogism. A knowledge of this is part of the necessary equipment of the arguer, *not in order that he may himself make use of it but that he may avoid it, and that the unwary may not be ensnared in the toils of sophistical argument;* in fact, Aristotle is carrying on the Socratic and early Platonic tradition by attacking the Sophists, who taught the use of logical fallacy in order to make the worse cause appear the better.[95]

The blanket statement that the arguer will not make use of sophistical arguments trades exclusively on the sentiments of the first of the two quotations which open this section. But plainly, according to the second, the arguer will make use of sophistical refutations under certain conditions.[96] These conditions are "in competitive argument and in meeting ambiguity," which is to say, when arguing with people one has branded sophists. Aristotle frequently exploits the common stereotype of sophists as merely contentious

---

93. Ibid., 175a.32–34, 41–46; 176a.19–24, italics mine.

94. *Rhetoric,* 1.1.14, my trans. Cf. LCL: "For what makes the sophist is not the faculty but the moral purpose." Kennedy has "for sophistry is not a matter of ability but of deliberate choice [*proairesis*] [of specious arguments]" (George Kennedy, *Aristotle* On Rhetoric: *A Theory of Civic Discourse* [New York: Oxford University Press, 1991], 35, brackets his). The latter translation, which could imply that anyone who chooses specious arguments is a sophist, is implausible unless Aristotle contradicts himself by later recommending that the non-sophist use such arguments when necessary.

95. *Aristotle,* 3.6, italics mine.

96. The extent of Aristotle's advocacy of sophistry is actually quite extensive. See Robert Wardy, "Mighty Is the Truth and It Shall Prevail?" in *Essays on Aristotle's* Rhetoric (ed. Amélie Oksenberg Rorty; Berkeley: University of California Press, 1996), 56–87.

people who want to gain fame and money from winning arguments by any and all means, including fraudulent ones. But, in a distorted echo of Furley's statement, we might say that Aristotle "taught the use of logical fallacy in order to make the [better] cause appear the better."

Even more strikingly, the motives of the sophist and the non-sophist for using sophistic argumentation actually overlap. In the chapter preceding the one where he will recommend deliberately arguing plausibly rather than truthfully, Aristotle suggests three reasons for studying sophistical arguments and their solutions. First, since they usually turn on language, they help us "appreciate the various meanings which a term can have and what similarities and differences attach to things and their names."[97] Second, they help us avoid such false reasoning in our own minds.[98] But the third reason is that "they establish our reputation (δόξαν), by giving us the credit of having left nothing untried."[99] It is not only the sophist, but also the philosopher who employs sophistic arts to acquire fame and glory.

A major component in sophistical argumentation is intentional ambiguity.[100] In fact, Aristotle places a discussion of the deceptive potential of "the power of names" near the beginning of On Sophistical Refutations.[101]

Some refutations do not affect their object but only appear to do so; this may be due to several causes, of which the most fertile and widespread division is the argument which depends on names. For, since it is impossible to argue by introducing the actual things under discussion, but we use the names as symbols in the place of the things, we think that what happens in the case of the names happens also in the case of the things, just as people who are counting think in the case of their counters. But the cases are not really similar; for names and a quantity of terms are finite, whereas things are infinite in number; and so the same expression and the single name must necessarily signify a number of things. As, therefore, in the above illustration, those who are not clever at managing the counters are deceived by the experts, in the same way in arguments also those who are unacquainted with the power of names

---

97. On Sophistical Refutations, 175a.5–9.
98. Ibid., 175a.10–13.
99. Ibid., 175a.13–14.
100. Of course, not all ambiguity and fallacies arising from it are intentional. A recent comprehensive "invitation" to the entire subject is provided by Douglas Walton, Fallacies Arising from Ambiguity (Applied Logic Series 1; Dordrecht, Boston, London: Kluwer Academic Publishers, 1996). Aristotle's On Sophistical Refutations laid the foundation for such investigations and remains influential.
101. Although Galen would have us believe otherwise (see Robert Blair Edlow, Galen on Language and Ambiguity: An English Translation of Galen's De Captionibus [On Fallacies] with Introduction, Text, and Commentary [Philosophia Antiqua 31; Leiden: E. J. Brill, 1977]), it was not Aristotle but rather the Stoics who analyzed ambiguity most thoroughly and effectively in antiquity (see Catherine Atherton, The Stoics on Ambiguity [Cambridge Classical Studies; Cambridge: Cambridge University Press, 1993]). The significance of their great reputation for detecting ambiguity for the interpretation of Acts 17 is discussed in the following chapter.

are the victims of false reasonings, both when they are themselves arguing and when they are listening to others.[102]

A large number of the species of sophistical argument discussed by Aristotle fall under this genus of linguistic ambiguity. Indeed, from his description of the relationship between things and names one might wonder if all discourse is inherently ambiguous, even deceptive, always both true and false, a notion to which I will return in the discussion of Gorgias' "doctrine of deception." But Aristotle does not go to this extreme.[103] As argued in *Rhetoric*, 3.2.1–7, truthful and sincere speakers can stick as closely as possible to "ordinary language," using nouns and verbs in their "prevailing" (κύριος) meaning.[104] One should avoid "excess," or more literally, too great a departure from "what is fitting" (τοῦ πρέποντος). Such excesses include "glosses" (γλώτταις), i.e., rare and foreign words; "double words" (διπλοῖς), i.e., compounds; and "coinages" (πεποιημένοις), i.e., words of one's own invention. Such excesses were considered sophistic traits, and most of Aristotle's negative examples will come from their writings.[105] But the epitome of excess with respect to the single term, *homonymy*, is most explicitly linked to the sophists.[106] According to Kennedy's delightful rendition "The kind of words useful to a sophist are homonyms (by means of these he does his dirty work)" (παρὰ ταύτας γὰρ κακουργεῖ).[107]

Here I would remind the reader what we saw Plato's Socrates do with χαλεπόν. Among its several possibilities, the word can mean, according to Socrates, either "hard" or "bad." Although the context of Simonides' poem clearly suggests the former, Socrates chose the latter and even succeeded in convincing the expert on such matters, the sophist Prodicus, that this was the correct meaning. It is by means of homonymy that Socrates does his dirty work in this case. His strategy is textbook sophistry by Aristotle's definition. Of course we could easily imagine other ways to exploit homonymy, especially where one has the freedom to make an uninterrupted speech or send an epistle not subject to immediate questioning. One might, for instance, use homonyms to send two very different messages to two very different factions within a single audience simultaneously, perhaps protecting oneself from the ire of one while at the same time ingratiating oneself with another,

---

102. *On Sophistical Refutations*, 164a–165a.

103. For a summary of *On Sophistical Refutations* and a brief discussion of "focal meaning," Aristotle's attempt to overcome the problems posed by homonymy, see Edlow, *Galen*, 17–31.

104. As Kennedy notes, modern literary critics have called this concept into serious question (Kennedy, *Aristotle*, 221).

105. Interestingly, some will come from Plato's usage.

106. Homonymy covers a multitude of sins in ancient linguistic theory, indeed every aspect of lexical ambiguity with respect to a single term. Thus what we would call polysemy, a diversity of possible meanings for what is, etymologically speaking, one word, is considered homonymy in ancient discussions (see Atherton, *Stoics*, 273–328, and Edlow, *Galen*, 21–22, 40–41).

107. Kennedy, *Aristotle*, 223.

or even use them to create factions within an audience.[108] In each of the following chapters I will present examples where Paul would appear to be exploiting such "sophistic" strategies. Such are the signs of a True rhetoric.

5. Cunning and Deception

Detienne and Vernant's *Cunning Intelligence in Greek Culture and Society* is one of the more impressive classical studies of our time. Sadly, it has not received the attention it deserves from Pauline scholars,[109] for to understand the cultural phenomena and issues it addresses is also to begin to understand why we should not only speak of a Socratic, but also of a sophistic Paul. What is cunning intelligence?

> There is no doubt that *mētis* is a type of intelligence and of thought, a way of knowing; it implies a complex but very coherent body of mental attitudes and intellectual behavior which combine flair, wisdom, forethought, subtlety of mind, deception, resourcefulness, vigilance, opportunism, various skills, and experience acquired over the years. It is applied to situations which are transient, shifting, disconcerting and ambiguous, situations which do not lend themselves to precise measurement, exact calculation or rigourous logic. Now in the picture of thought and intelligence presented by the philosophers, the professional experts where intelligence was concerned, all the qualities of mind which go to make up *mētis,* its sleights of hand, its resourceful ploys and its stratagems, are usually thrust into the shadows, erased from the realm of true knowledge and relegated, according to the circumstances, to the level of mere routine, chancey inspiration, changeable opinion or even charlatanerie, pure and simple.[110]

Much of Detienne and Vernant's work is concerned with myths of the Greek gods and heroes.

> However, it is in the world of men at grips with human problems that the intelligence of cunning comes into its own. When it operates in the sphere of Becoming it is constantly faced with unforeseen happenings and ambiguous situations. The unpredictable lies in wait for it and it must be sufficiently vigilant and polymorphic to reverse or divert to its own advantage the powers of cunning which plot to turn its own traps and nets against itself.[111]

Not surprisingly, such habits of mind are frequently associated with sophists. But no matter how much Plato ostensibly condemns sophistic cunning, his

---

108. And we should remember that homonymy is just one species of ambiguity. According to ancient linguistic/literary theory, such ambiguity can exist at the level of phrases and sentences as well. Modern theory would extend it to paragraphs and entire discourses (see Atherton, *Stoics,* 1–27).

109. A notable exception is Dale Martin's *Slavery as Salvation: The Metaphor of Slavery in Pauline Christianity* (New Haven: Yale University Press, 1990), 86–135.

110. Detienne and Vernant, *Cunning Intelligence,* 3–4.

111. Ibid., 306.

Socrates frequently embodies it, a fact not overlooked by Socrates' interlocutors. After quoting the passage in which Meno tells Socrates that it feels
like he is exercising magic and witchcraft upon him (*Meno*, 80A–B), and
that in any other country Socrates would be arrested as a wizard/magician
(γόης), Derrida rightly wonders, "What can be said about this *analogy* that
ceaselessly refers the socratic *pharmakon* to the sophistic *pharmakon* and,
proportioning them to each other, makes us go back indefinitely from one
to the other? How can they be distinguished?"[112] Is not Socrates' ambiguous
appearance a necessary byproduct of his "cunning" (μῆτις)?

> *Mētis* is itself a power of cunning and deceit. It operates through disguise. In
> order to dupe its victim it assumes a form which masks, instead of revealing,
> its true being. In *mētis* appearance and reality no longer correspond to one
> another but stand in contrast, producing an effect of illusion, *apátē*, which
> beguiles the adversary into error and leaves him as bemused by his defeat as
> by the spells of a magician.[113]

In *Cunning Intelligence* one mostly encounters "deception" (ἀπάτη) and
related terms in what Aristotle would have called their ordinary everyday or
prevailing (κύριος) sense. When we think of deception we tend to think first
of things like trickery and bold-faced lying. But now I want to discuss the
epistemologically loaded meaning ἀπάτη acquired in the hands of Gorgias, a
sense already anticipated above by the mention of the "sphere of Becoming."
An understanding of Gorgias' doctrine and the Platonic Socrates' supplementation of it will allow us to appreciate the similarities in Socrates and
Paul's worldviews, and the reasons both had an affinity for True rhetoric.

G. B. Kerford significantly advanced the reappraisal of the sophists as
competent philosophers with his study, *The Sophistic Movement*. What tar-
nished their reputation was not so much that Plato utterly misrepresented
them — many readers agree that he displays a grudging respect toward Gorgias and is even somewhat admiring of Protagoras — but that they simply
do not agree with Plato.[114] They refused his Socrates' "second voyage," that
is, metaphysics.[115] Throughout much of the intellectual history of the West,

---

112. Jacques Derrida, "Plato's Pharmacy," 119.

113. Detienne and Vernant, *Cunning Intelligence*, 21.

114. "In any of the dialogues, there are three or more points of view: those of each of the
two or more participants toward the other or others; and that of Plato toward them all. The
last is always the most difficult to fathom, for on occasion he appears to put such a man as
Gorgias or Protagoras in a good light, and at other times casts an unfavorable reflection upon
him. Even Socrates seems to be made to uphold a dishonest position, as in the *Hippias Minor*,
or to be hedging, as in the first speech that he gives in the *Phaedrus* (237–241d), or to be
somewhat hedonistic and utilitarian, as in parts of the *Protagoras* and the *Gorgias* itself. It is
neither easy nor candid to explain these away" (George Kimball Plochmann and Franklin E.
Robinson, *A Friendly Companion to Plato's* Gorgias [Carbondale: Southern Illinois University
Press, 1988], xxxv).

115. Kerford, *Sophistic Movement*, 67.

to reject this second voyage was not only to reject Plato, but, quite simply, to reject Truth itself.[116]

Kerford begins his discussion of Gorgias' "doctrine of deception" by noting that a fundamental change occurred in the second half of the fifth century B.C.E. in the understanding of language and how it works: " ... there was a growing understanding that what is very often involved is not simply a presentation in words of what is the case, but rather a representation, involving a considerable degree of reorganisation in the process."[117] This realization led to the development of the theory of literature and rhetoric in the sophistic period. Gorgias' treatise *On Nature* presents us with the most radical statement of the great divide that was sensed between discourse (λόγος) and reality. Kerford summarizes it well:

> What we communicate to our neighbors is never these actual things, but only a logos which is always other than the things themselves. It is not even, says Gorgias, speech that displays the external reality, it is the external object that provides information about the logos.
>
> It follows that Gorgias is introducing a radical gulf between logos and the things to which it refers. Once such a gulf is appreciated we can understand quite easily the sense in which every logos involves a falsification of the thing to which it has reference — it can never, according to Gorgias, succeed in reproducing as it were *in* itself that reality which is irretrievably *outside* itself. To the extent that it claims faithfully to reproduce reality it is no more than deception or *apátē*. Yet this is a claim which all logos appears to make. So all logos is to that extent Deception. ... [118]

Plato's Socrates is in complete agreement with Gorgias' doctrine as long as one limits its application to the phenomenal world, the sphere of Becoming. Logos can never effect a one to one correspondence with the phenomenal world. Furthermore, and consequently, he also agrees with the related Heraclitean and Protagorean notion that language which most accurately reflects the phenomenal world will of necessity be paradoxical and contradictory, because the phenomenal world, a place of becoming rather than being, is itself paradoxical and contradictory.[119] But Plato's Socrates goes beyond this agreement with sophists like Gorgias and Protagoras.

---

116. Of course the assimilation of Platonism by Christian theology reinforced this tendency.

117. Kerford, *Sophistic Movement*, 78.

118. Ibid., 80–81. This perspective on language and representation sounds quite avant-garde. Gorgias is no fifth-century Nietzsche or Derrida, of course, but the resemblance between sophistic and Derridean perspectives is close enough to cause Derrida to remind his readers that "One must thus minutely recognize the crossing of the border. And be fully cognizant that [my] reading of Plato is at no time spurred on by some slogan or password of a 'back-to-the-sophists' nature" (Derrida, "Plato's Pharmacy," 108). For a less restrained acknowledgment of the similarity between ancient sophistic and postmodern anti-foundationalist thought, see Gary A. Olson's interview with Stanley Fish, "Fish Tales: A Conversation with 'The Contemporary Sophist,'" in *There's No Such Thing as Free Speech*, 290–91.

119. Kerford, *Sophistic Movement*, 71–77.

The only fundamental point on which Plato is going to take issue with them is their failure to understand that the flux of phenomena is not the end of the story — one must look elsewhere for the truth which is the object of the true knowledge, and even for the understanding of the flux and its causes we have to go to more permanent, secure, and reliable entities, the famous Platonic forms. This in turn suggests that the real basis of Plato's enmity towards the sophists was not that they were wholly wrong in his eyes, but that they elevated half the truth to the whole truth by mixing up the source from which things come with its (phenomenal) consequences (*Phaedo* 101e1–3).[120]

Here we see that the issue of language and its relationship to the world of the senses takes us to the heart of the most distinctive aspects of Plato's philosophy. There was a time when this was largely unrecognized, a time when the *Cratylus,* subtitled *On the Correctness of Names,* could be dismissed as a marginal dialogue in the Platonic corpus dealing with the origin of language. But, as Kerford notes, since about 1955 a revolution has taken place, and its themes are considered of fundamental importance.[121] The dialogue is not about the origin of language, but, just as the subtitle says, about the problem of how names can be correct.

The dialogue opens with Hermogenes "first briefly stating the position of Cratylus the Heraclitean, according to which there is a natural rightness in names, the same for all, Greeks and barbarians, and then stating his own view, that the only rightness in names depends on what people agree at any one time to assign as the name of a thing."[122] Not surprisingly, Socrates, ever the instinctive foundationalist, is immediately attracted to the former opinion.

Socrates argues throughout that the correctness of names springs from their function of indicating the nature of the things named (see e.g. 422d1–2), and he supposes that they do their indicating by a process of imitation of the thing in question. But the things we encounter in our experience are cognitively unreliable in that they always both *are* and *are not*. This makes them unable fully to answer to the names that we use in meaningful discourse — the problem was already posed by Parmenides. Plato's solution however was neither that of renouncing language, nor that of abandoning altogether the world of experience, but rather the manufacture of a 'Third World,' that of the Platonic *Forms.*[123]

As Kerford later puts it, "This is Plato's contribution to the problem which he inherited from the sophists. He resolved the problem of correct language by altering reality to fit the needs of language, instead of the reverse."[124] Perhaps one should say, however, not that he altered reality, but that he

---

120. Ibid., 67.
121. Ibid., 74–75.
122. Ibid., 75.
123. Ibid., 76.
124. Ibid., 77.

supplemented it with another reality, an intelligible world so much more real than the phenomenal world that the phenomenal world is exposed as a shadow reality, a pale reflection and substitute of the really real that ideally would be replaced or escaped.[125]

But what could have emboldened Plato's Socrates to support such a manifestly fantastic solution to the correctness of names? Could one defend such a position on purely rational grounds? Certainly not. This solution is more a matter of faith than reason, as is already clear from an early passage in the *Cratylus*. Near the beginning of the dialogue, Socrates suggests, ironically, that the best procedure for finding out how names can be correct would be to ask the experts in such matters, the sophists. But Hermogenes does not have enough money to go that route. Then when Socrates suggests that he ask his brother who had studied with Protagoras, Hermogenes refuses because he rejects the kind of "truth" found in Protagoras's *On Truth*. Now that Plato has had his fun painting the sophists as intellectual merchants whose opinions on the subject of truth are ultimately worthless, "Socrates then says that Hermogenes should turn to Homer and the other poets where the doctrine that the gods used different names for things from those used by mortal men is clear evidence of a belief in names that are naturally right."[126] This is nothing short of an appeal to divine revelation, and it is hardly the only one in the dialogues. Another example, not unrelated to the present one, occurs with respect to the prisoner in the celebrated cave allegory, discussed briefly below. Plato, who clearly identifies Socrates with the prisoner by adding the detail that those who are still in chains will try to kill him upon his return from the light, does not portray him as having escaped from the chains which keep him from seeing the Truth by his own efforts, but as having been "released" (λυθείη) from them and "compelled" (ἀναγκάζοιτο) to see the light.[127]

The image of Socrates I am contemplating is one of several that emerge from the Platonic dialogues, one of those that tend to merge with Plato himself. It is not the only image found in the dialogues, and, in the opinions of some experts on the Socratic problem, it is an image that may be quite at odds with the historical Socrates who may have been sincere in his claim only to know that he knows nothing. But the Socrates I have in mind holds a conception of philosophy as "an ecstatic ritual process . . . religiously mo-

---

125. This macrocosmic move is quite literally the biggest example imaginable of what Derrida calls the logic of the supplement. The classic statement is in " . . . That Dangerous Supplement . . . ," in *Of Grammatology* (Baltimore and London: The John Hopkins University Press, 1974), 141–64, summarized very effectively in Jonathan Culler, *On Deconstruction: Theory and Criticism after Structuralism* (Ithaca: Cornell University Press, 1982), 102–7. The greatest danger of the supplement is that an endless chain of supplementation is required. This potential flaw in Plato's logic did not go unnoticed in antiquity. Must there not be a form of the form, and so on? See discussion in Rankin, *Sophists, Socratics, and Cynics*, 167–68.

126. Kerford, *Sophistic Movement*, 75.

127. *Republic*, 515c.

tivated by the desire to become divine...a lifelong quest for salvation," a quest that, like the mystery rites Plato's language betrays in the *Symposium* and elsewhere, requires "revelation" as well as reason.[128] It was this image of Socrates that was destined to have the longest career in the Greco-Roman world through Middle Platonism, Neoplatonism, and the church fathers. And I would argue that this Socrates is relevant for understanding the True rhetoric of a mystical apocalypticist like Paul. Despite the many philosophical, cultural, and personal differences between the two, both have reached a comparable worldview. Both have a fundamental mistrust of "this world"; both believe there is a better world which is, in fact, the source of this world; both believe that true knowledge of this better world is largely dependent on revelation; and, as I will argue in chapter three, Paul shares with this Socrates a mistrust of, and desire to transcend, both written and oral discourse.

With this provisional epistemological hypothesis in mind, it is intriguing to compare the Platonic critique of sophists voiced in the *Phaedo* with the Pauline critique of idolaters voiced in Rom 1. According to Socrates, the *antilogikoi* "mix up...the source" (φύροιο...ἀρχῆς) with its phenomenal consequences, and fail "to discover any of the realities; for perhaps not one of them thinks or cares in the least about these things" (*Phaedo*, 101e). According to Paul, the idolaters "exchanged the truth (μετήλλαξαν τὴν ἀλήθειαν) about God for a lie and worshiped...served the creation rather than the Creator" (Rom 1:25) and "did not see fit to acknowledge God" (1:28). Socrates and Paul, on the other hand, distinguish between the Source/Creator and the consequences/creation. Furthermore, this similarity extends beyond epistemology to ethics since both Socrates and Paul causally connect intellectual failure with moral failure. Right knowledge and right action are inextricably related. Judge has seen this very clearly.

> Virtue is knowledge. This was the Socratic thesis and the unity of all virtues becomes explicable in these terms; philosophy thus becomes a pious activity because it cares for the rational soul, which is the only element in man which partakes of the divine. *This itself, like the divine call, is a moral conviction, not arrived at by the process of rational criticism by which Socrates professes to be able to find things out, or at least to find out what is not the case.*[129]

Socrates and Paul, each in their own way, are "gnostics" who possess Truth about the cosmos that demands recognition and conversion, and that will lead not only to right knowledge but right (just) action as well.

---

128. Michael L. Morgan, "Plato and Greek Religion," in *The Cambridge Companion to Plato* (ed. Richard Kraut; Cambridge: Cambridge University Press, 1992), 232–35. "In the central passage of the *Symposium*, then, Plato, using terminology reminiscent of the Eleusinian Mysteries, depicts Socrates simultaneously as the interlocutor in a preliminary elenchus, as the recipient of a religio-philosophical teaching, and as an initiate in a mystery rite" (234).

129. Judge, "St. Paul and Socrates," *Interchange* 13 (1973): 113–14, italics mine.

Here is where Cole's perspective on Socratic/Platonic epistemological "confidence" can inform our understanding of Paul's mimetic rhetorical "missionary strategy." Paul, like Socrates, regarded both his enemies and potential converts as being in a state of ignorance borne of deception. In Socrates' case the problem is an ignorance endemic to our existence in the phenomenal world. Rosen expresses well the rather suspicious Platonic attitude toward the sphere of becoming: "The world as it appears is a sophist.... "[130] The sophists simply reflect and embody the phenomenal world they refuse to transcend. They are deceivers, but they themselves remain deceived through their rejection of the Truth. Since the deception is so severe that most have no idea how ignorant of the Truth they really are, Socrates must deceive the deceived — not just sophists, but everyone he meets — by becoming like them, i.e., by pretending to be ignorant himself. Then through an insinuative dialectic, he can gradually expose their ignorance both to themselves and others.

In Paul's case, however, the problem is even more acute. Ignorance is a state of diabolical deception: "...the god of this world has blinded the minds of the unbelievers..." (1 Cor 4:4a).[131] Humans are not so much the victims of a passive deception, attributable to the nature of the phenomenal world itself, as they are victims of an active deception, perpetrated by a "power" working within "this world." In fact, from Paul's description, one would have to conclude that *for him "the god of this world" is a sophist:* he seeks "to gain the advantage over" people through his "schemes" (2 Cor 2:11); he does not reveal his true identity, but rather he and his servants "disguise" themselves (2 Cor 11:13–15). The unworldly war Paul is waging (2 Cor 10:3–4) has the character of a philosophical/rhetorical debate: "We destroy arguments and every proud obstacle to the knowledge of God, and take every thought captive to obey Christ" (10:5). So it would appear that Paul had even more incentive than Socrates to deceive the deceived in order to lead them to the Truth.[132] I will further develop this perspective in chapter three and argue that it is a valuable interpretive key to 1 Cor 9:19–23.

---

130. Rosen, *Plato's Sophist,* 15.

131. Cf. Acts 26:16–18b. As discussed in the next chapter, this is one aspect of Paul's thought that Luke understood very well and liked so much that he made it an important theme in his narrative, especially, and surely not accidentally, in his speech to the philosophers in Acts 17.

132. And here we would do well to observe the rather fine line separating divine and diabolical deception in Paul, an idea to which I will return from time to time. Commenting on my use of 1 Cor 4:4a and what follows in the passage above, Paul Meyer remarks in a personal communication that deception is "Not always 'diabolical'; cf. 1 Cor 1:21! From this verse (are there not others in Paul?) one might even suggest that *God* (ὁ θεός), not just 'the god of this world,' 'is a sophist,' not only to overcome, or 'gain advantage' over people, but to transcend their criteria of perception, that very transcendence being his 'signature'?"

6. A Truly Socratic Paul

... we seem misleading and we are true ... (2 Cor 6:8c)[133]

Before audiences subject to manifold forms of demonic deception stood the Apostle with his "good news" of a crucified Christ (1 Cor 1:21), "scandalous to Jews and moronic to Gentiles" (1:23). His challenge was no less formidable than that of the prisoner in Plato's allegory of the cave who was released from chains and forced to see "the light" (τὸ φῶς).[134] If he were required to share his vision with his former bondsmen,

> would he not provoke laughter, and would it not be said of him that he had returned from his journey aloft with his eyes ruined and that it was not worth while even to attempt the ascent? And if it were possible to lay hands on him and kill the man who tried to release them and lead them up, would they not kill him?[135]

I think the similarity between this Socrates and Paul's rhetorical situations was not overlooked by Luke. Indeed, I would venture to add this passage to Loveday Alexander's list of popular Socratic traditions that may have influenced Luke's presentation of Paul.[136] Obviously, in both cases, the encounter with "the light" has dire consequences for the eyes and necessitates a period of readjustment (cf. Acts 9:8–19). But, furthermore, Plato's released prisoner appears disgraceful (ἀσχήμων) and ridiculous (γελοῖος) when "he is required in courtrooms or elsewhere to contend about the shadows of the Just (περὶ τῶν τοῦ δικαίου σκιῶν) or the images that cast the shadows and to wrangle in debate about the notions of these things in the minds of those who have never seen Justice (δικαιοσύνην) itself."[137] Perhaps Luke began preparing to present a Socratic Paul in his Gospel. Luke alone among the gospels (23:47) has the centurion say of Jesus, "Really this man was just" ("Οντως ὁ ἄνθρωπος οὗτος δίκαιος ἦν). Then in Acts we find out that Paul was chosen by God "to see the Just and to hear his own voice; for

---

133. Translation suggested by Max Zerwick and Mary Grosvenor, *A Grammatical Analysis of the Greek New Testament* (Rome: Biblical Institute Press, 1981), 546. In another personal communication, Paul Meyer, noting that there is really no basis for "seem," commends the NEB's "we are the imposters who speak the truth," and Luther's "als Verführer, und doch wahrhaftig."

134. Plato, *Republic*, 515C.

135. Ibid., 517A.

136. Taking her cue from Charles Talbert especially, Alexander brilliantly "argues that the Pauline narrative is continuously informed and shaped by the template provided by the biographical tradition relating to Socrates" (L. C. A. Alexander, "Acts and Ancient Intellectual Biography," in *Ancient Literary Setting*, vol. 1 of *The Book of Acts in Its First Century Setting*; ed. B. W. Winter, 31–63, especially 57–63). This has long been argued for Acts 17, and my sophistic take on Paul will generate new perspectives on this passage that will reinforce this "Socratic" reading in the following chapter.

137. Plato, *Republic*, 517D-E. Notice the paradoxical consequences for the True philosopher's image (σχῆμα). For both Socrates and Paul, one who has glimpsed the Truth and tries to tell about it cannot but appear disrespectable (ἀσχήμων).

you will be his witness to all the world of what you have seen and heard" (Acts 22:14–15; cf. 17:31; 24:25). But like the released prisoner who has seen Justice itself and must now address those who have not, he appears disgraceful or offensive to some (e.g., 22:22; 24:5), ridiculous or mad to others (17:32; 26:24). Many consider him worthy of severe punishment or even death.[138] So it was according to Paul himself: "Five times I have received from the Jews the forty lashes minus one. Three times I was beaten with rods [a Roman punishment]. Once I received a stoning" (2 Cor 11:24–25). He experiences "danger from my own people, danger from Gentiles," and "danger from false brethren" (11:26). Truly Paul had reason to "Give no offense to Jews or to Greeks or to the church of God," and to "try to please everyone in everything" (1 Cor 10:32–33).

But apart from changing his scandalous and moronic message — not an option as far as Paul was concerned — some offense was ultimately unavoidable. Penultimately, it was another matter. Certainly, as is often observed, his "adaptability" was all part of putting no obstacle in the way of the gospel of Christ (9:12). Since in the "new creation" (Gal 6:15), all the divisions of this present evil age are passing away (Gal 3:28), Paul feels perfectly free to masquerade in turn as an observant Jew, a proselyte, a Greek, or a less mature believer.[139] He seems to glory in this status ambiguity and mimetic freedom. Perhaps he saw it as mandated by "the law of Christ." As Theissen observes,

> Although the name Christ does not occur, it is clear that Paul is interpreting his life according to the role of Christ. For Christ also became a "slave" (Phil. 2:7*) like Paul. Christ also was "placed under the law" (Gal. 4:4*) — just as Paul places himself under the law. Christ is "weakness on God's part" (1 Cor 1:25*) — just as Paul intends to be weak with the weak. In all of this, he is an imitator of Christ (1 Cor. 11:1).[140]

But could 1 Cor 9:19–23 be about something more than mere accommodation and adaptation so as not to give needless offense? Could it be a rhetorical strategy, a rhetoric of body and voice aimed against the "elements" of this world that maintain these divisions mandated by law, by *the* Law?[141] In this already-but-not-yet apocalyptic existence, perhaps one cannot carry out a frontal assault on the passing but all too potent forms of this world. Perhaps one must always begin from within the world, no longer truly reflecting its image like the rest of the deceived, but miming and mod-

---

138. In all of this we could just as easily explore LXX intertexts, especially prophetic ones. This playful blending of Jewish and Hellenistic echoes is a constant feature of Luke-Acts. As we will see in the following chapter, in Acts 17 it becomes a high art.

139. My identification of the groups in 1 Cor 9:19–23 is discussed in chapter three.

140. Gerd Theissen, *Psychological Aspects of Pauline Theology* (Philadelphia: Fortress, 1987), 253.

141. Note that *every* division of humanity Paul lists in 1 Cor 9:19–23 is ultimately founded upon the Law.

eling it with a difference, a parodic and devious difference. Perhaps only a True rhetoric of ambiguity, cunning, and deception, a rhetoric of both body and voice, can infiltrate a world of ambiguity, cunning, and deception.

> But we speak God's wisdom, concealed in a mystery, which God decreed before the ages for our glory, a wisdom none of the rulers/founders of this age perceived. For if they had perceived it, they would not have crucified the Lord of glory (1 Cor 2:7–8).

God's incarnate wisdom, a wisdom of body and voice, was and is intended for an audience within an audience. For those who really know what God means, it results in "glory," but for those who lack the necessary gift of perception, it results in ruin.[142] God's concealed wisdom is a True rhetoric (cf. 1 Cor 1:21; Rom 8:28–30).

7. A Derridean Medi(t)ation

> As a "wizard and imitator," the Sophist is capable of "producing" "likenesses and homonyms" of everything that exists (234*b*–235*a*). The Sophist mimes the poetic, which nevertheless itself comprises the mimetic; he produces production's double. But just at the point of capture, the Sophist still eludes his pursuers through a supplementary division, extended toward a vanishing point, between two forms of the mimetic (235*d*): the making of likenesses (the *eikastic*) or faithful reproduction, and the making of semblances (the *fantastic*), which simulates the eikastic, pretending to simulate faithfully and deceiving the eye with a simulacrum (a phantasm), which constitutes "a very extensive class, in painting (*zōgraphia*) and in imitation of all sorts." This is an aporia (236*e*) for the philosophical hunter, who comes to a stop before this bifurcation, incapable of continuing to track down his quarry; it is an endless escape route for that quarry (who is also a hunter), who will turn up again, after a long detour, in the direction of [Luke's *Acts*]. This mimodrama and the *double science* arising from it will have concerned only a certain obliterated history of the relations between philosophy and sophistics.[143]

In the next chapter we will accompany a new Socrates as he once more walks the streets of Athens. Once more he will traffic in homonyms as he deceives the deceived (e.g., Acts 17:22). Once more the classic issue will arise: Who is the philosopher and who the sophist (Acts 17:18, 21)? Once more the talk will turn to images and faithful representation (17:23, 29). And once more we will have to ask if Socrates, either Plato's "original" or Luke's copy, is a genuine philosopher or a noble sophist, or if one can tell the difference in the mi(d)st of True rhetoric.

---

142. Whether the ruin is final or not depends, of course, on one's construal of Pauline universalism, an important, though not unambiguous, matter.

143. Jacques Derrida, "The First Session," in *Acts of Literature*, 134. "Luke's *Acts*" replaces "Mallarmé's 'Mimique.' "

II

Ambiguity in Athens
(A Two-Act Play)

---

ambiguous...**1.** Susceptible to multiple interpretation. **2.** Doubtful or uncertain. [Latin *ambiguus*, uncertain, "going about," from *ambigere*, to wander about: *ambi* -, around + *agere*, to drive, lead...].
— *The American Heritage Dictionary*

The *scene* in the book of Acts in which Paul preaches to the people of Athens (17:19–34) denotes, and is intended to denote, a *climax* of the book.
— Martin Dibelius (*Studies*, 26, italics mine)

As for the Text, it is bound to *jouissance*, that is to a pleasure without separation. Order of the signifier, the Text participates in its own way in a social utopia; before History (supposing the latter does not opt for barbarism), the Text achieves, if not the transparence of social relations, then at least of language relations; the Text is that space where no language has a hold over any other, where languages circulate (keeping the circular sense of the term).
— Roland Barthes (*Image-Music-Text*, 164)

Tragedy's site is the margin, and dramatists often treat the physical space which represents it in a way modern critics call "elastic" and *ambiguous*.
— Ruth Padel ("Making Space Speak," 359, italics mine)

TABLE 2
The Architexture of Acts 17:16–34

THEOS: [1]Jacob is my servant (παῖς); I will assist him. Israel is my chosen (ἐκλεκτός); my soul has accepted him. I have given my spirit (πνεῦμα) to him. [2]He will bring a crisis/judgment (κρίσιν) to the Gentiles. He will not cry out, nor raise his voice, nor let it be heard outside. [3]A bruised reed he will not break, and a smoking wick he will not quench, but bring a crisis/judgment (κρίσιν) regarding truth (εἰς ἀλήθειαν). [4]He will revive/reignite/shine forth (ἀναλάμψει) and not be weakened until he has established a crisis/judgment on the earth, and upon his name (ἐπὶ τῷ ὀνόματι αὐτοῦ) shall the Gentiles hope. [5]So says the Lord God who made the heaven (κύριος ὁ θεὸς ὁ ποιήσας τὸν οὐρανὸν) and fixed it, who made firm the earth and the things in it (τὴν γῆν καὶ τὰ ἐν αὐτῇ), who gives breath (πνοὴν) to the people upon it, and spirit to those who walk in it. [6]I the Lord God have called you in righteousness (ἐν δικαιοσύνῃ), and I will hold your hand and strengthen you. And I have given you for the covenant of a race (γένους), for a light of the Gentiles, [7]to open the eyes of the blind, to lead the bound and they who sit in darkness out of bonds and the prison house. [8]I am the Lord God (κύριος ὁ θεός), that is my name. I will not give my splendor (δόξαν) to another, nor my excellencies (ἀρετάς) to sculpted images. [9]See, the ancient things have come to pass, and new things (καινὰ) which I am announcing (ἀναγγελῶ). And before announcing them, I have revealed them to you. (Isa 42:1–9)

[16]Now while Paul was waiting for them in Athens, his spirit (πνεῦμα) within him was provoked, seeing that the city was full of idols. [17]So he dialogued in the synagogue with the Jews and the God-fearers, and in the market place every day with those who chanced to be there. [18]And also some of the Epicurean and Stoic philosophers conversed with him, and some said, "What would this dilettante (σπερμολόγος) say?" while others said, "He appears to be a proclaimer of strange gods" (Ξένων δαιμονίων) — because he preached Jesus and Anastasia. [19]And they took hold of him and brought him to the Areopagus saying, "Are we able to discern (Δυνάμεθα γνῶναι) what this new (καινὴ) teaching is which you present? [20]For strange things (ξενίζοντα) you bring to our ears; we wish therefore to know what these things mean." [21]Now all the Athenians and the visiting strangers (ξένοι) spent their time in nothing except telling or hearing something newer (καινότερον). [22]So Paul, standing in the middle of the Areopagus, said: "Men of Athens, I see how δεισιδαιμονεστέρους you are in every way. [23]For as I went through the city and looked carefully at the objects of your worship, I found among them an altar with the inscription, 'To an unknown god' (Ἀγνώστῳ θεῷ). What therefore you worship ἀγνοοῦντες, this I proclaim (καταγγέλλω) to you. [24]The God who made (ὁ θεὸς ὁ ποιήσας) the world and all things in it (τὰ ἐν αὐτῷ), he who is Lord (κύριος) of heaven and earth (οὐρανοῦ καὶ γῆς), does not live in shrines made by human hands, [25]nor is he served by human hands, as though he needed anything, since he himself gives to all mortals life and breath (πνοὴν) and all things. [26]From one ancestor he made all nations to inhabit the whole earth, and he allotted the times of their existence and the boundaries of the places where they would live, [27]so that they would search for God and perhaps grope for him and find him — though indeed he is not far from each one of us. [28]For 'In him we live and move and have our being'; as even some of your own poets have said, 'For we too are his race/kind (γένος). [29]Since we are God's γένος, we ought not to think that the divine (τὸ θεῖον) is like gold, or silver, or stone, an image formed by the art and imagination of mortals. [30]While God has ὑπεριδὼν the times of ἀγνοίας, now he παραγγέλλει all people everywhere to μετανοεῖν, [31]because he has fixed a day on which he will judge (κρίνειν) the world in righteousness (ἐν δικαιοσύνῃ) by a man whom he has appointed, having produced πίστιν for all by raising him from the dead." [32]When they heard of the resurrection of the dead, some scoffed; but others said, "We will hear you again about this." [33]So Paul went out from between them. [34]But some of them joined him and became believers, including Dionysius the Areopagite and a woman named Damaris, and others with them. (Acts 17:16–34)

THEODORUS: **A** According to yesterday's agreement, Socrates, we ourselves have come in timely fashion, and we bring also a certain stranger (ξένον), the race/kind (γένος) of/from Elea, a comrade of those attached to Parmenides and Zeno, and a real philosopher. SOC. Are you not unknowingly, O Theodorus, bringing no stranger (ξένον), but rather some god (θεόν), according to the word of Homer? **B** For he says that other gods — not least the god of strangers (τὸν ξένιον οὐχ ἥκιστα θεόν) who becomes a companion (συνοπαδὸν) to mortals who share in righteous (δικαίας) reverence — look down upon (καθορᾶν) both the insolence and lawfulness of humanity. So perhaps your companion may be one of the higher powers, who comes to watch over and refute us because we are worthless in argument — a kind of god of refutation. THEO. No, Socrates, that is not the stranger's way; he is more moderate than those who devote themselves to disputation. **C** And though I do not think the man is a god at all, he is certainly divine (θεῖος), for so I address all such philosophers. SOC. And rightly, my friend. However, I fancy it is not much easier, if I may say so, to distinguish (διακρίνειν) this race/kind (γένος) from that of God. For these men — not the plastic but real philosophers — appear in all sorts of shapes, thanks to the ignorance (ἄγνοιαν) of the rest of humanity, and visit the cities, looking down from above (καθορῶντες ὑψόθεν) on the life of those below, and they seem to some to be of no worth and to others to be worth everything. And sometimes they appear as politicians and sometimes as sophists, and occasionally they may produce the impression (δόξαν παράσχοιντο) in some that they are altogether mad. (Plato, *Sophist*, 216A–C)

1. Prologue

The reading of canonical works requires a sensitivity to the subtle and insidious way in which the institutional act of canonization serves to create and sustain reading communities that are dedicated, sometimes unconsciously, to the foreclosure of certain irruptions that occur in them, irruptions that would put at risk communal icons such as the works themselves, the persons they praise, and the values they exemplify for the community. By camouflaging the radically other at the heart of the supposed same, canonization thus functions as a strategy of prophylactic containment.[1] This phenomenon is well illustrated by classic studies, both "conservative" and "liberal," of Acts 17, the story of Paul in Athens.

Liberal readings of the Areopagus speech itself appear at first to emphasize the radically other by insisting that this "philosophical" Paul is not at all the same as the Paul of the genuine epistles, whereas more conservative readings attempt to conform the speech to Rom 1. And yet the liberal reading also falls under the canonical spell since it assumes that even Luke's hyper-Hellenized Paul will embody the highest philosophical and rhetorical standards of Greco-Roman humanism. The assumption of a saintly Socratic Paul, an Isocratean Socratic Paul, tends to anesthetize the liberal reading to the Clytemnestra-like ironic doublespeak that pervades his speech.[2] This radically other Paul does not appear to be either simply the Judeo-Christian apostolic Paul of conservative scholarship, or the Greco-Roman

---

1. See Tom Cohen, *Anti-Mimesis from Plato to Hitchcock* (Cambridge: Cambridge University Press, 1994), 262. Cf. Ernst Käsemann's remark, suggested to me by Paul Meyer, that "Sometimes exegesis betrays more what one does not want to see than what one has seen" (*An die Römer* [Tübingen: Mohr, 1973], 211, my translation). Also see George Aichele, *The Control of Biblical Meaning: Canon as Semiotic Mechanism* (Harrisburg, Pa.: Trinity Press International, 2001).

2. Barthes was fascinated by Jean-Pierre Vernant's demonstration of "the constitutively ambiguous nature of Greek tragedy, its texts being woven from words with double meanings that each character understands unilaterally...; there is, however, someone who understands each word in its duplicity and who, in addition, hears the very deafness of the characters speaking in front of him — this someone being precisely the reader (or here the listener)" ("The Death of the Author," in *Image-Music-Text* [New York: Noonday, 1977], 148). The relevance of this description of the tragic situation will be made clear in my analysis of the speech. Also relevant is Vernant's description of "another type of tragic ambiguity: veiled implications consciously employed by certain characters in the drama who in this way mask within the speech they address to their interlocutor another speech, the opposite of the first, whose meaning is perceptible only to those on the stage and in the audience who possess the necessary information" (Jean-Pierre Vernant, "Ambiguity and Reversal," in *Myth and Tragedy in Ancient Greece* [ed. Jean-Pierre Vernant and Pierre Vidal-Naquet; New York: Zone Books, 1988], 114). E.g., in Aeschylus' *Agamemnon,* Clytemnestra delivers an utterly duplicitous speech that Agamemnon understands in one way, but she and the audience in quite another. Tragedy and the Sophistic Movement were friendly siblings, and Luke's acquaintance with Tragedy has often been suggested on the basis of linguistic and thematic parallels. When Euripides or Aeschylus portrays a character who intentionally deceives his or her audience with ambiguous remarks, they know what type of rhetoric is being employed. Does not Luke?

philosophic Paul of liberal scholarship, but rather a Socratic-sophistic Paul, a Platonic-Socratic Paul, who breaks the canonical mold.

If the past century of scholarship on Acts 17 has taught us anything, it is that where Luke and his image of Paul are concerned, Athens has everything to do with Jerusalem. Paul is the middle man, the liminal man, the man of the (inner) margin. The main defect in Dibelius and Gärtner's strong readings of the Areopagus speech was their totalizing exclusivity. Gärtner tried to replace Dibelius's "total Stoic theology" with a total Old Testament theology.[3] Nonetheless, not either/or but both/and thinking is required to appreciate the double-tongued qualities of the speech.[4] Nauck's argument that 17:22–31 is influenced by Jewish-Hellenistic missionary propaganda is, as Haenchen observed, a step in the right direction.[5] But if such a step is taken with the intention of discovering the one unified, well circumscribed, pure system of discourse in which to give the speech its proper place, the polyphonic is still reduced to monophonic.[6] No, in both the narrative framework and the speech, Paul is standing in the midst, betwixt and between, or as Barthes would say, "in that space where no language has a hold over any other, where languages circulate (keeping the circular sense of the term)."[7]

And so is Luke. One only need inquire about the genre of Acts to realize this. Is Acts an attempt to imitate and extend "biblical" history, a specimen

---

3. According to Dibelius, "The real parallels to this sermon are to be found not in the Epistles of Paul, but in the writings of Cicero and Seneca and in those of their Greek predecessors" ("Paul in Athens," in *Studies in the Acts of the Apostles*, 82). This view is argued in detail in his "Paul on the Areopagus," 26–77. Contrast the following statement, typical of Gärtner: "...the criticism of idolatry follows the pattern often found in Old Testament and Jewish texts. Here, too, there is a striking likeness with Rom. 1, revealed in the function given to the natural revelation, as also in the genuinely Jewish doctrine that the creature may not be worshipped as if it were God" (Bertil Gärtner, *The Areopagus Speech and Natural Revelation* [Uppsala: Almqvist & Wiksell, 1955], 250).

4. See Mark D. Given, "Not Either/Or but Both/And in Paul's Areopagus Speech," *BibInt* 3.3 (1995): 356–72.

5. Ernst Haenchen, *The Acts of the Apostles: A Commentary* (Philadelphia: Westminster, 1971), 528. See Wolfgang Nauck, "Die Tradition und Komposition der Areopagrede," *ZTK* 53 (1956): 11–52. David Balch also finds Nauck's treatment among the best, but while "Nauck is basically correct, yet he is too negative about the possibility of Hellenistic-Stoic models having influenced the form. The influence of a Stoic model on Acts 17 can be convincingly shown" (David L. Balch, "The Areopagus Speech: An Appeal to the Stoic Historian Posidonius Against Later Stoics and the Epicureans," in *Greeks, Romans, and Christians: Essays in Honor of Abraham J. Malherbe* [ed. David L. Balch, Everett Ferguson, and Wayne Meeks; Minneapolis: Fortress, 1990], 73).

6. Because so much of Norden's investigation was concerned with redressing the underestimation of the Hellenistic component of the speech, he is often included among those who overlooked its debt to the OT. But this is not entirely fair. In the process of summarizing the results of his analysis, he says, "Denn es wurde auch gezeigt, daß diese Rede sich zusammensetzt aus zwei Bestandteilen: alttestamentlichen Gedanken und Zitaten, mit denen die apostolische Missionspredigt operiert hat, und theologischen Gemeinplätzen der Stoa, beide teils nebeneinander gestellt, teils ineinander geschoben" (Eduard Norden, *Agnostos Theos: Untersuchungen zur Formengeschichte religiöser Rede* [Stuttgart: B. G. Teubner Verlagsgesellschaft, 1956], 125). Norden's error was to attribute this curious cultural collage to a later redactor.

7. Barthes, "From Work to Text," in *Image-Music-Text*, 164.

of Hellenistic historiography, an institutional history, or the first Christian novel? Surely it is all of these and more, and that is why Pervo is on the right track when he calls it a historical novel.[8] For once one acknowledges just how "novel" Acts is, its generic impurity becomes even more apparent since the novel is the quintessential expression of the eclectic tendencies of the Hellenistic Age.

> Whoever wrote the first Greek novel did not create it out of nothing. Like his successors within the new genre, he was strongly influenced by what he had read and heard: by epic, historiography, and tales of travel, by drama and erotic poetry, by the rhetoric of his time.[9]

This description could apply almost as well to "bad" examples of Greco-Roman historiography.[10] Acts is neither simply history nor novel, nor simply a historical novel. It is all these things and, *ipso facto,* more.[11]

Before proceeding to the text, perhaps something should be said to those who continue to read biblical literature with little interest in anything other than important things like history and theology; those who venerate methodological and stylistic simplicity and purity; those who might look at the form of this chapter and consider it an eccentric obstacle impeding ready access to its content. To them I say, the eclecticism of the present chapter is an homage to the Lukan genius. Just as Luke and Acts and Luke-Acts inspire endless debate concerning their "unity," challenging the reader to find and/or create

---

8. Pervo, *Profit with Delight*, 136–38. Where he gets off the right track is in exaggerating Acts' lack of resemblance to a work of ancient historiography like the monograph. More equal weight should be given to the terms "historical" and "novel" in his genre description.

9. Tomas Hägg, *The Novel in Antiquity* (Berkeley and Los Angeles: University of California Press, 1983), 109. Hägg emphasizes that the strongest influence on the novel is Hellenistic historiography (111–14).

10. See now Bowersock's *Fiction as History: Nero to Julian* (Berkeley, Los Angeles, London: University of California Press, 1994), which could almost be characterized as a book-length meditation on the blurring of history and fiction in the Imperial period. Because he dates the advent of the novel later than many other classicists, Bowersock disagrees with Pervo's view of the genre of Acts only on which way the influence ran. He suspects that the Gospels and Acts influenced the novel, which in turn influenced later apocryphal Christian literature (e.g., 138–39).

11. Cadbury still has something to say to those who want to find one well-circumscribed genre in which to locate Luke-Acts (Henry J. Cadbury, *The Making of Luke-Acts* [New York: Macmillan, 1927], 127–54). Realizing that Luke-Acts resembles a lot of things in its literary environment, he tried to avoid the extremes of identifying it too closely with either "the popular literature of antiquity" or "contemporary formal historiography" (141–42). I am not saying that Acts is *sui generis,* but that its originality lies precisely in going farther than most literature of its time in mixing genre. This formal mixing tendency extends to content as well. Luke is rightly often labeled a universalist in various theological senses. But we must not neglect how true this is from an artistic and cultural perspective as well. He is not, however, a postmodernist in the sense of one who enjoys endless diversity for diversity's sake. As an apocalypticist, he, like most other early Christians, expected the differences of this world — religious, cultural, political, racial, ethnic, gender — one day to be either erased or harmonized in the Kingdom of God, "a social utopia" in which his Text "participates" before History, to use Barthes' language, but hardly a postmodern one. Still, Luke is certainly the most "worldly" of the evangelists, a critic, but nevertheless a consumer and producer of first-century popular culture.

that unity for him or herself, so must this chapter. A competent reader's response to Paul in Athens, a worthy doubling commentary, will be polymorphous and ambiguous. Luke transgressively combines literary, rhetorical, historical, hermeneutical, philosophical, theological, and even theatrical form and content in a creative pastiche. Lukewise, this chapter will let scholarly genre circulate freely, combining literary-critical, rhetorical-critical, and historical-critical form and content with hermeneutical, philosophical, and theological interests. Sometimes I will treat Paul in Athens as popular literature, sometimes as rhetoric, sometimes as history, sometimes as interpretation, sometimes as philosophy, sometimes as theology. And, taking a cue from the strong possibility that Luke echoes Euripides' *Bacchae* both verbally and thematically,[12] I have made this chapter, as I believe Luke made the narrative of Paul in Athens, structurally reminiscent of Greek Tragedy. It will be a kind of reader/viewer response and commentary on the unfolding drama.[13] The Lukan narrator's voice thus functions somewhat like a chorus. Paul and his interlocutors are the actors, and I am the rather noisy critical audience, an annoying characteristic not atypical of ancient ones.[14] To be sure, "Paul in Athens" is not a play. But, by reading it playfully, I hope to highlight certain aspects of Luke's writing that suggest a theatrical influence, especially the pervasive presence of what is often identified as tragedy's most characteristic feature — ambiguity.[15] As Vernant explains,

12. E.g., the use of the "fighting against God" (θεομάχος) topos in 5:39, the miraculous opening of prison doors and fetters in 16:25–26, and Jesus' Dionysus-like words to Paul about kicking against the goads in 26:14. With respect to the last example, notice that although Paul's conversion was already narrated by Luke and later recounted by Paul to a mainly Jewish crowd, the echo of the *Bacchae* is saved for Paul's most formal and elaborate defense speech, one set before an audience that includes a Roman governor, a host of pagan dignitaries, and a thoroughly hellenized Jewish king. Dibelius, ever the careful and cautious historian, notes that this example, as well as several other possible verbal and thematic allusions "are not sufficient to prove any immediate connection between the Acts and the *Bacchae*" (190), but he was clearly impressed by the arguments commentators have made for such a connection and rightly leaves it an open question. See references and discussion in Dibelius, "Literary Allusions in the Speeches in Acts," in *Studies in the Acts of the Apostles,* 186–90. See also P. Colaclides, "Acts 17:28A and Bacchae 506," *VC* 27 (1973). For a more skeptical response to finding an echo of the *Bacchae* in Acts 26:14, see A. Vogeli, "Lukas und Euripides," *TZ* 9 (1953).

13. On the "dramatic quality" of many of the narratives in Luke-Acts see Cadbury, *The Making of Luke-Acts,* 235–38. E.g., quoting J. de Zwaan approvingly, Cadbury says that "The frequent references both in Luke and in Acts to the feelings of the multitudes 'remind one in a remote way of the function of the chorus in Greek Tragedy'" (236). My procedure in this chapter is comparable to Rosen's in his commentary on Plato's *Sophist* (see above, p. 18). Although a Platonic dialogue is not technically a drama, he divides the *Sophist* into acts and scenes and pays careful attention to its dramatic qualities, realizing that the separation of form from content typical of more traditional commentaries is reductionistic.

14. See Bartsch, *Actors in the Audience,* especially "Oppositional Innuendo: Performance, Allusion, and the Audience," 63–97.

15. "Drama as we know it was, of course, another traditional area of literary fabrication, but the conventions of the stage and the verse in which the plays were written made them less easily assimilated to narrative history. Yet the scenes, denouements, and emotional excitements of the two genres could be remarkably similar" (Bowersock, *Fiction as History,* 16). Anyone

No literary genre of antiquity made such full use of the double entendre as did tragedy. . . . It may be a matter of an ambiguity in the vocabulary corresponding to what Aristotle calls *homōnumia* (lexical ambiguity); such an ambiguity is made possible by the shifts or contradictions in the language. The dramatist plays on this to transmit his tragic vision of a world divided against itself and rent with contradictions.[16]

Just before the "play" begins, observe that the *architexture* of Table 2 (p. 40) will serve a purpose comparable to the Greek "tent-background" (σκηνή) or Roman "scene front" (*scenae frons*) for this Athenian drama.

The *skene* (tent or hut) was in origin a simple structure for the convenience of the performers, which could also form a background for the plays. In the course of the fourth century it became a more solid building, ultimately acquiring a handsome architectural form with projecting wings. . . . Roman theatres conformed to a type which made a complete building, though, in larger examples, the auditorium — a semicircle — was probably only partly roofed. The stage, certainly roofed and close to the semi-circular "orchestra," was a wide and fairly deep raised platform, backed by a wall (*scenae frons*) as high as the top of the *cavea*, treated as an elaborate front toward the stage, with columns, niches, etc.[17]

The *scenae frons* developed from the Greek classical σκηνή and served a similar function. But with its increase of the number of passageways leading to "realities" limited only by the audience's informed imagination, the *scenae frons* provides the better analogy to the intertextual reading experience. The two "columns" flanking Paul as he stands "in between" are the background against which, and out of which, this reading is staged. But unlike a true σκηνή, this one is hardly simple and sparsely adorned.[18] When compared to a real σκηνή, my scene-painting (σκηνογραφία), painted with words, is more ornate and finely detailed.[19] And when compared to a real *scenae frons,* my architecture, built of words, is much larger and complex than can be re-presented on a single page. To simplify the discussion, I have reduced it to these two separate and representative columns. In truth there should be a colonnade.[20] But these two will serve as a gateway to an intertextual labyrinth I will explore from time to time.[21] Only as we first

familiar with Acts scholarship must be impressed with how often commentators fall into using descriptions like "highly theatrical," and terms like "scene" and *dramatis personae*.

16. Vernant, "Ambiguity and Reversal," 113. On *homōnumia,* see above, pp. 27–28. I hope to explore further similarities between tragic and apocalyptic worldviews in a future study.

17. Guy Cromwell Field, "Theatres, Structure," *OCD,* 1051–52.

18. For a discussion of what the audience may have seen when it looked at the σκηνή and σκηνογραφία see Padel, "Making Space Speak," 346–54.

19. "The third evangelist came to be regarded by tradition as a portrait painter" (Cadbury, *The Making of Luke-Acts,* v).

20. E.g., Norden begins to erect parallel columns to frame Paul almost from the very beginning of his work. Alongside portions of "Acta" 17 stand excerpts from "Poimandres," "Ode Salomos," "Kerygma Petri," and "Predigt des Barnabas" (Norden, *Agnostos Theos,* 6–7).

21. Cf. Derrida's theatrical image of "the quadrature of the text" with one face open to the audience like "the *frons scenae* of classical theater. . . . Although it passes itself off as the hearth

enter the theater will they steal the show, becoming the focus of attention itself. But the *scenae frons* is ever present, its system of chance allusions ever "circulating," surrounding Paul in Athens. Paul is the *con* of the *text,* "framed" as it were.[22] He is made to stand in the middle where and when Luke's intertextual worlds collide and coalesce — Socrates and the Septuagint, Theodorus and Theophilus, Theios and Theos — reminding us that "the Text participates in its own way in a social utopia; before History (supposing the latter does not opt for barbarism), the Text achieves, if not the transparence of social relations, then at least of language relations."[23]

> And, because Paul was of the same trade, he stayed with them, and they worked together, for by trade they were tentmakers (ἦσαν γὰρ σκηνοποιοὶ τῇ τέχνῃ).[24]

2. Parodos[25]

The Set(up)

[16]Now while Paul was waiting for them in Athens, his spirit within him was provoked, seeing that the city was full of idols.

Now the omnipresent narrator turns his omnipotent gaze toward the reader to share his omniscience. Such is the ancient recipe for a novel reading confection of presence, power, and pleasure. Popular novels of the Hellenistic

---

or focal point where the overall story gathers itself together, it has its own particular history just like each of the other surfaces" (*Dissemination,* 297–98). Thus the depth of the text, despite its surface appearance, is unlimited, making it paradoxically both finite and infinite, like the doubleness of the σκηνή. As Padel says of the audience's relation to the σκηνή, "The whole theatrical space, which they can see, contains another space which they cannot" ("Making Space Speak," 346).

22. "The expression framing the sign has several advantages over context: it reminds us that framing is something we do; it hints of the frame-up (falsifying evidence beforehand in order to make someone appear guilty), a major use of context; and it eludes the incipient positivism of 'context' by alluding to the semiotic function of framing in art, where the frame is determining, setting off the object or event as art, and yet the frame itself may be nothing tangible, pure articulation" (Jonathan Culler, *Framing the Sign: Criticism and Its Institutions* [Norman, Ok.: University of Oklahoma Press, 1988], xiv). And so a context is always, to some degree, a con text.

23. Roland Barthes, "From Work to Text," 164. I take responsibility for the construction of the *scenae frons.* I think Luke would approve, but it is my "architexture," my frame-up. I trust, however, that few will disagree with me that Isa 42 is an important part of the intertexture of Acts 17, and that popular Socratic texts and traditions are part of it as well. The choice of this particular selection from *The Sophist* is not meant to suggest that Luke is directly alluding to and building on it as I would argue he does with Isa 42. Rather, it is chosen to illustrate the well known topos in the Socratic tradition of the difficulty in distinguishing between philosophers and sophists, a topos I do think is utilized in this scene. On the strong similarity between this Greek topos and the Jewish theme of distinguishing between true and false prophets, as well as the tendency of Hellenistic Judaism to combine the two, see Betz, *Der Apostel Paulus,* 36–38.

24. Acts 18:3.

25. As defined s.v. by LSJ, 1341, "**III.** *coming forward, appearance,* esp. before the assembly...2. *first entrance* of a chorus in the orchestra, which was made *from the side wings*... **b.** *first song* sung by the chorus *after its entrance*... 3. *use of stage* for an artist's *performance*...."

and Imperial eras were quite different from modern ones. Usually the reader is informed from the outset as to what the plot will be, as well as the fate of the main characters.[26] The joy of reading is not in guessing the final outcome, but in sharing the author's apparent omniscience, his pervasive pres(ci)ence. This aspect of the Greco-Roman novel is also characteristic of its epic predecessors: "Often the narrator states in advance — in epic, in a regular *prooemium* — what is going to happen and how things will end. The feeling of suspense raised in the reader thus applies not so much to what will happen as to how it will happen; his attention is drawn to the actual course of events rather than to the outcome."[27]

Knowledge and pleasure are hardly strange bedfellows. To "know thyself" is a solitary pleasure, but to know all in advance is ultimate bliss, divine delight. From the beginning, the plot has been made known: "But you shall receive power when the Holy Spirit has come upon you; and you shall be my witnesses in Jerusalem and in all Judea and Samaria and to the end of the earth" (Acts 1:8).[28] The mystery that seduces the ancient novel reader, that engenders the desire for knowledge/pleasure, is not how the story will end, but how it will bend, for "It is not for you to know the chronology (χρόνος) or the critical events (καιρός) which the Author has fixed by his own authority" (1:7).[29] Such perverse pleasures, such following of the seductive twists and turns of an already undressed plot, feature the voyeuristic delights of dramatic irony.[30] For example, we know in advance that Paul, like Jesus, "must suffer" (Acts 9:16; cf. 3:18; Luke 9:22, et al.), but we also know that as bearer of "the Name" he cannot ultimately be stopped (Acts 5:38–39). Thus we are equipped to relish the certain demise of anyone foolhardy

---

26. Heliodorus' *Ethiopica* is an exception.

27. Hägg, *The Novel*, 111.

28. And, for those with ears to hear, a LXX intertextual matrix is made known: "*Be my witnesses* — and I am a witness — says the Lord God, and my servant whom I have chosen, so that you may know and believe and understand that I am. Before me there was no other god (ἄλλος θεός), and after me there will be none" (Isa 43:10; cf. Acts 1:8); "Do not hide and do not wander off. Did you not hear from the beginning and did I not tell you? *You are witnesses* if there is a god besides me" (Isa 44:8; cf. Luke 24:44–49); "Pay attention with your ears and follow my ways. Listen carefully to me and your soul will live in prosperity, and I will make with you an everlasting covenant, the sure guarantees of David. Look, *a witness among the Gentiles* I gave him. Nations which do not know you will call to you, and peoples which are not acquainted with you will run to you for the sake of the Lord your God, the Holy One of Israel, for he has glorified you" (Isa 55:3–5; cf. 49:6; Acts 13:47; 16:9). This entire intertextual matrix or semiotic circuit traces back to Isa 42:1–9, the first Servant Song (which, in turn, traces its semiotic power back to many other sources in an endless feedback loop).

29. "The asyndetic 'He said to them: It is not for you…' makes clear *to the reader* that Jesus is expressing a stern injunction which must be obeyed" (Ernst Haenchen, *The Acts*, 143, italics mine). "If there is a distinction between the two, the χρόνοι would refer to the interval before the consummation of the kingdom, the καίροι, to the critical events accompanying its establishment" (F. F. Bruce, *The Acts of the Apostles: The Greek Text with Introduction and Commentary* [3d rev. and enl. ed.; Grand Rapids: Eerdmans, 1990], 103).

30. Similarly in vol. 1, Luke's *bios*, the whole careers of both John and Jesus are foreshadowed early on, though perhaps more subtly (Luke 1:32–33; 76–77; 2:34–35).

enough to oppose the gospel. Free from suspense concerning the outcome, the reader can revel in pure spectacle.[31] How reassuring it must have been to identify with characters who suffer a myriad twists and turns of a cruel and seemingly inscrutable Fate, only to triumph in the end against all odds because they are "destined."[32]

This ancient novelistic characteristic of the narrative macrocosm that is Acts is also found at the microcosmic level of Paul in Athens. For here in this brief sentence (17:16), Theophilus, the beloved of God, is initiated into deeper mysteries. To know how Paul really feels as he sees, to know what he really thinks as he speaks, this is to escape the world of seeming, to be granted a temporary apotheosis.

Stage Left

But what of the strange manner in which his inner state is described: rather literally, "the spirit of him in him was provoked" (παρωξύνετο τὸ πνεῦμα αὐτοῦ ἐν αὐτῷ)? Certainly the phrase τὸ πνεῦμα αὐτοῦ ἐν αὐτω can be described as a "Hebraism" or Septuagintalism, even though the phrase itself occurs only once in the entire LXX.[33] But such a description of the spirit within should hardly be reduced to "simply *he*" was provoked as Zerwick and Grosvenor recommend[34] — at least not in the discourse of a New Testament author more intoxicated with spirits than any other save one, Paul himself. After all, Luke is quite capable of describing inner turmoil without such an obscure expression. Only one chapter earlier (16:18) he tells us in

---

31. See Pervo on "Adventure in the Acts of the Apostles" in *Profit with Delight*, 12–57.

32. "A belief in fate of a still more frightening kind assumes power in late Hellenism: fatalism, the conviction that some implacable force that directs the stars and planets has also *predestined* the life of every human being. The flight from this terrifying perspective often led to one of the new salvationist faiths.... Rootless, at a loss, restlessly searching — the people who needed and welcomed the novel are the same as those who were attracted by mystery religions and Christianity: the people of Alexandria and other big cities round the Eastern Mediterranean" (Hägg, *The Novel*, 86, 90, italics mine). Cf. "Paul's" message in Acts 13:47–48: "For so the Lord has commanded us, saying, 'I have set you to be a light for the Gentiles, so that you may bring salvation to the ends of the earth' [Isa 49:6; cf. 42:6b–7; Acts 26:18]. When the Gentiles heard this, they were glad and praised the word of the Lord; and as many as had been destined for eternal life became believers." The part of a personified malevolent Fate, or some well-known god who has become an enemy to the protagonist(s) in the Greco-Roman novel, is played by Satan in Luke-Acts.

33. Zerwick and Grosvenor, *A Grammatical Analysis of the Greek New Testament*, 409. The one occurrence of the phrase in the LXX is 1 Kgdms 30:12 (καὶ κατέστη τὸ πνεῦμα αὐτοῦ ἐν αὐτῷ, "the spirit of him in him was restored"). This restoration of a captured Egyptian is the result of receiving physical sustenance. When speaking of Paul's own physical restoration (9:19), i.e., in the kind of situation we might expect to find such an expression, Luke does not use it (καὶ λαβὼν τροφὴν ἐνίσχυσεν, "and taking food he was strengthened"). Furthermore, as we will see, regardless of grammatical similarity, the statement that "the spirit of him in him was provoked" belongs to a different semantic universe than 1 Kgdms 30:12, one in which Acts 2 would be the sun, and 9:17 a large planet.

34. Ibid., 409, italics theirs.

prim and proper Greek that "Paul was annoyed" (διαπονηθεὶς δὲ Παῦλος).[35] So why wait until Paul's appearance in Athens of all places to get suddenly Septuagintal?[36] Why introduce barbarism at the beginning of a chapter filled with Atticism?[37]

The clue to the appearance of this barbaric turn of phrase, "his spirit in him," is the accompanying verb παροξύνω ("to provoke," "irritate," "convulse"), a rare word in the NT, though not the LXX.[38] This term surely had special connotations to a LXX addict like Luke, especially when introduced in the context of idol-filled (κατείδωλος) Athens. It occurs forty-seven times in the LXX. Forty-one of these occurrences, i.e., about ninety percent of them, are employed in expressions of divine anger toward unbelief, disobedience, and idolatry.[39]

The largest number of occurrences in a single book is in Deuteronomy. Not insignificantly, the expression of divine displeasure with idolatry is frequent. The following Deuteronomic example is especially intriguing with respect to Paul in Athens.

> They provoked me (παρώξυνάν με) with strange gods;
> with their abominations they infuriated me.
> They sacrificed to *daimonia,* not to God;
> to gods whom they did not know.
> New (καινοί) and fresh ones came in, whom their fathers did not know.
> You have abandoned the God who begot you (γεννήσαντά δε),
> and forgotten the God who feeds you (Deut 32:16–19).[40]

Echoes of this influential passage from the Song of Moses (cf. Bar 4:7; *Odes Sol.,* 2:16–17; 1 Cor 10:20) can be heard in Acts 17. Verbal and/or thematic parallels are detectable in every phrase. In both texts, (1) divine provocation

---

35. Also cf. 10:17: "Now while Peter was perplexed within himself (Ὡς δὲ ἐν ἑαυτῷ διηπόρει ὁ Πέτρος) as to what the vision he had seen might mean...."

36. At the beginning of his discussion of variation of style in Luke-Acts, Cadbury observed that in comparison to other "literary men of antiquity...Luke's sensitiveness to style seems much less artificial and really more far-reaching" (*The Making of Luke-Acts,* 221; see also 221–33). Only an interpreter who does not fully recognize Luke's peculiar stylistic genius could possibly imagine that he unwittingly committed such an obvious stylistic blunder.

37. On Atticism in Acts 17, see Norden, *Agnostos Theos,* 332–36.

38. It occurs only here and in 1 Cor 13:5: "Love...is not easily provoked."

39. Cf. Seesemann: "It is normally used with ref. to God" ("παροξύνω," *TDNT* 5:857). Thus παροξύνω certainly qualifies as a *terminus technicus* in the LXX. The first occurrences are in Numbers (14:11, 23; 15:30; 16:30; 20:24).

40. Other occurrences in Deuteronomy expressing divine provocation caused by idolatry are 9:8, 18, 19; 31:20. All other occurrences except one refer to divine provocation caused by rebelliousness and other forms of disobedience (1:34; 9:7, 8, 22). The usage is different in Deut 32:41, "For I will sharpen (παροξυνῶ) my sword like lightning," but the subject is still God in his wrath. The word is also frequently used in the Psalms. E.g., "And they were joined also to Baal of Peor, and ate the sacrifices of the dead. And they provoked him (παρώξυναν αὐτὸν) with their practices. And destruction was multiplied among them" (Ps 106:28–29). Further occurrences in the Psalms expressing divine provocation caused by idolatry are 78:40, 41. The remaining occurrences, except the ones concerning enemies discussed later, refer to divine provocation caused by other acts of disobedience (9:25, 34; 106:11).

is caused by the presence of other gods and the abominations, which could also be translated idols, associated with them (lines 1–2; cf. Acts 17:16);[41] (2) gods are referred to as *daimonia*, a rare practice in both the LXX and the NT (line 3; cf. vv. 18, 22); (3) the subject of previously unknown gods is taken up (lines 4–6; cf. vv. 23, 19), and (4) the forgotten God is spoken of as the one who begets and provides sustenance (lines 7–8; cf. vv. 28–29, 25). Although these echoes are distorted, that is, some of the shared vocabulary and motifs function rather differently in Deut 32:16–19 and Acts 17:16–29, the number of parallels, combined with the clear allusion to Deut 32:8a in Acts 17:26, strongly suggests that Luke is playing (with) themes from the Song of Moses.[42] As odd as it may seem to us, Luke may well be applying prophetic anti-idolatry themes to the Athenians as though they were Israelites.[43] His Paul appears to imply, however absurdly, that pagans now worship gods, i.e., idols, whom some of their fathers did not know, and that they once had a more accurate knowledge of God that has been lost, forgotten, or rejected,[44] ironically making the true God the now unknown God.

But returning to our original provocation, even more intriguing is a LXX text where the subject provoked is "the Name." Psalm 73 is a lament over the destruction of "mount Zion where [God] tabernacled" (ὄρος Σιων τοῦτο ὃ κατεσκήνωσας ἐν αὐτῷ). In v. 7 the Psalmist says that the enemies have "burned your sanctuary to the ground; they have profaned the tabernacle of your Name (τὸ σκήνωμα τοῦ ὀνόματός σου)." Here we encounter the mysterious Deuteronomic "theology of the Name,"[45] whereby the immanence of God is expressed by the presence of his Name.[46] Therefore it is

---

41. "Where one appeals to the name of Yahweh any other divine presence has to be eliminated (e.g., Deut 12:2–3: '... you shall destroy their name out of that place'). The divine name of Yahweh does not tolerate any foreign divine name" (Martin Rose, "Names of God in the OT," *ABD* 4:1003).

42. Thus, in the spirit of Richard Hays who, like John Hollander, is especially sensitive to the trope of metalepsis in his analysis of literary allusions, I am trying to be sensitive to cases where a biblical author is not simply prooftexting, but is alluding to a whole complex of correspondences with the original context of an echo (Richard Hays, *Echoes of Scripture in the Letters of Paul* [New Haven and London: Yale University Press, 1989], 18–21).

43. Not surprisingly, then, the speech resembles earlier sermons made to Jews in Acts, and, as is often remarked, the pagan quotations in vv. 28–29 function much like the scriptural prooftexts of those earlier speeches.

44. "...Posidonius was one of the few philosophers in antiquity to stress that God is 'without form,' on the basis of which opinion he criticized representing the divine with images of animals or humans, a philosophical opinion according to Acts 17:25 and 29, despite the later Stoic rejections of this opinion argued in part in the second part of Dio Chrysostom's *Oration* 12. Luke-Acts guards the legitimate philosophical tradition against the Athenians who delight in novelties" (Balch, "The Areopagus Speech," 79). Balch argues that Paul tacitly appeals throughout his speech to Posidonius against contemporary Stoics who did not maintain his hard line against temples and images (69–71, 74).

45. See Rose, *ABD* 4:1003; H. Bietenhard, "ὄνομα," *TDNT* 5:255–58.

46. "In Deut Yahweh Himself, who dwells in heaven, is fairly clearly differentiated from His *shem*, which is localised in the holy place and which is His earthly representative. This

not surprising to find the Psalmist ask in v. 10, "How long, O God, will the enemy scoff? Will the opponent *provoke your Name* forever (παροξυνεῖ ὁ ὑπεναντίος τὸ ὄνομά σου εἰς τέλος)?"

With this "theology of the Name" in mind, let us recall that, in Acts, Paul's very identity was redefined by "the Lord" at his conversion as " . . . a chosen vessel/body (σκεῦος ἐκλογῆς) of mine to carry my Name . . . " (9:15).[47] Immediately afterward, this vessel is filled with the Holy Spirit (9:17), a term which, not insignificantly, is used interchangeably with the "Spirit of Jesus" on one occasion during Paul's adventures.[48] Thus, to say that Paul was filled with the Holy Spirit is also to say that he was filled with the Spirit of Jesus, filled with the presence of "my Name."[49] In short, Paul's "Spirit within him" is the One that is always "provoked" in the presence of other gods and their idols.[50] It is the One that filled him after his conversion ("the Holy Spirit," 9:17),

---

theologoumenon facilitates the increased later use of שם יהוה as an alternative for Yahweh and also prepares the way finally for the hypostatization of the *shem* as a relatively independent force compared with Yahweh" (Bietenhard, *TDNT* 5:258).

47. Bietenhard expresses the significance of the Name of Jesus succinctly: "In the NT the name, person and work of God are — with various differentiations — inseparably linked with the name, person, and work of Jesus Christ" (*TDNT* 5.271). The rootedness of this usage in the hypostatization of the divine Name in the MT/LXX is patent. To the use of σκεῦος here, cf. 2 Cor 4:7. Paul describes apostles as "earthen vessels" holding a treasure which is "the light of the knowledge of the glory of God in the face of Christ" (v. 6). This "light" is a "transcendent power" that comes from God, not themselves (ἡ ὑπερβολὴ τῆς δυνάμεως ᾖ τοῦ θεοῦ καὶ μὴ ἐξ ἡμῶν, v. 7). Because of it, although they constantly suffer, they also survive (vv. 8–9; cf. Acts 9:16). Paradoxically, then, they are always "*bearing about* in the body (ἐν τῷ σώματι περιφέροντες) the death of Jesus, so that the life of Jesus may also be manifested in our body" (v.10). This is an aspect of Paul's thought that Luke understood quite accurately.

48. In 16:6 the Holy Spirit blocks the way of Paul and his companions, while in the very next verse the same inhibiting action is attributed to the Spirit of Jesus. It would probably be wrong to choose between an objective and subjective genitive in this case. For Luke, after the resurrection, to some extent, the Spirit Jesus gives is the Spirit Jesus is.

49. Perhaps Luke's notion of Paul as the chosen "vessel" to bear the Name to the Gentiles throws some light on Paul's enigmatic remark that God "was pleased to reveal his Son *in* me" (Gal 1:16; cf. 2 Cor 4:7, discussed above, n. 47). Cf. 1 Cor 5:4: "When you are assembled, and *my spirit* is present with *the power of our Lord Jesus*. . . . " Consider also the intimate relationship — possibly parallelism — of Spirit and Name in the following remark: "But you were washed, you were sanctified, you were justified in the *Name* of the Lord Jesus Christ and in the *Spirit* of our God" (1 Cor 6:11). Other NT examples are worth noting: "But the Advocate, the *Holy Spirit*, whom the Father will send in my *Name*, will teach you everything, and remind you of all that I have said to you" (John 14:26). "If you are reviled for the *Name* of Christ, you are blessed, because the *Spirit* of glory and of God is resting on you" (1 Pet 4:14). Due to the influence of the LXX, Name and Presence, Name and Spirit, go together in the NT, and for early Christians that Name is Jesus (or his titles Lord and Son). Indeed, some of the miracles made possible by the gift of the Spirit in Acts are spoken of as occurring by the Name of Jesus (3:6; 4:10; 16:8). To invoke the Name is to invoke the Spirit. See entire discussion in Bietenhard, *TDNT* 5:271–80.

50. Johnson, apparently hearing the sort of Septuagintal echoes being explored here and realizing how appropriate a reference to the Holy Spirit would be in Acts 17:16, observes that "There are no *mss* that omit 'his' (*autou*), so the *pneuma* that is irritated is Paul's own and not the prophetic 'Holy Spirit' " (Luke Timothy Johnson, *The Acts of the Apostles* [SP 5; Collegeville, Minn.: Liturgical Press, 1992], 312). It should be clear why I do not agree with this conclusion and more argument will follow. It is Paul's unique relationship with the Holy

that moved him to blind Elymas the magician ("the Holy Spirit," 13:9), that forbade him from entering Asia ("the Holy Spirit," 16:6) and Bithynia ("the Spirit of Jesus," 16:7).[51] The line separating "my Name," "the Holy Spirit," "the Spirit of Jesus," and "the Spirit of him in him" is very fine indeed.[52]

That Name and Spirit should be so intimately linked in Acts is not surprising. Luke has a very pronounced and pervasive theology/Christology of the Name.[53] Like the Psalmist, he is under the influence of the Deuteronomic Name/Presence theology.

> And you will eat it [the tithe] in the place which the Lord your God will choose to have his *Name* called there ... and you will eat there in the *Presence* (ἐναντίον) of the Lord your God (Deut 14:23, 26).

> I know that the Lord will maintain the cause of the poor, and the right of the needy. Surely the righteous shall give thanks to your *Name;* the upright shall live with your *Presence* (σὺν τῷ προσώπῳ σου) (Psa 139[140]:12–13).[54]

According to the Deuteronomic perspective, to eat in the presence of the Lord is to eat in that one special place in which the Lord chooses "to have his Name called there," the Temple.[55] But for Luke, as for Deutero-Isaiah,

---

Spirit, the Spirit of Jesus, that suggests that "Paul's Spirit within him" is not simply a reference to his own spirit. Later, when we turn our attention to "Stage Right," I will present another reason why Luke resorted to this odd and intriguing expression.

51. Such a blurring of the Holy Spirit and the risen Jesus is already apparent in volume one of Luke-Acts. In Luke 12:12, Jesus says the Holy Spirit will teach the disciples what to say when brought before authorities, but in 21:15 Jesus says that *he* will give them a mouth and wisdom.

52. If the phrase "his spirit within him" is an unambiguous reference to Paul's human spirit, it is truly exceptional in Acts, for unless it is here, there is no occurrence of πνεῦμα in Acts that unambiguously refers to the human spirit. See Johnson's comments on ambiguous cases like Acts 18:25 and 19:21 (*The Acts,* 332, 346).

53. It is more prominent in Acts than Luke, very likely because the Name of Jesus (or the Lord) and the Spirit (of Jesus) overlap significantly after Jesus commends his Spirit into the hands of the Father (Luke 23:46). See especially Acts 2; 3:16; 4:7–30; 5:41; 15:14–18, and 26 (where ὄνομα is inaccurately translated "sake" in the RSV and NRSV); 19:13–17.

54. The intimate relationship between name and presence is expressed in the Psalm by typical Hebrew poetic parallelism.

55. The MT connects Name with presence more explicitly than the LXX, rather literally, "And eat before (לִפְנֵי) Yahweh your God, at the place that he will choose to make dwell (לְשַׁכֵּן) the Name of him there ... " (Deut 14:23). Obviously one could understand this to mean that Yahweh lives in the Temple, and commentators on the MT often explain that this is not what is intended; that the Hebrews, unlike their pagan neighbors, did not entertain such notions. The LXX rendering of לְשַׁכֵּן by ἐπικληθῆναι, "to have called upon," could be a deliberate mistranslation to guard against this misunderstanding. The LXX translates שׁכן as ἐπικαλέω nine times (Exod 29:45, 46; Deut 12:5, 11; 14:23; 16:2, 6, 11; 26:2), and in every case the idea that God or his Name dwells with a particular people, the children of Israel, or in a particular place, the Temple, is changed to the idea that He chooses to be called upon, or have His Name called upon, by a particular people, in a particular place. Cf. the similar tendency of Josephus, as noted by Levison, to avoid the idea that the Spirit dwells "in" people. Rather, it "accompanies" them (John R. Levison, "The Angelic Spirit in Early Judaism," [SBLSP 34; Atlanta: Scholars Press, 1995], 464–93, 489–90). Notice that the curious phrase in Acts 17:16 could be translated "the Spirit of him *with* him," a possibility to be considered later when we turn our attention to "Stage Right" (see below, pp. 56ff.).

the Temple is no more. God no longer chooses to have his Name called there. Yet also for Luke, as for Deutero-Isaiah, the Spirit has not departed. Instead it now rests upon the Servant/Child. For Deutero-Isaiah this Servant/Child is primarily exilic Israel.[56] For Luke it is primarily Jesus, the only one to be called the Servant/Child (παῖς) in Luke-Acts — others are slaves (δοῦλοι).[57]

Paul, however, is certainly more than just another slave, witness, or apostle. Indeed, the common opinion that Luke's sparing use of the title apostle (Acts 14:4, 14) for his hero is paradoxical results from failure to realize that, in Luke-Acts, being an apostle pales in comparison to Paul's superior status. As Jesus' "chosen vessel" who will "carry my Name" to the Gentiles, his intimacy with the Servant/Child is unique. Their destinies are so intertwined that one might well say in the words of another NT writer that Paul "completes what is lacking" (Col 1:24) in the suffering of the Servant: "for I will show him how much he must suffer for the sake of my Name" (Acts 9:16). To comprehend this intimacy better, we must gaze more intently at the Septuagintal side of the σκηνή, Isa 42:1–9.

The powerful influence of the Servant Songs on the Christology of the early church in general and Luke-Acts in particular is well known. Yet a perfect match between the careers of the Servant and Jesus was impossible. The first Servant Song is illustrative. It suggests that the Servant himself, exilic Israel, brings the knowledge of God to the Gentiles. But that is not what happened in Jesus' case, and both Matthew and Luke take steps to resolve this problem.

The problem was more difficult for Matthew since he portrays Jesus as forbidding a mission to the Gentiles (Matt 10:5), and even as voicing typical Jewish antipathy and prejudice toward them (see 6:7, 32; 18:17).[58] Still, Matthew clearly believed that Jesus fulfilled Isa 42:1–4 (see Matt 12:18–21), but only through his presence in the continuing activities of his disciples after the resurrection (28:19–20). Matthew's quotation from Isa 42 is apparently at least meant — there are several other possibilities — to explain Jesus' strange command "not to make him known" (Matt 12:16). Jesus will be able to "proclaim justice to the Gentiles" and "in his name the Gentiles will hope" precisely because, with respect to Israel in the present, he will not contend for their recognition, "he will not wrangle or cry aloud, nor will anyone hear his voice in the streets" (v. 19).[59]

Luke, however, deals with the problem more aggressively by introducing a very early allusion to the Servant Songs into the prophecies of the Spirit-filled

---

56. In some passages it could also be the prophet himself as representative of the exiles.

57. See Acts 4:29; 16:17.

58. And in light of 10:5, I would conclude that Matthew understands "the people who sat in darkness" of 4:16 to be limited to "the lost sheep of the house of Israel" located in Galilee and other predominantly Gentile regions, especially since Jesus is subsequently portrayed as "teaching in their synagogues" (4:23).

59. See Daniel Patte, *The Gospel According to Matthew: A Structural Commentary on Matthew's Faith* [Philadelphia: Fortress, 1987], 172–74.

Simeon concerning the destiny of "the servant/child (παῖς) Jesus" ("a light for revelation to the Gentiles," Luke 2:32a). Jesus' rejection at Nazareth in which he strongly implies that the benefits of the Kingdom are going to be enjoyed by Gentiles is made the first major episode of his ministry (4:16–30).[60] Furthermore, if Luke knew sayings of Jesus like Matthew's that negatively characterized Gentiles, he ignored them. Moreover, in spite of his affection for stories involving women, Luke omitted Mark's story of the witty Gentile Syrophoenician woman, probably not only because it portrays a Jesus who refers to Gentiles as dogs (7:26–30), something he could easily have altered, but even more likely because the story as a whole could leave the impression that Jesus is so unconcerned with Gentiles that he must be tricked into serving them.

Of course the list of pro-Gentile features of Luke could be lengthened considerably, but the point is that Luke goes well beyond Matthew in making Jesus as pro-Gentile as possible without denying what would appear to be the established fact that he himself did not preach to them. He also goes well beyond Matthew in making "Servant" a title for Jesus.[61] Nevertheless, he still does not suggest that Jesus directly performs the Servant's task of opening the Gentile's eyes nor, for that matter, gathering the dispersed tribes of Jacob and Israel (Isa 49:5–6, 12).

Luke, however, had a distinct advantage over Matthew where the Servant was concerned: volume two, The Acts (of Paul).[62] By establishing the most intimate relationship possible between Jesus and Paul, that is, by making Paul the chosen bearer of the Name to the people and the Gentiles, Luke suggests that Jesus is able to fulfill his Servant role in/with Paul. Notice how Luke "frames" Paul's prophetic ministry with references to the Servant Songs in his first and last major speeches. The Pisidian Antioch speech climaxes with "For so the Lord has commanded us, saying, 'I have set you for a light for the Gentiles, that you may bring salvation to the uttermost parts of the

---

60. If one resolves the difficult text-critical problem in Luke 10:1 in favor of "seventy-two" rather than "seventy," then unlike Matthew's Jesus who explicitly forbids a mission to the Gentiles, Luke's Jesus may well be symbolically anticipating a mission to the traditional number of the nations. The fact that he sends the disciples ahead to cities he is about to visit himself is no obstacle to this symbolic interpretation since the Spirit of Jesus is with the apostles and disciples as they spread the gospel to all nations in Acts. See discussion in Robert C. Tannehill, *The Narrative Unity of Luke-Acts: A Literary Interpretation* (2 vols.; Philadelphia: Fortress, 1986), 1:232–33.

61. Matthew uses the title in 12:18 only, while Mark does not use it as a title at all. Cf. Acts 3:13, 26; 4:27, 30. In light of these occurrences in Acts, it is tempting to hear an echo of the Servant theme when "the παῖς Jesus" or simply "the παῖς" is used in Luke's birth narrative, especially in 2:27 and 34 in the context of Simeon's prophecies. Finally, Luke alone uses παῖς for Israel (Luke 1:54) and David (Luke 1:69; Acts 4:25), possibly suggesting some special relationship between them and the παῖς Jesus.

62. "There can be no doubt that Paul is the hero of Luke-Acts. One might even be tempted to call Acts the 'Acts of Paul' instead of 'The Acts of the Apostles' " (J. Christiaan Beker, *Heirs of Paul: Paul's Legacy in the New Testament and in the Church Today* [Minneapolis: Fortress, 1991], 48).

earth' " (Acts 13:47; Isa 49:6; cf. 42:6–7). Likewise the speech before Festus and Agrippa concludes with this theme (Acts 26:18, 23). In the latter case the special relationship between Jesus and Paul is conveyed in a subtle and highly artful manner. In v. 18, the risen Lord Jesus gives Paul the Servant's task of turning the people and the Gentiles to "the light." But as Paul concludes his defense, he summarizes his message as "that the Christ must suffer, and that, by being the first to rise from the dead, *he* would proclaim light both to the people and to the Gentiles" (v. 23). *In the space of five verses we have the risen Jesus proclaiming that Paul will fulfill the Servant's task and Paul proclaiming that the risen Jesus will fulfill the Servant's task.*[63] Paul is not the Servant, but the risen Jesus can be the Servant through, or better in/with, Paul.[64]

This is why Paul in Athens, the drama that begins by having Paul argue with both Jews and pagans because of (μὲν οὖν in 17:17) idolatry, opens with the statement that "his Spirit in him was provoked," and indeed "was being provoked" throughout the entire episode.[65] For it is really the Servant, the Spirit of Jesus, the Name that Paul the chosen vessel bears, that will now play His scripted role in grand style before dispersed Jews and the Gentiles. In the spiritual heart of pagan antiquity, in the city famed to have more gods than men, the Servant will now speak for "the Lord God" (Isa 42:5, 8, κύριος ὁ θεός; cf. Acts 17:24, ὁ θεὸς . . . κύριος) and "proclaim new things" (Isa 42:9, καινὰ ἃ ἐγὼ ἀναγγελῶ;[66] cf. Acts 17:18–19, καταγγελεὺς, εὐαγγελίζω, ἡ καινὴ αὕτη . . . διδαχή, v. 23, καταγγέλλω) in order to "bring a crisis/judgment" to the Gentiles (Isa 42:2, ἐξοίσει κρίσιν; cf. Acts 17:31, μέλλει κρίνειν). He is the one who was called/appointed "in righteousness" for this task (Isa 42:6, ἐκάλεσά σε ἐν δικαιοσύνῃ; cf. Acts 17:31, ἐν δικαιοσύνῃ ἐν ἀνδρὶ ᾧ ὥρισεν), and who proclaims "the Lord God who made the heaven and fixed it, who made firm the earth and the things in it, and who gives breath to the people upon it" (Isa 42:5; cf. Acts 17:24–25).[67] The Servant proclaims the Lord God's message that "I will not

---

63. Once this special relationship between the Servant and Paul is fully realized, it is easy to see why Luke may have distorted the facts by making Paul's ministry almost consistently one to both Jews and Gentiles. Since Jesus did not fulfill the Servant's task toward either the Gentiles or the dispersed Jews, Paul, as his Name bearer, must do both. If Luke knows anything of an ethnic division of mission between Peter and Paul (Gal 2:7–8), he must ignore it to maintain his Christology/Servantology/Paulology.

64. For parallels between Jesus and Paul in general, see Walter Radl, *Paulus und Jesus im lukanischen Doppelwerk: Untersuchungen zu Parallelmotiven im Lukasevangelium und in der Apostelgeschichte* (Frankfurt: Peter Lang, 1975); A. J. Matill, "The Paul-Jesus Parallels and the Purpose of Luke-Acts: C. H. Evans Reconsidered," *NovT* 17 (1975): 15–45.

65. In response to the reading offered in my "Stage Left," Paul Meyer suggests the possibility that the choice of the imperfect tense rather than an expected aorist for παροξύνω in Acts 17:16 is significant. It is not merely Paul's spirit that remains "provoked" throughout this episode, but the Spirit of the Name he bears, the Spirit that must remain provoked while in the presence of idols. See above, pp. 48–50.

66. The speaker is actually "the Lord God" in Isa 42:9.

67. On the echo of Isa 42:5 in Acts 17:24–25 see E. Fudge, "Paul's Apostolic Self-

give my glory to another, nor my praises to sculpted images" (Isa 42:8; cf. Acts 17:29). And "upon his name the Gentiles will hope" (Isa 42:4, ἐπὶ τῷ ὀνόματι αὐτοῦ ἔθνη ἐλπιοῦσιν; cf. Acts 17:18, Ἰησοῦς, v. 31, ἀνήρ).[68] And all of this is possible because he has been "revived" (Isa 42:4, ἀναλάμπω; cf. Acts 17:31, ἀνίστημι).[69]

No wonder then that, as is often observed, the distinctive Christian message plays such a small role in the speech. The Servant's first and main task where the Gentiles are concerned is to turn them "from darkness to light, from the power of Satan to God" (Acts 26:18a). Then, as he says, "they may receive forgiveness of sins and a place among those who are sanctified by faith in me" (Acts 26:18b). From Luke's perspective, it was necessary for Paul to make this appearance in Athens, not so much because he was the great Apostle to the Gentiles, as Paul himself probably would have said, but because he is the chosen vessel that bears the Name upon which the Gentiles will hope, because of the chosen Servant's mission, because of "his Spirit in him."[70]

Stage Right

But all this is merely one side of the cultural equation. "His spirit in him" should not be interpreted on the basis of LXX intertexts alone. One should also ask what intertexts "his spirit in him" might conjure up in the context of a Paul who dialogues in the agora with whoever chances by, layperson or philosopher, and will later be characterized as one who appears to introduce foreign δαιμονία. Can readers who are able to hear these Socratic echoes remain deaf to the δαιμόνιον?

The "divine thing"[71] of Socrates was a perennial hot *topos* in religio-

---

Consciousness in Athens," *JETS* 14 (1971): 193–98. This echo can easily be observed in the *architexture* of my *scenae frons* (see Table 2, p. 40 above).

68. Of course, Acts 9:15 (τὸ ὄνομά μου) is the key here. And, as is so often the case in Isa 53 as well, the difference of the LXX from the MT is crucial for Christian interpretation. Where the MT has "And the coastlands will wait expectantly for his law," the LXX has "And upon his Name the Gentiles will hope."

69. Luke could easily have equated ἀναλάμπω with ἀνίστημι ("to rise"). Consider some of the possible translations for ἀναλάμπω in the context of Isa 42:4: "to flame up," "take fire," "break out anew," "revive," or "shine forth." It is hard to imagine that given the profound influence of this Servant Song on Luke that he would not have noticed that Isa 42:4 epitomizes his entire second volume: "He will revive/reignite/shine forth and not be weakened until he has established a judgment on the earth, and upon his name will the Gentiles hope." Notice also the possibility of associating it in more than one sense to the risen Jesus as Luke portrays him. It could refer to his resurrection, the fiery advent of his Spirit at Pentecost, or his shining forth "light" to the Gentiles.

70. This is not to say, however, that Paul would have objected to being so closely associated with the Servant. E.g., cf. Gal 1:15, "But when God, who had set me apart before I was born and called me through his grace, was pleased to reveal his Son in me, so that I might proclaim him among the Gentiles..." with Isa 49:1, "Listen to me, islands, and pay attention, Gentiles. After a long time it will happen, says the Lord. From my mother's womb he has called my name...."

71. Vlastos expresses the common opinion that the proper translation in Plato is always non-substantival, and quotes John Burnet's opinion that δαιμόνιον is never a noun-substantive

philosophical circles.[72] Both Plato and Xenophon chose this vague term for Socrates' divine "sign," but Plato never personified it as Socrates' deity, or δαίμων.[73] Xenophon and later writers were not so cautious. As Vlastos observes, "In Xenophon its promptings to Socrates are not restricted to dissuasion; they also give positive injunctions and, what is still more striking, the δαιμόνιον affords Socrates an intelligence service he can use to benefit third parties as well.... "[74] In the pseudo-Platonic *Theages*, the δαιμόνιον becomes a full-fledged deity to be propitiated by prayer and sacrifice.[75] Interestingly,

> The mentality of the writer of this curious work is indicated by the fact that a young man is supposed to make moral progress simply by being in the same house with Socrates and much greater if [he] sat at Socrates' side and most of all when sitting right next to Socrates, touching him (130E).[76]

It is not hard to see the implications. The δαιμόνιον is in or with Socrates. It is a divine presence whose benefits can "rub off" on someone in a spiritual/magical fashion. Much later, Plutarch will write a sort of combination historical novel and philosophical essay called *On Socrates' Personal Deity* that, in a manner reminiscent of the *Phaedrus*, will put reflections in the mouths of Socrates' acquaintances like these by Theocritus:

> I don't think that anything that Pythagoras is said to have done as a seer is as important or as divine. I mean, Homer in his poem has Odysseus "attended in all his struggles" by Athena, and exactly the same goes for Socrates: throughout his life his personal deity seems to have afforded him the kind of perceptiveness which, all by itself, "leads the way and sheds light" — to have given him this guide as a companion whenever he was in situations which were opaque and unfathomable by human intelligence, in the course of which his personal deity invariably communicated with him and made his decisions inspired.[77]

---

in Classical Greek. Thus it is Socrates' enemies who, nevertheless, (mis)understood him as referring to δαιμόνια καινά (Gregory Vlastos, *Socrates*, 280–81). And yet, Vlastos goes on to affirm that in Xenophon the word is a quasi-substantive (281).

72. " ...the topic of psychological daimonology was extremely popular through the first century BC to the second century AD, and produced a number of different and fascinating versions" (Ian Kidd, "On Socrates' Personal Deity: Introduction," in *Plutarch: Essays* [trans. Robin Waterfield; London: Penguin, 1992], 306).

73. For a good discussion of Plato's version of the δαιμόνιον that differs somewhat from that of Vlastos, see Thomas C. Brickhouse and Nicholas D. Smith, *Plato's Socrates* (New York: Oxford University Press, 1994), 189–95. In a nutshell, although Vlastos acknowledges that modern classical scholars have often unfairly tried to eliminate an acceptance of religion and the supernatural from the historical Socrates because it offended their own epistemological sensibilities, Vlastos himself continues to argue that divine revelation is not a source of any of his ideas. Brickhouse and Smith allow it some minimal contribution. For my purposes, it is irrelevant whether or not the real Socrates was inspired by God or "the god" Apollo. That Isocrates and later writers thought so is indisputable. It is this legendary Socrates that is relevant here.

74. Vlastos, *Socrates*, 281.

75. Ibid., 282.

76. Ibid.

77. Plutarch, *De Genio Socratis*, 580D.

It was these more daring versions of the δαιμόνιον, ones that turn it into an accompanying god or spirit, that were to capture the imagination of later generations and have the more pervasive influence, one that extended even to Hellenistic Judaism. As Levison demonstrates, both Philo and Josephus model the presence of the divine Spirit in or with certain gifted individuals on the same Socratic model as Plutarch.[78]

> ... Josephus and Philo proffer independent instances in which the divine spirit is interpreted as an angelic being who accompanies and inspires people. The model presupposed in this exegetical transformation can be ascertained from Plutarch's De genio Socratis, in which daemonic beings inspire the minds of the daemonic race.[79]

Because they wrote at a time when Socrates had become a full-fledged pagan saint, as much a popular religious as a philosophical hero, the analogies between the activities of the Socratic δαιμόνιον and the Angelic Spirit were too obvious for Josephus and Philo to ignore.[80] I doubt that Luke was any less aware of them.

For example, we have already had occasion to mention the curious passage in Acts 16:6–7 where the Holy Spirit "hinders" Paul and company from entering Asia, and the Spirit of Jesus "did not permit" them to enter Bithynia.[81] Similarly in 20:23, the Holy Spirit "solemnly testifies" to Paul that bonds and afflictions await him. In Acts 27:21–26, "a messenger of the god I belong to and serve" functions very much like Socrates' δαιμόνιον. And, as so often is the case in Socratic legends, the point is emphasized that dire consequences follow from failing to heed Paul's divinely inspired advice (27:9–11).[82]

The Spirit in Luke-Acts is never the source of purely irrational emotional and ecstatic experiences. Rather its benefits, like those of Socrates' δαιμόνιον, are rational and epistemological.[83] Luke's tendencies in this mat-

---

78. Levison discusses Philo, Vit. Mos. 2.265 and Som. 2.251–252; Josephus, Antiquities 10.239; Wars 1.69; Contra Apion 2.262–64 ("The Angelic Spirit," 489–92).

79. Levison, "The Angelic Spirit," 492. For complete discussion and further bibliography see 488–93 where Levison convincingly demonstrates that for Josephus "the divine spirit which accompanied Daniel was a daemonic being which, in a manner parallel to Socrates and John Hyrcanus, remained in close association with Daniel," and that "Philo's account of his experience [of the divine spirit] ... resonates with Socrates' experience, as it is interpreted by Plato and Plutarch" (491).

80. Interestingly, δαιμόνιον is first clearly used as a noun in the LXX. This probably contributed to the fact that Josephus and Philo understand Socrates' δαιμόνιον as an independent spiritual being. Notice also that πνεῦμα is very similar to δαιμόνιον in its ambiguity. Both can refer in a rather vague way to "the divine," to "spirits," or to supernatural powers, whether good or evil. Similarly, δαιμονία and πνεύματα can be used interchangeably. Luke himself does so in Luke 10:17, 20.

81. Also indicated as a possible reference to Socrates' δαιμόνιον by Alexander, "Acts and Ancient Intellectual Biography," 59.

82. E.g., Theages, 129b–c.

83. For a good brief argument for why the Pentecost experience of glossolalia in Acts 2 should be understood as a miraculous gift for speaking in foreign languages, not as irrational

ter can already be observed in his Gospel. While Matthew says that when the disciples are brought to trial "what you are to say will be given to you in that hour; for it is not you who speak, but the Spirit of your Father speaking through you" (Matt 10:19b–20), Luke's version of this Q logion says "do not become anxious how or what you should speak in your apology (τί ἀπολογήσησθε), or what you should say; for the Holy Spirit will teach you (διδάξει ὑμᾶς) in that very hour what you ought to say" (Luke 12:11b–12). We see here in Luke the same aversion that Philo, influenced by the Platonic Socrates' discussion of divine inspiration, displays to forms of inspiration wherein the mind of the prophet is inactive. For Philo and Luke, the Spirit does not speak through people as passive mouthpieces like the priestess of Apollo or Balaam, rather it "teaches" them "to make an apology," a formal defense speech.[84] This mode of inspiration is a distinguishing characteristic of Socrates' δαιμόνιον. His divine inner voice,

> belonged to neither recognized class of divination: it was not an external sign open for interpretation by technical divination, since it was a personal phenomenon not available to others. Nor was it in the accepted form of direct natural communication from a god, which took the form of possession when you were out of your mind, or of dreams and the like when asleep or unconscious. Socrates was awake with all his wits about him when it occurred. Plato rightly said that it was unique (*Republic* 496c); indeed dangerously so in a democracy, since it sounded as if Socrates claimed a personal line to God.[85]

It may sound "new" and "strange" to suggest that Luke wants the reader with ears to hear to take Paul's "spirit in/with him" as a playful reference to Socrates' accompanying δαιμόνιον, but we should remember that little is not strange in the text at hand. Normally δαιμόνιον refers to the demonic in the NT, but here Paul is taken for a proclaimer of foreign divinities (δαιμόνιον). He will even praise the Athenians for their *daimōn*-fearing (δεισιδαιμονεστέρους) disposition and quote pagan poetry like Scripture. So by not ascribing Paul's motivation to the "Holy Spirit" or "the Spirit of Jesus" as is typical in Acts, but rather ambiguously to "the spirit of him in/with him," Luke has opened up a space where the allusive play on the ever elusive Socrates can continue to unfold, a space the new Socrates jumps into with both feet in the very next verse.

To overlook either the Jewish or Hellenistic aspects of the set(up) is to choose between Stage Left and Stage Right, to see only half the "play," to

---

ecstatic utterance like at Corinth, and not as a "hearing miracle," see James B. Polhill, *Acts* (NAC, vol. 26; Nashville: Broadman, 1992), 98–100.

84. Therefore, Fitzmyer's "curious parallel" to Luke 12:12, Philo's version of the angel's comments to Balaam wherein the angel says "I shall prompt the words you need without your mind's consent," is actually an illustration of the model of inspiration Luke is trying to avoid (Joseph A. Fitzmyer, *The Gospel According to Luke* [AB 28A; New York: Doubleday, 1985], 966).

85. Kidd, "On Socrates' Personal Deity: Introduction," 304–5. Cf. Levison, "The Angelic Spirit," 488–89.

refuse to see Paul standing "in the midst." Then Paul is either a Servant of the Lord or a new Socrates. But to carefully look over the set(up) is to recognize that unlike in previous acts, Paul the double agent, prophet and popular philosopher, is now fully exposed — in the Synagogue and the Agora (17:17).

3. Act One: Dialogue[86]

This *double meaning* or lack of sharpness in the description continues all through and is part of the individual character of this *scene.*[87]

[17]So he dialogued (διελέγετο) in the synagogue with the Jews and godfearers, and in the agora every day with those who chanced to be there. [18]And some also of the Epicurean and Stoic philosophers conversed with him. Some said, "What would this dilettante (σπερμολόγος) say?" while others said, "He appears to be a proclaimer of foreign divinities" (δαιμονίων) — because he preached Jesus and Anastasia.

The verb "dialogue" (διαλέγομαι) appears only three times in the NT outside of Acts.[88] Strikingly, it occurs ten times in Acts, and always with reference to Paul (17:2, 17; 18:4, 19; 19:8, 9; 20:7, 9; 24:12, 25). The first occurrence in 17:2 refers to his dialoguing in the synagogue of Thessalonica on three Sabbaths.[89] In 17:17 he dialogues both in the synagogue and the agora. It is hardly accidental that Luke has introduced this word at just this time and restricted it to Paul. For Luke, Paul is the first and foremost Christian dialectician. Only Apollos is given a similar, though by no means equal, honor. Apollos's "powerful refutations" (διακατελέγχομαι) are mentioned but not narrated (18:28).[90] Paul, on the other hand, dialogues with Jews (17:2, 17; 18:4, 19; 19:8), philosophers and other frequenters of the Athenian agora (17:17–18), attendees of his formal lecture series (19:9), fellow workers (20:7, 9), and a Roman governor (24:25). This image of Paul as master dialectician, recently introduced (17:2) and now repeated, is an important interpretive key to the ensuing encounter with the philosophers of

---

86. Or, First Episode.

87. Haenchen, *The Acts,* 517, italics mine. This comment immediately follows his observation that "συμβάλλω [in Acts 17:18] can mean 'to converse with' but also to 'engage in an argument' (Bauer, *WB* 1539)."

88. Mark 9:34; Heb 12:5; Jude 9.

89. It is intriguing that the frequent description of Paul as one who dialogues crops up soon after the beginning of the so-called "we-source." But the solution that perhaps most naturally suggests itself, that such vocabulary and the resultant image of Paul derive from this hypothetical source, is complicated by dramatic considerations: perhaps Luke introduced the image of Paul as dialectician precisely at this time in preparation for his encounter with philosophers and pagans in general. Of course, these explanations need not be mutually exclusive.

90. Considering what we know about first century C.E. Alexandrian Judaism and its intellectual heritage, Luke's concise descriptions of Apollos exude an undeniable overdetermination. See below, p. 93.

Athens. Commentators usually concentrate upon the contrasting cosmological and theological ideas of the Epicureans and Stoics, as well as the relative incompatibility or compatibility of their ideas with those expressed in the ensuing speech. This is, of course, an important contextual perspective for a competent reading, and I will assume it here. What is missed, however, is the rhetorical significance of Paul the dialectician confronting representatives of the two philosophical schools which had the least in common where linguistic theory in general, and dialectic in particular, are concerned. While Epicurus, and the school he founded, was lampooned by rival schools for a naïve and totally inadequate theory of language, the Stoics were, and still are, recognized as having the most highly developed linguistic theory in the history of Greco-Roman philosophy. They were indeed the philosophers of the Word (λόγος), and were especially renowned for their dialectic. This interest in lexical precision is certainly related to the fact that, as Catherine Atherton explains, the Stoics provide the first surviving definition of the linguistic phenomenon known as ambiguity (ἀμφιβολία), one that is remarkable for its "complexity, subtlety, and precision."[91] Why were the Stoics the ones to take such a keen interest in this subject?

> Stoic interest in ambiguity was the inevitable consequence of the basic doctrines about human nature, language, and rationality on which the whole Stoic system was based.... The point was that seeing or missing an ambiguity could make a difference to one's general success as a human being.[92]

Since they were the first philosophical school to study the subject systematically, it is not surprising that the Stoics took considerable pride in their ability to detect ambiguities.

> Stoic dialectic is able to distinguish what is said ambiguously (D.L. 7.47 31B7), as if nothing else could, and no person but the man with dialectical knowledge — an extraordinary claim, whose remarkableness lies rather in its ambition than its uniqueness. Behind it lie Stoicism's pretentions to authoritativeness in philosophy, in the principles of science, and in all linguistic matters.[93]

Epicurus's reputed attitude toward dialectic and the importance of detecting ambiguity was quite different.

> Epicurus' famous hostility to dialectic (*e.g.* D.L. 10.31(191); Cicero *acad.* 2.97 (201)) was blamed for his failure to teach "how ambiguities are distinguished," "qua via ... ambigua distinguantur," or to fix the meaning of such a key term as *pleasure* despite his frequent assertion "that the force of words

---

91. Atherton, *The Stoics*, 1.
92. Ibid., 2–3.
93. Ibid., 127.

should be carefully expressed," "diligentia oportere exprimi quae vis subiecta sit vocibus" (Cicero *fin.* 1.6, 22 (19H)).[94]

In light of the well-known Stoic pretensions to dialectical mastery and expertise in detecting ambiguities and sophisms, as well as the equally well-known shortcomings of the Epicureans in such matters, Luke's casting of Paul in the role of a new Socrates, the returned father of dialectic, is not likely coincidental. Neither can his portrayal of the philosophers as grossly misunderstanding Paul's message through failure to disambiguate ἀνάστασις.[95] Intriguingly, one ancient criticism of the Stoic analysis of ambiguity was its weakness in detecting intentionally ambiguous sophistical refutation.[96]

Some immediately passed judgment on Paul by referring to him as a σπερμολόγος. The word often refers to a sparrow who picks up seeds and scraps in the street, but when applied to a person it takes on a variety of negative connotations, the least insulting of which implies that someone is a frivolous gossip. But on the lips of philosophers critiquing the promulgator of a "new teaching," it could well mean something a great deal more insulting: Paul is a philosophical dilettante, maybe even one who "*retails* scraps of knowledge."[97] If so, they are provisionally branding him an ignoble sophist.[98] Perhaps Luke is hinting that some of the philosophers suspect Paul's religious reformer image is only a disguise. The arrival of such strangers was apt to generate suspicion. Compare Protagoras's remarks to Socrates shortly after the former arrived in Athens.

> ... when one goes as a stranger (ξένον γὰρ ἄνδρα) into great cities, and there tries to persuade the best of the young men to drop their other connexions, either with their own folk or with foreigners, both old and young, and to join one's own circle, with the promise of improving them by this connexion with oneself, such a proceeding requires great caution; since very considerable jealousies (φθόνοι) are apt to ensue, and numerous enmities (δυσμένειαί) and plots (ἐπιβουλαί). Now I tell you that sophistry is an ancient art, and those men of ancient times who practised it, fearing the offensiveness of it, disguised it in a decent dress, sometimes of poetry, as in the case of Homer, Hesiod, and Simonides; sometimes of mystic rites and prophecies, as did Orpheus, Musaeus and their sects. ... [99]

---

94. Ibid., 110. This estimate of Epicurus could be inaccurate and unfair polemic, but it was a common opinion. See A. A. Long, *Hellenistic Philosophy: Stoics, Epicureans, Sceptics* (2d ed.; Berkeley: University of California Press, 1986), 30.

95. "Is Luke being facetious again? Does he make the audience misunderstand Paul as if he were bringing a new pair of oriental divinities, as if Anastasis were (mis)understood as a proper name?" (Hans Conzelmann, "The Address of Paul on the Areopagus," in *Studies in Luke-Acts* [ed. L. E. Keck and J. L. Martyn; Nashville: Abingdon, 1966], 229–30).

96. Atherton, *The Stoics*, 99–103.

97. LSJ, 1627, italics mine.

98. "Paulus wird zwar von den athenischen Philosophen auch als Goet betrachtet, worauf die verächtliche Bezeichnung 'σπερμολόγος' hindeutet, aber er ist ja nicht der erste, über den ein solches Urteil ausgesprochen worden ist" (Betz, *Der Apostel Paulus*, 38; see also p. 34, n. 139).

99. Plato, *Protagoras*, 316C–317A.

This passage reminds us that jealousy and plots against Paul are topoi Luke exploits on more than one occasion with a Paul who bears a striking resemblance to an itinerant sophist (ζῆλος: Acts 13:45; 17:5. ἐπιβουλή: 9:24; 20:3; 20:19; 23:30; cf. 5:17).[100] Religious innovation is a prominent accusation against him (16:21; 17:6–7; 18:13; 19:26; 21:21; 21:28; cf. 6:13–14).

But others on the Areopagus are not quite sure what to make of Paul and exhibit more caution. "He seems (δοκεῖ) to be a proclaimer of foreign divinities" (17:18). But is see(m)ing be(liev)ing? If the message seems strange, no less does the messenger. Luke is probably playing with another topos in this case, that of the perils associated with recognizing the true identity and character of newly arrived strangers. In other contexts Luke employs this topos on a popular level. Paul (and associates) are easily mistaken for gods by common folk (14:14; 16:30; 28:6).[101] But in Athens, in the presence of philosophers, the issue is different. Unlike simple folk, philosophers know that human beings are not "gods" (θεοί). For many Epicureans the very notion would be ludicrous. Stoics, however, would say that all human beings are somewhat divine since they are permeated by "spirit" (πνεῦμα), and it is toward this point of contact that the speech will later gravitate. But the Platonic Socrates would not have agreed with this pantheistic anthropological leveling. In the well-known Platonic worldview, while all human beings have an immortal soul, certain human beings, true philosophers, are "divine" (θεῖοι).[102] Perhaps Luke is suggesting that the challenge facing the philosophers is not only whether they can discern Paul's new teaching, but whether or not they can recognize this new Socrates and the fact that the divine is as present and active in this one as it was in the old.[103]

Long before Luke, Plato had used this topos of discovering the true identity of the stranger to introduce *The Sophist*, a dialogue concerned mainly with the difficulty of distinguishing originals from copies, the real from the fake.[104] Distinguishing philosophers from sophists is the first and foremost illustration of the problem. In 216B Socrates echoes two passages from *The*

---

100. About the resemblance between Paul and other itinerant "sophists" see E. A. Judge, "The Early Christians as a Scholastic Community: Part II," 125–28.

101. On Acts 14:14, see especially Amy L. Wordelman, "The Gods Have Come Down: Images of Historical Lycaonia and the Literary Constructions of Acts 14," unpublished Ph.D. diss., Princeton University, 1994; discussed in Robbins, *Tapestry*, 201–7. On 16:30, see Haenchen, *Acts*, 497.

102. *Sophist*, 216C.

103. "Recognition, *anagnōrisis* of persons whose identities were unknown or mistaken is, of course, a typical and even focal device of tragic action. But this kind of recognition is the overtly theatrical event that condenses the epistemological bias of the entire phenomenon of drama. Thus recognition extends along a far wider spectrum, embracing the world, the other, and the self" (Froma Zeitlin, "Playing the Other: Theater, Theatricality, and the Feminine in Greek Drama," in *Nothing to Do with Dionysos?*, 84).

104. See above, pp. 18–19. Is it significant that both Plato's Stranger and Luke's Paul remain nameless in Athens?

Odyssey. The first is spoken by Odysseus to the Cyclopes, the second by the suitors after one of them struck Odysseus.

> Do not deny us, good sir, but reverence the gods; we are your suppliants; and Zeus is the avenger of suppliants and strangers — Zeus, the strangers' god — who walks in the footsteps of reverend strangers (9.269–72).

> Antinous, you did not do well to strike the unfortunate wanderer. Doomed man that you are, what if perchance he be some god come down from heaven? And the gods do, in the guise of strangers from afar, put on all manner of shapes, and visit the cities, beholding the violence and righteousness of men (17.483–87).

Plato takes these mythical motifs and makes them an analogy for the *modus operandi* of real philosophers.[105] Just as gods disguise themselves as strangers of various sorts in order to observe the insolence and lawfulness of humanity, so also philosophers disguise themselves in such unexpected and unlikely forms as politicians and sophists. Socrates hints that they may appear in the latter form to refute those who are worthless/careless (φαῦλος) in argument. These real philosophers are able to visit the cities, "appearing disguised in all sorts of shapes, because of the ignorance of the others" (διὰ τὴν τῶν ἄλλων ἄγνοιαν), "beholding from above the life of those below" (216C).[106] When reading this description of real philosophers who appear as sophists, one is reminded of Socrates who was lampooned in the theater as a sophist (Aristophanes, *Clouds*), condemned on charges appropriate to an ignoble sophist (Plato, *Apology*), and who utilized sophistic *antilogic* in his *elenchus*.[107] He was truly a model of ambiguity in Athens.

All this is quite intriguing when made the backdrop of Paul's appearance on the Athenian stage. Members of the two most famous philosophical schools of the day meet him and mistake him for either a σπερμολόγος or a promoter of strange gods. The same crisis is being played out in Athens all over again. Only too late did the Athenians figure out that Socrates was "a kind of gift to the city from the god" (*Apology*, 31B; cf. 30D); that he was doing what "the god commands," and performing a "service" (ὑπηρεσίας, λατρεία in 23C) to the god (30A). He warned them that should they dispose of him, their only hope was that the god, in his care, "should send some other" (31B; cf. 30D).[108] All this sounds strangely familiar. In his speech

---

105. As discussed in my conclusion, "Reel Paul," Plato unequivocally condemns this metamorphic theology in *The Republic* (381C–D). But such shape-shifting will be deemed commendable when exercised by certain privileged humans.

106. Socrates goes on to say in 216D that they will give some the impression that they are worthless, others that they are worth everything, and still others that "they are altogether mad" (παντάπασιν ἔχοντες μανικῶς; cf. Acts 26:24).

107. See Kerford, *The Sophistic Movement*, 59–67.

108. It is not unlikely that Luke was influenced by the *Apology*. See Haenchen on Acts 4:19 (*Acts*, 219, n. 11).

before the Sanhedrin, Stephen dwells on Moses as the one the Israelites rejected, and who predicted that "A prophet shall God raise up to you from among your brethren, like me" (7:37). Is Luke again assimilating the Athenians to the Israelites?[109] Is he suggesting that Socrates was a Greek Moses? He describes Moses as "he who was in the congregation in the wilderness with the angel who spoke to him at Mount Sinai, and with our fathers; and he received living oracles to give us" (7:38). Thus Moses, like the legendary Socrates, was accompanied and inspired by a divine messenger on a continuing basis. When the Israelites rejected him, they immediately fell into idolatry (vv. 39–41), which is also the present state of the Athenians. Stephen then continues with an attack on temple worship (vv. 42–50) that is often compared to Acts 17:24–25. Is Luke casting Paul in the role of a new Socrates because he thinks Paul with "his Spirit within him" is that "other" God might send, a divinely inspired philosopher like Socrates? Furthermore, is the crisis brought to the Athenians by the presence of Paul analogous to the crisis brought to Jerusalem by the presence of Jesus?

> [19]And they took hold of him and brought him to the Areopagus saying, "Are we able to discern (γνῶναι) what this new teaching is which you present?[110] [20]For strange things you bring to (εἰσφέρεις) our ears; we wish therefore to know what these things mean."

The line is cast; the bait taken. The philosophers are hooked. For good reason, some commentators have taken their request to be spoken with tongue in cheek. Are we to suppose that pretentious philosophers, some of whom have branded Paul a charlatan, others the proclaimer of a new cult, are sincerely asking if they have the wit to discern what Paul is teaching? If not, the roles have been temporarily reversed. They are trying on the mask of the mockingly ironic Socrates for the moment.[111] But the joke will ultimately be on them. Dramatic irony has the last word. They have already proven that they lack discernment by taking this new teaching about Jesus and Anastasia to be the proclamation of two strange δαιμονία, rather than the resurrection of one.[112] Nor do they have any idea of the deeper significance of their saying that Paul is bearing strange things to their ears.[113] Only Theophilus and

---

109. See above, pp. 49–50.

110. An indicator of Luke's dramatic expertise is his attention to place and movement. His plays often divide into two acts distinguished in part by place changes. In Tragedy, "[t]he acting space is seen in several ways at once. 'Space as well as time had a certain elasticity.' The setting seems to waver sometimes: between, for instance, the Akropolis and the nearby Areopagus" (Padel, "Making Space Speak," 359–60). Or, in the case of Paul in Athens, between the Agora and the nearby Areopagus.

111. See above, pp. 15–22.

112. The possibility that the latter is the "right" interpretation of the speech, what those who joined Paul and believed understood, will be discussed below, p. 76.

113. Cf. περιφέροντες in 2 Cor 4:10. See above, p. 51, n. 47.

the reader can recognize the irony: Paul, the "bearer" of the Name, is indeed "bearing" strange things.[114]

These strange things, these foreign objects extend beyond Jesus and Anastasia to include both the proclaimer and even the text itself. To judge by the reactions of some interpreters, "Paul in Athens" might well be gesturing toward its own strange and foreign quality. For Norden it was quite literally a foreign object inserted by a strange hand. He thought it had been modeled on a second-century biography of Apollonius. Although no one accepts this re-source-ful theory anymore, the opinion that Paul in Athens is a Lukan fiction persists on other, more intrinsic grounds. In Gärtner's words, "...scholars have read into the Areopagus speech a total Stoic theology, leading them to regard it as a 'foreign body' in the framework of the New Testament texts."[115] But for Gärtner the fault lies not with the text but with the interpreters: "...what really makes Rom 1:29 and Acts 17 so difficult to interpret is the number of terms familiar to us from Greek philosophy. This philosophical sense *intrudes* as we read, so that we may easily give the words a connotation that *does not fit* the context. When interpreting the texts, therefore, it is important not only *to penetrate* to the true meaning of the terms, but also *to define clearly* the functions of the theories involved."[116] One must not be penetrated by a foreign object (philosophical sense), but rather "to penetrate." Such is manly biblical criticism. It is monological, phallocentric, and, hence, tragic.

> Earlier I defined the tragic universe as one that is other than the self originally imagined it to be. Going one step further, we may add that tragedy is the epistemological form par excellence. What it does best through the resources of the theater is to chart a path from ignorance to knowledge, deception to revelation, misunderstanding to recognition. The characters act out and live through the consequences of having clung to a partial, single view of the world and themselves.[117]

Scholars like Gärtner resist the doubleness in the world of the text just as the majority of Paul's tragic Athenian interlocutors resist the doubleness in the text of the world. It is probably no accident that Stoics and Epicureans are made to be the unwitting dupes of this new sophistic Socrates. For all their differences, these schools shared a naïve realism. For the Stoics, the Cosmos is in principle a simple place, a perfectly logical and harmonious structure, and our personal logos can mirror that harmony and perfection since both are united by the same Logos, the same Spirit.[118] Disunity and ambiguity are only apparent, a temporary failing on our part, not the

---

114. βαστάζω and φέρω belong to the same semantic field.

115. Gärtner, *The Areopagus Speech*, 145.

116. Ibid., 82, italics mine.

117. Zeitlin, "Playing the Other," 76.

118. "For the Stoics the whole world is the work of immanent *logos* or reason, and in his power of articulate thought a man [*sic*] is supposed to have the means to formulate statements

World's. For the Epicureans, the quintessential materialists, the world is also a fairly simple place, completely knowable in principle.[119] Both Stoics and Epicureans were thus optimistic and confident about human attainment of unambiguous perception and expression. This contrasts sharply with the Platonic-Socratic and Sophistic views of the phenomenal world as a place of inherent ambiguity, shadow, and deception. It also contrasts sharply with those of a new-fangled apocalyptic Socrates, the Paul of Acts.

4. Stasimon[120]

[21]Now all the Athenians and the visiting strangers (ἐπιδημοῦντες ξένοι) spent their time in nothing except telling or hearing something newer (καινότερον).

As commentators are fond of pointing out, Luke's portrait of Athens is "classic." The sights are cites, citings, a series of (ex)citations:[121] a city filled with gods and temples, rival philosophical schools, a latter day Socrates accused of bringing in new divinities, and now Athenians "in the agora inquiring if anything newer is being said" (Demosthenes, *Philippic* 1.43). With the invocation of this last well-known topos, Luke tells us, if there was ever any doubt, who he considers the real σπερμολόγοι, the dilettantes, the "real" fakes. Now he will present Paul in the middle of the Areopagus, addressing Stoics and Epicureans on their own turf, in their own dialect, especially the former, acknowledging Athenian religiosity, quoting pagan dedications and poets with seeming approval. The more one becomes aware of the intertextual labyrinth that forms the *scenae frons* of Paul in Athens, the more a simple mimetic representational reading appears quite naïve. What Luke provides is no straightforward, historical attempt to recount Paul's adventures in Athens. For just as his artisan, Paul, weaves his σκηνή with the threads of many texts as he attempts to recast an ambiguous icon, the altar of an unknown God, so Luke himself weaves with other texts in

which mirror cosmic events. Language is part of nature and provides man [*sic*] with the medium to express his relationship with the world" (A. A. Long, *Hellenistic Philosophy*, 125).

119. "In brief, Epicurean methods of scientific inquiry assess empirical evidence on the basis of a prephilosophical, pretheoretical body of naturally-formed words and meanings deriving its authority from its causal proximity to the external world and to language users' own internal states — the result of what Goldschmidt 1978:157 calls 'un véritable dédoublement du monde réel' represented by the *simulacra*, and thus by the preconceptions which, somehow, they go to form" (Atherton, *The Stoics*, 114–15). This epistemology is perfectly suited to Epicurus's ethical goal of freeing humanity from fear and anxiety. A cosmos that cannot easily be observed in all its aspects and senses that cannot be trusted are fine epistemological catalysts for traditional piety and superstition.

120. As the word suggests, a *stasimon* is performed by the chorus standing alone. In it they do not interact with the actors as in the episodes, and they frequently comment or "take a stand" on the situation as Luke does here.

121. As A. D. Nock said, " . . . brilliant as is the picture of Athens, it makes on me the impression of being based on literature, which was easy to find, rather than on personal observation" (Haenchen, *Acts*, 520).

an attempt to recast another icon, an unknown Paul. Act Two of Luke's Athenian drama, the centerpiece of his entire second volume, will be the scripting of a rhetorical act(or), the sculpting of a verbal icon.

5. Act Two: Monologue[122]

Every word is by nature ambiguous.[123]

It is crucial at this point that we distinguish between the narrator, the orator, the oratees, and the narratee. As readers we are about to enter into what is arguably the most sophisticated speech composed by the most accomplished narrator and speech writer in the NT. It will not do to be insensitive to the fact that this speech is to be heard on two levels: that of the oratees who are inquisitive and philosophically inclined pagans, and that of the narratee, Theophilus, who, like the implied reader, is now, on the basis of his reading of Acts up to this point, an insider. We often speak of the omniscient narrator, but in this case the narratee's knowledge of the orator and what he represents is so superior to that of the oratees, who are even made to admit their ignorance explicitly in v. 20, that we may go so far as to speak of the narratee's shared omniscience with the narrator. This sets up a situation which the narrator fully exploits to create a highly entertaining reading experience. Much of that entertainment is derived from double entendres created by ambiguous words and phrases which have one set of associations for insiders in the Christian movement such as the orator and narratee, and another for outsiders such as the oratees of this speech.

My approach to the speech in this section will be primarily literary and rhetorical. It will come as no surprise to the reader by now that I assume those readings that have emphasized the Jewish intertexture of the speech on the one hand and the Hellenistic intertexture on the other are equally valid.

[22]So Paul, standing in the middle of the Areopagus, said: "Men of Athens, I see how δεισιδαιμονεστέρους you are in every way."

The orator opens his *proem* or *exordium* with the conventionalized vocative *salutio* "Men of Athens."[124] Then, in his *captatio benevolentiae* ("currying of favor") he employs an ambiguous word, a homonym that occurs only twice in the NT, both times in Acts: δεισιδαίμων (v. 22).[125] It has

---

122. Or, Second Episode.

123. Chrysippus according to Gellius 11.12.1, in A. A. Long and D. N. Sedley, *Greek and Latin Texts with Notes and Bibliography* (vol. 2 of *The Hellenistic Philosophers*; Cambridge: Cambridge University Press, 1987), 230; see also Atherton, *The Stoics*, 298.

124. On the possibility that this was not an appropriate *salutio* in this situation, see Kennedy, *New Testament*, 130. For a discussion of the rhetorical terms of arrangement employed in the following analysis see ibid., 23–24.

125. See entry under δεισιδαιμονέω, LSJ, 375. δεισιδαιμονία appears in Acts 25:19.

long been recognized that the translation of this one double word, this *dittos* in Aristotle's terminology, establishes the tone of the whole speech.[126] The assumption is almost always that Paul means either to compliment or insult. Since the credo of most biblical interpreters is "The Lord our God (*Logos,* meaning) is One," δεισιδαίμων must have either a positive or a negative connotation. When the orator says, "I perceive that in every way you are thoroughly *daimōn*-fearing," does he mean "thoroughly religious," or "thoroughly superstitious"? The latter option would make things much less complicated from a historical point of view, for it is how many Pauline scholars would have expected Paul the Jew to respond in this situation. Unfortunately, the immediate context argues strongly against such a simple solution. Most commentators have enough rhetorical sensitivity to realize how unlikely it would be for Luke to portray Paul as beginning his speech with an insult. So the "thoroughly religious" choice is more popular even though it creates more difficulties.[127] If one concludes that Paul in all sincerity complimented the Athenians for their pagan religiosity, however unenlightened he considered it to be, some scholars will immediately find the speech to be neither authentic history nor even plausible fiction in light of Rom 1.

But there is a more sophisticated way of understanding Paul's "compliment." Paul may indeed want most of his Athenian oratees to take it that way, but he does not really mean it. The narratee, Theophilus, and other readers can hear the irony and know that Paul is saying one thing, very religious, while thinking just the opposite — very superstitious.[128] So if, as many say, the translation of δεισιδαιμονιστέρους sets the tone for the entire speech, and if in this context the word is irreducibly double, what we have is a Truly rhetorical Paul, one who is addressing and/or creating an audi-

---

126. E.g., A. T. Robertson, *Word Pictures in the New Testament* (Nashville: Broadman, 1930), 285.

127. E.g., Haenchen, *The Acts,* 520, decides in favor of "the cautiously appreciative 'religious.' " Cf. Bruce, *The Acts,* 380: "[δεισιδαιμονιστέρους] was as vague as Eng. 'religious,' and here one may best translate 'very religious,' 'uncommonly religious.' But KJV 'too superstitious' is not entirely wrong; to Paul the Athenian religion was mostly superstitious...." It is not really accurate to say δεισιδαιμονιστέρους was as vague as "religious" since in general usage, according to Webster's, "religious" carries no connotation of superstition. (Of course, certain neo-orthodox theologians would dissent.) One must prefix a qualifier like "overly" to "religious" to arrive at an approximation to superstitious. Not even "pious" is analogous, since its negative connotation is rather "hypocrisy." We simply have no suitable word available. Bruce's most valuable observation is the one he does not develop: "Cf. δεισιδαιμονία in 25:19, where it might have one meaning for the speaker and another for the person addressed."

128. Cf. Conzelmann: "The speech starts with the *captatio benevolentiae* (vs. 22). How this tactful beginning is to be understood has already been indicated in vs. 16. Of course, δεισιδαίμων here does not mean *superstitious* (Theophrastus' character of δεισιδαιμονία!), but rather *devout.* The Christian reader of course hears the irony in it" ("The Address of Paul on the Areopagus," 220). Though he does not develop this laconically expressed perspective, it seems likely that Conzelmann understood Luke's Paul to be speaking deceptively to his audience. See also Dean Zweck, "The *Exordium* of the Areopagus Speech, Acts 17.22,23," *NTS* 35 (1989): 102.

ence within an audience through the use of a homonym. Indeed, if Zweck is correct in suggesting that the "Epicurean auditors may have picked up an ironical intent in the epithet (at the same time approving the speaker for it), since in their literature the word has the connotation of 'superstitious,' "[129] Paul may be sowing the seeds of division in his speech right from the beginning in a way roughly analogous to his approach with the Pharisees and Sadducees in Acts 23.[130] The double word becomes a double cross. After all, division is not an unintentional consequence of the gospel in Luke-Acts, something to be avoided if possible. Rather, it is always expected. It is God's dia-logue (Luke 12:51–53).

Recognizing that the author has chosen to have the orator begin his speech with an intentional ambiguity, the reader is faced with the task both of deciding how the oratees would interpret this ambiguity and how the narrator expects the narratee to interpret it. As remarked above, due to the conventions of rhetoric, in this case the *captatio benevolentiae*, the oratees can hardly be imagined to expect the orator to begin by insulting them. Even less so if the situation portrayed is not deliberative but forensic as George Kennedy suspects.[131] Based on similar rhetorical situations in Acts, we can probably conclude that if Luke wanted us to think the audience responded with anger, he would have told us so. Of course, the audience might well be suspicious of this orator's sincerity if they recognized that he has appeared in their midst as another Socrates. But the narrator gives us no reason to suppose they are that perceptive. On the contrary, an important theme of the entire play is the Athenians' inability to recognize this new Socrates. So from their perspective, unless he is a fool, or exceedingly arrogant, he must be complimenting them.

The narratee, however, is operating in a different space, that of the entire narrative of Acts to this point. He (Theophilus) knows by now who the orator really is and what he represents. Indeed, solely on the basis of the subnarrative unit we are examining, the narratee, informed at the outset by the narrator, knows that the orator strongly disapproves of Athenian religion (v. 16), and can hardly be sincerely commending it. With this superior knowledge the narratee is in a position to be entertained by this wily orator who simultaneously compliments and insults, leaving the oratees confused, if not oblivious, but the narratee in stitches. And so from the very beginning of this speech the narratee is made aware that the orator is capable of addressing his audience with tongue in cheek. Now that Theophilus is sensitized to this capability, he will be on the lookout for it. He will know that should more such ambiguities appear, their interpretation will not likely involve an either/or but a both/and. He will not have long to wait.

---

129. Zweck, "The *Exordium* of the Areopagus Speech," 102.

130. The Sanhedrin speech will be discussed below, pp. 78–82.

131. Kennedy, *New Testament*, 129–30. This also appears to be Bruce's position (Bruce, *The Acts*, 377–78).

²³For as I went through the city and looked carefully at the objects of your worship, I found among them an altar with the inscription, "To an unknown god" (Ἀγνώστῳ θεῷ). What therefore you worship ἀγνοοῦντες, this I proclaim to you.

In the orator's narration of the facts (v. 23) he calls attention to the altar dedicated "To an unknown God," and states his intention: "What therefore you worship ἀγνοοῦντες, this I proclaim to you." We are already faced with our second ambiguity.¹³² ἀγνοέω has both a positive and negative connotation. It can mean a straightforward, non-culpable epistemic failure resulting in a lack of knowledge, or a culpable moral failure of acting ignorantly in regard to what is right, to act amiss.¹³³ When the orator says "What therefore you ignorantly worship, this I proclaim to you," does he mean "What you worship unknowingly," or "What you worship improperly/shamefully"?¹³⁴ The answer is both/and. The oratees are kept in confusion, unsure whether they are being excused or accused of ignorance, while the narratee's expectations generated by the first example of double entendre are satisfied by a second.

²⁴The God who made the world and all things in it, he who is Lord of heaven and earth, does not live in shrines made by human hands, ²⁵nor is he served by human hands, as though he needed anything, since he himself gives to all mortals life and breath and all things.

Now the orator comes to the proposition, that which the speaker wishes to prove (vv. 24–25). His convictions are expressed through three sets of oppositions which contrast positive views pertaining to God, which are, of course, the orator's, with negative views belonging to the oratees. First, in v. 24 the positive view that God makes a dwelling place for human beings is opposed to the negative view that human beings make a dwelling place for God. Second, in v. 25 the positive view that God sustains human beings is opposed to the negative view that human beings sustain God.

²⁶From one ancestor he made all nations to inhabit the whole earth, and he allotted the times of their existence and the boundaries of the places where they would live, ²⁷so that they would search for God and perhaps grope for him and find him — though indeed he is not far from each one of us. ²⁸For "In him we live and move and have our being"; as even some of your own poets have said, "For we too are his race/kind" (γένος). ²⁹Since we are God's race/kind, we ought not to think that the divine/deity (τὸ θεῖον) is like gold, or silver, or stone, an image formed by the art and imagination of mortals.

---

132. See Gärtner, *The Areopagus Speech,* 236–37.

133. See entry ἀγνοέω in LSJ, 11–12.

134. Fortunately, unlike the first example, this double entendre can be reproduced in English by the use of "ignorantly," which can carry epistemic and/or moral connotations. The RSV ("What therefore you worship as Unknown") has introduced a univocality not found in the Greek. Indeed, this translation is grammatically insupportable since ἀγνοῦντες is in agreement with the plural εὐσεβεῖτε, not the singular ὃ whose antecedent is θεῷ.

Verse 26 elaborates on the radical dependence of human beings on God and introduces the idea that God intends for human beings to seek after God. At this point the orator turns the tables on the oratees by constructing his strongest proof from quotations of their own poets.[135] Their poets know that God is intimately close to human beings and that human beings are God's race/kind. This supports the third and final opposition that is a powerful refutation of an opposing view. The positive view that humankind are representative of God's kind is opposed to the negative view that inanimate objects (idols) are representative of God's kind.

Notice that Satan is not mentioned in the speech. This might appear surprising considering the pervasive presence of the role of the Opponent throughout Acts.[136] Since the narratee already knows that Satan is the power opposed to God (5:3; 10:38; 13:10), he might wonder why Satan is not now explicitly associated with idolatry. How natural such an association would be is confirmed later in the orator's description of his commission as being sent by Jesus to open the Gentiles' eyes, "that they may turn from darkness to light and from the power of Satan to God, that they may receive forgiveness of sins and a place among those who are sanctified by faith in me" (26:18). So why is Satan not explicitly mentioned in the Areopagus speech? Satan has been occulted for rhetorical effectiveness. The narrator revels in portraying the orator as a master of ambiguity. One of the functions of this ambiguity is to obscure the offensiveness of his discourse. The very opposite of this strategy would be to have the orator state point blank, "You are devil worshipers!"[137] From the narrator's perspective, Paul is far too sophisticated for that.[138]

³⁰Indeed, the times of ἀγνοίας God having ὑπεριδὼν, now παραγγέλλει all people everywhere to μετανοεῖν, ³¹because he has fixed a day on which he will

---

135. Such a maneuver was not without its dangers: "Quotations of poetry and citations of historical precedent could enliven a speech and help to buttress the argument by the inspired wisdom of the poet and the authority of past practice.... But when using poetic and historical examples, the Athenian orator had to avoid taking on the appearance of a well-educated man giving lessons in culture to the ignorant masses" (Josiah Ober and Barry Strauss, "Drama, Political Rhetoric, and the Discourse of Athenian Democracy," in *Nothing to Do with Dionysos?*, 251).

136. See Given, "Not Either/Or but Both/And in Paul's Areopagus Speech," 360–63.

137. "He did not, as Witsius observes, in the heat of his zeal break into the temples, pull down their images, demolish their altars, or fly in the face of their priests; nor did he run about the streets crying 'You are all the bond-slaves of the devil,' though it was true; but he observed decorum, and kept himself within due bounds, doing that only which became a prudent man" (Matthew Henry, *Acts to Revelation* [vol. 6 of *Matthew Henry's Commentary on the Whole Bible*, New Modern Edition; Peabody, Mass.: Hendrickson, 1996], 181).

138. Indeed, Paul is far more astute in this respect than any other orator in Acts. This suggests careful attention to characterization, a technique which was long denied to the author of Luke-Acts. But see now James M. Dawsey, *The Lukan Voice: Confusion and Irony in the Gospel of Luke* (Macon: Mercer University Press, 1986); Darr, *On Character Building*; David B. Gowler, *Host, Guest, Enemy and Friend: Portraits of the Pharisees in Luke and Acts* (ESEC 1; New York: Peter Lang, 1991), esp. 173–76, 297–319.

judge (κρίνειν) the world in righteousness (ἐν δικαιοσύνῃ) by a man whom he has appointed, having produced πίστιν for all by raising him from the dead" (17:30–31).[139]

The orator's *peroration* begins with a third and fourth use of double entendre, the former playing on an ambiguity noted earlier, only now with the substantive ἄγνοια (v. 30). Does the phrase "the times of ignorance" refer epistemologically to "the times of misconception" or morally to "the times of culpable error?"[140] Once again, the answer is both/and.

The fourth double entendre appropriately enough has been "overlooked" in recent exegesis of the Areopagetica.[141] The verb ὑπεροράω is a *hapax legomenon* in the NT. It can mean "to overlook" or "to despise."[142] Is the orator saying "God, having overlooked the times of misconception, now commands all people everywhere to change their minds," or "God, having despised the times of culpable error, now commands all people everywhere to repent." Not either/or but both/and.

Regardless of which way the oratees hear the orator, the narratee knows that God does not "wink at" idolatry, to quote the KJV. This is not the

---

139. The NRSV and NASB are much better than the RSV, NIV, and KJV at the beginning of v. 30. The latter three seriously weaken or even ignore μὲν οὖν which should be construed either as mostly concessive-adversative in relation to the following clause (NRSV: "While God has overlooked...now"), or mostly confirmative-asseverative in relation to the preceding clause (NASB: "Therefore having overlooked...now"). My choice of "Indeed" reflects a preference for, and strengthening of, an asseverative construal (notice further that the case for the concessive rendering is weakened by the absence of δέ, ἀλλά, or a similar adversative particle in the following clause). Perhaps the asseverative translation has been less attractive because of the failure to recognize the negative connotations of ὑπεροράω (see below). "Therefore the times of ignorance God having overlooked" does sound rather surprising immediately after a sentence, or an entire speech, proclaiming that one "ought not to think" (v. 29) the Deity is like an idol. But, as we shall see, "overlooked" is not the only possible translation.

140. See ἄγνοια in LSJ, 12.

141. "Recent" is the operative word. In preparation for the article on which this section is based, I consulted a selection of recent standard commentaries. None mentioned the antithetical connotations of the word. But cf. Matthew Henry: "These times of ignorance God *winked at*. Understand it [1.] As an act of divine justice. God *despised* or *neglected* these times of ignorance, and did not send them his gospel, as now he does. It was very provoking to him to see his glory thus given to another; and he *detested* and *hated* these times. So some take it" (*Matthew Henry's Commentary*, 6:186).

142. See ὑπερόρασις in LSJ, 1867, and ὑπεροράω in BAGD, 841. LSJ lists the neutral meaning first and the negative meaning second while BAGD lists the negative first, making it all the more surprising that NT scholars and translators regularly overlook it. An extensive random survey of the occurrences of this word in the LXX, Philo, Josephus, and classical authors confirms that if lexical meanings were arranged by frequency of occurrence, BAGD would have the correct order. The vast majority of occurrences are of the negative "to despise or disdain." Yet I have also found that many of the occurrences of the neutral "to overlook or disregard" are not neutral at all, but are used in situations where overlooking or disregarding someone or something results in harm to that person or thing. Finally, note that the Vulgate does not render ὑπεροράω with *praeterire* or *neglegěre*, the most natural choices to express "to ignore," but rather *despicěre*, "to look down on, despise," a word which is not only similar to ὑπεροράω in construction, but also in its preponderantly negative connotations.

first speech the narratee has read in Acts that characterized God's attitude toward idolatry. In Stephen's speech (7:1–53) the orator says,

> And they made a calf in those days, and offered a sacrifice to the idol and rejoiced in the works of their hands. But God gave them over to worship the host of heaven (7:41–42).

Not only does this orator identify enslavement to astral deities as punishment for idolatry, but the exile as well. Both Stephen and Paul are reliable orators in Acts, at least from the narrator and reader's perspective. They can be fully depended on to express views that the narrator approves. Since Stephen's speech explicitly affirms that God punishes idolatry, we can hardly expect another reliable orator in Acts to contradict this affirmation. The oratees at the Areopagus are left guessing whether or not God has overlooked or despised their conduct in the past, although the immediately following call for "change of mind/repentance" leaves no doubt as to what God's attitude will be from now on. But there can be no doubt in the omniscient narratee's mind as to God's attitude toward idolatry, past, present, or future. The narratee knows which sense of ὑπεροράω expresses the convictions of the orator and the narrator on this subject. Once again the narratee, the insider, knows what the orator is really saying. An oratee, on the other hand, must repent and follow Paul before the insider's insight will become possible.

The *coup de grace* of the use of double entendres is saved for the final clause of the speech where they come fast and furious (17:31). The antithetical meanings of πίστις are well known.[143] It can mean, among other things, "faith" or "proof." Does the orator proclaim that God is "supplying proof by raising him from the dead" or "supplying faith by raising him from the dead"? Both/and. The oratees have been identified as philosophers. For them πίστις is a guarantee or a means of persuasion — a proof.[144] But the narratee recognizes that the entire *peroration* is composed of technical insider jargon. Indeed, the narratee is now a gnostic *par excellence*. In contrast to the philosophically inclined oratees, he knows that μετάνοια is not simply a change of mind (2:38),[145] δικαιοσύνη is not simply fulfillment of legalities (13:38), and πίστις is not simply a logical proof (3:16, passim). These words mean one thing to the philosophical oratees, but quite another to the insider, and those Athenians who were destined to see the light even through the mask of Paul's Ambiguity in Athens.

---

143. See πίστις in LSJ, 1408.
144. Bruce, *The Acts*, 340, notes that "Vettius Valens 277.29f. provides an example of πίστιν παρέχω in the same sense."
145. See also 3:19; 5:31; 8:22; 11:18; 13:24.

6. Exodus

Luke's story concludes on an ambiguous note.[146]

[32]When they heard of the resurrection of the dead, some scoffed; but others said, "We will hear you again about this." [33]And so Paul went out from between them. [34]But some of them joined him and became believers, including Dionysius the Areopagite and a woman named Damaris, and others with them (17:32–34).

Given the generally triumphalistic tone of Acts, it is quite unlikely that Luke meant to offer Paul in Athens as some sort of failure for Paul, and few interpreters hold this opinion anymore. On the contrary, it was an ambiguous success, just the sort of tragic triumph that Luke always presents. The notion of a resurrection from the dead caused diverse reactions, and it would be a mistake to think that all philosophers would have found the notion objectionable.[147] Nothing is said here about the nature of this resurrection from the dead.[148] For all they know, Paul is speaking of the ascension of the soul.[149] Therefore some, surely the Epicureans, laugh at him, not because of the nature of the resurrection from the dead, but because survival of any kind is absurd from their point of view. Others, however, probably the Stoics, do not find this notion or that of a coming judgment wholly worthless and want to hear more.[150]

What did those who "joined Paul and believed" believe? What had they understood that others did not? This question admits of no one or certain answer, but I would introduce a new teaching. Notice that the speech does not end where it began. Based on the contents of the narration and proposition, we would expect the peroration to return to the theme of the unknown God. Instead it offers new information about a proof given by this God involving the resurrection of a man. The climax of the speech hearkens back not to its beginning, but to the original encounter with the philosophers and their misunderstanding of Jesus and Anastasis. Thus the proclamation of the unknown God is only a foundation for clarifying what these two terms really signify: a man, Jesus, and his return from the dead.[151] Those who "get it" now understand that Paul is not preaching about two gods/spirits but an

---

146. Johnson, *The Acts*, 320.

147. For a reappraisal of the received opinion on this matter, see Martin, *The Corinthian Body*, 110–23.

148. When νεκρός is found in the plural it usually refers collectively to "the dead" as opposed to the living, or to the realm of the dead, not to corpses *per se* as is often the case with the singular. Again, there is enough ambiguity in Paul's discourse to allow some to (mis)take him to mean a resuscitation of corpses and others something more refined.

149. See Oepke, "ἀνίστημι," *TDNT* 1:369.

150. See Howard Clark Kee, "Pauline Eschatology: Relationships with Apocalyptic and Stoic Thought," in *Glaube und Eschatologie* (ed. Erich Grässer and Otto Merk; Tübingen: J. C. B. Mohr, 1985), 135–58.

151. The D scribe's toleration of Paul's ambiguities wore thin in Acts 17:31. For "man" he substitutes "Jesus."

event concerning one.[152] And if Paul would later tell them more of Luke's story of Jesus, this would become even clearer to them. For then they would know that this new Socrates is telling them about a being very much like those the old Socrates brought up in his defense speech.

> But do we not think the spirits (δαίμονας) are gods or children of gods (θεῶν παῖδας)? Yes, or no? "Certainly." Then if I believe in spirits, as you say, if spirits are a kind of gods, that would be the puzzle and joke which I say you are uttering in saying that I, while I do not believe in gods, do believe in gods, since I believe in spirits; but if, on the other hand, spirits are a kind of illegitimate children of gods, by nymphs or by any others, whoever their mothers are said to be, what man would believe that there are children of gods, but no gods.[153]

Luke is fully aware that from a Gentile perspective, Jesus is a δαίμων, a παῖς θεοῖ, a child of a human mother and, in this case, *the* God, as Paul's speech has established.[154] And if Paul were to tell the Athenians of the refusal of the residents and leaders of Jerusalem to pay him proper respect, perhaps they would be reminded of a classic story about another "new *daimōn*" (τὸν νεωστὶ δαίμονα Διόνυσον ὅστις ἔστι, *Bacchae* 219–20) who was not recognized as "the Son of God" by the leaders of his own land. This god was made to "suffer" (*Bacchae*, 492, 500, 801) along with his followers, and judgment followed.[155]

This brings me to a final feature that has fascinated readers for centuries, the two named converts, Dionysius and Damaris. The pseudepigraphical career of Dionysius is well known and, as Haenchen remarks, "Pious fantasy became preoccupied with [Damaris]. Since Chrysostom she has passed for the wife of Dionysius. According to Zahn (608f.) she could have been 'the wife or mother of one of the presumably young "philosophers." ' "[156] But should our imaginations be exercised on the identity of supposedly real historical persons represented by these names,[157] or should we not rather reflect upon the words themselves? Is it a coincidence that an encounter touched off by the subject of the meaning of two names, masculine and feminine, now ends with two more intriguing names, masculine and feminine? Perhaps if

---

152. Alexander observes that Paul never denies the charge that he is introducing new δαιμόνια ("Acts and Ancient Intellectual Biography," 59).

153. Plato, *Apology*, 27D.

154. See also Luke 1:35.

155. As failure to recognize and acknowledge Dionysus results in the destruction of the house of Cadmus in the *Bacchae* (e.g., 1376), so Jesus predicts that Jerusalem's "house is forsaken" (Luke 13:35) because "you did not know the time of your visitation" (Luke 19:19; cf. *Bacchae*, 1345: "See! You know me, but at the time it was required, you knew not"; also 1340–43). "Because the residents of Jerusalem and their leaders did not recognize him (τοῦτον ἀγνοήσαντες) or the utterances of the prophets that are read every Sabbath, they fulfilled them by condemning him" (Acts 13:27).

156. Haenchen, *Acts*, 527.

157. See, e.g., J. G. Griffiths, "Was Damaris an Egyptian? (Acts 17:34)," *BZ* 8 (1964): 293–95.

Luke was being "facetious," as Conzelmann put it, in the case of the first coupling, now he is being ludic. For just as the first two names are susceptible to (mis)interpretation, as the philosophers demonstrate, so are the last. After so theatrical an episode in his narrative, is Luke playfully suggesting that the whole scene in some sense "belongs to Dionysus," (Διονύσιος) the god of the theater?[158] Has he coined a name otherwise unattested in all of Greek literature to pair with Dionysius, one that looks to be based on δάμαρ, a common word for "wife" in Tragedy, subtly reminding the reader that this whole scene began with the philosophers' ignorance in taking Anastasis to be a proper name, a divine consort of Jesus? Perhaps Luke is telling us, and has been telling us all along, "from the beginning" (Luke 1:1), in his own playful way that,

> Many are the forms of divine things,
> and many things the gods bring to pass unexpectedly;
> and the things expected have not happened,
> but the god has found a way for doing unexpected things.
> So this matter turned out.[159]

7. Epilogue: Paul the Character
–or– The Acts of Paul

Sensitivity to the sophistic quality of Paul's rhetorical strategies in Acts 17 and elsewhere is heightened by comparison with other speech-making characters in the narrative. This idea once would have sounded rather unlikely given the amount of emphasis some scholars placed on the homogeneity of the speeches in Acts. Eduard Schweizer's treatment was long considered definitive, but the careful reader must be struck by the number of exceptions to the rule of homogeneity even in his own analysis.[160] It is not, however,

---

158. Interestingly, Barrett, using clues from both Acts and the Epistles, suspects that Paul arrived in Corinth in March (C. K. Barrett, *The First Epistle to the Corinthians* [BNTC; Peabody, Mass.: Hendrickson, 1973], 5). That would put Paul's visit to Athens in the Spring, the time of the Great Dionysia, which was famous for having been the festival at which the new plays were debuted in classical times.

159. *Bacchae*, 1390. Cf. Acts 13:40–41: "Beware, therefore, that what the prophets said does not happen to you:

> Look, you scoffers!
> Be amazed and perish,
> for in your days I am doing a work,
> a work that you will never believe,
> even if someone tells you."

160. Eduard Schweizer, "Concerning the Speeches in Acts," in *Studies in Luke-Acts*, 208–16. In light of the maturation of classically informed rhetorical criticism among NT scholars, Schweizer's efforts, devoid of any attempt at formal analysis of the speeches according to contemporary rhetorical categories, now appear inadequate. An analysis of all the speeches in one volume is now available (Marion L. Soards, *The Speeches in Acts: Their Content, Context, and Concerns* [Louisville: Westminster John Knox, 1994]). While finding certain themes to be

the issue of whether such analyses have overemphasized the supposed same-ness of *logos* among the witnesses in Acts that interests me here. The more serious problem is the preoccupation with matters of *logos* to the detriment of sensitivity to differences in *pathos* and *ethos*.[161] Indeed, the very notion that these dimensions of rhetoric can be separated save in the most artificial way as one step in the critical process betrays a logocentric bias that severely reduces the breadth, length, height, and depth, that is to say, the body, or texture, of the text. Does Luke attempt not only to create appropriate dis-course for particular situations based on logical exigencies, something that no one can seriously doubt, but also to fit the discourse to the passion and character of the speaker?

As for *pathos*, few would contest that varied emotional states are con-veyed in Luke's portrayal of both speaker and audience even within the same scene. Yet, until recently, attention to such matters tended to be ignored by *serious* scholarship and left over, as is considered proper for all such excess, to the imaginative and edifying domain of devotional commentary. What intrigues me most, however, in light of my reading of the Areopagus speech, is the *ethos*-related question of whether Luke reserved such a virtuoso dis-play of sophistic wiles, in this case mainly the cunning use of ambiguity, for Paul alone in his narrative, and whether there are other incidents in Paul's career where Luke imagined Paul to have demonstrated sophistic cunning. A full analysis of this question is beyond the scope of this chapter, but a provisional answer can be provided by a brief comparison of speeches given before the Sanhedrin by Peter, Stephen, and Paul.

Apart from the simple play on "save" (σῴζω) in 4:9 (cf. 4:12), Peter's speech in 4:8–12 is devoid of playful subtleties. Furthermore, the audience is unambiguously addressed as the murderers of Jesus and "you builders" who rejected the cornerstone. In response to such a speech, Luke imagines that the Sanhedrin would have noticed both the "boldness/brashness" (παρρησία) of the disciples — not necessarily the compliment that many commentators assume — and the fact that they were illiterate and untrained. Even a reader with no knowledge of rhetorical etiquette has little trouble understanding why the Council found this speech brash. But how do the Council's members arrive at the conclusion that Peter and John are illiterate and untrained? After all, the speech features a quotation from a text! The key is to realize that the descriptions, illiterate and untrained, are hardly unrelated. Peter and John speak boldly but recklessly. That a well-read, well-bred person, without provocation, would begin a defense speech by unambiguously insulting the court in an opening statement seems very unlikely to Luke, and he has the

---

recurrent and pervasive in most of the speeches, Soards does justice to the considerable amount of structural and functional differences between them.

161. Fortunately, this tendency in biblical criticism may be changing. See Thomas H. Olbricht and Jerry L. Sumney, eds., *Paul and Pathos* (SBLSS 16: Atlanta: SBL Press, forthcoming in 2001).

Council voice the obvious conclusion that these defendants are ignorant and untrained. Furthermore, they show a complete disregard for any sane rhetorical strategy by immediately associating themselves quite explicitly with a recently convicted and executed criminal!

Stephen's speech in Acts 7 is also ultimately insulting, though Luke portrays this "Hellenist" as far more rhetorically astute than Peter and John. His speech begins as a relatively straightforward and simple narration of Israelite history (7:1–19), but when he gets to Moses, if not before, he begins to weave a thick web of ambiguity and insinuation (7:20–50).[162] Increasingly it becomes clear that Stephen is seeing Jesus' rejection foreshadowed in that of Moses. The speech then concludes in a openly denunciatory and insulting fashion (7:51–53). The effect on the audience is predictable.

Is this the way Luke imagines all his witnesses behaving before this court? Not at all. Paul also appears before the Sanhedrin in Luke's narrative (22:30–23:11). Staring at the Council, he begins by forthrightly declaring his innocence, to which the high priest responds by commanding that he be struck. To be sure, Paul does respond by insulting the presider. But when he is told that it is the high priest of God that he has insulted he immediately issues an apology, complete with an appropriate scriptural quotation (Exod 22:27). Whether we choose to detect irony in Paul's words or not, Luke shows us a Paul who is aware of what is proper behavior in this situation and who acts accordingly. Can we really imagine Peter and John responding this way based on Luke's portrait? But the fun has only begun.

Completely bypassing the charges at hand, Paul pits the two parties of the Council against each other by crying out, "Brothers, I am a Pharisee, the son of Pharisees. On account of the hope and resurrection of the dead I stand before the court" (23:6). Paul, who on the basis of his portrait in Acts to this point, not to mention the portrayal of Christian Pharisees as his opponents at the Jerusalem Council, surely cannot sincerely claim to be a Pharisee, chooses a strategy of deception according to Luke. As John Darr perceptively remarks,

> This is all a clever, irony-laden ploy consisting of partial truths (he never did turn in his membership card, and he does indeed still believe in resurrection), and based on the insight that the Pharisees are susceptible to a display of external religious criteria (lineage, education, membership, doctrinal orthodoxy) but are blind to the deeper truths of the situation. The reader realizes that what Paul fails to tell the Sanhedrin about himself (his conversion, belief in Jesus as Christ, argument that Gentile converts do not have to be circumcised, etc.) is much more significant than what he tells them. Furthermore, the reader is well aware that Paul never talks of his Pharisaism *except* in these desperate

---

162. See especially Ben Witherington III, *The Acts of the Apostles: A Socio-Rhetorical Commentary* (Grand Rapids: Eerdmans, 1998), 260–78, and J. Dupont, "La structure oratoire du discours d'Étienne (Actes 7)," *Bib* 66 (1985): 153–67. Also see Soards, *The Speeches in Acts*, 57–70.

situations where such information might help him survive, just as he never mentions his Roman citizenship until he is about to be lashed (22:25–30).[163]

The fact that he casts himself as a Pharisaic champion of the doctrine of resurrection without mentioning Jesus only magnifies the ambiguous, cunning, and deceptive qualities of Paul's defense.[164] Let us recall that Peter and John did not hesitate to mention Jesus by name before the Council. It is very difficult not to think of Paul before the Sanhedrin when reading the following description.

> Mētis — intelligence which operates in the world of becoming, in circumstances of conflict — takes the form of an ability to deal with whatever comes up, drawing on certain intellectual qualities: forethought, perspicacity, quickness and acuteness of understanding, trickery, and even deceit. But these qualities bring into play the weapons which are their own particular attribute: elusiveness and duplicity, like spells which they use to oppose brute force. A being of mētis slips through its adversary's fingers like running water. It is so supple as to be polymorphic; like a trap, it is the opposite of what it seems to be. It is ambiguous, inverted, and operates through a process of reversal.[165]

Historical-critical scholars have resisted this reading. Typical is Haenchen who, citing Phil 3:5–9 as evidence, simply declares that "No proof should really be necessary that here it is not the historical Paul who speaks. . . . Just as little should there be need for proof that Luke does not here want to show a clever rabbinical trick by his hero."[166] Substitute sophistical for rabbinical and I would contend that regardless of what Luke wants, this is what he gets. Haenchen, like most commentators, believes that Luke's Paul, in stark contrast to the historical Paul, is serious about his claim to be a Pharisee. He believes it is part of a Lukan strategy of showing that Christianity and Pharisaism are not incompatible. Highly conservative commentators who uphold the reliability of Acts usually affirm that Paul really agreed with this notion on some deeper level and thus was not really lying in claiming to be a Pharisee. Yet F. F. Bruce did not shy away from linking this incident directly to 1 Cor 9:23.[167] Why are some scholars more willing than others to believe that the historical Paul "put on an act" in certain situations?

---

163. Darr, *On Character Building*, 123. Darr convincingly argues against the widespread notion that Luke portrays the Pharisees rather favorably (85–126). His perspective tends to support the likelihood that Paul's occasional espousal of Pharisaism is feigned and opportunistic (122–26).

164. Cf. his convenient omission of the fact that the new *daimonion* he proclaims in Athens suffered crucifixion before his resurrection.

165. Detienne and Vernant, *Cunning Intelligence*, 43–44.

166. Haenchen, *Acts*, 643.

167. Bruce, *The Acts*, 465. Bruce, however, was not unaware of the danger of linking this account with the "all things to all people" policy: "It is overscrupulous to blame Paul for his action on this occasion (whether he be the historical Paul or the Lukan Paul), as if his sole purpose were by a disingenuous claim to set his accusers by the ears . . . " (Bruce, 466). Implicit here is the assumption that Paul has other purposes that justify his action.

I suspect that Calvin, as reformer, orator, and lawyer, can help us answer this question with what he has to say about Paul's appearance before the Sanhedrin. Of Paul's rhetorical strategy in this case, he says,

> Paul's *strategem*, which Luke reports, seems out of keeping with a servant of Christ. For the *astuteness*, which he used, was closely related to a *feint*, that was not far removed from *lying*. He says that the circumstances of his case turn on the resurrection of the dead. But we know that the issue was about other matters, that he abrogated the ceremonies, and admitted the Gentiles to the covenant of salvation.[168]

So far Paul can be grateful that Calvin was not counsel for the Sanhedrin. But he quickly switches to advocacy:

> I reply that *even if those things are true, yet he did not lie*. For he does not deny that he was accused of the things, and he does not resolve the dispute on this one issue, but truly acknowledges that the Sadducees are hostile to him, because he affirms the resurrection of the dead....Therefore we must note that Paul began by wishing to explain his whole situation frankly and sincerely, and that he did not *cunningly* avoid a clean and honest confession, such as the servants of Christ should have given. But we must also observe that, because an opening was barred, and no hearing was granted to him, he used *an extreme remedy* to make it plain that his adversaries were being swept off their feet by a blind hatred....If anyone nowadays obscures the light of sound doctrine, *and uses Paul's example as an excuse for his own cunning*, his is easily refuted. For it is one thing to look to one's personal interests, at the expense of the truth, but another to bring professed enemies of Christ from attacking Him, to fighting among themselves.[169]

Notice the considerable ambiguity in Calvin's own position here. He insists that Paul did not intend to be cunning ("he did not cunningly avoid a clean and honest confession"), but the situation dictated "an extreme remedy." Then, by his stern warning to any who would use Paul's example as a pretext for their "own cunning," Calvin clearly assumes that Paul *was* being cunningly deceptive. What made Paul's subterfuge permissible for Calvin was the selfless goal of it. The noble end justified the ignoble means.[170] Indeed, the implication seems to be that Paul "did not lie," because a noble lie, a "golden lie," is not a true lie. Perhaps it is a True lie.

I began this Epilogue asking whether Luke presents Paul's rhetoric as substantially different from that of any other character in Acts. By now it

---

168. John Calvin, *The Acts of the Apostles: 14–28* (London: Oliver and Boyd, 1966), 230, italics mine.

169. Calvin, *The Acts*, 230–31, italics mine.

170. Cf. Luther: "What harm would it do, if a man told a good strong lie for the sake of the good and for the Christian church [...] a lie out of necessity, a useful lie, a helpful lie, such lies would not be against God, he would accept them." Quoted in Sissela Bok, *Lying: Moral Choice in Public and Private Life* (New York: Pantheon Books, 1978), 48. See ibid., p. 309, n. 9 for full reference.

should be clear that Paul's rhetoric is unique. Paul is a new Socrates before philosophers, and he is like a slippery sophist in court.[171] Anyone who believes that the "real" Paul could not have behaved this way must dismiss the rhetorical implications of Luke's stories of Paul before the Areopagus and Sanhedrin, in Athens and Jerusalem. But, as I will suggest in the next two chapters, although Luke's portrait of a sophistic Paul may be fanciful, it is not necessarily fantastic.

> Role playing is what actors must literally do in the theater as they don their costumes and masks to impersonate an other — whether king or servant, mortal or god, Greek or barbarian, man or woman. But the reverse side of the coin is to be dubbed an actor, a *hypokritēs,* who is only playing a role, offering only a persona (a *prosōpon*) to the other that does not match what lies behind the mask.[172]

After this Paul left Athens and went to Corinth (Acts 18:1).

---

171. "Even when they are caught animals may, thanks to their *mētis,* themselves remain traps: they have all the cunning of the sophist, the *poikílos* schemer 'who is never without a way (*pórous eumēchanos porízein*) of escaping from difficulties (*amēchánōn*).' Their *mētis* even rivals Promethean cunning 'capable of extricating itself even from the inextricable' " (Detienne and Vernant, *Cunning Intelligence,* 33).

172. Zeitlin, "Playing the Other," 84.

III

Cunning in Corinth

Socrates in the dialogues of Plato often has the face of a *pharmakeus*. That is the name given by Diotima to Eros. But behind the portrait of Eros, one cannot fail to recognize the features of Socrates, as though Diotima, in looking at him, were proposing to Socrates the portrait of Socrates (*Symposium*, 203*c,d,e*). Eros, who is neither rich, nor beautiful, nor delicate, spends his life philosophizing (*philosophōn dia pantos tou biou*); he is a fearsome sorcerer (*deinos goēs*), magician (*pharmakeus*), and sophist (*sophistēs*). A being that no "logic" can confine within a noncontradictory definition, an individual of the demonic species, neither god nor man, neither immortal nor mortal, neither living nor dead, he forms "the medium of the prophetic arts, of the priestly rites of sacrifice, initiation, and incantation, of divination and of sorcery (*thusias-teletas-epōdas-manteian*)" (202*e*).

— Derrida, "Plato's Pharmacy," 117.

For we are the aroma of Christ for God among those being saved and those being destroyed, to one a fragrance from death for death, to the other a fragrance from life for life (2 Cor 2:15–16).

For even though we walk about in the flesh, we are not fighting in a fleshly manner. For the weapons of our struggle are not fleshly but rather have divine power to destroy strongholds, destroying arguments and every proud obstacle to the knowledge of God, taking captive every thought to obey Christ (2 Cor 10:3–5).

We are always carrying around the death of Jesus in the body so that the life of Jesus may also be manifested in our bodies (2 Cor 4:10).

Yet among the perfect/initiates (τελείοις) we do speak wisdom (σοφίαν), but wisdom not of this age or of the rulers of this age who are being disempowered. But rather we speak a wisdom of God hidden in a mystery which God appointed before the ages for our glory (1 Cor 2:6–7).

1. Protect

The previous chapter began by calling attention to the institutional act of canonization and its powerful yet often surreptitious effects on interpretation. I concentrated on "breaking the canonical mold" by providing a new reading of Acts 17:16–34 that sought to demonstrate that both its Hellenistic and Jewish components are even more pervasive and complex than previously recognized, and that Luke has combined them in a creative cultural pastiche that reminds one of Barthes' definition of the Text. The Paul that emerges from this pastiche, the Lukan Paul, is a highly complex, multidimensional and multi-cultural character, whose discourse is often a True rhetoric, a multi-layered rhetoric intentionally designed to be heard different ways by different people. Luke's Paul also walks a thin line between adapting his message to his audience and cunningly conforming himself to his audience, and one could easily suspect that he probably crossed that line from time to time. The "Epilogue" pointed out that Acts 17 is not the only example of such a Paul in Luke's second volume. But to what extent is the Lukan Paul the "real" Paul where rhetorical strategy is concerned?

This chapter and the next begin to answer that question. It is only a beginning because more passages and issues could be discussed than space and time allow here, and because I must introduce the crucial issue of how Paul's worldview, his apocalypticism, relates to his unique exploitation of writing and rhetoric. If my arguments about apocalypticism and rhetoric in Paul succeed, by the end of chapter four, "Deception in Rome," it should be clear why Romans must always leave us with more questions than answers. If there is deception in Rome, and True rhetoric is Paul's ambiguous and cunning response to deception, then Romans is True rhetoric, a message designed to be heard differently by different actors in the audience, some more and some less deceived. Thus our problem is not that the text has no meaning, but that it has an excess of meaning, meaning that is indeterminate in the sense that its determination is a matter of perspective.

A steady undercurrent in the present chapter will be a concern with the way the needs of institutions created and sustained by the canonical machine serve to foreclose certain readings generally deemed unconducive to institutional aims, readings that support the troubling image of Paul as a master of True rhetoric. I will be modifying and championing views of some contested texts in the Corinthian correspondence over other views that seem more subject to canonical and ecclesiastical constraint. These chosen texts are 1 Cor 1–4, 9:19–23, and 2 Cor 2:14–4:6, although others will come into play. A concluding section will further investigate the issues raised by the discussion of the 2 Cor 2:14–4:6 passage concerning the relationship between speech and writing, especially as they relate to Paul's apocalypticism. This will serve as a bridge to my treatment of Romans.

Protecting Paul — from himself, his enemies, and even well-meaning but misguided friends like myself — is the oldest profession of Pauline interpreters. Early canonical protectors include "Luke," the "Pastor," and "Peter" (e.g., 2 Pet 3:15–16), and modern examples are not hard to find. For example, with respect to 1 Cor 9:19–23, one of the most dangerous Pauline passages, Peter Marshall observes that

> Since H. Chadwick's seminal work on vv. 19–23 a number of articles have appeared, though scholars generally have not recognized the importance of the passage for our understanding of Paul.... As if in recognition of the dilemma of his enemies, but *protective of Paul,* scholars have chosen to describe his behavior as flexible, chameleon-*like, apparently* inconsistent or contradictory.[1]

But are such interpreters protecting Paul, or rather protecting the Church from a less assimilable Paul who is often a thorn in the flesh? As Käsemann argued long ago with respect to Paul's doctrine of justification by faith, the justification of the ungodly,

> It is never long, to be sure, until orthodoxy and enthusiasm again master this Paul and banish him once more to his letters. However the Church continues to preserve his letters in her canon and thereby latently preserves her own permanent crisis. She cannot get away from the one who for the most part only disturbs her. For he remains even for her the apostle of the heathen; the pious still hardly know what to make of him. For that very reason his central message is the voice of a preacher in the wilderness, even in Protestant Christianity, which today stands much nearer early catholicism than it supposes or is willing to believe.[2]

Käsemann's remarks represent some of the most incisive insights of the liberal Protestant tradition, the home turf of the historical-critical method. Indeed, his remark about the church preserving a crisis in her canon sounds rather postmodern in its critical disposition.[3] But such internal ecclesiastical recognition of the radical Paul on this and other subjects remains the exception rather than the rule.

Let me be clear that I am not claiming always to know when Paul's interpreters consciously intend their work to protect the Church from Paul in order to further institutional aims. Sometimes they declare their intentions, sometimes not. To some extent, of course, it is a matter of perspective. While in this chapter I use E. P. Sanders's reading of 1 Cor 9:19–23 as an example of Pauline protection, certainly few traditional Lutheran and Reformed interpreters would think of Sanders as protecting Paul. What interests me is the protective effects of these discourses, regardless of the authors' conscious or unconscious intentions. Indeed, all interpreters must strive to become more

---

1. Peter Marshall, *Enmity,* 315, italics mine.
2. Ernst Käsemann, "Paul and Early Catholicism," in *New Testament Questions of Today* (Philadelphia: Fortress, 1969), 250.
3. Cf. my remarks at the beginning of chapter two (p. 41), inspired by a passage by Tom Cohen.

aware of certain investments that control their work. Thus a constant and rigorous self-analysis is required.[4]

With these comments, and in light of much of my study to this point, many readers will have noticed a deconstructive influence on my project. This aspect of my work may already have raised some questions. How can one who quotes Derrida on a regular basis show so much interest in intentional ambiguity? Is not deconstruction disinterested or even antithetical to the concept of authorial intention? I have already addressed this misunderstanding in chapter one.[5] Or, how can a writer who is interested in the *history* and *thought* of Paul and Pauline Christianity associate himself with deconstruction? Is not deconstruction concerned only with texts and the unfettered play of the signifier? In short, is the combination of historical criticism and deconstruction found in this work "legitimate"?

2. A Methodological Interlude: Deconstruction — as Inscribed Here

In the early nineties, Stephen Moore asked the question, "Deconstruction — what will it have been?"[6] By then it had already been many things to many people, indeed, so much so that even Derrida had distanced himself from some of what went by the name. But Moore could still say that deconstruction was largely ignored and/or marginalized by mainstream biblical scholarship, for "with regard to this sect we know that everywhere it is spoken against."[7] Since then, little has changed except that Moore's own work has perhaps increased fear and loathing, occasionally contempt, of this unwelcome stranger in what has otherwise become an increasingly interdisciplinary field. The answer to the question of what deconstruction will have been can be stated in one word: misunderstood. For this reason, I provide the following comments about what deconstruction is not in my work. In the process, I will make a number of contrasts between what deconstruction is in my work as opposed to Stephen Moore's, the scholar perhaps most associated with deconstruction in biblical studies.

Deconstruction, as inscribed here, is not an arbitrary procedure: "The *incision* of deconstruction, which is not a voluntary decision or an ab-

---

4. An apparent poststructuralist objector to this procedure is Stanley Fish, who refers to this notion as "the critical self-consciousness fallacy" (see his "Critical Self-Consciousness, Or Can We Know What We're Doing," *Doing What Comes Naturally*, 436–67). But, rightly understood, Fish's argument does not exclude the sort of self-examination envisioned here. Fish is rather objecting to the notion that one can occupy a position outside oneself or one's discipline while carrying out such evaluation, that one can transcend his or her situation *tout court*.

5. See p. 3, n. 7.

6. Stephen D. Moore, *Mark and Luke in Poststructuralist Perspectives: Jesus Begins to Write* (New Haven and London: Yale University Press, 1992), xiii.

7. Ibid., xiv.

solute beginning, does not take place just anywhere, or in an absolute elsewhere."[8] The charge of arbitrariness can be brought on a stylistic and/or methodological level. In terms of style, some deconstructors leave the impression of arbitrariness by failing to balance the Dionysian/Nietzschean with the Apollonian/Heideggerian aspects of Derrida's project. Parts of Moore's *Mark and Luke in Poststructuralist Perspective* appear so bizarre to the uninitiated that surely more than one reader has complained of the "occasionally lurid word play," "his extreme approach," and has been moved to say that "we can be thankful that deconstruction has perhaps already passed its prime in secular literary study."[9] Deconstruction is trivialized when it tends to be presented as an endless series of puns illustrating the free play of the signifier. This critique, of course, is not entirely fair to Moore's *Mark and Luke*. But when he drifts into his neo-Joycean mode, his claim "to [be] reply[ing] to the gospels in kind, to write in a related idiom," strikes even me as more than a little arbitrary.[10] One should not forget that Derrida's most celebrated neo-Joycean essay was a response to Joyce's text.[11] Derrida himself has spoken out strongly against the notion that deconstruction is arbitrary and can make a text say whatever one wants.[12] As for the methodological charge of arbitrariness, some deconstructors left the impression that deconstruction itself is a method, indeed, an alternative method to every "traditional" method, including, of course, historical criticism.

Deconstruction, as inscribed here, cannot be accused of "not wanting to go any further than the text itself."[13] The formulation of this charge, and the failure to realize its irony, reveals a complete misunderstanding of deconstruction. According to Riddel, Yale school deconstruction — he singles out de Man and Miller — was partly responsible for this misreading of Derrida. "There is no outside the text" actually means that Derrida "textualize[s] the world" — so long as "world" is not construed as a *uni*verse, a new totality.[14] Leitch summarizes the point well:

> Since language serves as ground of existence, the world emerges as infinite Text. Everything gets textualized. All contexts, whether political, economic, social, psychological, historical, or theological, become intertexts; that is, out-

8. Jacque Derrida, "Positions," *Positions* (Chicago: The University of Chicago Press, 1981), 93.

9. Stanley E. Porter, "Literary Approaches to the New Testament: From Formalism to Deconstruction and Back," in *Approaches to New Testament Study* (JSNTSup 120; ed. Stanley E. Porter and David Tombs; Sheffield: Sheffield Academic Press, 1995), 110–11.

10. Moore, *Mark and Luke*, xviii.

11. Jacques Derrida, "Hear Say Yes in Joyce," in *James Joyce: The Augmented Ninth. Proceedings of Ninth International James Joyce Symposium* (ed. Bernard Benstock; Syracuse: Syracuse University Press, 1988), 27–75.

12. Idem, *Limited Inc,* 146. See also Seeley, *Deconstructing the New Testament.*

13. Porter, "Literary Approaches," 111.

14. Joseph N. Riddel, "Re-doubling the Commentary," *Contemporary Literature* 20 (Spring, 1979), 242.

side influences and forces undergo textualization. Instead of literature we have textuality; in place of tradition, intertextuality.[15]

Deconstruction, as inscribed here, does not treat texts deemed worthy of its attention with contempt. Moore compiles the following quotation from Derrida's *Ear of the Other:*

> I love very much everything that I deconstruct...; the texts I want to read from the deconstructive point of view are texts I love, with that impulse of identification which is indispensable for reading. They are texts whose future, I think, will not be exhausted for a long time.... My relation to these texts is characterized by loving jealousy and not at all by nihilistic fury (one can't read anything in the latter condition).[16]

I strongly concur with this attitude and feel this way not only toward Paul's texts, but also the texts of his interpreters examined in this chapter.[17]

Finally, and above all, deconstruction, *as inscribed here,* is no enemy of historical inquiry. On the contrary, it "depends upon an historical analysis."[18]

> What we must be wary of, I repeat, is the *metaphysical* concept of history. This is the concept of history as the history of meaning, as we were just saying a moment ago: the history of meaning developing itself, producing itself, fulfilling itself.... we must first distinguish between history in general and the general concept of history. Althusser's entire, and necessary, critique of the 'Hegelian' concept of history and of the notion of an expressive totality, etc., aims at showing that there is not one single history, a general history, but rather histories *different* in their type, rhythm, mode of inscription — intervallic, differentiated histories. I have always subscribed to this, as to the concept of history that Sollers calls "monumental."[19]

In this light, Barr's devastating critique of the "essentially synthetic method" of the "Biblical Theology" movement sounds quite Derridean at times.[20]

---

15. Vincent B. Leitch, *Deconstructive Criticism: An Advanced Introduction* (New York: Columbia University Press, 1983), 122.

16. Moore, *Mark and Luke,* 3.

17. One of Moore's works, however, seems far removed from this Derridean attitude. After totalizing the Bible by means of an utterly one-sided view of its God, he concludes, "For if what I have been arguing about the Bible is indeed the case — that its God is a singularly pure projection of the will to power — then the biblical critic might have no choice but to clutch his or her scalpel defensively, to brandish it threateningly, as the hypermasculine hulk that is the biblical God lumbers across the examining room, an imperious frown furrowing his perfectly handsome features, and a pair of handcuffs dangling ominously from his weight-lifting belt, which is cinched around his bloodstained butcher's apron, from the pocket of which a blindfold protrudes. 'You do not believe because you have seen me,' he intones. 'Blessed are those who have not seen and therefore believe'" (*God's Gym: Divine Male Bodies of the Bible* [New York: Routledge, 1996], 139–40).

18. Derrida, "Positions," 93. See also Seeley, *Deconstructing the New Testament,* 159–60.

19. Ibid., 56–58.

20. James Barr, *The Semantics of Biblical Language* (London: SCM, 1961), 270, passim.

Käsemann was also uncompromising in his rejection of an "enthusiastic theology of history" with its inevitable blindness to history's horror.[21]

Someone has said that the problem with the historical-critical method is that it never really was all that historical or critical. Apparently many poststructuralist biblical interpreters would concur. But this attitude appears mistakenly to assume that "historical criticism" is some sort of monolith, that there is one thing called historical criticism and one unified school of its practitioners. Oddly enough, such totalizations of historical criticism often come from poststructuralist interpreters who complain loudly, and rightly, about the dangers of such totalizations. It is simplistic and sad that deconstruction and poststructuralism more generally, in all their diversity, are often portrayed as the enemy of some sort of monolithic monster named "historical criticism." The final paragraph of Moore's *Poststructuralism and the New Testament* is illustrative.

> What, then, is the precise relationship of poststructuralism to historical criticism? As I see it, poststructuralism is temperamentally unsuited to be yet another handmaid (a French maid?) to historical criticism. Neither is poststructuralism poised to become historical criticism's slayer (historical criticism is much too massive for that, occupying entire city blocks at the national conferences; it crushes its enemies by sitting on them). Rather, in the context of biblical studies, poststructuralism would be historical criticism's id, the seat of its strongest antiauthoritarian instincts — historical criticism unfettered at last from the ecclesiastical superego that has always compelled it to genuflect before the icons it had come to destroy.[22]

While at least granting that historical criticism has antiauthoritarian instincts, one would never guess from the last sentence the controversial role historical criticism has already played in Christian denominations over the past three centuries. What about those scholars who either voluntarily or, more often, involuntarily, gave up their positions in church-related colleges, universities, and seminaries because of their relentless pursuit of the historical-critical approach and refusal to bow to ecclesiastical authority? Historical criticism at its best has hardly been beholden to the Church, nor has it been unacquainted with a searching self-examination of its presuppositions.[23] To a great extent, deconstruction is a never-ending process of

---

21. See Roy A. Harrisville and Walter Sundberg, *The Bible in Modern Culture: Theology and Historical-Critical Method from Spinoza to Käsemann* (Grand Rapids: Eerdmans, 1995), 246–47.

22. Moore, *Poststructuralism*, 117. See also the mostly polarizing discourse in The Bible and Culture Collective, *The Postmodern Bible*, 1–8.

23. E.g., "In this way exegetical work does indeed become dependent on the work of philosophy. But it would be an illusion to suppose that any exegesis could be carried out independently of some profane conceptuality. Every exegete is dependent — usually unreflectively and uncritically — on some conceptuality . . . " (Rudolf Bultmann, "On the Problem of Demythologizing," in *New Testament and Mythology and other Basic Writings* [selected, ed., trans. Schubert M. Ogden; Philadelphia: Fortress, 1984], 107). Cf. *The Postmodern Bible*, 278, 302.

breeching authoritarian institutional limits and an intense probing of their often unconsciously internalized effects.[24] In that respect, it resonates rather strongly with the legacy of some historical criticism. Only by furthering an ongoing process of lifting the canonical and ecclesiastical veil will we be prepared to catch more than a glimpse of a sophistic Paul and imagine the consequences of such a transgression.[25] "Intervention" is indispensable and interminable, and that is affirmed by both deconstruction and the best and most uncompromising examples of historical criticism.[26]

3. Containing Cunning in 1 Cor 1–4

This is a cunning intelligence for which hunting and fishing may originally have provided the model but which extends far beyond this framework as the figure of Odysseus, the human embodiment of *mētis*, in Homer, clearly shows. There are many activities in which man [*sic*] must learn to manipulate hostile forces too powerful to be controlled directly but which can be exploited despite themselves, without ever being confronted head on, to implement the plan in mind by some unexpected, devious means: they include, for example, the stratagems used by the warrior the success of whose attack hinges on surprise, trickery or ambush, the art of the pilot steering his ship against winds and tides, the verbal ploys of the sophist making the adversary's powerful argument recoil against him...."[27]

When I came to you, brothers and sisters, I did not come proclaiming the mystery of God in lofty speech or wisdom. For I decided to know nothing among you except Jesus Christ and him crucified. And I (be)came in weakness and in much fear and trembling to you. And my speech and my proclamation were not in persuasive words of wisdom, but in a demonstration of the Spirit and power, so that your faith might not be in human wisdom, but in the power of God. Yet we do speak wisdom to the perfect/initiates, though it is not a wisdom of this age or of the rulers of this age who are being disempowered.

---

24. A major theme in Vernon Robbins's recent description of a comprehensive socio-rhetorical approach is the detection and destruction of such boundaries. See, e.g., his critique of exegesis based on severely limited definitions of "intertextuality" like Michael Fishbane's model of "inner biblical exegesis" (*Tapestry*, 97–102; see also 142–43, 192–236).

25. Earlier transgressors of the veil often placed over 1 Cor 9:19–23 include Marshall, who concludes that charges of inconstancy are not entirely without substance and that Paul really was part chameleon (Marshall, *Enmity*, 401–2, quoted below), and Dale Martin, who concludes that "Paul's self-portrayal as Christ's managerial slave, who must preach the gospel by compulsion and not from free will, is a clear rejection of the moral philosophical discourse that spoke of the leader as the benevolent, patriarchal wise man" (*Slavery*, 117–18). Rather than the latter respectable model of leadership, Paul espouses the highly controversial and frequently disreputable populist or demagogic model. See esp. "The Enslaved Leader as a Rhetorical Topos," and "Slave of All in 1 Corinthians 9," in *Slavery*, 86–116, 117–35. I might add that this model is often closely associated with sophistic rhetoric.

26. "Deconstruction, as I have insisted, is not *neutral*. It *intervenes*" (Derrida, "Positions," 93, italics his).

27. Detienne and Vernant, *Cunning Intelligence*, 47–48.

But rather, we speak the hidden wisdom of God in a mystery which God appointed before the ages for our glory (1 Cor 2:1–7).

The applicability of the first quotation to 1 Cor 1–4 may not be immediately apparent. Those who are familiar with rhetorically informed interpretations of 2 Cor 10–13 might rather have thought of that passage while reading this definition of cunning intelligence.[28] In that case there is considerable agreement that, whether influenced by a Socratic model or not, Paul turns the arguments of the Corinthian "sophists" and the "super-apostles" against them.[29] He does not confront them head on, but rather takes on their own style in an ironic, parodic fashion, thereby demonstrating their "real" foolishness through his own feigned foolishness.[30] Thus Paul repeats their foolishness with a difference. But I will argue that Paul's strategy in 1 Cor 1–4 is yet more cunning.[31]

Recent studies of 1 Cor 1–4 suggest that even before the "super-apostles" arrived in Corinth, the same socio-cultural factors that attracted some of the Corinthians to them were already at play in the division between "those of Paul" and "those of Apollos."[32] Their contrasting rhetorical styles and abilities may well have attracted some to one and some to the other.[33]

The Rhetorical Situation

When Paul founded the church in Corinth, most of his converts were probably pagan. Some likely came from the ranks of God-fearers.[34] Only a few were Jews.[35] Therefore, most would not already have had a firm ground-

---

28. I have already discussed Betz's important work on this passage. See above, pp. 11–13.

29. See discussion and bibliography in Winter, *Philo and Paul*, 224–28.

30. See especially Christopher Forbes, "Comparison, Self-Praise and Irony: Paul's Boasting and the Conventions of Hellenistic Rhetoric," *NTS* 32 (1986): 1–30.

31. On the veiled quality of Paul's rhetoric in 1 Cor 1–4 more generally, see Benjamin Fiore's excellent article, " 'Covert Allusion' in 1 Corinthians 1–4" *CBQ* 47 (1985): 85–102. Fiore suggests that Paul is using the rhetorical figure of *logos-eschēmatismenos* (see 1 Cor 4:6) in these chapters out of "respect for the dignity of the persons charged with faults" (95). But Fiore recognizes that this theory does not fit well with the level of irony and sarcasm encountered from time to time in this passage. His explanation is that perhaps the crisis was so severe that Paul had to be more explicit at points: "In any event, Paul's concern is for the good of the community, and not for the purity of rhetorical forms" (96).

32. Winter, *Philo and Paul*, 170–78, passim, provides a full development of this perspective.

33. Relying on a study by Robert W. Smith, *The Art of Rhetoric in Alexandria: Its Theory and Practice in the Ancient World* (The Hague: Martinus Nijhoff, 1974), Pogoloff hypothesizes that Apollos used a rough and ready demagogic Alexandrian rhetoric, appropriate to drinking parties, while Paul was calmer and more sententious (Stephen M. Pogoloff, *Logos and Sophia: The Rhetorical Situation of 1 Corinthians* [SBLDS 134; Atlanta: Scholars Press, 1992], 183–95). Aside from the fact that what little evidence we have about Apollos suggests just the opposite to most interpreters, one clearly cannot say anything with any confidence about his rhetorical style on the basis of a huge generalization about what kind of rhetoric was predominant in Alexandria, for there were, nevertheless, many styles present.

34. On the God-fearer issue, see below, p. 145.

35. This is the picture that emerges based on evidence from Acts and the Corinthian correspondence. See discussion in Gordon D. Fee, *The First Epistle to the Corinthians* (NICNT; Grand Rapids: Eerdmans, 1987), 3–4.

ing in Jewish morality, an observation surely not unrelated to the libertine nature of several of the problems in the church. So the cultural and ethnic makeup of these converts was analogous to those Paul had recently made when he wrote 1 Thessalonians.[36] A comparison with 1 Thessalonians may cast some light on facets of the rhetorical situation in 1 Corinthians.

First, despite the fact that 1 Thessalonians does contain a few echoes of Scripture, reminding us of how thoroughly Paul's very diction betrays his years of immersion in the LXX, this letter still suggests that Paul did not encourage a Scripture-based ethic and hermeneutic in his congregations.[37] Certainly Paul's Jewish roots are much in evidence when he reaches the parenetic section where he exhorts in rather traditional rabbinic terms, especially on the subject of marriage (4:4–5).[38] And yet he does so without citing relevant biblical authority to support his *halakah*. Most revealing of all, Paul says they really do not even need anyone to write to them "for you yourselves have been 'God-taught' to love one another" (4:9). Here in Paul's earliest surviving correspondence, we already see his overly optimistic confidence that the Spirit will take care of things, rendering superfluous written texts like the Law. In the last section of this chapter I will develop the idea that as a mystical apocalypticist who longed for all forms of mediation to give way to perfect spiritual presence, Paul naturally had a low view of writing itself.

Second, Paul's reminder of what had transpired while he was among the Thessalonians cannot fail to remind one of some of the very points he makes to the Corinthians about his initial work there. His gospel came "not only in word, but also in power" (1:5; cf. 1 Cor 2:4); the message appears to have been quite simple, for its effect can be summarized simply that they "turned to God from idols, to serve a living and true God, and to wait for his Son from heaven, whom he raised from the dead, Jesus who delivers us from the wrath to come" (1:9–10; cf. 1 Cor 2:2);[39] and he pictures himself

---

36. On the Thessalonian audience, see Robert Jewett, *The Thessalonian Correspondence: Pauline Rhetoric and Millenarian Piety* (Philadelphia: Fortress, 1986), 118–19.

37. See John Knox, *Marcion and the New Testament: An Essay in the Early History of the Canon* (Chicago: University of Chicago Press, 1942), 15–17; J. Louis Martyn, "John and Paul on the Subject of Gospel and Scripture," in *Theological Issues in the Letters of Paul* (Nashville: Abingdon, 1997), 209–30, esp. 217. Apparently Martyn also thinks that Paul was not the one who introduced Scripture to the Galatians: "It was in the Teachers' sermons, in fact, that the Galatian Gentiles first heard about Abraham, Sarah, Hagar, Ishmael, and Isaac" (222). But if the evidence of 1 Thessalonians and Galatians, as well as Philippians, Colossians, and Philemon for that matter, not to mention the fact that Paul never mentions the practice of Scripture-reading in worship — if all these could suggest that Paul did not introduce a preoccupation with Scripture into his churches, why is it used so much in 1 Corinthians? The description of the rhetorical situation being set forth here could answer that question.

38. See Raymond F. Collins, "The Unity of Paul's Paraenesis in 1 Thess. 4.3–8. 1 Cor. 7.1–7, a Significant Parallel," *NTS* 29 (1983): 420–29. Perhaps he also echoes Jesus traditions in v. 9.

39. Notice, however, that the similarity is in the simplicity, not the content. This difference is significant, and I will return to it below.

as a nurse taking care of children (2:7; cf. 1 Cor 3:1). In short, in both cases he is writing to new and immature converts.

But little did Paul know that this act of adapting and condescending to the infantile spiritual level of his new converts in Thessalonica and Corinth would come back to haunt him in his relationship with the latter community. Unlike in Thessalonica, Paul was followed by "a native of Alexandria . . . an eloquent man . . . well versed in the Scriptures" (Acts 18:24). If Apollos lived up to this reputation among Paul's recent converts, he surely would have made quite an impression.[40] Unlike Paul, he probably would have promoted a preoccupation with Scripture and its interpretation.[41] And though the description of Apollos in Acts is rather slim, it immediately calls to mind Philo of Alexandria, making one wonder if Apollos spoke and wrote a similarly polished Greek and practiced Platonically informed allegorical exegesis.[42] These possibilities would remain idle speculations if not for the fact that they can help make sense of a number of aspects of 1 Cor 1–4 and 1 Corinthians more generally, as we will see later. So let us assume for the moment that when Apollos began to "water" what Paul had "planted" (1 Cor 3:6), he began to impress some of the Corinthians so much with his rhetoric and "wisdom" that they began to think of him as Paul's superior, leading to the formation of divisions (σχίσματα, 1 Cor 1:10) and rivalries (ἔριδες, 1:11). Nothing indicates that this was his intention, and Paul apparently feels he can to some extent present himself and Apollos as amicable associates who equally disapprove of such developments. But we cannot just assume that there was perfect harmony between these two. Some of what Paul writes in 1 Cor 1–4 can easily be read as veiled criticism of Apollos (4:6), and one should not overlook the fact that while at one point in his argument Paul appears to put Apollos on the same level as himself (3:5–9, 21–23), this section ends with an assertion of Paul's paternal authority over the congregation and a threat toward those who would contest it (4:14–21). So, while I agree with Margaret Mitchell that 1:10, Paul's appeal for unity, is the πρόθεσις (thesis statement) for the entire letter, its relationship to 1:11–

---

40. I am essentially in agreement with Witherington's construal of the Apollos factor in the rhetorical situation Paul faced in Corinth. See Ben Witherington III, *Conflict and Community in Corinth: A Socio-Rhetorical Commentary on 1 and 2 Corinthians* (Grand Rapids: Eerdmans, 1995), 83–87, 124, 130.

41. Or perhaps a convert from the synagogue had begun to do this already (Acts 18:8). Of course, I am not saying that Paul himself did not use Scripture in his initial work in Corinth. Part of his message in the synagogue would certainly have been that the Christ event was "according to the Scriptures" (1 Cor 15:3–4). Such "proofs" from an ancient and revered sacred text would even have been effective with pure pagans. But this is hardly the same thing as teaching converts to regulate their lives according to the Scriptures.

42. Like Witherington, though he is not the first to suggest it, I am attracted to the hypothesis that Apollos wrote Hebrews (*Conflict and Community in Corinth*, 127). But see the critique of Montefiore's version of this hypothesis in C. K. Barrett, *The First Epistle to the Corinthians* [BNTC; Peabody, Mass.: Hendrickson, 1973], 8–11.

4:21 is especially important.[43] Before Paul can set about to restore harmony (ὁμόνοια) through addressing the wide range of divisive behavior at Corinth, he must first reestablish his authority among those elements of the community that have come to regard him as weak and inferior on the basis of *his initial appearance* among them.

But before discussing Paul's response to this rhetorical situation, I will close this section with an illustration of how even rhetorically informed scholarship can attempt to contain Paul's cunning. Witherington totally rejects Castelli's argument that Paul is reestablishing his authority in 1 Corinthians 1–4.[44]

> Paul believes that his role and status are established by God. 1 Corinthians 1–4 is not an *apologia* or an attempt to reestablish a lost authority. Paul distinguishes himself both from the sort of father figure the emperor might be and from the sort other teachers, especially Sophists, might be, especially by means of his hardship catalog (vv. 9–13). Unless one wants to argue that all fathers are bad parents and inherently oppressive and that therefore all father-figure imagery is necessarily the imagery of coercion and manipulation, Castelli's argument will not stand.[45]

First Corinthians 1–4 is certainly not a defense in the technical sense. Paul does not respond to a long list of accusations and insults leveled against him as he does at times in 2 Corinthians (e.g., 2 Cor 3–6 and 10–12). But Witherington's denial that Paul is reestablishing a lost authority is curious, especially coming from a rhetorically sensitive and astute interpreter who has such a firm grasp on the divisive rhetorical situation at Corinth. Consider the following passage concerning 4:6:

> Verse 6c should probably not be taken to mean that the Corinthian Christians should not get puffed up ("inflated with air") about Apollos over Paul, simply because he uses a certain kind of Greek rhetorical skills or Hellenistic wisdom ideas in his gospel presentation. The phrase "for the one . . . and against the other" should not be underestimated. Paul is countering factiousness that included rivalry, quarrels, boasting, and other sorts of bad behavior all too common during the empire among students of rival Sophistic rhetors.[46]

How can an interpreter with this understanding of the situation at Corinth not conclude that Paul must first reestablish his authority? Paul will have no hope of solving the long list of problems he will address in this letter, let alone of exercising the sort of frightening authority manifested in 5:1–

---

43. Mitchell, *Paul,* 65–70.

44. Elizabeth Castelli, *Imitating Paul: A Discourse of Power* (Literary Currents in Biblical Interpretation; Louisville: Westminster John Knox, 1991), esp. 97–111.

45. Witherington, *Conflict and Community,* 145.

46. Ibid., 141.

13 (cf. 2 Cor 10:8–11), until the factions once again recognize his paternal privileges.[47]

Underlying Witherington's objection to Castelli's position that Paul is seeking to reestablish his authority, especially through a call to imitation (μίμησις) and paternalistic ideology, is the same old tendency of Pauline scholarship that she exposes so effectively. In Witherington's case there is between the interpreter and Paul "no ironic distance whatsoever; Paul is the speaker-who-is-supposed-to-know, and his voice is cast as objective."[48] Any analysis of Paul's rhetorical strategy that would tend toward detecting in it a manipulative and coercive dimension, a cunningly insinuative strategy for regaining control over a situation in which the subject himself has a personal stake, must be avoided. An illustration of this tendency is the way practically everyone else in the Corinthian situation, even Apollos, can be tarred with the title "sophistic," but Paul must always be predictably "anti-sophistic."[49] In the final analysis, Witherington's reading of Paul, for all its undeniable rhetorical sensitivity, is ultimately not very rhetorical-*critical,* at least where Paul is concerned.

The Rhetorical Strategy

Faced with the exigence outlined above, what strategies did Paul devise in order to persuade? First, no interpreter should fail to recognize and appreciate Paul's initial strategy in a passage that rightfully stands among the most original and inspiring contributions to Christology in the NT (1:17–31). So there is no need to dwell upon this legendary passage here. Briefly stated, sensing that many of the Corinthians are beginning to consider themselves superior to others by their possession and/or progress in "eloquent wisdom" (ἐν σοφίᾳ λόγου, 1:17), Paul first cuts everyone down to size, perhaps even some of those "of Paul," by reminding them that the wisdom which really counts, God's wisdom, Christ-crucified, is the exact opposite of that praised in this world, and is, in fact, "foolishness," when measured by those standards (1:18–31). Nevertheless, "the foolishness of God is wiser than human beings, and the weakness of God is stronger than human beings" (1:25).

But immediately after this section, Paul begins to introduce in 2:1–5 a second strategy, intimately though rather tacitly related to the first, in which

---

47. Cf. Nils Dahl: "...one aim of what Paul has to say about the strife in Corinth, about wisdom and foolishness, and about the function of Christian leaders, is to re-establish his authority as apostle and spiritual father of the church at Corinth" ("Paul and the Church at Corinth in 1 Cor. 1:10–4:21" in *Christian History and Interpretation: Studies Presented to John Knox* [ed. W. R. Farmer, C. F. D. Moule, and R. R. Niebuhr; Cambridge: Cambridge University Press, 1967], 321). My agreement with other aspects of Dahl's conclusions about 1 Cor 1–4 will be readily apparent in this section (see ibid., 329). I see myself as merely adding a more fully rhetorical-critical dimension to his reading, especially by demonstrating even stronger links between these chapters and later passages in 1 Corinthians.

48. Castelli, *Imitating Paul*, 97–98.

49. Witherington, *Conflict and Community,* 85.

he claims to have a deeper wisdom that he can share only with those who have advanced beyond the basics (2:6–3:4) and are truly worthy of the word "spiritual." On the surface, this creates some tension with his first strategy. Therefore, some interpreters dismiss out of hand the possibility that Paul is claiming to have access to deeper mysteries he has not yet divulged because they think he would be contradicting his own position in his first strategy. But I rather suspect that what we have here is one of those classic cases where Paul is having it both ways, and very effectively I might add.[50] He first demolishes everyone else's definition of wisdom and then claims to be the conduit of a wisdom that is so beyond the human imagination that even "the rulers of this age" cannot understand it. Whatever or whoever these "rulers" are, they are certainly superior to the Corinthians, and perhaps that is Paul's point. If even those who are wisest in this age cannot comprehend it, what hope do the Corinthians have apart from a steward of mysteries like Paul? Then he sophistically "seduces the sophists," so to speak, by claiming that this wisdom is only the beginning of what is available to those who accept it.

The way Paul presents himself here tends to align him with the venerable "Sophists" of the past.

> From the beginning *sophia* was in fact associated with the poet, the seer and the sage, all of whom were seen as revealing visions of knowledge not granted otherwise to mortals. The knowledge so gained was not a matter of technique as such, whether poetic or otherwise, but knowledge about the gods, man and society, to which the "wise man" claimed privileged access.
>
> From the fifth century B.C. onwards the term *'sophistēs'* is applied to many of these early 'wise men' — to poets, including Homer and Hesiod, to musicians and rhapsodes, to diviners and seers, to the Seven Wise Men and other early wise men, to Presocratic philosophers, and to figures such as Prometheus with a suggestion of mysterious powers. There is nothing derogatory in these applications, rather the reverse. It is to this honourable tradition that Protagoras wishes to attach himself in the passage already quoted from Plato's dialogue the *Protagoras* (316c5–e5).[51]

And perhaps like Protagoras, if Socrates' suspicion was right about him, one must truly be Paul's disciple in order to hear the deeper meaning of his doctrines. Concerning Protagoras's famous and perplexing man-measure dictum, Socrates exclaims, "By the Graces! I wonder if Protagoras, who was all-wise (πάσσοφός), did not utter this enigma (ἠνίξατο) to the common mob like ourselves, but speak 'the truth' in secret to his disciples" (Plato,

---

50. See above, p. 23, n. 86. The compatibility between the two strategies will become clearer below, pp. 99–101.

51. Kerford, *The Sophistic Movement*, 24.

Theaetetus, 152C).[52] Maybe if the Corinthians want True wisdom, they must prove themselves faithful children of a True sophist.

Before speaking further of how the second strategy unfolds in 2:6–3:4, however, something more must be said about 2:1–5. Paul's remarks here about his *modus operandi* are almost always understood as if they were about the rhetorical content and form he displayed not only on the occasion of his first visit to Corinth, but at all times in every place he went. I do not agree for two reasons.[53]

First, as for content, the notion that "Christ *and him crucified*" was always the main emphasis of Paul's missionary preaching is controverted not only by the Areopagus speech — admittedly evidence easily dismissed by those who put little stock in Luke's presentation of Paul — but by 1 Thessalonians as well. As is well known, Paul's report in 1 Thess 1:9–10 sounds more like the result of a God, resurrection, and judgment-centered message such as Paul reportedly preached in Athens than the result of an utterly cross-centered message such as he claims to have preached in Corinth (1 Cor 2:2).[54]

Notice also that Paul says he "decided" (ἔκρινα, 2:2) to know nothing but this. Why does he put it that way? Why did he not just say, "I knew nothing among you except Jesus Christ and him crucified"? Could it be because he wants the Corinthians to realize that he could have preached a much more complex and impressive version of his message if he had "decided" to do so, if he had judged them capable of digesting it (3:1–2)? If they had been mostly God-fearers who knew the Scriptures well, would he not have taken

---

52. "The truth" is an allusion to the title of one of Protagoras's books. Vernon Robbins also quotes the exclamation of Socrates about Protagoras given above in his discussion of the secrecy motif in Mark (*Jesus the Teacher: A Socio-Rhetorical Interpretation of Mark* [Minneapolis: Fortress, 1992], 137–38).

53. In an earlier publication I registered my skepticism concerning Marshall's suggestion that even the gospel itself had a certain relativity for Paul ("True Rhetoric," SBLSP 36 [Atlanta: Scholars Press, 1997], 549). I now feel that, under the influence of Bornkamm's "Missionary Strategy," I rejected this possibility too hastily. As long as one understands this to mean that Paul might have put more initial emphasis on the cross in one situation, the resurrection in another, imminent judgment in another, and so forth, "a certain relativity" seems warranted by the evidence.

54. See, e.g., David Wenham, "The Paulinism of Acts Again: Two Historical Clues in I Thessalonians," *Themelios* 13 (1988): 53–55. As Bart Ehrman cogently remarked in a seminar at the University of North Carolina, we should be careful about treating this passage as a *Cliff Notes* version of Paul's sermon. But the absence of a cross-centered message is characteristic of the entire letter. How odd that a letter that mentions Jesus' death in the context of ongoing persecution and suffering does not even hint at the salvific benefits associated with such experiences. Instead, the response to this suffering is an emphasis on the hope of the soon coming of the Lord. Perhaps if 1 Thessalonians is as early in Paul's missionary career as some think (mid-forties), he had not yet come to terms with the possibility that sustained suffering rather than its quick alleviation by the *parousia* might be the will of God. Perhaps at this early stage his theology was more one of resurrection and glory, than of crucifixion and suffering. Perhaps Luke gives us more of an early than a late Paul.

a more advanced approach, one that compared more favorably with that of Apollos?

Second, as to form, notice that Paul does not say "And I *was* (ἤμην) with you in weakness and in much fear and trembling" (cf. Mark 14:49) but that "I *(be)came* (ἐγενόμην)" this way. Here we should note two things: (1) Both here and in 2:1 (ἦλθον), Paul chooses aorists to narrate his past activity among the Corinthians. Perhaps he is emphasizing that the way he appeared to them on that particular occasion, preaching a simple message in weakness, is not always the way he appears or will appear in the future.[55] (2) Context determines whether γίνομαι, when used in the past tenses, retains its radical sense of coming to be and changing from one state to another, or is simply synonymous with the past tense of "to be." In this case we should notice a pattern. First Corinthians 1:30 speaks of "Christ Jesus, who *became* wisdom to us from God" with the result that the one who boasts will boast in the Lord (v. 31). By becoming wisdom for us, Paul means that Christ became weak and submitted to the cross (1:23–25). Surely Paul is setting up a parallel with his own ministry.[56] He did not come to the Corinthians in strength and worldly wisdom, but rather he too, like Christ, *(be)came* in weakness (2:3) with the result that their faith, analogous to the "boast" in 1:31, will be in God (2:5). Notice also that every other occurrence of γίνομαι in chapters 1–4 clearly refers to an act of becoming (4:9, 13, 15, 16). Verses 9 and 13 refer to the apostles becoming a spectacle and like scum. *Strikingly, the next past tense examples are in 9:20 and 22 where Paul speaks of having become like various groups.* Paul not only wants the Corinthians to see that the unsophisticated message he preached is not all he knows—he "decided" on this message—but he also wants to hint that the unimpressive rhetoric he displayed is not all he is capable of—he "became" this way in this particular situation. Indeed, viewed in this light, the later appearance of 1 Cor 9:19–23 in this letter may also function, in addition to its immediate contextual purpose, as another reminder that one cannot conclude that to see Paul perform in a particular situation is to behold all the glories of Paul.

Paul is not implying that if he had judged his Corinthian audience capable of appreciating it, he would have presented his message "in the grand style." Recent rhetorical studies convincingly argue that Paul did shy away from an overly ornate style,[57] though the conclusion that this was due to some perceived inherent incompatibility between eloquence and the gospel is not

---

55. As pointed out to me by Paul Meyer in personal communication.

56. On Paul's "down-up soteriology," see "Paul's Self-Enslavement as His Salvation" in Martin, *Slavery,* 129–32.

57. See, e.g., Michael A. Bullmore, *St. Paul's Theology of Rhetorical Style: An Examination of 1 Corinthians 2.1–5 in Light of First Century Greco-Roman Rhetorical Culture* (San Francisco: International Scholars Publications, 1995), 223–25.

as certain as many think.[58] At least one critic suggests that it was because he might have been incapable of it, at least on a sustained basis.[59] But what I am saying is that Paul wants the Corinthians to know that he could have appeared to be much more rhetorically sophisticated, spiritually wise, and scripturally learned, had he wanted to do so. And, as we shall see, he will prove it in this letter.

Rhetorical sophistication and a claim to spiritual wisdom are demonstrated above all in 2:6–3:4 (other examples will follow). But just how Paul accomplishes this feat is subject to a polarizing debate among interpreters. After redefining wisdom as "a secret and hidden wisdom of God" which, of course, "*we* speak," Paul launches into a discussion of wisdom available only to the "spiritual" (2:6–3:2). Some argue that Paul is forthrightly claiming to have "a secret and hidden wisdom of God" (2:7) imparted only to the "perfect," and thus, in effect, claiming to be more of a "gnostic" than the Corinthian enthusiasts themselves. But others object to this reading, surely the most "literal" one, since it would appear to make Paul guilty of claiming the same sort of pretentious wisdom he has just sought to demolish (1:18–2:5). Such objectors often argue on the basis of the pervasive presence of irony in this passage.[60] Hays, for example, strongly and deftly emphasizes the biting irony that pervades 2:6–3:4, and he succinctly states the attendant danger:

> Irony is the most dangerous of rhetorical devices, because it employs semantic misdirection; the author relies upon the audience to pick up the clues that what is meant is not exactly what is said. Thus the risk of misunderstanding is great:

---

58. A typical example is Duane Litfin, *St. Paul's Theology of Proclamation: 1 Corinthians 1–4 and Greco-Roman Rhetoric* (SNTSMS 79; Cambridge: Cambridge University Press, 1994). This very common idea, which mostly stems from treating the rhetorical implications of Paul's statements in 1 Cor 2:1–5 as if (1) they were always true of Paul's proclamation instead of a strategy Paul was using in this particular situation, and (2) one must treat whatever Paul says at face value, can lead even a rhetorically competent interpreter who knows that Paul can be quite rhetorical in his letters to amazing conclusions: "Paul would not present his gospel rhetorically for reasons carefully spelt out in 1 Corinthians 2.1–5, but felt free to employ accepted rhetorical forms in his writings. It thus appears that, to borrow a notion from Philodemus, Paul felt compelled to renounce not rhetoric itself but the deceit (ἀπάτη) which all too often accompanied its spoken manifestation, especially of the sophists" (Winter, *Philo and Paul,* 217). Apparently we are supposed to conclude that written discourse is less prone to deception than oral, an assumption Plato, for one, would have found ludicrous. Cf. Gooch's more contextual and less dichotomous understanding of the rhetorical implications of 2:1–5 (Paul W. Gooch, "Faith, Wisdom, and Philosophy: 1 Corinthians 1–4," in *Partial Knowledge: Philosophical Studies in Paul* [Notre Dame: University of Notre Dame Press, 1987], 16–51, esp. 47–49).

59. "It may just have been his foreign accent (cf. Luc. *Nav.* 2), but more probably also the problem of grammatical slips (which must also have been obvious in his spoken language) and a general lack of literary sophistication (e.g., in terms of carefully crafted hypotactic, especially periodic, sentence construction)" (R. Dean Anderson Jr., *Ancient Rhetorical Theory and Paul* [CBET 18; Kampen: Kok Pharos Publishing House, 1996], 250–51). Anderson immediately goes on to suggest that Greek was "*very possibly* a second language to Paul" (italics his), but if that were so, why would the LXX so clearly be Paul's Bible?

60. Fee is very sensitive to irony in this passage (*First Epistle to the Corinthians,* 97–120).

> Readers who are not tuned in to the situation of the author and audience may miss the clues and drastically misread the text.[61]

In this case, it is assumed that staying sensitive to the irony in this text solves the problem of a Paul who appears to be too much like his opponents. Only a drastic misreading, a non-ironic reading, could make the mistake of thinking that Paul himself is claiming access to deeper truths through possession of the Spirit.

I am not convinced by this either/or type of reasoning. Interpreters who argue that the wisdom Paul speaks of in 2:6 is *only* the wisdom of God he just defined as "Jesus Christ and him crucified" (2:2; cf. 1:30) are not entirely wrong. They just too quickly foreclose the possibility of intentional ambiguity in Paul's ironic argument and thereby miss the real genius of Paul's *cunning* rhetorical strategy.[62] I see this foreclosure to be the result of trying to protect the Church from the type of Paul I am arguing for, a Paul who really means what he says when he speaks of having deeper wisdom reserved for the more advanced.[63] Regardless of what Paul may have intended to result from the use of such language, it is obviously a recipe for division, and that has been its effect from time to time. This Pauline cunning must be contained for the sake of the Church.

Yes, "the mystery of God" (2:1) proclaimed by Paul is first and foremost "Jesus Christ and him crucified" (2:2). This is indeed the "secret and hidden wisdom of God, which God decreed before the ages for our glorification" (2:7), secret and hidden enough to be completely misunderstood by "the rulers of this age" (2:8). The only way it can be understood correctly, not as scandal or folly (1:23), is through the activity of the Spirit. This emphasis on Christ crucified as the wisdom of God is *fundamentally* right. I say fundamentally right because I think Paul is suggesting that this spiritual wisdom is the foundation for other "spiritual doctrines" (2:13), gifts of knowledge available only to those who truly have "the mind of Christ" (2:16). It is the Spirit alone which can reveal to the believer the paradox that the crucifixion of the Messiah is God's triumph over the rulers of this age. But after this crucial first step, the one who receives the Spirit continues to be taught by the Spirit. New spiritual truths continue to flow from the fundamental truth

---

61. Richard Hays, *First Corinthians* (IBC; Louisville: John Knox, 1997), 40.

62. E.g., Hays, *First Corinthians,* 39–41. See also Judith L. Kovacs, "The Archons, the Spirit and the Death of Christ: Do We Need the Hypothesis of Gnostic Opponents to Explain 1 Cor. 2:6–16?" in *Apocalyptic and the New Testament: Essays in Honor of J. Louis Martyn* (JSNTSup 24; ed. Joel Marcus and Marion J. Soards; Sheffield: Sheffield Academic Press, 1989). Kovacs makes a strong argument that Paul's "wisdom" is not of the "gnostic" but of the apocalyptic variety. But how this rules out the possibility that Paul is trying to outbid his opponents in esoteric knowledge is not apparent.

63. See also Fred W. Burnett, "The Place of 'The Wisdom of God' in Paul's Proclamation of Salvation (1 Cor 2:6–16)" in *Reading Communities Reading Scripture: Essays in Honor of Daniel Patte* (Harrisburg, Pa.: Trinity Press International, forthcoming).

that the crucified Christ is the wisdom of God.[64] We cannot easily dismiss the strong possibility that Paul is claiming here to have access to "depths" of divine wisdom (2:10) that he has not shared with the Corinthians because they "were not ready for it" (3:1).[65] And why should we find this at all surprising? Later, near the very end of this long letter he will reveal a "mystery" (15:51–57). One wonders if he saved it till the end so as to suggest subtly to the Corinthians that they have a long way to go before they are ready for such wisdom.

Why do some interpreters strongly resist this image of Paul? Perhaps because this is not a canonically and ecclesiastically friendly Paul. This Paul is *too* cunning, spiritually arrogant (2:15–16), and potentially divisive. A Paul who might say and do one thing in the company of "baby" Christians and quite another among "the mature," just as he appears one way to Jews, another to Gentiles, and another to "the weak" (1 Cor 9:19–23). This is a Paul who will easily be co-opted later by the Gnostics and become the patron saint of many divisive spiritual elites throughout church history.[66] Surely "Saint Paul" himself bears no responsibility for such developments.[67] Paul's cunning must be contained.

If I am reading Paul's strategy correctly, if he is serving notice to the Corinthians that he only *appeared* to be lacking in spiritual power, wisdom, and eloquence on his first visit because of his condescension to their elementary level, then we might expect him, in spite of the fact that he tells the Corinthians that they are still not ready for it, to seek to demonstrate that he is far from deficient in these areas. And because much of that wisdom is probably associated with Scripture for the Corinthians through the influence of Apollos's example, we might expect him to show that he too is powerful in the Scriptures. Does he undertake a demonstration of such things? Notwithstanding the fact that much of the subject matter of his letter had been determined ahead of time by the need to respond to an oral report of problems and a written list of questions, Paul still manages to show

---

64. "Instruction in its deeper dimensions seems here (*pace* many commentators) reserved for mature believers, who are ready for 'solid food' — though Paul evidently wants all the Corinthians to attain to that level (3:1ff.)" (Markus N. A. Bockmuehl, *Revelation and Mystery in Ancient Judaism and Pauline Christianity* [Grand Rapids: Eerdmans, 1997] 165).

65. On this entire passage, see especially Robin Scroggs, "Paul: Σοφός and Πνευματικός," *NTS* 14:1 (1967): 33–55.

66. On Gnostic interpretation of 1 Corinthians 1–4, see Elaine Pagels, *The Gnostic Paul* (Philadelphia: Trinity, 1992), 53–64.

67. See Fee, *The First Epistle to the Corinthians*, 120, for a typical example of interpretation that assigns all the blame to "misapplication" of Paul's "intent." I certainly agree with Fee that much of the present day nonsense he mentions being perpetuated on the basis of this passage would hardly meet with Paul's approval. What I am saying, however, is that Paul assumes that some in the Church truly have the Spirit and the revelatory knowledge available through it, and others do not. Taking this seriously means that divisions in congregations between those who are truly spiritual and those who are not are inevitable. How do we know Paul himself thought so? See 1 Cor 11:18–19.

that he is not at all inferior in any of these areas. Let us recall a few salient examples.

Is he spiritually powerful? In dealing with the first reported problem among the Corinthians, Paul speaks of himself as being "absent in body" but "present in spirit" (5:3). In fact, when they are assembled together, *his* "spirit is present with the power of our Lord Jesus" (5:5). The Corinthian enthusiasts equate speaking in tongues with being spiritually powerful, but Paul tells them he "speaks in tongues more than all of you" (14:18). This claim is one of the most rhetorically cunning moves Paul makes. Rather than opposing this spiritual exercise, Paul presents himself as even more adept at it than the Corinthians so that he can enhance his authority for regulating it.

Is he spiritually wise? Paul may not always know what "Jesus according to the flesh" said about something, but as one "taught by the Spirit" (2:13), he can dispense authoritative advice on subjects like proper behavior for the unmarried and widows (7:25–40) since, as he says facetiously, "I think I *too* have the Spirit of God" (7:40).

Is he eloquent? It is no accident that 1 Cor 13 appears in this particular letter. Nowhere else in the Pauline correspondence has Paul addressed a problem in one of his churches with such artistic élan.[68] It shows that if Paul wants to be eloquent, he can "demonstrate a still more excellent way" (12:31), both spiritually and rhetorically. Appropriately enough, this truly inspired passage has been called an "encomium on love," for it is nothing less than "an epideictic showpiece."[69]

Is he learned in the Scriptures? First Corinthians is littered with clear allusions to Scripture and, unlike 1 Thessalonians, it also has many quotations. As suggested above, the necessity of demonstrating his competence in Scripture was probably brought about by the impression Apollos made on the Corinthians. Thus it is hardly fortuitous that a scriptural injunction to boast only in the Lord (1 Cor 1:31, echoed in 3:21) and scriptural quotations aimed against human wisdom and cleverness (1:19; 3:19–20) form the backbone of Paul's counsel to the Corinthians "not to go beyond the things that are written" (1 Cor 4:6).[70] If Scripture is playing a major role in some of the Corinthians' pretensions to wisdom, then Paul quite sophistically uses their own weapons to demolish these pretensions. Even more telling is the presence of a sophisticated typological exegesis of an OT text (10:1–13).[71]

---

68. A classic study of the rhetorical virtues of this passage, still very much worthy of reading, is J. Weiss, "Beiträge zur paulinischen Rhetorik," in *Theologische Studien J. Weis* (ed. C. R. Gregory, et al.; Göttingen: Vandenhoeck & Ruprecht, 1897), 196–200.

69. See Witherington, *Conflict and Community*, 264.

70. J. Ross Wagner greatly strengthens the case for taking this apparently mysterious phrase, ἵνα ἐν ἡμῖν μάθητε τὸ Μὴ ὑπὲρ ἃ γέγραπται, as a reference to the Scriptures Paul quotes or alludes to in chapters 1–3, especially 1:31, in his " 'Not Beyond the Things Which are Written': A Call to Boast Only in the Lord (1 Cor 1:4.6)," *NTS* 44 (1998).

71. See E. Earle Ellis, "A Note on 1 Cor 10,4," in *Prophecy and Hermeneutic in Early Christianity* (Grand Rapids: Baker, 1993), 209–12.

He thus demonstrates not only that he is skilled in contemporary modes of interpretation, but also that he knows popular rabbinic lore and can use it creatively for his own purposes (10:4). He is no inferior to Apollos where Scripture and its interpretation are concerned.

In conclusion, 1 Cor 1–4 show that Paul is a cunning rhetor. He does not deny that he seemed unwise and unsophisticated when he was among the Corinthians, but instead subtly attributes his retrospectively inferior appearance to the necessity of adapting to their own level at the time. He strongly criticizes the type of wisdom they have begun to aspire toward apart from his guidance, and instead casts himself as the conduit of a genuinely spiritual wisdom to which they have yet to attain, and will not attain apart from him. One might say he utilizes "the verbal ploys of the sophist making the adversary's powerful argument recoil against him.... "[72] Throughout this section, and 1 Corinthians as a whole, Paul demonstrates that he is far more sophisticated than some Corinthians might think as he sophistically seduces the sophists.

4. Domesticating Deception in 1 Cor 9:19–23

Mētis is itself a power of cunning and deceit. It operates through disguise. In order to dupe its victim it assumes a form which masks, instead of revealing, its true being. In metis appearance and reality no longer correspond to one another but stand in contrast, producing an effect of illusion, *apátē*, which beguiles the adversary into error and leaves him as bemused by his defeat as by the spells of a magician.[73]

[19]For though I am free from all, I have enslaved myself to all in order that I might win/gain the more. [20]I became like a Jew to the Jews in order to win/gain the Jews; to those under the law like one under the law — though not myself being under the law — that I might win/gain those under the law; [21]to the lawless like the lawless — not being without God's law but within Christ's law — that I might win/gain the lawless. [22]I became weak to the weak that I might win/gain the weak. I have become everything to everybody that I might by all means save some. [23]But I do it all for the sake of the gospel, in order than I may become a shareholder in it (1 Cor 9:19–23).

For reasons explored later in this section, a few interpreters take Paul's comments in these verses quite "literally," despite their embarrassing potential. They are thus said to express Paul's "chameleon principle," and to suggest an image of Paul as a Christian Proteus.[74] But how are we to understand such a Paul? As Marshall remarks,

---

72. Detienne and Vernant, *Cunning Intelligence,* 47–48.
73. Ibid., 21.
74. Wayne Meeks, "The Christian Proteus," in *The Writings of St. Paul* (Norton Critical Edition; New York: W. W. Norton, 1972), 435–44, especially 437–39.

A healthy respect for the dilemma felt by both Greeks and Jews over Paul may help us to be cautious in planting him too firmly in either tradition and may lead us to see something of his remarkable individuality.... It is here that we ourselves face a dilemma of definition. How do we describe Paul's inconsistency? I doubt whether this creative and elusive edge to his character can be defined and limited by such terms as 'principle' or 'strategy' or vague ideas such as 'higher consistency.' The chameleon in Paul must be allowed its full range of colours.[75]

We now have a wealth of social and cultural information available to help us understand why both friends and enemies were likely to be taken aback by such slavish/knavish behavior.[76] But after this material has been fully digested and one may even have gone so far as to admit that charges such as inconstancy, flattery, and demagoguery are not entirely inappropriate in this case, how Paul could have justified such behavior remains baffling. Until a better answer is given to this question, some scholars will remain more comfortable with assuming that Paul's remarks should not be taken too seriously in this case. I have already laid the groundwork for explaining Paul's "inconsistency" with the concept of a True rhetoric, and I will briefly return to this subject later in this section. But my main focus will be on readings that have the effect of taming this wild text. In the process of critiquing them, I will offer counterarguments to strengthen the case that we should take 1 Cor 9:19–23 "at face value."

Aside from ignoring it, there are mainly two ways of domesticating deception in 1 Cor 9:19–23. The first way is to say that all Paul really means is that he was flexible, adaptive, or accommodating, and that the degree of this adaptation was far too mild to be construed as cunning or deception. This is the tendency Marshall notes above.[77] The second is to say that Paul cannot

---

75. Marshall, *Enmity*, 401–2. The problem of Pauline inconsistency was already recognized and reflected upon by the church fathers. See Margaret M. Mitchell, "ποικίλος τις καὶ παντοδαπός ('A Variable and Many-sorted Man'): John Chrysostom's Treatment of Pauline Inconsistency" (paper presented at the annual meeting of the AAR/SBL, Philadelphia, Pa., November 1995). In this fascinating paper, Mitchell demonstrates, on the basis of passages from several of Chrysostom's homilies, that his defenses of Paul's inconsistency "correlate almost exactly (with few exceptions) with the means... which are employed by modern scholars who seek to explain Paul's putative inconsistency" (6). Like most Pauline protectors, Chrysostom usually argues that the inconsistencies are only apparent, not real. But in *de laudibus sancti Pauli* 5.4 and 5, he praises Paul for being "a variable and many-sorted man." And just like modern Pauline protectors who take Paul's "adaptability" epitomized in 1 Cor 9:19–23 seriously, all is justified by v. 22b. His intriguing Christological and *Theological* justification as provided by Mitchell will be presented below, p. 180, n. 33. Unfortunately, Mitchell's recently published monograph on Chrysostom and Paul was not yet available to me at the time the present work was being completed. See idem, *The Heavenly Trumpet: John Chrysostom and the Art of Pauline Interpretation* (HUT 40; Tübingen: J. C. B. Mohr, 2000).

76. See Marshall, *Enmity*, 70–90, 278–325; Martin, *Slavery*, 86–135; Glad, *Paul and Philodemus*, 15–52, 237–332.

77. See above, p. 85.

really mean what he says at all. It is just hyperbole.[78] Some find it incredible, if not impossible, that Paul radically changed lifestyles on a regular basis.

Domesticating Deception I: Accommodation

As an example of the first view, that Paul simply means he was flexible and accommodating, I have chosen a recent book by Clarence Glad. In his published dissertation, *Paul and Philodemus: Adaptability in Epicurean and Early Christian Psychagogy,* Glad provides a valuable and very able comparison of Epicurean and Pauline discourses of psychagogic guidance. The study owes much by way of inspiration to the pioneering work of Malherbe on the relationship of Paul's parenesis to Greco-Roman moral philosophy, as well as to Stowers's investigations of the relationship of Paul's rhetoric to established Greco-Roman rhetorical forms. Yet while many of the Pauline texts chosen by Glad are quite apt for illustrating the similarity of Epicurean and Pauline psychagogy — that is, adaptability for the purpose of caring for and improving the souls of a wide variety of persons in varying situations — his prime example, 1 Cor 9:19–23, the one around which the entire study revolves, is not one of them. There are several difficulties with Glad's reading of this text. Here I wish to address two that are especially evident.

First, Glad rather consistently interprets Paul's recurrent expression "I became like" (ἐγενόμην...ὡς) as if it merely meant "I associated with," or "I adapted to the psychological disposition of." This tendency is easily observed in his detailed analysis of Paul's psychagogic adaptability in chapter six of his book. For example,

> Contrary to the "wise" in Corinth, Paul subscribes to an affable and versatile leadership model both in "recruitment" and "psychagogy." Paul's flexible recruitment practice which included *association* with different character types, including the immoral, was seen as reprehensible and somewhat askew to his earlier recommendation to the Corinthians.[79]

Glad goes on to make "general remarks on Paul's flexible life and adaptability in the epistolary and hortatory context of 1 Corinthians," as a prelude to "discussing the form and function of 1 Cor 9:19–23 and the motifs of adaptation, versatility, and association, evident both in this pericope and its larger context."[80] Over and over again, Glad returns to the motif of the limits of association both within and outside the community, since this is an important issue in the wider context, and since Paul's own liberal practices of association are modeled on those of his Lord.

---

78. Even Marshall's exegesis reduces the scandal of Paul bragging about his behavior by developing Chadwick's passing suggestion that 9:19–23 might not be Paul's own choice of words, but rather an ironic echo of charges made against him (Marshall, *Enmity,* 308–17).

79. Glad, *Paul and Philodemus,* 240, italics mine.

80. Ibid.

None of this discussion, however, not even that of the concepts of adaptation and versatility which, as Glad acknowledges, involve significant ethical risks from the perspective of ancient rhetorical theory, really comes to terms with the most serious charge that could be brought against Paul's "recruitment" strategy, namely that he acts like a con-man (πανοῦργος), or an impersonator/imposter (γόης). Betz connects the appearance of the former term in 2 Cor 12:16 directly with becoming all things to everyone ("allen alles zu werden") in 1 Cor 9:22, and his ensuing discussion documents the linkage of both terms with polemics against rhetors/sophists.[81] Glad, however, makes no reference to Betz's discussion of 1 Cor 9:19–23. While γόης and κόλαξ ("flatterer") do belong to a close semantic range as Glad states,[82] and can be used in the same breath to describe the conduct of one individual, they also can be used to describe quite different behaviors owing to differing motives. For example, it is one thing to flatter like a sycophant, i.e., to speak opportunistically rather than truthfully, and quite another to impersonate, i.e., to pretend to be someone or something one is not. The Gospels portray Jesus as one who associated freely with tax collectors and sinners, but he is never portrayed as temporarily assuming the identity of a tax collector or a sinner in order to "gain" tax collectors or sinners. That the expression ἐγενόμην...ὡς strongly suggests the latter conduct will be demonstrated by a brief survey of this usage below.[83] For now it will be sufficient to note that even though Glad claims that "Paul's 'language of becoming' in this text has baffled scholars,"[84] all of the scholars he cites — Barrett, Conzelmann, Hall, and Gooch — have in common the understanding that "becoming like" means temporarily assuming a different identity, not merely adapting a little, being versatile, or being liberal enough to associate with those who for varying reasons are "other."[85] What bafflement there is arises precisely from this shared understanding of the Greek. For example, Conzelmann and Hall want to know how Paul can *become like* a Jew when he is a Jew? The key is to understand that in this context Paul is not talking about becoming a Jew in the sense of becoming like a descendant of Abraham, as if his ethnicity was something Paul could change, but of practicing Judaism. Therefore, Barrett's solution is entirely satisfactory: "His Judaism was no longer of his very being, but a *guise* he could adopt or discard at will."[86] This is why Paul speaks of becoming "like" a Jew. He can

---

81. Betz, *Der Apostel Paulus*, 104–6.
82. Glad, *Paul and Philodemus*, 122.
83. See below, p. 109.
84. Glad, *Paul and Philodemus*, 252.
85. See Gooch's excellent study, "For and Against Accommodation: 1 Corinthians 9:19–23," in *Partial Knowledge*, 124–41. As he puts it, "[Paul's] point is that he has himself taken on different ways of behaving, assumed different identities. His accommodation embraces more than the epistemological; in fact it is primarily *practical* accommodation that he describes" (134, italics his).
86. Barrett, *The First Epistle to the Corinthians*, 211, italics mine. As Glad notes, Gooch's

temporarily and cunningly "become like" a practicing Jew, but he cannot actually "become" a practitioner of Judaism again (Gal 1:13; 2:18).

This brings us to the second difficulty. Glad goes against the majority of interpreters who understand the "lawless" (ἄνομοι) of 1 Cor 9:21 as Gentiles and argues instead that they are immoral persons in general. Relying on Stowers, he rightly notes that οἱ ἄνομοι is not a technical term for Gentiles in Jewish literature before 70 c.e.[87] There are two problems, however. First, neither Stowers nor Glad pays sufficient attention to the fact that ἄνομοι nevertheless can be applied specifically to Gentiles as in Wis 17. And notice especially Acts 2:23, an example neither Stowers nor Glad mentions, where it seems most natural to understand οἱ ἄνομοι to refer specifically to Gentiles. The meaning of a term depends above all on the immediate context. In this case, Peter is addressing a crowd that has committed the immoral act of crucifying and killing Jesus. He does not, however, call this Israelite crowd in 2:22 ἄνομοι, but instead reserves that term for those who had the power to carry out such an act, the Gentiles. Context is decisive in Rom 2:12 as well. Here ἄνομοι occurs in the midst of a discussion of God's impartial judgment of Jew and Gentile (2:9–11,13–14).[88] It refers to Gentiles who are "without the law," in contrast to Jews who are "under the law."

I understand "Jews" in 1 Cor 9:19–23 to refer to Jews who practice Judaism; "those under the Law" to refer to proselytes and God-fearers;[89] "those outside the Law" to refer to pagan Gentiles; and "the weak" to refer to those in the church, whether ethnically Jew or Gentile, whose lack of knowledge and maturity puts their fragile faith at risk through their own and others' conduct.[90] Thus Paul's categorization is comprehensive, cover-

---

explanation is similar. Paul is quite capable of distinguishing between being ethnically a Jew — according to the flesh — and practicing the religion of Judaism — his former life (see also J. Louis Martyn, *Galatians* [AB 33A: New York: Doubleday, 1997], 153–54; 163–64). The first he mostly embraces, the second he mostly rejects. Both impulses, however, are subject to (un)certain qualifications. The distinction comes through in his contrasting attitudes toward Abraham and Moses. His attitude toward Abraham, the father of the Jews, is very positive, while his attitude toward Moses, the father of Judaism, is at best ambiguous, possibly hostile (see later discussion of 2 Cor 3). Moreover, this distinction between Jews and Judaism is crucial in any discussion of supposed anti-Semitism in Paul.

87. See Stanley K. Stowers, *A Rereading of Romans: Justice, Jews, and Gentiles* (New Haven: Yale University Press, 1994), 134–38.

88. For a proper stress on context as the determiner of the meaning of ἄνομος in 1 Cor 9:21, see Fee, *First Corinthians*, 429.

89. It is context that strongly suggests this identification. The other three designations clearly refer to separate and easily identifiable groups. So while the second designation could, *by itself*, simply be another way of speaking of practicing Jews (but why the redundancy?), here it serves as an apt designation for the one class of humanity Paul "becomes like" that would otherwise not be included, a group that was certainly an important focus of Paul's missionary activity.

90. The mention of "the weak" last is probably not accidental since giving those "with knowledge" an example of how they should behave toward the weak is a major purpose of ch. 9 in the context of chs. 8–10. My understanding of issues at stake between weak and strong believers in 1 Cor 8–10 is quite different from most other commentators. I have set

ing every conceivable situation of impersonation or adaptation in which he found himself and appropriately culminates with the summary statement, "I have become all things to everyone, that I might by all means save some."[91] In Rom 15:1 he categorizes himself as among "the strong." He probably does not explicitly do so here so as not to align himself too closely with the strong in Corinth, whose conduct he criticizes. Glad follows the now widely accepted view of 1 Cor 9 as an integral part of a sustained argument running through 1 Cor 8–10 that "persons of knowledge," that is, strong persons, should not let their liberty "trip up" (σκανδαλίζω) people with "a weak conscience." In short, they should *condescend* toward them as Paul does.[92]

If Paul's language of becoming (ἐγενόμην...ὡς) means what many interpreters have assumed, that Paul temporarily changed identities as a "missionary strategy," then Glad's definition of ἄνομοι would force us to contemplate a Paul who temporarily becomes like the immoral in order to win the immoral. How does Glad avoid this difficulty? Once again by ignoring what the Greek actually says — "I became like," the language of becoming — in favor of the language of association.

> Paul's advice concerning "outsiders" and "insiders" in 1 Cor 5 is congruent with his remarks in 9:19–23 which shows the need for association with immoral persons — ἄνομοι — *outside* the community in order to recruit or benefit them. That such behavior was seen as "lawless" by some goes without saying. Paul emphasizes that such a conduct is upright and law-abiding, congruent

---

forth my views in a paper delivered at the 1999 Annual AAR/SBL Meeting entitled "All Things to All People All at Once: Paul's Ambiguous Rhetorical Strategy in 1 Cor 8:1–11:1," and I intend to publish a revision of it soon. Here I will only state my conclusion that the weak believers of 1 Cor 8 are Christians whose consciences are weak because of a lack of knowledge. (Malherbe also emphasizes the cognitive aspect of their weakness in his "Determinism and Free Will in Paul: The Argument of 1 Corinthians 8 and 9," *Paul in His Hellenistic Context* [ed. Troels Engberg-Pedersen; Minneapolis: Fortress, 1995], 238–39.) They do not yet possess the knowledge that "no idol in the world really exists," that "there is no God but one," that God is not one God among many, and that Jesus Christ is not one Lord among many (see 8:4–6), therefore putting them at great risk when eating meat that has been offered to idols. There is no real evidence that the weak of 1 Cor 8 already know, consciously or unconsciously, that eating idol meat is wrong and that they consequently suffer a crisis of conscience after partaking. On the other hand, while the weak of Rom 15 are also to be considered weak because of inadequate knowledge, in their case the symptoms are the observance of a variety of legalistic and scrupulous customs.

91. As Hays explains well, the presence of "the weak," a group within the church, among those whom Paul is "winning" or "saving" is not a problem if one understands Paul's soteriology (see *First Corinthians*, 155). Everyone in the church, both strong and weak, is *being* saved, and both groups are endangered in 1 Cor 9–10. More specific reasons for why the weak can so easily be listed with the unconverted will be discussed below, pp. 115–17.

92. Richardson and Gooch call attention to the use of συγκαταβαίνειν in early exegesis of Paul's letters, but as Mitchell observes, they "treat this accommodation in terms of Paul's *behavior*, without attention to the *rhetorical strategy* involved in Paul's call for accommodation here in 1 Cor" (*Paul and the Rhetoric of Reconciliation*, 248). Exclusive focus on either word or deed tends to lessen the controversial dimensions of Paul's strategy.

with the "law of Christ" and explains the need for associating with different types of people in light of recruitment.[93]

The language of becoming cannot be sidestepped this easily. Paul did not say "I associated with" (e.g., ἐκολλήθην), he said "I became like" (ἐγενόμην...ὡς). Consider the following examples of expressions used to express association. In Acts 10:28 we read, "...and he [Peter] said to them, 'You yourselves know how unlawful it is for a Jew to associate with (κολλᾶσθαι) or to visit with a Gentile.'" Rom 12:6 says, "Live in harmony with one another; do not be arrogant, but associate with (συναπαγόμενοι) the lowly." In 1 Cor 5:9 (see also 5:11), Paul reminds the church that "I wrote to you in my letter not to associate with (μὴ συναναμίγνυσσθαι) the immoral." Ephesians 5:7 says, "Therefore do not be associated with them (μὴ οὖν γίνεσθε συμμέτοχοι αὐτῶν)." Other ways of expressing association are found in Wis 6:23; 8:4; Sir 9:4; 13:2; 13:16. But is the ἐγενόμην...ὡς construction used to express a willingness to associate? There are many constructions similar to Paul's ἐγενόμην...ὡς found in the LXX. Two are especially significant since they are concerned with cultural assimilation: "Only on these terms will we conform to you, and live among you: that you become as we are (ἐὰν γένησθε ὡς ἡμεῖς), in that every male of you be circumcised" (Gen 34:15); "So Bagoas left the presence of Holofernes, and approached her and said, "Let this pretty girl not hesitate to come to my lord to be honored in his presence, and to enjoy drinking wine with us, and to become today like (γενηθῆναι ἐν τῇ ἡμέρᾳ ταύτῃ ὡς) one of the Assyrian women who serve in the palace of Nebuchadnezzar" (Jdt 12:13). There are also many examples that speak metaphorically and retrospectively of change. For example, Mic 7:1: "Woe is me! For I have become like (ἐγενόμην ὡς) one who, after the summer fruit has been gathered, after the vintage has been gleaned, finds no cluster to eat; there is no first-ripe fig for which I hunger." Consider also Isa 63:19: "We have become like (ἐγενόμεθα ὡς) those over whom you have never ruled, like those who are not called by your name." *There is, in fact, no example in the NT or LXX where this construction is used simply to express a willingness to associate with someone.* Whether it is used in a literal or figurative mode, it refers to concrete, observable changes. Not surprisingly, Glad never produces the translation of the entire phrase that his interpretation of ἄνομοι requires, that is, "I became like the immoral in order to gain the immoral." The more usual interpretation of "the lawless" as Gentiles is far less problematic and far more convincing. As seen in the quotation above, Glad wants to define ἄνομοι in 9:19–23 by linking it with 1 Cor 5 and 6. But 1 Cor 5 and 6 actually work against his interpretation of ἄνομοι because while these chapters contain a long list of names for various kinds of immoral people, they are never referred to there as ἄνομοι.

---

93. Glad, *Paul and Philodemus,* 260.

Paul became like a Gentile, a recruitment situation, so as to remove any obstacles between them and Christ. Food matters are probably meant, and this example works well with the other groups mentioned. In the presence of practicing Jews and proselytes ("those under the law"), what Glad calls a recruitment situation, or in the presence of weak Christians — which in some but not all situations meant Christians who abstained from certain foods — what Glad calls a psychagogic situation, Paul could have become like these by observing *kashrut*.[94] We would have to suspect that a mixed group of Christians containing both those who do and do not observe food laws would precipitate a crisis, and Gal 2:11–14 confirms this.[95] But in this case the "man-pleaser" (1 Cor 10:31–33) finds that no one can please all of the people all of the time, and his more fundamental values are exposed by whom he chooses to please when he cannot please all of the people, both Jew and Greek, all of the time.[96]

On the basis of a convergence of evidence from Acts and the Epistles I think the extent of his "becoming like" goes beyond this minimal dietary example.[97] I have argued that ἐγενόμην...ὡς really "means what it says," so to speak, "I became like," not "I associated with," or "I adapted to the psychological disposition of," and, if this is so, ἄνομοι in the context of 1 Cor 9:19–23 surely does not mean the immoral in general. Glad's reading of 1 Cor 9:19–23 creates more problems than it solves and, by reducing Paul's admissions to merely having associated with all types of people, blunts the long-recognized, and thus carefully regulated, offensive potential of Paul's language of becoming, a language that goes far beyond the respectable adaptability of the philosopher or physician.[98] Glad is aware of

---

94. It is revealing, however, that Paul's language does not distinguish between a recruitment and a psychagogic goal in reference to these groups. Weak believers, no less than Jews, proselytes, and Gentiles, need to be "gained," or as he glosses the term, "saved" (9:22).

95. "When it came to cases Paul's easy tolerance, which he effortlessly maintains in theory — it is a matter of individual conscience what one eats and whether one observes 'days' — could not work" (E. P. Sanders, *Paul, the Law, and the Jewish People* [Minneapolis: Fortress, 1983], 178).

96. "Given a direct conflict between living as a Gentile and as a Jew, with no possibility of changing one's practice to suit present company, Paul viewed it as the only behavior in accord with the truth of the gospel to live as a gentile" (ibid.).

97. So too did Bornkamm. Regarding Paul's participation in the purification ceremony of four Nazarites in Acts 21:23–26, he says that "Even though the author of the source or Luke himself may have used the report for his own purposes, there are good reasons for believing that Paul did in fact respond to the request made of him, and that at this point he actually practiced his maxim to become a Jew to the Jews in the sense of I Cor. 9:20" ("Missionary Strategy," 204).

98. "Paul's self-portrayal as Christ's managerial slave, who must preach the gospel by compulsion and not from free will, is a clear rejection of the moral philosophical discourse that spoke of the leader as the benevolent, patriarchal wise man" (Martin, *Slavery*, 117–18). Rather than the latter respectable model of leadership, Paul espouses the highly controversial and often disreputable populist or demagogic model. See especially "The Enslaved Leader as a Rhetorical Topos," and "Slave of All in 1 Corinthians 9," in *Slavery*, 86–116, 117–35. This model is closely associated with sophistic rhetoric.

the perennial battle between philosophy and rhetoric/sophistic.[99] By reducing 1 Cor 9:19–23 to a description of respectable *philosophical* psychagogy, his interpretation, intentionally or not, protects Paul's rhetorical respectability. Paul's "language of becoming" actually raises the specter of a Paul who is beyond the bounds of a respectable philosophic rhetoric, a Paul who is willing, at least temporarily, to leave the realm of being for that of seeming.[100] Pauline psychagogy goes well beyond the bounds of philosophical respectability, and 1 Cor 9:19–23 is best understood as a frank admission of this *slavish*, and, in his enemies' eyes, *knavish* (πανοῦργος), conduct. First Corinthians 9:19–23 is not merely the prime example of a psychagogic, but also of a sophistic Paul.[101]

Domesticating Deception II: Hyperbole

Another way of domesticating deception in 1 Cor 9:19–23 is to dismiss it as mere hyperbole.[102] E. P. Sanders cites Paul's hyperbolic account of his missionary activity in Rom 15:19 for an analogy, but this is not convincing. For a statement to appear as hyperbole instead of falsehood, it needs to have a significant amount of truth about it. We can classify Paul's claim to have fully preached the gospel from Jerusalem as far round as Illyricum as hyperbole rather than an empty boast because he truly had covered a lot of land and sea. If, however, Paul only on rare and exceptional occasions enslaved himself to others as Sanders thinks, 1 Cor 9:19–23 would not qualify as hyperbole, but hypocrisy. But why is Sanders so convinced that Paul is indulging in hyperbole?

> The problem is the practical one which we noted above: how could he have been a Jew to the Jews and Gentile to the Gentiles *in the same church?*
>
> We may put the matter this way: Paul doubtless observed the laws of *kashrut* when he was in Jerusalem. But where else would he have been in a strictly Jewish environment? Obviously in the Diaspora synagogues. But Paul's purpose in the Diaspora was to win Gentiles, and, on the basis of Gal. 2:11–14, we can be sure that, when with Gentiles, he did not observe dietary laws. In other words, to consider 1 Cor 9:19–23 to be literal description of his behavior, we would have to suppose that he observed the law for a token period of time in each new city, intending to give it up as soon as a Gentile was attracted to the gospel, or that he established two different churches and

---

99. Glad, *Paul and Philodemus,* 57, 116. The deceptive character of this battle was addressed in my first chapter.

100. "Brethren, I beseech you, become as I am, for I also have become as you are" (Gal 4:12).

101. By no means am I denying Glad's main thesis that the Greco-Roman art of psychagogy, and especially the Epicurean form of it, is illuminating with regard to Paul's pastoral methods. On the contrary, it is a remarkably convincing and valuable thesis. I am only saying that this model alone is inadequate for understanding the extent of Paul's radical adaptability.

102. E.g., Wilfred L. Knox, who held that Paul always lived as a Pharisee, complains that "The rhetorical tone of the passage obscures the facts" (*St. Paul and the Church of Jerusalem* [Cambridge: Cambridge University Press, 1925], 122).

commuted between them, observing the law in one and not in the other. To my knowledge, no one has ever proposed the second of these possibilities as the way in which Paul actually behaved. But is the first any more likely?[103]

Of course it is ridiculous to imagine that Paul switched back and forth between a Jewish and a Gentile way of life *in the same church*. And certainly this is no more likely than the notion that he founded two churches, one Jewish and one Gentile. But why does Sanders assume that 1 Cor 9:19–23 must be interpreted from the standpoint of how Paul behaved in a church at all?[104] The first three groups listed show that Paul is mainly using his recruitment strategy as an example. One cannot use the Galatian incident, *a dispute within a church*, to argue that when he entered a Diaspora synagogue he would suddenly break *kashrut* the moment a Gentile showed some interest in the gospel. After all, any Gentile likely to be present would be a proselyte or God-fearer, one who respects Jewish customs and Jews who faithfully observe them, and one who would not likely be impressed if Paul showed up acting like a Jewish apostate. I think that scholars who see a fair amount of continuity between the strategy of 1 Cor 9:19–23 and the long series of expulsions from the synagogue in Acts are right.[105] Paul entered the synagogue of a new city appearing as, that is, becoming like, an observant Jew. Then, either through formal preaching and teaching, or through informal debate — Luke imagines them all — Paul's controversial views about Judaism and Torah eventually become all too apparent and he is punished and occasionally expelled. This is why he leaves the synagogue according to Acts, not because a Gentile had been attracted to the gospel. With no future missionary prospects within the local Jewish community, he no longer observes Jewish customs while continuing to work among whatever converts, mostly Gentiles, he has made from the synagogue, and carries out the purely Gentile mission that Sanders wants to make his only mission.[106] This stereotyped scenario of Acts even agrees with the (equally stereotyped?) sequence of 1 Cor 9:19–23. First, in the synagogue, Paul becomes like a Jew, proselyte, or God-fearer to Jews, proselytes and God-fearers; then, out of the synagogue, he becomes like a Gentile to Gentiles. Sporadically, he finds himself among weaker believers, either ethnically Jew or Gentile, who observe various legalistic customs, and becomes like the weak.[107]

---

103. Sanders, *Paul, the Law, and the Jewish People,* 185–86.
104. The exception of "the weak," the group certainly within the Church, will be discussed below.
105. E.g., Bornkamm, "Missionary Stance," 200.
106. "In all probability, when he entered each city, he went to Gentiles, he preached to them with some success, and he lived like a Gentile" (Sanders, *Paul, the Law, and the Jewish People,* 186).
107. The conditions for a conflict such as occurred in Antioch — a mixture of law-observant Christian Jews and law-free Christian Gentiles — very likely would be rare since there are virtually no signs of Jews in Paul's own congregations (see Sanders, *Paul, the Law, and the Jewish People,* 190). Indeed, in light of Paul's views on this incident as expressed in Galatians,

Is the practice of going to Diaspora synagogues first in cities that had them incompatible with Paul's almost universal self-description as the apostle to the Gentiles, as Sanders thinks? Not at all. If, as Sanders believes, Paul really thought of his ministry as a priestly service on behalf of the Gentiles so that their eschatological offering would be acceptable, there could be no better place to begin than among those Gentiles who had already turned to the God of Israel. With their attraction to Jewish monotheism, but understandable reluctance to convert fully, it would be only natural to consider them ripe for the picking. So to accept the testimony of Acts that Paul usually began his work in the synagogue is not necessarily "to make Paul first and foremost an apostle to the Jews in the Diaspora who failed and only then turned to the Gentiles...."[108]

The only group already within the church that Paul mentions is "the weak." It is unlikely that this example can be written off as hyperbole since this is not the only time Paul recommends such "accommodation" within the church.[109] Is it likely that Paul repeatedly recommended this "becoming like" if in fact he never really did so himself? I think not. Sanders never faces the difficulty this example presents for his hyperbole theory since his treatment of the various groupings tends to reduce them simply to unconverted Jews and Gentiles.[110]

If Sanders's reduction of 1 Cor 9:19–23 to hyperbole were accepted, what would be the effect on our image of Paul? His character would appear far less questionable and his integrity enhanced. He would appear far more *consistent*.

We see, thus far, *a consistent picture:* Paul was an apostle to the Gentiles, his mission was a success, the mission to the Jews was relatively unsuccessful, he addresses that failure as a fresh problem for the first time in Romans 9–11, he

---

it is readily apparent that for all practical purposes a Jew would have to cease observing Jewish customs in order to participate in a Pauline congregation: "Thus it seems that we must modify somewhat Davies' statement that 'In Christ Jews remain Jews and Greeks remain Greeks. Ethnic peculiarities are honoured.' That is true as long as ethnic peculiarities did not come into conflict. When they did, the factors which separated Jews from Greeks must be given up by Jews" (178). This fact alone could have given birth to the charges expressed in Acts that Paul was teaching "all the Jews who are among the Gentiles to forsake Moses, telling them not to circumcise their children and obey the customs" (Acts 21:21), charges that I tend to think are essentially correct, though I doubt Paul ever taught such things with much *parrēsia*.

108. Sanders, *Paul, the Law, and the Jewish People,* 190. Of course, the fact that there is so little evidence from Paul's letters of Jewish Christians in his congregations is not insignificant. But even in Acts, Paul's success in the synagogues is minimal. Although Luke thinks Paul's efforts often began in synagogues, the rule, illustrated well by the results of Paul's first and last sermons in Acts, is that the majority of Jews will reject his message while many Gentiles will listen (Acts 13:44–47; 28:23–28). The expected result would be precisely what prosopography of Paul's letters show: a handful of Jews in largely Gentile congregations.

109. Cf. 1 Cor 8:7–13; Rom 15:1–2. The principle of accommodation is the same in each case, even though the weak of 1 Cor 8 and Rom 15 are distinct phenomena. What unites them is defective knowledge. See n. 90 above on the differences.

110. The designation "the weak" never occurs in his discussion of "Paul's Missionary Practice" (Sanders, *Paul, the Law, and the Jewish People,* 179–90).

rearranges the eschatological sequence so that it accords with the facts, and only indirectly does he give himself a role in the salvation of Israel.[111]

For the sake of consistency, Sanders is willing to sacrifice the convergence of independent evidence in 1 Cor 9:19–23 and Acts, as well as other loose ends in the Pauline corpus that might support this convergence.[112] Rather than the troubling image of a Paul who repeatedly masquerades in the synagogue as an observant Jew just long enough to insinuate his radical message that, in Sanders's words, "denies two pillars common to all forms of Judaism: the election of Israel and faithfulness to the Mosaic law,"[113] we have a Paul who "entered each city,... went to Gentiles,... preached to them with some success, and... lived like a Gentile."[114] Instead of a Paul who changes identities almost as frequently and easily as a tragic actor changes masks, we have a Paul with unveiled face, who only rarely puts on a mask so as not to blind his less liberated brethren to the gospel with his emancipated glory.[115] Paul the perpetual contradiction disappears.

And yet, ironically, Paul's consistency in missionary practice is purchased at the cost of placing him in a permanent state of hypocrisy, for Sanders also asserts that Paul remained "a loyal member of the synagogue."[116] Is it not incongruous to find it an "intrinsic improbability," even "almost impossibility," to believe that "Paul was Torah-observant for a short period of time, and then stopped observing at least aspects of the law when the first Gentile entered the church," while apparently seeing no problem with the notion that he remained "a loyal member of the synagogue" while living as a Gentile, preaching a law-free gospel? Surely this would be to "build up again those things which I tore down," and "prove myself a transgressor" (Gal 2:18).[117]

Both Glad and Sanders's treatments of 1 Cor 9:19–23 appear at first to protect Paul's integrity, whether intentionally or not, but wind up making matters worse. Glad would reduce Paul's "becoming like" to mere adaptation to, and association with, different types of people, including the

---

111. Sanders, *Paul, the Law, and the Jewish People*, 185, italics mine.
112. See references in ibid., 182.
113. Ibid., 208.
114. Ibid., 186.
115. See 2 Cor 3:17–18. Paul seems to have an affinity for the mask: "Even if our gospel is veiled, it is veiled only to those who are perishing" (2 Cor 4:3).
116. Sanders, *Paul, the Law, and the Jewish People*, 199. Sanders is right to insist that any theory must account for evidence that Paul accepted disciplinary punishment by the synagogue (see ibid., 190). But accepting, or should we say suffering, such discipline hardly proves that Paul remained "a loyal member," if by that one means that he kept attending the synagogue all the time he worked in a given city. Such "discipline" when it occurred may not have been exactly voluntary, and we cannot simply assume that Paul returned to the particular synagogue or was even welcome there any longer. Sanders can only make this leap because he has entirely rejected the evidence from Acts that Paul regularly preached in synagogues.
117. See Marion Soards, "Seeking (*zētein*) and Sinning (*hamartōlos* and *hamartia*) according to Galatians 2.17," in *Apocalyptic and the New Testament: Essays in Honor of J. Louis Martyn* (JSNTSup 24; ed. Joel Marcus and Marion L. Soards; Sheffield: Sheffield Academic Press, 1989), 237–54.

immoral. But if we take the language of becoming seriously, this means we must contemplate the possibility that he acted like the immoral in order to gain the immoral. Sanders would reduce Paul's "becoming like" to mere hyperbole.[118] But if we suppose that Paul continuously attended synagogue while simultaneously living like a Gentile, his temporary states of hypocrisy become a permanent one. This is especially true for the Paul of Sanders, who denies the pillars of Judaism and probably considered "the third race" the "true Israel."[119]

Many Pauline interpreters actually do not take Paul's language of becoming much more seriously than does Glad or Sanders. Some are not troubled by it because they cannot really imagine that it means anything more than that he adapted his style a little for his different audiences as any good moral philosopher should, neither talking over their heads nor offending unnecessarily.[120]

Demonic versus Divine Deception in an Apocalyptic World

The key to understanding how Paul justified his deceptive missionary strategy is to comprehend fully Paul's apocalyptic assessment of his audiences. Consider the weak, for example. Glad argues cogently that what distin-

---

118. Perhaps Glad is really not far from Sanders on this point. Consider this curious and convoluted passage aimed at Martin's *Slavery as Salvation*: "It has been suggested that Paul's use of the populist model of leadership reflects the position of a visionary egalitarian and not of a benevolent patriarch. The accommodation of the latter is not 'real' but only pretended for tactical purposes; the accommodation of the demagogue is, on the other hand 'real.' Paul's own social self-lowering, exemplified by his trade, for example, had a tangible social dimension. *But 1 Cor 9:19–23 does surely not yield information concerning the social 'reality' of Paul's adaptation. Paul's connection of 'weakness' with 'knowledge' and 'consciousness' also shows that his concern is cognitive rather than social. The fact that Paul's adaptation is a form of literary adaptation should also make us be on our guard against any facile attempt to determine the social tangible 'reality' of Paul's accommodation. We cannot step outside of Paul's own intertextuality!*" (Glad, *Paul and Philodemus*, 327, italics mine).

119. Sanders, *Paul, the Law, and the Jewish People*, 171–79. Witherington incorrectly gives Sanders's view on this issue as just the opposite of what is stated above (*Conflict and Community*, 119). Actually there is some ambiguity as to whether Sanders is saying that Paul did or did not think of Christians as a third race, an ambiguity that I would take to be an accurate reflection of Paul's own. Sanders's conclusion is illustrative: "Paul's view of the church, supported by his practice, *against his own conscious intention,* was substantially that it was a third entity, not just because it was composed of both Jew and Greek, but also because it was in important ways neither Jewish nor Greek" (179, italics mine).

120. "Discrimination in speech is already seen in Pythagoras' practice of teaching his disciples to speak to children in childlike terms, to women in womenlike terms, to governors in governmental terms and to ephebes in ephebic terms. Such concerns are also present in the moralists' focus on different types of students and by rhetoricians in their discussion of character portrayal. Because of this, and in light of the intricate connection between the philosopher's σχῆμα and λόγος, *we should be careful* not to focus solely on adaptation in behavior when explicating Paul's statements on adaptability" (Glad, *Paul and Philodemus*, 273, italics mine). Although Glad's thesis is that 1 Cor 2:22b "is part of a tradition in Greco-Roman society which underscores, in light of human diversity, the importance of adaptability in conduct *and* speech" (ibid., 1, italics mine), he tends to focus solely on speech. Indeed, the citation in n. 118 above would appear to foreclose *any* investigation of behavior.

guishes Paul from the strong in Corinth is the advocacy of a gentle rather that a harsh psychagogy.[121] Though Paul rejected their methods, Glad thinks that he concurred with the strong that the weak must be reformed. But Glad does not explore why Paul felt this way. A glance at the Galatian situation shows us why. According to Gal 4:10–11, not only are the Galatians considering circumcision, but to Paul's horror, they already "observe days, months, and seasons, and years!" (Gal 4:10–11). As Betz explains, Paul is here drawing on a common religious topos in the ancient world concerning religiously scrupulous and superstitious people. After stating that "In any case, a religious behavior such as Paul describes is the very opposite of what the 'sons of God' ought to do," Betz calls attention to similar and related descriptions of religious scrupulosity in 1 Cor 8:7ff., 10:23ff., and Rom 14:1ff., the very passages with which Glad is concerned while discussing the wider phenomenon of "the weak" in Paul.[122] In Galatians, the life or death, salvation or damnation, gravity of this situation is underscored by Paul's statement that "I am afraid I have labored over you in vain" (Gal 4:11). As Betz comments, "If they engage in such superstition, his work and the salvation of the Galatians will come to nothing…" (219). This is how Paul *really* feels about practices typical of weaker believers, and so it is not surprising that he lists them along with Jews and Gentiles as those he tries to "win/gain," or "save." They are still partially blinded by the god of this world.

Paul's advice to the strong, based on his own example, is to pretend to be weak in the presence of the weak (1 Cor 10:27–30), but he never explains where one would go from there.[123] Yet just as we can be sure that he does not become like a Jew or a Greek indefinitely, eventually they must be "saved," so must we assume that his becoming like the weak is not an end in itself.[124]

---

121. Glad, *Paul and Philodemus*, 334.

122. Betz, *Galatians*, 219.

123. Perhaps in light of the inconsiderate behavior the strong have displayed toward the weak, Paul does not instruct them further because he thinks they have neither the aptitude nor the right attitude to practice his form of psychagogy.

124. While I agree with Martin's brilliant argument that "the theological and ethical disagreements between Paul and the Strong over issues related to eating and sex can be understood by sketching their respective assumptions about the body, its boundaries, and its susceptibility to pollution" (*The Corinthian Body,* 164), his application of it in 1 Cor 8–10 is problematic. Martin contends that Paul himself believes that *gnosis* is a talismanic prophylactic against daemonic pollution available only to high status individuals like the strong. In essence, the weak never had it, never will (189). The implication is that they are irreformable. Paul, however, says nothing about pollution in this case, but rather of the danger of "provoking the Lord to jealousy" (1 Cor 10:22a). His monotheistic background and assumptions are never more evident than throughout 10:1–22. Furthermore, since 10:1–22 is clearly addressed to the whole community, Paul probably assumes that *all* are endangered by idolatry, regardless of their *gnosis* (note the thinly veiled insult aimed at those who consider themselves strong in 10:22b). I think what Paul is up to in 1 Cor 8–10 is more rhetorically complex than Martin assumes. Briefly stated, I would argue that the oft noted tensions, possibly contradictions, in these chapters result from an unfortunate attempt to be strong to the strong and weak to the weak simultaneously. Here Paul the chameleon "morphs" into Paul the peacock. We should always bear in mind that,

The most plausible answer is that after Paul identified with the weak by becoming like them, he followed an insinuative rhetorical strategy similar to that imagined by Luke with respect to Jews and Gentiles, and that Paul himself has already followed at the beginning of this letter (see discussion of 1 Cor 1–4 above). Unlike the strong, his words and deeds would at first be "veiled" and intentionally ambiguous.

Just as Plato's Socrates feels free to break the rules of dialectic if necessary in order to win an argument, and Aristotle can counsel the use of sophistic *elenchus* to defeat sophists on their own terms, so Paul feels free to leave the world of being for that of seeming, "to become all things to everyone," in order to propagate the Truth, his gospel Truth. However different the reasons for their conviction that Truth is real and knowable, however differently they define the Truth, the rhetorical effect is rather analogous: a willingness to employ intentional ambiguity, cunning, and deception to disseminate the Truth, a willingness to employ True rhetoric. The deceived must first be deceived for their own good.

Finally, let us observe that a few scholars have no trouble accepting the deceptive metamorphoses implied by 1 Cor 9:19–23. Perhaps some are not troubled by them because they are in complete sympathy with Paul's goal, to spread a law-free gospel. Barrett, who, as we saw above, does not hesitate to call Paul's Judaism a "guise," falls in this category, as would, no doubt, many Evangelicals. F. F. Bruce, for example, states that

> Truly emancipated souls are not in bondage to their emancipation. Paul conformed to the customs or departed from them according to the company, Jewish or Gentile, in which he found himself from time to time, making the interests of the gospel the supreme consideration.[125]

Here we encounter a phenomenon not restricted to the battle between philosophy and rhetoric. When one is "right," and all others are self-deceived, or in the case of an apocalyptic worldview, demonically deceived, the end justifies the means. "Behold, I send you out as sheep in the midst of wolves; so be cunning as serpents and innocent as doves" (Matt 10:16). Means of persuasion that seem blameworthy when employed to support a position with which we do not agree are deemed praiseworthy, or at least excusable, when employed to support the "True" position — ours.[126]

---

presumably, Paul's letters are intended to be heard by the *whole* church, e.g., both strong and weak. Such situations surely presented Paul with difficult rhetorical challenges. In this case, one did not have the luxury of simply choosing "to welcome one who is weak in faith, but not for diacritical dialogue" (Rom 14:1). I have addressed this problem in my unpublished essay, "All Things to All People All at Once" (see n. 90 above).

125. F. F. Bruce, *Paul: Apostle of the Heart Set Free* (Grand Rapids: Eerdmans, 1977), 346.

126. For a critique of this tendency of Pauline criticism see Elisabeth Schüssler Fiorenza, "Rhetorical Situation and Historical Reconstruction in 1 Corinthians," 388–90.

5. Avoiding Ambiguity in 2 Corinthians 2:14–4:6

It [i.e., a popular Greek riddle] is an example of those two-edged sayings such as Plato uses to define the sphere of opinion *dóxa,* the intermediary world which participates both in Being and in Non-Being, where the dark and the bright are mixed and confused and where the true and the false are closely linked. These two-headed statements that pull in contrary directions (*emamphoterizein*) are sometimes called "crab words" because they are so oblique and never come straight to the point.[127]

¹Therefore, having this ministry as ones who have received mercy, we do not act badly. ²On the contrary, we have given up disgraceful concealments, not practicing cunning nor disguising the word of God, but rather by a manifestation of the truth we commend ourselves to everyone's conscience before God. ³*But even if our gospel is veiled,* it is veiled only to those who are perishing. ⁴In their case the god of this world has blinded the minds of the unbelievers, to keep them from seeing the light of the gospel of the glory of Christ, who is the image of God (2 Cor 4:1–4).

Second Corinthians 4:1–4, a passage that somewhat ironically announces itself as the conclusion of an argument (Διὰ τοῦτο), qualifies as "crab words." It is a two-headed statement that pulls in contrary directions: vv. 1–2 versus vv. 3–4. As such, it is a fitting conclusion to one of the most ambiguous passages in the Pauline corpus, 2 Cor 3, the focus of attention in this section. Is Paul's gospel concealed or not? Does he act badly or not?[128] Or is it that in this intermediary world "where dark and the bright are mixed and confused and where the true and the false are closely linked," where the god of this world uses the law of God to blind minds, a world where what appears to be glorious and divine one moment appears inglorious and demonic the next — is it that in this world such matters are never clearly black or white? I will briefly return to such questions at the end of this section, but in order to answer them we must first contemplate 2 Cor 3 with an unveiled face.

I am especially indebted to two readings of this passage, though I differ from each significantly. The reading that has influenced me most is a chapter entitled "A Letter from Christ," in Richard Hays's *Echoes of Scripture*

---

127. Detienne and Vernant, *Cunning Intelligence,* 304.

128. The translation of ἐγκακέω as "to lose heart" found in the NRSV, RSV, NIV, and NASB makes little sense in this context. If one translates it this way in v. 1 while retaining the ἀλλὰ in v. 2, as do the NIV and NASB, one is left wondering how not losing heart can be the contrary of renouncing shameful things. Instead, the ἀλλὰ at the beginning of v. 2 would have to be left untranslated — precisely what the RSV and NRSV do! Grundmann, "ἐγκακέω," *TDNT* 3:486, correctly gives the word's primary meaning as "to act badly," or "to treat badly," and this clearly works better. Oddly enough, he then goes on to suggest that the word can mean "to grow weary" on the basis of its use in 2 Cor 4:1! Actually, it has become almost the rule to translate ἐγκακέω practically everywhere it appears in the NT as "to lose heart" or something equivalent. Balz and Schneider list only this meaning and BAGD does not include anything approximating "to act badly" at all! But in several cases in the NT, "to act badly" would work much better.

in the Letters of Paul.[129] Broadly characterizing Paul's hermeneutic, Hays argues that "Paul...offers helter-skelter intuitive readings, unpredictable, ungeneralizable."[130] Surely this is nowhere more evident than 2 Cor 3. While typology is "a central feature of his interpretive strategy,"[131] more systematic procedures like allegory and midrash are very uncommon.[132] Consequently, while one may posit that an intertextual matrix "generated" Paul's reading in some cases, serious distortion results from undertaking a systematic and sustained exegesis of an intertext in an effort to show *in detail* how that text *controlled* Paul. The explicit rejection of this caution by Scott Hafemann leads to predictably disastrous consequences in his exegesis of 2 Cor 3:6–18.[133]

The second reading from which I have profited is Carol Stockhausen's *Moses' Veil and the Glory of the New Covenant: The Exegetical Substructure of II Cor. 3,1–4,6.*[134] Like Hays and Hafemann, Stockhausen is convinced of the crucial role Scripture plays in Paul's argument in this passage. And although the language and conceptualities of intertextuality play no role in her study, she independently reaches many of the same conclusions as Hays with regard to Paul's hermeneutics in general and his exegetical moves in this particular passage. She is much closer to Hays than is Hafemann in her sensitivity to Paul's exegetical freedom.[135] But what is most impressive about Stockhausen's reading is her acceptance of the possibility that the oft-noted ambiguity of this passage is not unintentional. She concludes that "The wisest course is simply to admit that when Paul uses an

---

129. Hays, *Echoes*, 122–53.

130. Ibid., 160.

131. Ibid., 161.

132. As Hays reminded me in a personal communication, it is debatable whether even midrash should be spoken of as systematic. See Daniel Boyarin, *Intertextuality and the Reading of Midrash* (Bloomington: Indiana University Press, 1990).

133. "...it has been argued throughout this study that Paul's view of the letter/Spirit contrast and his understanding of their respective ministries in 2 Cor 3:6–18 have been consistently derived from a careful contextual reading of Exodus 34:29–35 in accordance with its *original canonical intention* [!]" (Scott J. Hafemann, *Paul, Moses, and the History of Israel* [Peabody, Mass.: Hendrickson, 1996], 453, italics mine). Hafemann, who at least acknowledges that his conclusion is "very conservative," transforms Paul into an exegete and theologian of *Heilsgeschichte*. The continuity between Moses and Paul is so over-stressed that he can write a section called "The Essential Contrast between the Ministries of Moses and Paul (2 Cor. 3:12–13)," containing not a single contrast (ibid., 336–47)! Instead, it presents half a dozen ways in which Paul is *like* Moses. Fortunately, Hafemann's conclusion that Paul is controlled by the "original canonical intention" of the OT, an intention amazingly compatible with Reformed theology it seems, does not nullify many of the fine exegetical observations made along the way. But perhaps the greatest strength of this mammoth study is its encyclopedic discussion of previous research in copious footnotes.

134. Carol Kern Stockhausen, *Moses' Veil and the Glory of the New Covenant: The Exegetical Substructure of II Cor. 3,1–4,6* (Roma: Editrice Pontificio Istituto Biblico, 1989).

135. Notwithstanding the fact that she later wrote an article aimed at counteracting Hays's conclusion in *Echoes* that he found no systematic exegetical procedures at work in Paul's reading of Scripture. See Stockhausen, "2 Corinthians and the Principles of Pauline Exegesis," in *Paul and the Scriptures of Israel* (JSNTSup 83:1; Sheffield: JSOT Press, 1993), 143–64.

ambiguous term or form, he means to play upon that very ambiguity. We must allow him to do so."[136]

Both of these studies, and Hafemann's as well, have made important progress on the translation difficulties of 3:4–18, and I now offer my own translation incorporating some of their suggestions, while advancing others.

> [4]Such is the confidence that we have through Christ toward God. [5]Not that we are competent of ourselves to claim anything as coming from us; our competence is from God, [6]who has made us competent to be ministers of a new covenant, not of script but of Spirit; for the script kills, but the Spirit gives life.[137] [7-8]Now if the ministry of death, engraved in letters on stone, came in glory so that the people of Israel could not look into Moses' face because of the glory of his face — a glory being disempowered[138] — how much more will the ministry of the Spirit come in glory?[139] [9]For if there was glory in the ministry of condemnation, much more does the ministry of justification abound in glory! [10]Indeed, what had glory did not have glory in this respect, for the sake

---

136. Stockhausen, *Moses' Veil,* 126–27.

137. "My translation of *gramma* as 'script' — which should be read as a verbal noun meaning 'that which is inscribed' — is an attempt to capture the wordplay that links verse 6 back to verse 3. Just as Christ's epistle is not 'inscribed' (*eggegrammenē*) with ink or on stone, but written by the Spirit on hearts, so Paul's ministry of the new covenant is not of the 'script' (*gramma*) but of the Spirit" (Hays, *Echoes,* 130). Unfortunately for Hays, the choice of this translation of *gramma* is *disseminative.* Who can read "script" in this context and not think of *the* Script(ure)?

138. The not so bright idea that καταργέω can mean "fade," is fading fast. The NRSV corrects the RSV on this point, while the KJV had it right all along (see Hays, *Echoes,* 133–34). Hafemann now provides us with a thorough word study of καταργέω (*Paul,* 301–9), concluding that "Paul's frequent and consistent use of καταργέω warrants its consideration as a Pauline *terminus technicus* to express the meaning of the coming and return of Christ in relationship to the structures of this world on the one hand, and its significance for the effects of those structures on the other" (309). Therefore, I have suggested a translation of καταργέω that stays close to the Greek word's components (κατά + ἀργέω, the verb being derived from ἀ-εργός), and implies the rendering ineffective of something that once had power to achieve an intended result (see also Hübner, "καταργέω," *EDNT,* 2:267–68). The glory of Moses' face, the glory of the old covenant, its power to kill, is now "disempowered." The glory does not simply become inoperative, it is *made* inoperative. Linda L. Belleville makes similar observations about the word's meaning, but mistakenly seems to conclude that the "fading glory" interpretation can be supported on this basis ("Tradition or Creation? Paul's Use of the Exodus 34 Tradition in 2 Corinthians 3.17–18," in *Paul and the Scriptures of Israel,* 165).

139. The verb καταργέω occurs as a present tense participle in 3:7, 11, and 13. Since in v. 7 it is governed by ἀτενίσαι, general principles of usage would suggest that the participle refers to a simultaneous process of "being disempowered" (*pace* Hays, *Echoes,* 219). The decisive proof of this occurs in v. 11 where the opposite of τὸ καταργούμενον is τὸ μένον, "that which remains" in force. I am deeply indebted to Paul Meyer for this insight. This is precisely what I would expect since I maintain that Paul is speaking not only of the covenant, but insinuatively of the entire Mosaic law in this passage, one of the many powers of this age that are still effective but *in the process* of being disempowered (cf. 1 Cor 7:31). On the question of the subject of the participle in each verse there is considerable consensus. In this first occurrence it clearly agrees in gender with the glory (δόξα) of Moses' face, which is, of course, related to the glory of the old covenant itself. And so the second and third occurrences in the neuter would appear to speak generally of the whole phenomenon being discussed, i.e., the glory of the old covenant.

of the surpassing glory;[140] [11]for if what is being disempowered came through glory, how much more what remains in glory! [12]Since, then, we have such a hope, we act with great candor, [13]and not like Moses, who put a veil over his face to keep the people of Israel from comprehending "the end" of what is being disempowered. [14]But rather their minds were hardened. For to this very day, that same veil remains upon the reading of the old covenant lest it be discovered that in Christ it is disempowered.[141] [15]Indeed, to this very day whenever Moses is read, a veil lies over their heart; [16]but when one turns to the Lord, the veil is removed. [17]Now the Lord is the Spirit, and where the Spirit of the Lord is...freedom! [18]And all of us, with unveiled faces, seeing the glory of the Lord as though reflected in a mirror, are being transformed into the same image from one degree of glory to another; for this comes from the Lord — the Spirit.

Beginning in 2:14, Paul starts reflecting on his ministry: the spreading of the fragrance of a knowledge (γνῶσις) of Christ which issues in either life or death to those who breathe it. This elicits the question "Who is competent for these things?" (2:16), a question he is still answering at the beginning of the passage quoted. But immediately after asking this question, it becomes clear that the answer is going to be a matter of *synkrisis,* i.e., of showing who *is* competent through comparison and contrast with who *is not* competent (οὐ γάρ ἐσμεν ὡς οἱ πολλοί, 2:17). Those not competent are "the many" who retail the word of God, while Paul and his colleagues are persons of sincerity, sent from God. With such credentials, Paul does not need letters of recommendation, "as some do" (3:1).

More specifically, Paul does not need "letters of recommendation" written "with ink." His recommendation is written "not on tablets of stone but on tablets of human hearts" (2 Cor 3:1–3). Thus he starts with a polemic against false ministers who need to carry letters of recommendation written

140. The RSV/NRSV and the NIV all illustrate the danger of departing significantly from a fairly literal translation in this verse. E.g., the NRSV says, "Indeed, what once had glory has lost its glory because of the greater glory." Stockhausen's translation is better, but she also simplifies on the assumption that ἐν τούτῳ τῷ μέρει εἵνεκεν, "in this regard, for the sake of," is redundant (*Moses' Veil*, 88). The KJV is much better: "For even that which was made glorious had no glory in this respect, by reason of the glory that excelleth." Paul appears to be distinguishing between two different glories, one of condemnation, the other of justification (cf. the differentiation and gradation of glory in 1 Cor 15:40–41). The point is that while the ministry of condemnation indeed had one kind of glory, a glory of condemnation, it *never* had a superior glory of justification. Cf. Rom 2:20a: "For no one will be justified in his sight by works of the law." The glory of justification was withheld from the ministry of condemnation for the sake of the surpassing glory that was to come. Schlatter understood this verse much as I do (see C. K. Barrett, *The Second Epistle to the Corinthians* [BNTC; Peabody, Mass.: Hendrickson, 1973], 118).

141. Many scholars have favored treating ἀνακαλυπτόμενον as a nominative or accusative absolute referring to παλαιᾶς διαθήκης. See references in Stockhausen, *Moses' Veil*, 88. The plausibility of this reading is enhanced by her suggestion that μή should be translated "lest." I will not go into the details of her arguments in favor of this translation here, but note how nicely the result agrees with the theme of "hardening" introduced in the preceding clause.

in ink, and proceeds to a denigration of letters written on stone tablets.[142] Only a little later Moses will be cast as a minister bringing "a ministry of death, carved in letters on stone" (3:7). We cannot easily dismiss the shocking possibility that Paul is placing his opponents and Moses together on the negative side of a binary opposition with his own ministry on the positive side.[143] Paul is probably already anticipating the later direct contrast of his own *modus operandi* with that of Moses (3:12–13).

After reiterating the theme of competency (3:4–6), Paul launches into his contrast of "the ministry of death" and "the ministry of the Spirit" (3:7–11), and their continuing effects (3:12–18). It is in this context that we find Paul's explicit contrast of himself with Moses:

> Since, then, we have such a hope, we act with great candor, and not like Moses, who put a veil over his face to keep the people of Israel from comprehending "the end" of what is being disempowered (3:12–13).

My translation tries to capture an intentional ambiguity in the use of τέλος.[144] I agree with Hays who wants to construe τέλος in the sense of "goal," "purpose," "result," and "outcome," though I do not agree that the translations such as "end," "cessation," or "termination," are thereby ruled out.[145] The use of quotation marks may seem a bit daring, but this passage has a philosophical ambience, and Greek writers depended on context alone to indicate autonymy, i.e., linguistic reflexivity.[146] I also have tried to favor the investigative intellectual flavor that ἀτενίζω ("to comprehend") often takes on when it is not being used of physical sight.

Interpreters who are attracted to the "goal" rendering often appear motivated by a desire to rescue the Script(ure), all too closely associated with the old covenant, from Paul's deeply devaluative rhetoric.[147] Perhaps Paul meant that Moses was trying to hide the glory of Christ as the "goal" of the old covenant, but that now, with the veil removed, Christians can see

---

142. "In these contrasts, written letters of recommendation fall implicitly on the side of the superceded Mosaic writing, clearly inappropriate for a minister of the new covenant" (Stockhausen, *Moses' Veil*, 72). The possibility of an inherent devaluation of writing itself in this passage will be discussed later.

143. On the likely connection between Paul's opponents and popular Mosaic traditions, see Dieter Georgi, *The Opponents of Paul in Second Corinthians* (Philadelphia: Fortress, 1986), 246–71.

144. Stockhausen also sees a double meaning here (*Moses' Veil*, 126–27).

145. Hays, *Echoes*, 137. See Furnish, *II Corinthians*, 207, for references to other interpreters who choose "goal."

146. See discussion of the Stoic doctrine of autonymy in Atherton, *The Stoics on Ambiguity*, 323–28.

147. Hafemann is explicit: " . . . if this study can be sustained, the salvation-history paradigm presented here for understanding Paul's view of the Law and his OT hermeneutic may be considered an essential key to a coherent and positive reading of Paul, the Law, and the history of Israel. In turn, Paul may be recovered as a model for us as well. For from the vantage point of 2 Cor. 3, the other 'problem' passages in Paul concerning the Law and his OT hermeneutic take on a decidedly different perspective" (*Paul*, 459).

his glory *in* the text.[148] But this idea leaves open the possibility that Moses was being intentionally deceptive toward the Israelites concerning the true nature of the old covenant. Actually, such an insinuation on Paul's part is a strong possibility. Furnish suggests that Ulonska's reading, according to which Paul is warning the Corinthians not to be misled by his opponents as Moses misled the Israelites, is probably ruled out by v. 14a.[149] But v. 14a is just another specimen of the manifold ambiguity in this passage. It is not at all clear that the hardening of the Israelites' minds was their own doing as Furnish assumes, thus relieving Moses of any responsibility. Furthermore, it is far more likely that v. 14a ultimately means that God hardened their hearts (cf. Rom 11:25) so that they would not be able to see through Moses' deception, a deception in which, therefore, God is complicitous since ultimately God is the one instituting this "ministry of death" (cf. Gal 3:21–22; Rom 3:20b; 4:15; 5:20a). And so, according to those who would counter the possibility of an insinuative attribution of impure motives to Moses, and the rather uncomfortable theological implications just discussed, perhaps he was only trying to shield the people from a glory that would kill them because of their sinfulness, but that now, Christians, already in the process of being transformed by the Spirit, can behold the unveiled glory *in* the text. To put the matter in terms of the exigencies of modern Christian canonical, ecclesiastical, and apologetic discourse, surely the Torah remains inspired Scripture for Paul, and surely Paul's occasionally anti-Judaistic rhetoric did not extend even to a denigration of Scripture.[150]

But such interpretations bypass a contextually sound yet unrecognized reading that their championing of the translation of τέλος as "goal" makes possible.[151] The fact is that Paul has already explicitly stated the purpose/result of "the disempowered thing" (τοῦ καταργουμένου), of the *gramma*, of the old covenant, of "Moses." It is *condemnation* and *death.* "The script kills," it is a "ministry of condemnation," a "ministry of death." That is its goal. In contrast, Paul's ministry offers a teleology of "hope" (3:12), not "death." It "gives life," because it is "a ministry of the Spirit," and "the Spirit gives life." This is why he can be so candid, unlike Moses who, quite understandably, tries to hide the τέλος of his ministry, both in the sense of its temporary status and death-dealing purpose.[152]

Paul's play on τέλος is only the most obvious example of ambiguity in

---

148. "At the same time, readers who do by the aid of the Spirit discover the glory of God *in* Scripture are necessarily transformed by the experience" (Hays, *Echoes,* 148, italics mine).

149. Furnish, *II Corinthians,* 232–33.

150. The problem of the ambiguous relationship between the Old Covenant, Law, and Scripture will be discussed in the next section.

151. Hafemann's criticism of Hays for relying more on his interpretation of τέλος in Rom 10:4 than on the immediate context to decide its meaning in 2 Cor 3:13 has some validity (*Paul,* 350), but Hafemann himself is open to a similar criticism for letting his interpretation of Exod 34:29–35 blind him to the immediate context.

152. We should not overlook the fact that the germ/term τέλος is also a euphemism for death,

this passage. Commentators have frequently observed that the passage as a whole is pervaded with it, and the long list of translation difficulties testifies to the fact.[153] But why does this passage seem so veiled? Is it simply because the subject matter is difficult and profound? Or is it that Paul knows that what he is trying to say to an audience that has become more and more enamored with Scripture in the years since Apollos's original appearance among them is potentially offensive?[154]

While pondering these questions, it will help to circle back to where we began this section, 2 Cor 4:1–4. While commentators often observe isolated parallels between 2 Cor 4:1–6 and 3:12–18, the synoptic presentation in Table 3 will show that the relationship is even more intimate and extensive than previously realized. A thorough discussion of this synopsis will have to await another time.[155] For now I trust that the reader can see not only that some parallels exist, as commentators realize, but that Paul is following an amazingly similar pattern of thought in both passages. This pattern has implications for the contrast Paul is making between himself and Moses.

Commentary on the entire passage from 2 Cor 2:14–4:6 is littered with references to implicit and explicit parallels Paul appears to be creating between himself and Moses, and often stress is laid on how much Paul is like Moses, as if Paul were making an overall positive comparison. As we saw in Hafemann's case at the beginning of this section, this stress can be total. Hays and Stockhausen, however, do justice to the negative aspects of the comparison while finding positive aspects present though, we might say, veiled.[156] Hays's sensitivity to the ambiguity of the overall effect of the comparison is unsurpassed.

> The more elaborately Paul develops the images spun from Exodus 34, the more the reader begins to wonder why he is telling us all this, if indeed his ministry is really so unlike that of Moses. Rhetorically, the act of positing a dissimile and then lavishly developing it has a backlash effect: by distancing his ministry from Moses, Paul paradoxically appropriates attributes similar to those that he most insistently rejects; connotations bleed over from the denied images to the entity with which they are discompared.[157]

This complex effect is readily observable in the parallel passages printed below. The contrast between the ministries of Paul and Moses is stark at the

etymologically linked to τελευτάω, one of the Greek verbs for dying. Perhaps a playful Paul has managed a triple entendre regarding the law: goal/end/death.

153. See Stockhausen, *Moses' Veil*, 35.

154. See above, pp. 93–94. Also, if Georgi is right about the nature of Paul's opponents, Paul knows that what he is trying to say to an audience that has become attracted to these Moses-like divine men is potentially offensive (see above, p. 122, n. 143).

155. Notice, e.g., the typical Pauline paradox of slavery and freedom in the Lord expressed through the parallel in vv. 5 and 17.

156. Both Hays and Stockhausen argue that Moses is functioning as the paradigm of the believer who is glorified by turning to the Lord.

157. Hays, *Echoes*, 142.

TABLE 3
A Synoptic Parallel of 2 Cor 4:1–6 and 2 Cor 3:12–18

2 Cor 4:1–6	2 Cor 3:12–18
[1]Therefore, having this ministry as ones who have received mercy, we do not act badly.	[12]Therefore, since we have such a hope, we act with great candor,
[2a]On the contrary, we have given up disgraceful concealments, not practicing cunning or disguising the word of God,	[13]and not like Moses, who put a veil over his face to keep the people of Israel from looking into "the end" of what is now disempowered.
[2b]but rather by a manifestation of the truth we commend ourselves to everyone's conscience before God.	[14]But rather their minds were hardened.
[3]*But even if our gospel is veiled,* it is veiled only to those who are perishing.	For to this very day, that same veil remains upon the reading of the old covenant lest it be discovered that in Christ it is disempowered.
[4]In their case, the god of this world has blinded the minds of the unbelievers,	[15]Indeed, to this very day whenever Moses is read, a veil lies over their heart;
to keep them from seeing the light of the gospel of the glory of Christ, who is the image of God.	[16]but when one turns to the Lord, the veil is removed.
[5]For we are not proclaiming ourselves but Jesus Christ and ourselves as your slaves for the sake of Jesus.	[17]Now the Lord is the Spirit, and where the Spirit of the Lord is . . . freedom!
[6]For it is the God who said, "Let light shine out of darkness," who shined in our hearts	[18]And all of us, with unveiled faces, seeing the glory of the Lord as though reflected in a mirror, are being transformed into the same image from one degree of glory to another;
to give the light of the knowledge of the glory of God in the face of Christ.	for this comes from the Lord — the Spirit.

beginning in 2 Cor 4:2a and 3:13. Paul claims to have renounced concealment, cunning, and disguise, while Moses puts on a veil to hide his ministry's "end." But something strange and unexpected happens in 4:2b–4 and 3:14–16. At first Paul continues the contrast, portraying himself as the manifester of unveiled truth. But then, astonishingly, he concedes the possibility that his gospel *is* veiled (4:3), and this concession is parallel to the assertion that Moses' veil remains over the old covenant to this very day (3:14)! So Paul appears to allow that, at least in the case of those who are doomed, his ministry is just as veiled and deadly as that of Moses. Then 4:4 explains why those who are perishing cannot see the light through the veil — their minds are blinded by the god of this world. However, the presence of Paul's conceded veil is not denied here. But for those whose minds are *not* blinded, the veil does not have the same effect. Somehow they see the light of the gospel. Here let us recall the "pharmaceutical" passage quoted on the title page of this chapter: "For we are the aroma of Christ for God among those being saved and those being destroyed, to one a fragrance from death for death, to the other a fragrance from life for life" (2 Cor 2:15–16). Paul's gospel is Paul's "pharmacy."[158] Just as one and the same *pharmakon* is deadly to one and salvific to another, so also with the gospel. For Jews and Gentiles who take the gospel "at face value," who do not penetrate the mask, *who are not aware of the mask as mask at all,* it is scandalous and moronic, *prima facie.* But for Jews and Gentiles who take the gospel [as] *para-dox,* who — by grace — do penetrate the mask, *who are aware of the mask as mask,* it is the power and Wisdom of God (1 Cor 1:23–24).[159] The former have seen the facile truth: the gospel is patently absurd. But the latter have unmasked the mask. They know that the gospel is like light from darkness, treasure in earthen vessels (4:6–7). They have experienced the apocalypse of ambiguity.

6. Apocalyptic Logocentrism

One often finds emphasis placed on the difference between letter (γράμμα) and script (γραφή). To be sure, they are not exactly the same thing, but the contrast between the two can be exaggerated.[160] The possibility of a metonymical overlap between "Script," "Scripture," "Law," "Old Covenant," and "Moses" tends to be ignored. For example, since Hays, using texts like Gal 3:8, wants to claim that "Paul thinks of *Graphē* (Scripture) as alive and active," he must radically separate it from *gramma.*[161] But Paul says a veil lies over the Israelites' minds when the old covenant is read in 2 Cor 3:14 and when *Moses* is read in the next verse.[162] Are we really to suppose that the γράμμα, the old covenant, and "the read Moses" are easily separable from one another, or all three from γραφή? One wonders where

---

158. "Only a little further on, Socrates compares the written texts Phaedrus has brought along to a drug (*pharmakon*). This *pharmakon,* this "medicine," this philter, which acts as both remedy and poison, already introduces itself into the body of the discourse with all its ambivalence.... Operating through seduction, the *pharmakon* makes one stray from one's general, natural, habitual paths and laws" (Derrida, "Plato's Pharmacy," 70).

159. "If a speech could be purely present, unveiled, naked, offered up in person in its truth without the detours of a signifier foreign to it, if at the limit an undeferred *logos* were possible, it would not seduce anyone" (ibid., 71).

160. Probably in reaction to the exaggeration of their equivalence, for example, in Käsemann, "The Spirit and the Letter," in *Perspectives on Paul* (Mifflintown: Sigler Press, 1996), 143. But see p. 159 in the same article for a more nuanced statement on Scripture and Law.

161. Hays, *Echoes,* 106.

162. Indeed, Hays himself, in a brilliantly suggestive passage, declares that "a coherent reading of 2 Cor 3:12–18 is possible only if we recognize that in these verses a metaphorical fusion occurs in which Moses *becomes* the Torah," and shortly thereafter speaks of "the dreamlike transfiguration of Moses from man into text" (Hays, *Echoes,* 144–45, italics his).

the Law (νομός) would fit into this neat dichotomy of γράμμα/γραφή especially when confronted with a text like Gal 3:22–23 where the very same constraining function is attributed to both γραφή and νομός.[163] Or what about Rom 3:19–20? Here Paul clearly makes reference to the immediately preceding list of denunciations quoted mainly from the Psalms (also Ecclesiastes, Proverbs, Isaiah, and Leviticus). Yet in doing so he says, "Now we know that whatever *the Law* says it speaks to those who are under the Law, so that every mouth may be stopped, and the whole world may be accountable to God. For no flesh will be justified in his sight by works of the Law, since through the Law comes knowledge of sin." "The Law," in this case, is a metonym for Scripture.

The errors attendant upon turning the γράμμα/γραφή distinction into a firm exegetical principle are exemplified by Schrenk when he says "The word which is near (R. 10:8) is not the γράμμα but Scripture, which is self-attesting through the Spirit of Christ."[164] But the very verse cited, Rom 10:8, explicitly defines "the word which is near" not as Scripture, but as "the word of faith which we preach." It is "on the lips" and "in the heart." So while Scripture can play a corroborating role in presenting the "word which is near," Paul presupposes that this word is only available through proclamation (Rom 10:14–17): "So faith comes from hearing, and hearing by the *preaching* of Christ" (10:17). Here we begin to sense Paul's phonologism/phonocentrism. Scripture on its own cannot bear "the Word." The voice, "preaching," is privileged over writing. And, both consequently and necessarily, faith comes through *hearing*.

This connection of Paul with the typical Western privileging of speech over writing resonates with a reading of him associated with Luther and most fully developed in neo-orthodoxy, especially by Bultmann. Appropriately enough, at the heart of Bultmann's *Theology of the New Testament*, that is, at almost the exact middle of the two-volume work, stands the following programmatic passage.

> But if it is true that the proclamation of the salvation-occurrence is not a preparatory instruction which precedes the actual demand for faith, but is, in itself, the call for faith or the challenge to give up one's previous self-understanding or the cry, "Be reconciled to God!" — if that is so, then that means that *the salvation-occurrence is nowhere present except in the proclaiming, accosting, demanding, and promising word of preaching.* A merely "reminiscent" historical account referring to what happened in the past cannot make the salvation-occurrence visible. It means that the salvation-occurrence continues to take place in the proclamation of the word. The salvation-

---

163. See Bernardin Schneider, "The Meaning of St. Paul's Thesis 'The Letter and the Spirit,' " *CBQ* 15 (1953): 163–207, which shows, on the basis of a survey of the use of γράμμα before and during Paul's time, that it was used for particular written laws and for written law taken as a whole (188–91).

164. "γράμμα/γραφή," *TDNT* 1:768.

occurrence is eschatological occurrence just in this fact, that it does not become a fact of the past but constantly takes place anew in the present. It is present not in the after-effect of a significant fact of world history but in the proclamation of the word, which, unlike world events, does not get absorbed into the evolution of the human mind. Paul expresses this by saying that at the same time that God instituted reconciliation He also instituted the "message (lit. "word," KJ) of reconciliation" (II Cor. 5:18f.). Consequently, in the proclamation Christ himself, indeed God Himself, encounters the hearer, and the "Now" in which the preachèd word sounds forth is the "Now" of the eschatological occurrence itself (II Cor. 6:2).[165]

"Word" and "presence," along with many equivalent expressions, return again and again in tandem in the following thirty pages as Bultmann goes on to discuss "The Word, the Church, the Sacraments," "The Structure of Faith," "Life in Faith," and "Faith as Eschatological Occurrence." References to Rom 10 are predictably frequent,[166] and Rom 10:8–10 may be fairly characterized as the catalyst of two passages crucial for understanding Bultmann's theology, his discussions of faith as "confession" and "hope."[167] While he acknowledges that these verses support a "dogmatic" or "knowledge" component in the concept of faith, he quickly moves on to his preferred concept in which "Ultimately 'faith' and 'knowledge' are identical as a new understanding of one's self." This prepares the way for his statement of faith's "undogmatic" character.

> "Faith," that is, also has, on the other hand, "undogmatic" character insofar as the word of proclamation is no mere report about historical incidents: It is no teaching about external matters which could simply be regarded as true without any transformation of the hearer's own existence. For the word is *kerygma,* personal address, demand, and promise; it is the very act of divine grace (§34, 1). Hence its acceptance — faith — is obedience, acknowledgment, confession. That is the reason why "grace" as well as "faith" can likewise be named as the opposite of "works" to designate the basis of rightwising (§30, 2); for "faith" is what it is only with reference to the "grace" which is actively present in the word.[168]

This passage presupposes a reading of Rom 10:6–8 that takes us to the heart of Bultmann's word-presence Christology, that is, his own Pauline-aided, and Heideggerian-abetted, phonologism/phonocentrism. Indeed, it is practically a commentary on these verses. One does not require a mediator to ascend into heaven or descend into the abyss to make Christ present (vv. 6–7). For Bultmann, this would no doubt be trying to establish faith

---

165. Rudolf Bultmann, *Theology of the New Testament* (one vol. ed.; New York: Charles Scribner's Sons, 1955), 301–2, italics his.
166. Ibid., 301, 306, 307, 312, 314 (twice), 316 (twice), 317 (twice), 318 (twice), 319, 320.
167. Ibid., 317–20.
168. Ibid., 318–19.

by searching for the Christ "according to the flesh" (2 Cor 5:16), the historical Jesus. Therefore, as he says above, the "word of proclamation" can be "no mere report about historical incidents." Instead, grace itself is *"actively present in the word,"* since *"the word is near"* (Rom 10:8). Or, as he remarks in the last sentence of the longer block quotation above, "in the proclamation Christ himself, indeed God Himself, encounters the hearer," a thought encountered repeatedly throughout this section of his work. Certainly, as Bultmann concedes, he has gone beyond Paul in his insistence on the degree to which the "salvation-occurrence" in the "Now" of the "word of proclamation" eclipses the importance of "the mere report of historical incidents."[169] Nevertheless, it seems that Bultmann is reflecting a comparable phonological desire for immediate presence found in Paul's own Christology, a desire strongly rooted in Paul's apocalypticism.[170]

Of course, Bultmann wanted to strip away the mythological aspects of this apocalypticism while retaining its "eschatological" essence, but, not surprisingly, what is retained is the promise of direct encounter with God through "the preached word," immediate "present-ness."[171] I cannot agree with Bultmann that Paul's apocalyptic worldview can be demythologized while staying true to his thought.[172] What I take to be the real insight of Bultmann's (mis)reading, however, is the implication that the essence of Paul's apocalypticism is a desire for im-mediate presence. Paul's apocalyptic expectation is the underlying — or should we say, *fore* lying — cause of his phonocentric symptoms. And while we might well expect this present and near future-oriented desire to reduce, even to curtail, interest in producing written accounts of the events of Jesus' life, it hardly leads to a demotion

---

169. For example, ibid., 319. This preoccupation with "present-ness," the "Now," "self-understanding," and "authenticity" reflects Bultmann's well-known debt to existentialism. For an excellent introduction to his hermeneutic, see the essay collection, *New Testament and Mythology and Other Basic Writings.*

170. A similar phonological desire, but not the same, since Bultmann's desire is hardly for a presence through the word in any sense of which Paul would have approved. Between Paul and Bultmann stands Heidegger's "destruction" of the metaphysics that would allow for a real presence like Paul's Spirit, a destruction whose influence motivates Bultmann to argue erroneously that Paul is already beginning to reject the notion of Spirit "as a material" (*Theology,* 334).

171. It is difficult to understand what Bultmann could possibly mean by statements that say Christ himself and God himself are present, even actively present, in the word. He has gone far enough down the path of the "other" Heidegger, the de(cons)tructive Heidegger, to have begun to hollow out any *substance* at all to talk about the presence of the Holy Spirit (see the previous note). Indeed, one could argue that a faithful following out of Bultmann's lead, surely more faithful than Bultmann's following of Paul's, would lead in the direction of John D. Caputo's brilliant and provocative *The Prayers and Tears of Jacques Derrida: Religion without Religion* (Bloomington and Indianapolis: Indiana University Press, 1997). This profoundly Bultmannian book, which oddly enough hardly mentions Bultmann (perhaps he appears occasionally in the guise of Paul, Luther, Kierkegaard, and Heidegger), could be further subtitled, *Faith without Content* or *Hope without Object.* According to Caputo, with manifold justification from the more recent Derrida, deconstruction "is," among other things, "faith," in "an apocalypse without apocalypse."

172. See J. Christiaan Beker's critique in *Paul the Apostle: The Triumph of God in Life and Thought* (Philadelphia: Fortress, 1984), 140–43, 146–49.

of the account of the originary salvific events themselves to a "mere report of historical incidents" ("if Christ has not been raised, then our preaching is in vain and your faith is in vain," 1 Cor 15:14). Bultmann does not take seriously enough the fact that the *kerygma* itself is a rehearsal of "once and for all" salvific events. But what remains true to Paul is the notion that mouth and ear is the proper medium for this message. If so, then what might we expect Paul's attitude to be toward a record of *heilsgeschichtlich* events "engraved in letters on stone" (2 Cor 3:7)? The expected answer is implicit when Paul violently reinscribes Deut 30:12–14 as a text about Christ, not the Law (Rom 10:6–8). In context, Deut 30:12–14 is precisely about the nearness, the present-ness, and the *life*-giving or *death*-dealing effects of the Law. No one needs to ascend into heaven or cross the sea to obtain it.[173] It is "in your mouth and in your heart." But Paul has transferred the life-giving or death-dealing pharmaceutical present-ness of the Law to the "word of faith" (Rom 10:8; cf. 2 Cor 2:16). The Word supplements by filling up what is lacking in the Law; it is the "goal" prepared for but unreachable through the Law. And by taking the Law's place, it is the Law's "end."

Speaking for the moment with a Johannine accent, Paul no longer searches the Scriptures thinking that "in them you have life" (John 5:39).[174] Perhaps he is in the same boat with John, for there is something slightly "Fishy" about Paul's reader-response theory.[175] Though one may read the old covenant/Moses for centuries, its "true" signified, Christ, will never be found there (2 Cor 3:14–15). But this is not because *the text* is veiled, at least not in the sense that Christ the spiritual signified is subsisting incognito in the living Text, revealing himself only to those whom he chooses, but rather because *the mind of the reader* is hardened. This reader lacks competency and the text awaits a reader or community of readers who are competent. Only by the reader being equipped with something outside this world, and here the Fish flops out of the boat, outside the cosmic (textual) apparatus, only by first turning away from the text toward the Lord, the Master of Meaning, can the true signified be "found" (2 Cor 3:16). Is it any surprise that the Lord the reader turns to is also the Spirit (2 Cor 3:17)?

---

173. Though Paul structures his discourse in Rom 10:6–8 according to the pattern of Deut 30:12–14, he is very likely working from memory and forgetfully, yet creatively, substitutes the descending into the abyss of Ps 107:26 for the crossing of the sea in Deut 30:13, a "forgetting" all the more understandable since it allows him to introduce the resurrection theme.

174. Notice that Paul shows no interest in sustained verse by verse commentary, either allegorical or midrashic. He operates with a de facto "canon within the canon" (see Hays, *Echoes*, 162), and not even his typologies are, strictly speaking, methodical (161). Perhaps there was a time when he, like Philo and the Rabbis, regarded the Law as "the likeness (μόρφωσις) of knowledge and truth" (Rom 2:20), and practiced a comprehensive hermeneutic commensurate with such a conception. But for Paul that likeness is no longer found in a pre-existent Torah, but rather a pre-existent Christ, who was "in the form (μορφή) of God" (Phil 2:6a). *Paul longs for his children to "morph"* (μορφόω) *Christ, not the script* (Gal 4:19).

175. See Stanley Fish, *Is There a Text in This Class: The Authority of Interpretive Communities* (Cambridge: Harvard University Press, 1980).

For Paul, in a certain way, spiritual exegesis must be spiritual eisegesis. The reader can only possess the meaning by virtue of the down payment deposited in herself (ἀρραβῶνα, 2 Cor 1:22; 5:5). The Spirit is the source of her reader competency, a power that has united her with a new community of readers.[176] Only the Spirit can penetrate the veil. Spirit *in* Paul is not comparable to a rational Hegelian principle pervading the universe.[177] Neither is the Spirit simply a new hermeneutical principle, presumably allegoresis.[178] Spirit is an active material power that can invade persons, re-image them, and give them abilities they never had before.[179] It is nothing less than the active power and presence of God, something that from Paul's perspective has only recently become widely available.[180]

Heirs of the Enlightenment find it difficult to grasp and hold on to this point. For example, Hays grasps the point well: "When Paul contrasts Spirit to *gramma*, he is not opposing the basic intent of Scripture to its specific wording, as in our familiar distinction between 'the spirit and the letter of the law.' Nor is he thinking, like Philo or Origen, about a *mystical latent sense concealed beneath the text's external form.*"[181] And later he says, "If the gospel is *hidden in Scripture*, Scripture must be understood as richly allusive in character, hinting the kerygma, prefiguring it metaphorically. The biblical text must be read as a vast texture of *latent promise*, and the promise must be recovered through interpretive strategies that allow *the hidden word* to become manifest."[182] These two passages are not contradictory for Hays since the crucial word present in the first passage is "mystical" while the crucial word absent from the second is "spiritual." For a Philo

---

176. Just as the Spirit is the source of Paul's competency (e.g., 2 Cor 3:5–6). But before we begin to think that spiritual interpretation of Scripture is something Paul envisions as a normative activity in his congregations, we should not overlook the fact that interpretation of Scripture is not among the gifts listed in 1 Cor 12.

177. See Martin, *The Corinthian Body*, on the subjects of "The Pneumatic Body" in Greco-Roman culture (21–25), and "The Nature of Paul's Resurrected Body" (123–28). "No physical/spiritual dichotomy is involved here, much less a material/immaterial one. Rather, Paul has a hierarchy of essences, probably all assumed to be stuff, but of varying degrees of density or 'stuffness.' Paul would have thought of *all* of it as 'material' — if, that is, he had been able to think in such a category without a material/immaterial dichotomy. At any rate, all the 'stuff' here talked about is indeed stuff" (128). Apparently when it comes to spirit, Paul is closer to Stoicism, the dominant philosophy of his time, than to Plato or Hegel.

178. *Contra* Daniel Boyarin, who tends to turn Paul into a Philo, Origen, or Augustine with respect to hermeneutics (*A Radical Jew: Paul and the Politics of Identity* [Berkeley: University of California Press, 1994], 13–15, 104–5).

179. "For I will not venture to speak of anything except what Christ has accomplished through me to win obedience from the Gentiles, by word and deed, by the power of signs and wonders, by the power of the Holy Spirit..." (Rom 15:19); "My speech and my proclamation were not with plausible words of wisdom, but with a demonstration of the Spirit and of power..." (1 Cor 2:4).

180. "And we have received *not the spirit of the world, but the Spirit which is from God,* that we might understand the gifts bestowed on us by God" (1 Cor 2:12).

181. Hays, *Echoes*, 150, italics mine.

182. Ibid., 155, italics mine.

or an Origen, the concealed "sense" of Scripture is a spiritual presence, a metaphysical entity, while for Paul it is not. This crucial distinction can still be maintained even when Hays uses words like "latent" and "hidden" in both passages, since one can certainly speak of latent or hidden meanings without meaning latent or hidden presences. But when he uses the phrase "interpretive strategies that allow *the hidden word to become manifest,*" I find myself wondering if Hays is losing his grip and falling back unconsciously into a "mystical" hermeneutic. The italicized words carry a lot of theological freight, intentionally or not — perhaps they are an echo of "the Word became flesh"? — and they remind me that Hays wants to maintain that for Paul, and probably for Hays, Scripture is "alive and active."

But Paul can ask those who want to be under the Law, "Does he who supplies the Spirit to you and works miracles among you do so by works of the Law, or by *hearing* with faith?" (Gal 3:5). "Works of the Law," a writing with the flesh and on the flesh, is opposed to "hearing with faith," a spiritual writing with the heart and on the heart.[183] *For Paul, no Life, no Power, no Presence, is ever to be expected from writing, the letter, the Law.* If it were, the Law would be against the promises of God, which is also to say, in conflict with Paul's doctrine of justification by faith alone: "for if a law had been given *which could make alive,* then righteousness would indeed be by the Law" (Gal 3:21). What makes righteousness possible? What is able to "make alive"? The Spirit. Why can the Law not make alive? Because the Law is devoid of Spirit. *There is nothing in the text.*

I am not saying that for Paul the text is meaningless apart from the meaning with which the competent reader *in-spires* it. To use a not irrelevant example, Derrida was often misunderstood by superficial readers to be saying that texts have no meaning when he used the arresting aphorism that there is nothing in the text. Derrida's point was rather that texts are not conveyors of metaphysical presences, transcendent entities that can be passed from mind to mind; they are not loci of presence.[184] I am saying that Paul held a not dissimilar view of the dead(li)ness of the script: "The script kills, but the Spirit gives life" (2 Cor 3:6b).

Also, I am not saying that Paul does not consider, in a certain way, much of Scripture to be "the words of God" (Rom 3:2). He certainly believes that God said *much* of what God is reported to have said there.[185] But these words of God are not the "Word of God" for Paul. The latter designation

---

183. "He is a Jew who is one inwardly, and real circumcision is a matter of the heart, spiritual and not literal. His praise is not from men but from God" (Rom 2:29).

184. It would be far more accurate to say that, for Derrida, texts are too meaningful; that because every word is marked by the trace of every other word in the texture that is discourse, no author can fully control meaning.

185. I agree, however, with Martyn that Paul may not consider every commandment in Scripture to be from God. See below, p. 155, n. 49. Furthermore, given the state of the canon in Paul's day and his highly selective usage of it, how would we know exactly where Paul draws the line between what is and is not Scripture?

for Scripture belongs to the later church, not Paul.[186] The "Word of God" is something Paul hears and proclaims in the present. To put the matter only a little too simply, that present Word sometimes resonates with the words of Scripture, and in those cases Paul is happy to acknowledge that what God said is what God now says. But sometimes that Word does not resonate with the words of Scripture, and in those cases he decides that what God said then is not what God says now. The reason is profoundly theological: *what is "alive and active" for Paul is not Scripture, but God.* I cannot develop this perspective more fully here, but the implication in the present context is clear. Scripture is often of use to Paul because it does indeed testify to what God has said and done in the past. A particularly telling example of this is his use of Scripture as "promise." Paul certainly believes that "the Old Testament already contained signals, orientations, anticipations [of the Christian reality] that can be discovered there."[187] But,

> Here we must make a rudimentary but fundamental distinction. . . . Now, the distinction is between texts and realities, the book and history. Paul does not actually think so much that the promise is contained in the Old Testament as a book as that it is present in the events it reports, and so has an existential, not just verbal, dimension.[188]

To reiterate, for Paul, *there is nothing in the text.* Recognition of this point is crucial. If we miss this, we will be tempted to turn him into Philo or a church father, neither of whom shared his apocalyptic pessimism toward the things — even the good things — of this world. Paul never searches for the Spirit in the Letter as do others.[189] The reason he does not emerges from the preceding discussion: *the text has no agency, no power, no life, of its own.* That is why it can be co-opted at will by Sin. We cannot know for sure at what point in his life Paul came to feel that Sin had used the very commandment that was supposed to lead to life for him to thoroughly deceive (ἐξαπατάω) and kill him.[190] But this realization had a profound and

186. For that matter, there is no place in the New Testament where writing of any kind is referred to as the "Word of God." One of my favorite assignments for students, especially those from very conservative Christian backgrounds, is to have them search an online New Testament for the phrase "word of God" and summarize its range of meanings.

187. Romano Penna, "Paul's Attitude Toward the Old Testament," in *Paul the Apostle* (Collegeville, Minn.: Liturgical Press, 1996), 2:77.

188. Ibid.

189. See Wai-Shing Chau, *The Letter and the Spirit: A History of Interpretation from Origen to Luther* (American University Studies 7.167; New York: Peter Lang, 1995).

190. I suspect it was a pre-conversion development. Thus in the terminology of the current debate, I tend to move from "plight" to "solution," and not as E. P. Sanders advocates, from "solution" to "plight." But, in agreement with Sanders, I do not accept explanations of the "plight" grounded upon a supposed impossibility for Paul or anyone else to keep the Law "blamelessly." For a detailed statement of the erroneous view that fulfilling the whole law is impossible and inevitably leads to disobedience and a curse, see Frank Thielman, *From Plight to Solution: A Jewish Framework for Understanding Paul's View of the Law in Galatians and Romans* (NovTSup 61; Leiden: Brill, 1989).

shocking effect on his attitude toward the Law. The commandment is not to be trusted. *Moses* is not to be trusted. Paul's attitude is anything but Pharisaic. Indeed, it is not "Christian." This is a Paul who must be banished to his "letters."[191] The minister of a covenant "not of Script but of Spirit," must be transformed by the Church into the ultimate man of letters. The one who would have cried out "God forbid!" (μὴ γένοιτο) at the very thought of a new covenant in *Script,* must become its premier author.[192]

As far as I can see, a pneumatic Script (γραφή) is really unnecessary for Hays's overall perspective and should be abandoned. One might say it sounds more Christian than Pauline. Hays usually argues as though Paul's spiritual hermeneutic is a new reader competence, the result of something added to the interpreter, the Spirit, not something dwelling in a semi-hypostatized meaning-ful Text.[193] Hays charges those who dismiss the hypostatization of Scripture found in Gal 3:8 (where Scripture "foresees" and "preaches") as merely figurative with reductionism. But even if we would grant this point, though I would not, it does not follow that what Paul does with Scripture in this example shows that Scripture is alive and active, capable of carrying out its own will. I would argue, rather, that Paul's assertion that the Scripture "preached the gospel" to Abraham is patently absurd and graphically illustrates the weakness and helplessness of the material signifier. As in the example of Rom 10:6–8 above, Paul would seem to be demonstrating that if Sin can co-opt the Law for destructive purposes, he, through the power of the Spirit, can just as easily co-opt it for salvific ones. Ultimately, however, Paul's characteristic attitude toward "the Writing" should not be determined simply by collecting and weighing all the positive and negative examples against one another. The decisive factor, in my opinion, is the inherent logocentrism and phonocentrism of Paul's worldview.

But is this logocentrism mainly the result of Hellenistic influence upon Paul with its inevitable privileging of speech over writing? Certainly many interpreters have suspected this when reading Paul's letter/Spirit contrast.[194] But recently Brian Ingraffia has attempted to protect Paul and John from the postmodern critique of onto-theo-logy by insulating them from any substantive Greek influence:

> The *Religionsgeschichtliche* school has interpreted Paul's distinction between heaven and earth as a sign that he, or his followers, began to think in Hellenistic categories of thought. But I want to follow those scholars who focus

---

191. Käsemann, "Paul and Early Catholicism," 250.

192. And when Christians think at once of the Bible when they hear the phrase "the Word of God," the transformation/deformation of Christianity, at least from Paul's perspective, is complete.

193. Hays, *Echoes*, 150.

194. E.g., while commenting on 1 Cor 3:6, Furnish refers to the "oft-cited passage from Plato's *Phaedrus,*" i.e., 275D-276E (*II Corinthians,* 195).

instead on the continuity of the Bible's *Heilsgeschichte*. Rather than arguing that the Greek language and worldview transformed Paul's thought, I will be arguing that Paul transformed the Greek language and worldview through the eschatological categories of his gospel.[195]

Unfortunately for Ingraffia, the rigid dichotomy of Hebrew and Hellenistic categories of thought undergirding the logic of this passage has long been rejected by responsible scholarship. In fact, some scholars are once again taking seriously the possibility that Paul was profoundly influenced by popular philosophy even in such fundamental matters as his anthropology.[196]

Ingraffia also wants "to demonstrate here that Derrida's deconstruction of the logocentrism of Western thought undermines only the human *logos* of Greek and modern rationalism, not the divine *logos* of biblical, Christian theology."[197] The key to this demonstration, in his opinion, is the "eschatological categories of Paul's gospel." But it should be clear by now that Paul's eschatology and apocalypticism, far from protecting him from the logocentrism and phonocentrism clearly evidenced in the preceding discussion, actually contributes to it *more* than Hellenism. We can further understand why this is so by paying attention to a recurrent characteristic of Paul's description of the apocalyptic goal toward which all of creation is heading. *Over and over again, Paul's eschatology features the overcoming of anything and everything that separates and divides.*

In 1 Thessalonians, probably the earliest extant letter of Paul, we first catch a glimpse of Paul's eschatological utopia. From the moment of the presence/arrival (τὴν παρουσίαν) of the Lord (1 Thess 4:15; cf. 5:23), believers "will always be with the Lord" (4:17; cf. 5:10). In 1 Cor 13, Paul contrasts the provisional and partial nature of prophecy, tongues, and knowledge with what will happen when "the perfect" comes: "For now we look through a mirror into an enigma, but then face to face" (13:12). Abuses involving prophecy, tongues, and knowledge are precisely what is *dividing* the Corinthians. Over against this Paul sets images of intimate reciprocity

---

195. Brian D. Ingraffia, *Postmodern Theory and Biblical Theology: Vanquishing God's Shadow* (Cambridge: Cambridge University Press, 1995), 71.

196. See Boyarin, *A Radical Jew,* 57–85, and Martin, *The Corinthian Body,* 104–36. It should be observed, however, that Boyarin finds Paul's anthropology to be rather Platonic while Martin finds him closer to the Stoics. Martin's arguments are more convincing, though a Platonic influence is not to be discounted. In any case, as Martin points out in a personal communication, these parallels should not be spoken of as "influences," if one means by this that Paul is consciously aligning himself with particular philosophical schools: "All that Paul has in common with them (e.g., 'astral bodies') he could get from the wider culture more generally."

197. Ingraffia, *Postmodern Theory and Biblical Theology,* 213. Ingraffia's reference to "the human *logos* of Greek ... rationalism" reveals to an embarrassing extent just how little he understands the concept of "logocentrism." The Greek *logos* was every bit as much a theological concept as the Christian one. What did *logos,* or should we say *Logos,* mean to the Stoics?!

like "face to face," and "knowing fully as I have been fully known."[198] In 1 Cor 15, the ultimate goal after all opposition to God and his Christ is destroyed is that "God may be all in all" (15:28). In 2 Cor 3, life under the new covenant is pictured as a continual process of being metamorphosized into the image of the Lord from one degree of glory to another (3:18), a process that will be completed when he appears (Phil 3:21). And at the end of Rom 8, Paul waxes especially eloquent as he asserts that "I am convinced that neither death, nor life, nor angels, nor rulers, nor things present, nor things to come, nor powers, nor height, nor depth, nor anything else in all creation, will be able to separate us from the love of God in Christ Jesus our Lord" (8:38–39). The very dimensions of the universe will give way to direct and eternal encounter.

In short, what Paul looks forward to is an unmediated and uninterrupted experience of the presence of Christ: *parousia*, perfect presence. Occasionally this desire is so intense that total assimilation seems envisioned, hardly a surprising image for one who likes to speak of being "in Christ." Although Ingraffia is aware that the desire for presence is part of Derrida's description of logocentrism, it is not at all clear that he comprehends the far-reaching implications of this. He does not seem to realize that this longing for pure presence is actually *the* major symptom of logocentrism and the one Paul most fully exhibits. Far from insulating him from logocentrism and phonocentrism as Ingraffia would like to think, Paul's eschatology ensures that his case of it will be especially acute. To understand Paul's apocalyptic hope is to understand why he must have an ambivalent attitude at best toward Scripture as well as writing more generally, and why the living "breath" of divinely inspired speech, the Word, the Gospel, must be favored.

7. Collusion

There are two important conclusions I would draw from this chapter, conclusions that should be borne in mind when approaching the subject of the next chapter, "Deception in Rome."

The first conclusion is that Paul was indeed cunning, more so than many interpreters care to admit. Whether due more to adequate formal training or natural talent, he was a master rhetorical strategist. He was capable of co-opting his opponents' arsenal in order to trump them (1 Cor 1–4); he was capable of deceiving his audience by presenting himself, at first, as what they are, so that they might eventually become what he is (1 Cor 9:19–23; cf. Gal 4:12); and he was capable of using intentional ambiguity to lessen the offensiveness of his radical opinions on subjects like Moses and "the end"

---

198. Though Paul would certainly argue that by *agapē* he means something far more "spiritual" than physical intimacy, we can hardly rule out the possibility that sexual imagery is influencing his expression here, as is so often the case in mystical religious language. And marriage, of course, is spoken of as *"two becoming one"* in Paul's culture.

of the Law so as to allow those who have been called to penetrate the veil through the power of the Spirit while others remain blinded by the god of this world (2 Cor 3–4).

The second conclusion to be drawn is that Paul exhibits classic symptoms of logocentrism/phonocentrism, and that his apocalypticism ensured that his case would be particularly acute. His powerful desire for unmediated presence goes hand in hand with his devaluation of the Law and his insinuative remarks concerning the masked Moses, mediator of the text and metaphor of the text.[199] Writing and hiding, writing and deception: such activities have an affinity for one another and are complicitous in a world corrupted by separation and alienation.

---

199. See above, p. 126, n. 162. For an application of Derrida's critique of phonocentrism to several figures in church history stretching from Tertullian to Bultmann, see Seeley, *Deconstructing the New Testament*, 8–15.

IV

Deception in Rome

A text is not a text unless it hides from the first comer, from the first glance, the law of its composition and the rules of its game.

— Derrida, "Plato's Pharmacy," 63

...one can deceive a person about the truth, and (remembering old Socrates) one can deceive a person into the truth. Indeed when a person is under an illusion, it is only by deceiving him that he can be brought to the truth.

— Kierkegaard, as quoted in Vlastos, *Socrates,* 132

1. The Rhetorical Situation: Deception in Rome

Why Romans? That is the perennial and multifaceted question that sparks "the Romans debate."[1] If Paul had mainly wanted to inform the Romans of his planned visit, why not a short communiqué, basically Rom 1:1–15 and 15:17–16:16? Indeed, why not consider everything in between a monstrous interpolation by some later disciple who wanted to provide a compendium of Pauline doctrine? Would not such a letter flow much better? Would not the heart of this imagined letter have done the trick?

> I want you to know, brothers, that I have often intended to come to you (but thus far have been prevented), in order that I may reap some harvest among you as I have among the rest of the Gentiles. I am a debtor both to Greeks and to barbarians, both to the wise and to the foolish — hence my eagerness to proclaim the gospel to you also who are in Rome. For in Christ Jesus...I have reason to boast of my work for God. For I will not venture to speak of anything except what Christ has accomplished through me to win obedience from the Gentiles, by word and deed, by the power of signs and wonders, by the power of the Spirit of God, so that from Jerusalem and as far around as Illyricum I have fully proclaimed the good news of Christ (Rom 1:13–15; 15:17–19).

Is this not all that was necessary? Just a subtle hint that no matter what gossip they may have heard, he actually "has reason to boast." Then in the intimacy of the personal presence he ostensibly desires ("For I long to see you...I have longed for many years to come to you...I hope to see you...to be refreshed in your company," 1:11; 15:23, 24, 32), he could enter into a more con*fid*ent(ial) dialogue ("that we may be mutually encouraged by each other's faith," 1:12). Nevertheless, he is not content to declare his eagerness to come to Rome to preach his gospel and leave it at that. Why not?

Furthermore, the matters discussed in the last section of the previous chapter add another dimension to the "Why Romans?" question. If Paul exhibits logocentric/phonocentric symptoms, why did he choose to introduce himself to the Romans in the body of a text, in the form of a letter? If the gospel is something spiritual that should, or rather must, be "heralded" and "heard," how can he get ahead of himself in [a] dead letter and "preach" the gospel he is so anxious to proclaim in person? Or is that what he is doing?

For several reasons relating to the nature of the beast, a written introduction was appropriate. In the first place, Paul, like Rousseau, knew the advantages of *absence* and *writing*.

Starobinski describes the profound law that commands the space within which Rousseau must move:

---

1. See Karl P. Donfried, ed., *The Romans Debate* (revised and expanded ed.; Peabody, Mass.: Hendrickson, 1991).

How will he overcome the misunderstanding that prevents him from expressing himself according to his true value? How escape the risks of improvised
speech? To what other mode of communication can he turn? By what other
means manifest himself? Jean-Jacques chooses to be *absent* and to *write*. Paradoxically, he will hide himself to show himself better, and he will confide in
written speech: "I would love society like others, if I were not sure of showing
myself not only at a disadvantage, but as completely different from what I am.
The part that I have taken of *writing and hiding myself* is precisely the one that
suits me. If I were present, one would never know what I was worth" (*Con-
fessions*). The admission is singular and merits emphasis: Jean-Jacques breaks
with others, only to present himself to them in written speech. Protected by
solitude, he will turn and re-turn his sentences at leisure.[2]

To be sure, Paul was no Rousseau. He by no means always sought to avoid
the risks of improvised speech. Still, he does not so overvalue personal presence, even when it is possible, that he will always choose it over graphic
mediation. Paul knew that "being there" was not always best, and that
sometimes a *substitute* for personal presence was better than the real thing.
On occasion, writing and hiding himself was the best choice as, for example,
the "painful letter" to the Corinthians demonstrates.

> So I made up my mind not to make you another painful visit. For if I cause
> you pain, who is there to make me glad but the one whom I have pained?
> And I wrote as I did, so that when I came, I might not suffer pain from those
> who should have made me rejoice; for I am confident about all of you, that
> my joy would be the joy of all of you. For I wrote you out of much distress
> and anguish of heart and with many tears, not to cause you pain, but to let
> you know the abundant love that I have for you (2 Cor 2:1–4).

If Paul were present, they might get the wrong idea. Abundant love
manifested in personal presence might rather appear as pain inflicting pain.
    Maybe too, as many suppose, there was the risk that "If I were present,
one would never know what I was worth." As Paul's enemies say, "His letters
are weighty and strong, but his bodily presence is weak, and his speech of
no account" (2 Cor 10:10). Paul, of course, immediately takes issue with
this criticism ("Let such people understand that what we say by letter when
absent, we will also do when present," 2 Cor 10:11), but later he will subtly
acknowledge the possibility that judged by the standards of these "super-
apostles" at least, his personal presence might still be considered inadequate:
"I may be untrained in speech, but not in knowledge; certainly in every way
and in all things we have made this evident to you" (2 Cor 11:6). Writing
one of his "weighty and strong" letters to the Romans first would give Paul
the chance to put his best foot forward, to put his knowledge before his
speech.

---

2. Derrida, " . . . That Dangerous Supplement . . . ," 142.

There are still other reasons a well-constructed letter of self-introduction might have been appropriate in this case. Is not Romans to some extent the defense and confirmation of Paul and his gospel?[3] Perhaps Paul is saying, "You may have heard it said that I should be ashamed of my law-free gospel, but I want you to know that 'I am not ashamed of the gospel; it is the power of God for salvation to everyone who has faith, to the Jew first and also to the Greek' (Rom 1:15–16). And so I give you Romans 1–8. You may have heard that I am unconcerned, even hostile, toward my own people, but I want you to know that 'I am speaking the truth in Christ, I am not lying; my conscience bears me witness in the Holy Spirit, that I have great sorrow and unceasing anguish in my heart. For I could wish that I myself were accursed and cut off from Christ for the sake of my brethren, my kinsmen by race' (9:1–3). And so I give you Romans 9–11. You may have heard it said that my gospel encourages arrogance and division within the body of Christ, but I want you to know that 'by the grace given to me I bid every one among you not to think of himself more highly than he ought to think, but to think with sober judgment, each according to the measure of faith God has assigned him' (12:3–4). And so I give you Romans 12–15."

Every major section of Romans addresses sensitive subjects for Paul. We would know this on the basis of clues strewn throughout Romans alone, a frequently defensive tone where the law, ethics, and Judaism are concerned (Rom 1:16; 3:8, 31; 6:1–2, 15; 7:7, 13; 9:1–3; 10:1; 11:1, 11), but the evidence from other Pauline letters is overwhelming. Is he afraid the Roman Christians have heard about "Corinthianized" Christianity? Is he afraid they have heard some of the things he has said about Jews who oppose his gospel (e.g., 1 Thess 2:14–16; cf. Acts 13:46)? He is afraid they have heard things he has said or at least implied about Judaism, its law and covenants, in his battles with Judaizers in Galatia?

But I also suspect that another reason Paul chose writing in this case is its deceptive potential. This is an aspect of writing with which Paul was well acquainted. For example, the "painful letter" already referred to was ostensibly aimed at solving some crisis in the Corinthian congregation. But only after the crisis was past did Paul tell them the *real* intention of his letter: "For this is why I wrote, that I might test you and know whether you are obedient in everything" (2 Cor 2:9).[4] Here, in the only correspondence apart from Romans in which "obedience" has any prominence, the word is closely linked with Paul's personal authority and a letter he has sent as a test

---

3. For this perspective see especially Ernst Käsemann, *Commentary on Romans* (Grand Rapids: Eerdmans, 1980), and Peter Stuhlmacher, *Paul's Letter to the Romans: A Commentary* (Louisville: Westminster John Knox, 1994).

4. I find partition theories that make 2 Cor 10–13 part of "the painful letter" to be the most convincing. Furnish too easily dismisses evidence in favor of such hypotheses (*II Corinthians*, 37–38). For an excellent history of the literary and historical problems presented by 2 Corinthians and the proposed solutions, see Hans Dieter Betz, *2 Corinthians 8 and 9* (Hermeneia; Philadelphia: Fortress, 1985), 3–36.

of personal loyalty: "So although I wrote to you, it was not on account of the one who did the wrong, nor on account of the one who was wronged, but in order that your zeal for us might be made known to you before God" (2 Cor 7:12). The letter was a self-test that the Corinthians did not even know they were taking until they had passed it. It was a test given so that zeal for Paul might be revealed *to themselves* ("that your zeal might be made known *to you*"). This letter to the Corinthians was not simply an altruistic attempt to solve specific problems, but a cunning and deceptive test of obedience aimed at rescuing the Corinthians from deception.

Similarly, when Paul speaks to the Romans of "the obedience of faith," he is not simply talking about conversion. The obedience of faith is an ongoing process in which Paul sees himself as the premier spiritual authority where Gentiles are concerned:

> I urge you, brothers and sisters, to keep an eye on those who cause dissensions and offenses, in opposition to the teaching that you have learned; avoid them. For such people do not serve our Lord Christ, but their own appetites, and by smooth talk and flattery they deceive the hearts of the innocent/naïve. *For while your obedience is known to all, so that I rejoice over you, I want you to be wise in what is good and guileless in what is evil* (Rom 16:17–19).

Paul does indeed think he has something to "impart" to the Romans, "some spiritual gift to strengthen" them (1:11). He speaks of the Romans' obedience not merely as a profession of faith, but as having "become obedient from the heart to the type of teaching (τύπον διδαχῆς) to which you were entrusted" (6:17). When one considers Paul's long list of friends and fellow-workers now in Rome (16:3–15), it seems possible that some of these Pauline Christians had a hand in establishing some of the very house churches Paul is addressing.[5] This would help explain why he does not seem to feel he is building "on another's foundation" (15:20) while preaching there. The "type of teaching" in Rome that Paul would like to encourage over other competing types would already be essentially Pauline. But while he is thankful to God (6:17) that they have accepted this "type of teaching," so that he rejoices over them (16:19), the "hearts of the innocent/naïve" (16:18) must be protected. There are other types of teaching in Rome, possibly more pervasive than the Pauline type. Until all the Romans accept Paul's wisdom, some will remain vulnerable to other gospels. Obedience to the "teaching you have learned," which subtly includes the content of Romans itself, appearing as it does at the end of what David Aune has aptly described as a "speech of exhortation" (*logos protreptikos*) and Karl Donfried

---

5. For strong arguments in favor of accepting most of Rom 16 as belonging to Romans, see especially Harry Gamble, *The Textual History of the Letter to the Romans* (SD 42; Grand Rapids: Eerdmans, 1977). As Dunn observes, most recent commentators are convinced that chapter 16 belongs to Romans, though the notion that it was originally directed to the Ephesians is still supported by some (*Romans 1–8*, lx).

a "letter essay," will enable them to be "wise in what is good and guileless in what is evil" (16:19).[6] As Aune concludes, "Thus Romans is protreptic not only in the sense that Paul is concerned to convince people of the truth of Christianity, but more particularly in the sense that he argues for his version of Christianity over other competing 'schools' of Christian thought."[7] The letter becomes not only a protreptic but a prophylactic against the type of teaching and type of enemies Paul constantly combats.

But if they pass this test of obedience, they will have been caught in Paul's web, for the letter to the Romans is also a textual Trojan horse.[8] Paul introduces himself as a slave, one of his favorite self-designations. What could be more disarming, less threatening, less potentially domineering, than a slave? But Paul's master is "Jesus Christ our Lord, through whom *we have received grace and apostleship to bring about the obedience of faith among all the Gentiles* for the sake of his name, *including yourselves* who are called to belong to Jesus Christ" (1:4b–6; cf. 15:8). How cunning! Paul is no ordinary slave, but a commissioned steward in Christ's household.[9] Romans is an invitation to the Romans to recognize fully Paul's claim upon them, to recognize his special commissioning, his divinely sanctioned authority over all Gentile Christians.[10]

But such "deceptions," and we have only scratched the surface here, are necessary only because part of the audience is already subject to, or at least threatened by, deception. What is the actual or potential "Deception in Rome"? Essentially the same one that Paul had faced in his own congregations: Judaistic forms of Christianity promulgated by apostles who in Paul's estimation were false. But to address this danger, Paul had to indulge in a little cunning deception of his own, especially since (1) he knew that some of the Gentile congregations in Rome already had a strongly Judaistic

---

6. See David Aune, "Romans as a *Logos Protreptikos*," in *The Romans Debate*, 278–96; Karl P. Donfried, "False Presuppositions in the Study of Romans," in *The Romans Debate*, 121–25.

7. Aune, "Romans as a *Logos Protreptikos*," 279.

8. "My hypothesis, if correct, would oblige us to recognize the fact that the primary function of written communication is to facilitate slavery. The use of writing for disinterested purposes, and as a source of intellectual and aesthetic pleasure, is a secondary result, and more often than not it may even be turned into a means of strengthening, justifying or concealing the other" (Claude Lévi-Strauss, "A Writing Lesson," in *Tristes Tropiques* [New York: Atheneum, 1984], 299).

9. Speaking of the contrasting metaphorical senses of slavery in Galatians, Martin says, "In one case, the aspects of slavery that provide the meaning are labor, drudgery, the unconditional obedience to a merciless master. In the other case, however, the aspect of slavery that provides the meaning is the role of slave agents as indispensable, authoritative representatives of the powerful owner" (Dale Martin, *Slavery as Salvation*, 60).

10. I see much merit in Günther Klein's thesis that Paul did not feel he was building on someone else's foundation in Rome because the churches there lacked an apostolic foundation ("Paul's Purpose in Writing the Epistle to the Romans," in *The Romans Debate*, 29–43). I would add, however, that from Paul's perspective, if churches were predominantly Gentile, they already had an apostolic foundation whether they knew it yet or not.

character,[11] and (2) he suspected that they had already heard of his severe criticisms of the Law and Judaism. Indeed, although many aspects of the situation of Romans are contested, most interpreters would now acknowledge that Paul's reputation for harsh attitudes toward the Law, Judaism, and unrepentant Jews, fully deserved or not, is to be included among them. The reason for Paul's diplomacy in Romans, however, is not to be explained by positing a primarily Jewish audience, an argument that always requires explaining away a great deal of rather obvious evidence to the contrary.[12] Instead, I hold to the more traditional arguments for a primarily, though not exclusively, Gentile audience.[13] And I would conclude from Paul's address of this primarily Gentile audience as "ones who know the Law" (Rom 7:1) that many probably came from the ranks of the "God-fearers."[14] Such people came under the sway of Christianity precisely because of their prior admiration and respect for Jews and Judaism. Far from being the sort of Gentiles who would be tempted to "boast over the branches" while contemplating the present plight of Israel (Rom 11:18), they were likely "Judaeophiles." This explains Paul's diplomatic attitude toward Judaism in Romans without resort to strained arguments for a primarily Jewish audience. In light

11. See discussion of the composition of the community in Werner Georg Kümmel, *Introduction to the New Testament* (rev. ed.; Nashville: Abingdon, 1989), 309–11.

12. See, e.g., Steven Mason, "Paul, Classical Anti-Jewish Polemic, and the Letter to the Romans," in *Self-Definition and Self-Discovery in Early Christianity: A Study in Changing Horizons* (Lewiston, N.Y.: Mellen, 1990), 181–223, esp. 195–223. An interpreter is hard-pressed to make the case for a primarily Jewish audience in light of Rom 1:13; 11:13–25, and 15:15–16. Furthermore, it is a mistake to use 2:17–29 to prove a Jewish audience since the Jew addressed here is an imaginary dialogue partner in Paul's diatribe. Thus in light of Rom 1:13, 11:13–25, and 15:15–16, one should conclude that Paul's parenthetical remark in 7:1, that he is speaking to those who know the Law, does not mean he is speaking primarily to Jews, but rather to Gentiles who know the Law, probably former God-fearers (see below, n. 14, on the problem of "God-fearers"). From Paul's standpoint, even such Gentiles must "die to the Law" just like Jews (7:4–6).

13. Stowers, *Rereading*, 29–33, makes an interesting but overstated argument concerning the audience of Romans. Relying on concepts derived from reader-response criticism, Stowers distinguishes between the encoded and the empirical audiences of the letter, and avers that the implied author addresses an exclusively Gentile encoded audience (see references in the preceding footnote). Stowers concedes that this by no means rules out the presence of some Jews in the empirical audience — the presence of a Jewish-Christian minority is quite likely — but he insists that at no point does Paul address them directly (32–33). Hays raises the weighty objection against this position that Romans is addressed "to *all* God's beloved in Rome, who are called to be saints" and that surely includes Jewish and Gentile Christians (*CRBR* [1996]). But while Stowers has overstated his case for an exclusively Gentile encoded audience, his argument does remind us that very little of Romans addresses Jewish Christians in a direct way, and I have to wonder how they would have felt about that, especially in light of Paul's remarks to the "Strong" in 14:1 and 15:1a.

14. See Dunn's discussion of the recipients (*Romans 1–8*, xliv–liv). I continue to use the term God-fearers while Dunn, following Trebilco, prefers the term God-worshipers. But, as Dunn observes, whatever we choose to call them, evidence of many Gentiles attaching themselves to Jewish synagogues is not in doubt. Furthermore, Kraabel's opposition to the term God-fearer has been undermined by recent archaeological discoveries. A full treatment of the subject is now provided by Irina Levinskaya, *Diaspora Setting* (vol. 5 of *The Book of Acts in Its First Century Setting;* ed. B. W. Winter; Grand Rapids: Eerdmans, 1996).

of Paul's reputation in these matters, *this audience identification is the key factor in the rhetorical situation of Romans,* and will be a constant reference point in the readings offered here. Very likely Paul's anti-Judaistic polemic had gotten out of hand in the eyes of many (Acts 21:20–21, 27–28), and he had reason to suspect that his reputation for harsh rhetoric toward unrepentant Jews (e.g., 1 Thess 2:14–16) would be a hindrance to gaining the Roman Christians' support for his projected mission to Spain. He must offer an apology for his anti-Judaistic and occasionally anti-Jewish rhetoric, but it must be a veiled apology so he will not appear to be admitting openly the mistakes of the past and confirming the accuracy of rumors about himself.

But does Paul really fear that the Romans' positive attitude toward the Law could lead them into deception? The place to begin to answer this question is Rom 7, the New Testament's premier discussion of deception. Here we find Paul's description of Sin's deceptive expropriation of the Law, and the continuance of Paul's somewhat deceptive representation to the Roman house churches of his own attitude toward the Law (cf., 2:13; 3:31). But in order to appreciate fully these deceptions, especially the latter, I will first have to examine Krister Stendahl's highly influential re-reading of this text, a re-reading intended to prove that (1) the profound psychological and anthropological insights found there are more the product of eisegesis than exegesis; (2) Paul himself never experienced the divided "I" most commentators find dramatized here, and (3) Paul's true purpose is to offer an encomium of the Law. To anticipate, the problem with the last point is not that Stendahl is incorrect in seeing a more positive attitude toward the Law expressed in Paul's discourse in Rom 7, but that he fails to take the rhetorical situation into account and instead takes Paul's remarks "at face value," not asking for what reason Paul might want or need to appear to be defending the Law at this point in his career and to this particular audience. I will then consider another text, Rom 9:1–5 (especially vv. 4–5), that is frequently used with little regard to the rhetorical situation of the letter to prove that Galatians and 2 Cor 3 are anomalous where the subject of Judaism is concerned and that, in spite of what he had written in the past, Paul really has a highly appreciative attitude toward Judaism. To dramatize how the rhetorical situation complicates interpretation of these verses, I will read them in the spirit of an unsympathetic Judaistic critic, a "weak" reader, who has been paying careful attention to Paul's remarks on Judaism and the Law to this point in his letter and who also has some knowledge about what he has said about these matters in the past. Finally, I will consider another text, Rom 14:1–15:13, that is also frequently used with insufficient regard to the rhetorical situation of the letter to prove that Paul is trying to heal divisions in and among the Roman house churches. Those who are not convinced by this increasingly popular perspective are faced with the difficult task of explaining why Paul appears to give advice to the "strong" concerning the "weak" if he really knows nothing of actual conflicts among competing groups in Rome, but my understanding of the rhetorical situation offers another explanation. To dramatize how the rhetorical situation complicates interpretation of these verses, I will try to read them in the spirit of a "strong" reader. Fitzmyer suggests that "Paul's letter is not an abstract, dogmatic treatise or a dialogue with Jews who do not accept his gospel; it is rather a didactic and hortatory letter, *intended for discussion* by Jewish and Gentile Christians of Rome, for their understanding and for their conduct."[15] My "weak" and "strong" readings are an attempt to imagine some of that discussion.

What is the point of this exercise? To prove that Paul really was an antinomian and/or anti-Judaistic? God forbid! Rather, the point is that the "truth" of such charges is a matter of one's perspective. Perhaps some members of Paul's Roman audience were satisfied by what Paul had to say on these subjects. Some probably concluded that although he may have a rather creative and original understanding of the Law and Judaism, he nevertheless does, in his own way, "uphold the Law" and respect Judaism. Surely some Romans, however, would not have been satisfied. Perhaps particularly those who already knew something about Paul's "published" views on controversial issues in the past would have wondered what Paul really thought when faced with his complex and occasionally rather ambiguous discourse in Romans. To be sure, such readers might well sound like early practitioners of a "hermeneutics of suspicion." But in light of what we have learned so far in this study, can we quickly rule out the possibility that such a reading would necessarily be less "competent" than the former? Could the key to Romans be to hear it in the diverse ways its originally diverse audience heard it, a diversity of which Paul was well aware and for which he designed this somewhat deceptive communication?

2. Is "I" I in Romans 7?

According to Krister Stendahl, the sober reflections on the "I" in Rom 7 have both everything and nothing to do with Paul.[16]

> The theologian would be quite willing to accept and appreciate the obvious deepening of religious and human insight which has taken place in Western thought, and which reached a theological climax with Luther — and a secular climax with Freud. He could perhaps argue that this Western interpretation and transformation of Pauline thought is a valid and glorious process of theological development. He could even claim that such a development was fostered by elements implicit in the New Testament, and especially Paul.[17]

---

15. Joseph A. Fitzmyer, *Romans* (AB 33; New York: Doubleday, 1993), 79, italics mine.

16. For a thorough recent survey of interpretive positions and issues in Romans 7, see Michael Paul Middendorf, *The "I" in the Storm: A Study of Romans 7* (Saint Louis: Concordia Academic Press, 1997).

17. Stendahl, "Introspective Conscience," in *Paul among Jews and Gentiles,* 95.

But what he cannot claim, according to Stendahl, is that Paul himself experienced "man's or his own cloven ego or predicament."[18] On the contrary, "the rather trivial observation that every man knows that there is a difference between what he ought to do and what he does," has been elevated by many Pauline interpreters to "the golden truth of Pauline anthropology," when in reality this anthropology is only the "means for a very special argument about the holiness and goodness of the Law."[19] He concludes,

> Unfortunately — or fortunately — Paul happened to express this supporting argument so well that what to him and his contemporaries was a common sense observation appeared to later interpreters to be a most penetrating insight into the nature of man and into the nature of sin.[20]

Let us be clear on the magnitude of Stendahl's claim. For at least sixteen centuries, at least from the time of Augustine, interpreters of Paul have credited him with profound anthropological insights into the essentially divided nature of the human self,[21] insights that when demythologized are strikingly similar to modern psychological conflict theories of human personality, thus making Paul to some extent a forerunner of Freud. Now we are being told that Paul deserves no such (dis)credit. Indeed, such notions are diametrically opposed to what Paul really thought since Paul's argument in Rom 7 is actually "one of *acquittal of the ego*, not one of utter contrition.... In Rom. 7 the issue is rather to show how in some sense 'I gladly agree with the Law of God as far as my inner man is concerned' (v. 11); or, as in v. 25, 'I serve the Law of God.' "[22] In contrast to Stendahl's careful "historical" reading of Rom 7, "This Western interpretation reaches its climax when it appears that even, or especially, the will of man is the center of depravation. And yet, in Rom. 7 Paul had said about that will: 'The will (to do the good) is there...' (v. 18)."[23]

Methodologically speaking, what Stendahl considers to be the great virtue of his reading, that it is historical rather than theological, should be recognized as its weakest and most (self?) deceptive feature:

> We should venture to suggest that the West for centuries has wrongly surmised that the biblical writers were grappling with problems which no doubt are ours, but which never entered their consciousness.
>
> For the historian this is of great significance. It could of course always be argued that these ancients unconsciously were up against the same problems as we are — man being the same through the ages. But the historian is

---

18. Ibid., 92.
19. Ibid., 93.
20. Ibid.
21. "Especially in Protestant Christianity — which, however, at this point has its roots in Augustine and in the piety of the Middle Ages — the Pauline awareness of sin has been interpreted in the light of Luther's struggle with his conscience" (ibid., 79). See also, 83–86.
22. Ibid., 93, italics mine.
23. Ibid.

rightly anxious to stress the value of having an adequate picture of what these people actually thought they were saying. He will always be suspicious of any "modernizing," whether it be for apologetic, doctrinal, or psychological purposes.[24]

The historical advice offered here is sound. The biblical world is not our world. But does Stendahl follow his own advice? In contradistinction to interpreters who read Rom 7 differently than he, and who apparently for that reason must be theologians rather than historians, Stendahl "the historian," would claim access to "the Pauline original."[25] The (self?) deceptive nature of this gesture must not be missed. The fact is that Stendahl himself, like those interpreters he is castigating, is by trade *both* historian *and* theologian. And we may rest assured that other interpreters, those who detect profound anthropological insights in Rom 7, sincerely believe that they too, as theologians *and* historians, have "an accurate picture of what these people thought they were saying." They would no doubt remind Stendahl that difficult problems are hardly to be resolved by "a simple reading of the text,"[26] as though this is what a historical reading is, least of all when at least sixteen centuries of debate amply testifies that the text in question simply is not simple.[27] Actually, none of us can escape some form of "modernizing," regardless of our motives, since we are all (post)modern interpreters.[28] Few interpreters dispute this mundane observation in theory, but it is easy to forget in practice. Often the one who accuses others of modernizing for some purpose or another fails to apply the same hermeneutic of suspicion to himself or herself. Such is the case here. Stendahl elsewhere describes his work as being shaped by two "overarching concerns": hermeneutics and relations between the Church and the Jewish people. These concerns are clearly interrelated, and determinative:

> The responsibility of interpretation is a grave one, and these essays are an attempt at minimizing the risks of misuse, thus setting the texts free for peaceful, liberating, and salvific use. I believe that the *first* and indispensable step in any such enterprise is to insist on a clear distinction between what a text *meant* according to its original intention, and what it came to mean and/or might mean at any later point in history or the future.[29]

24. Stendahl, "Introspective Conscience," 95.

25. Ibid., 96.

26. Stendahl, "Paul Among Jews and Gentiles," in *Paul Among Jews and Gentiles,* 7.

27. Cranfield lists six interpretive options for understanding Paul's use of the first person singular in 7:7–13, and seven possibilities in vv. 14–25. None can be excluded with absolute confidence, and Cranfield himself goes against the majority who accept Kümmel's position that the "I" has nothing to do with either Paul's biography or the Christian life, opting instead for the classic Lutheran interpretation (C. E. B. Cranfield, *The Epistle to the Romans* [2 vols., ICC; Edinburgh: T. & T. Clark, 1975], 1:342–44).

28. The title of the SBL series, *The Bible and Its Modern Interpreters,* delightfully admits to more than a strictly chronological interpretation.

29. Stendahl, "Sources and Critiques," in *Paul Among Jews and Gentiles,* 127.

What began as a scholarly and intellectual curiosity led me to recognize how the Christian use of Scripture, and not least of the Pauline epistles, had caused developments of satanic dimensions. The first two essays in this book are partly an attempt to get at some of the roots of Christian anti-Semitism.[30]

Notice the thoroughly modern nature of these overarching concerns. Furthermore, there appears to be an underlying assumption, very likely a theological conviction, that the NT itself can be absolved of anti-Semitism and, as seen below, anti-Judaism.[31] Though Satan ("developments of satanic dimensions") is active in the (mis)use of Scripture, Scripture itself is always salvific:

> We note how the biblical original functions as a critique of inherited presuppositions and incentive to new thought. Few things are more liberating and creative in modern theology than a clear distinction between the "original" and the "translation" in any age, our own included.[32]

The real problem cannot be with the original intention but only with later interpretation.

> When the first two essays in this book assert that Paul's argument about justification by faith neither grows out of his "dissatisfaction" in Judaism, nor is intended as a frontal attack on "legalism," I believe that I am striking at the most vicious root of theological anti-Judaism.[33]

Clearly Stendahl has sallied forth on a hermeneutical crusade. There are certain inconvenient readings that simply cannot be what Paul intended. While I agree whole-heartedly with Stendahl (and E. P. Sanders, who stated the case more effectively) that "legalism" is not Paul's problem with Judaism, the textual evidence that Paul experienced some sort of "dissatisfaction" with Judaism is not so easily dismissed. So it is not surprising that "gett[ing] at the roots of Christian anti-Semitism" in his famous essays, "Paul Among Jews and Gentiles," and "The Apostle Paul and the Introspective Conscience of the West," occasionally requires a sort of blindness that does not yield insight.[34]

---

30. Ibid., 128.

31. Stendahl often uses the terms as if they were synonymous. This practice is erroneous and causes problems, but sadly the terms continue to be confused and misapplied in various ways. Because Stendahl practically equates the two, it is difficult to find Paul anti-Judaistic because he is not anti-Jewish. I thoroughly agree with Stendahl that Paul is not anti-Jewish. He may get very angry and frustrated with those of his brothers and sisters "according to the flesh" who do not agree that Jesus is the Messiah (1 Thess 2:14–16!), but he does not hate them, and certainly not because they are sons and daughters of Abraham. Even in Galatians where Paul teaches that ethnic distinctions are ultimately meaningless in Christ, he does not hesitate to speak of "We ourselves, who are Jews by birth and not Gentile sinners . . ." (2:15). Yet, Paul can be shockingly anti-Judaistic at times, and observing how Paul negotiates this anti-Judaism in Romans is fascinating.

32. Stendahl, "Introspective Conscience," 96.

33. Ibid., "Sources and Critiques," 127.

34. Indeed, the hermeneutical investments that require the "I" not to be I in Rom 7 continue to produce readings that overlook obvious evidence to the contrary. E.g., Stowers invokes some

Consider a couple of examples. In his influential argument for considering Paul's Damascus road experience a "call" rather than a "conversion," Stendahl quotes Gal 1:13–16 in order to show that Paul's language echoes that of Isaiah and Jeremiah's prophetic calling, thus highlighting Paul's continuity with Judaism. The point is well taken, but where Paul and Judaism are concerned, one cannot choose so easily between continuity and discontinuity. How does Stendahl explain Paul's language at the beginning of this passage: "For you heard of *my former life* in Judaism (Ἰουδαϊσμός)..."? He does not. He simply ignores it.[35] In order to *free* Paul from any traces of anti-Judaism, apologists are often tempted (1) to *erase* as many traces of it as possible through selective reading, or (2) to *save* the remaining repulsive texts by re-covering them.[36]

While Stendahl's reading of Gal 1:13–16 illustrates the first option, his reading of Phil 3:5–9 illustrates the second. Consider this salutary passage:

> In Philippians, he stresses that he is "a Hebrew born of Hebrews, as to the law a Pharisee, as to zeal a persecutor of the church, as to righteousness under the law blameless" (Phil. 3:5–6). *Yet without casting doubts as to the worth of his background* but pointing out that his former values, great as they were, are as nothing in light of his knowledge and recognition of Christ, he continues, "But whatever gain I had, I counted as loss for the sake of Christ. Indeed I count everything as loss because of the surpassing worth of knowing Christ Jesus my Lord. For his sake I suffered loss of all things and count them as dung in order that I may gain Christ and be found in him, not having a righteousness of my own, based on law, but that which is faith in Christ, the righteousness of God that depends on faith..." (Phil. 3:7–9).[37]

---

patristic commentary to show that ancient readers did not think Paul was including himself in the "I" of Rom 7. His prime example is Origen. Yet the first thing we learn about Origen's exegesis from Stowers is that "Origen says that Paul does not speak of himself *alone* in 7:7–8 but of every person" (*Rereading*, 266, italics mine). Simple logic dictates that if Paul is speaking of every person he is including himself. But, curiously, four sentences later Stowers concludes that "Clearly for Origen the speaker of 7:7–25 does not speak autobiographically of Paul." Origen, in fact, does maintain Paul as the "I" in chap. 7 (see Middendorf, *The "I" in the Storm*, 265–66).

35. Ibid., "Paul Among Jews and Gentiles," 8.

36. Of course, the opposite is possible. Selective reading can be used to make a NT author more anti-Judaistic or anti-Jewish than he really is. Jack T. Sanders argues in *The Jews in Luke-Acts* (Philadelphia: Fortress, 1987) that Luke-Acts is not only anti-Judaistic, but anti-Semitic as well. And yet, he does not discuss Acts 1:6, one of the most potentially damaging verses to his thesis. Here the risen Jesus in no way discourages the notion that one day he will restore the kingdom to Israel. Someone who ignores such evidence hardly has confirmed Haenchen's opinion that Luke has "written the Jews off." Acts 1:6 reminds us that the possibility of "holy remnant" theology in Luke-Acts, so quickly dismissed by Sanders (235), cannot so easily be ruled out. For a far more exegetically sound discussion of the Jews in Luke-Acts, see especially Robert C. Tannehill, "Rejection by Jews and Turning to the Gentiles: The Pattern of Paul's Mission in Acts," in *Luke-Acts and the Jewish People: Eight Critical Perspectives* (ed. Joseph B. Tyson; Minneapolis: Augsburg, 1988), 83–101.

37. Ibid., 8–9, italics mine.

Stendahl will go on to conclude on the basis of his readings of these passages from Galatians and Philippians that "It thus becomes clear that the usual conversion model of Paul the Jew who gives up his former faith to become a Christian is not the model of Paul but of ours."[38] Granted, this "usual conversion model" is an oversimplification. But how can one who speaks of his "former life in Judaism" not be, in some sense, giving up his "former faith"? How can one who counts all his Jewish credentials as "dung" not be "casting doubts as to the worth of his background"?[39] How can one who speaks of past privileges of which he has suffered "loss" not be speaking of a transition more profound than a prophetic calling? How can Stendahl be so sure that one who evaluates these past achievements as "having a righteousness of my own, based on law" does not find in a "righteousness from God that depends on faith," the answer to "a 'dissatisfaction' in Judaism"?

Of course, the trump card often played to prove that Paul had experienced no dissatisfaction in Judaism is Phil 3:6, where the pinnacle of Paul's glorying in his Jewish past — now relegated to the inferior realm of "flesh" by the way — is his claim that "as to righteousness under the Law" he was "blameless."[40] To be sure, Phil 3:6 does refute one theory of Paul's dissatisfaction with Judaism: that he had "difficulties in fulfilling what he as a Jew understood to be the requirements of the law."[41] Kümmel used Phil 3:6 to refute decisively *this* autobiographical interpretation of Rom 7.[42] But this

---

38. Ibid., 9.

39. While some find it easy, too easy, to dismiss the psychoanalytical arguments that Paul underwent a radical conversion, sociological arguments are harder to ignore. Such excessive devaluation — dung and loss — of one's past is precisely what sociology has taught us to expect from converts. After listing David Snow and Richard Machalek's four "rhetorical indicators" of conversion, Segal notes that "Only one indicator — biographical reconstruction, where the subject actively reinterprets past experiences or self-conceptions from the vantage point of the present in such a way as to change the meaning of the past — is a clear indicator of religious conversion" (Segal, *Paul the Convert*, 79).

40. Not surprisingly, Phil 3:6 is Stendahl's first and foremost weapon taken up against the idea that Paul had an introspective conscience ("Introspective Conscience," 80).

41. Stendahl, "Paul Among Jews and Gentiles," 13. One of the weaknesses of Theissen's *Psychological Aspects* is his attempt to reconcile Rom 7:7–23 and Phil 3:4–6: "The thesis defended here, therefore, is that Phil. 3:4–6 reflects the consciousness of the pre-Christian Paul, while Romans 7 depicts a conflict that was unconscious at the time, one of which Paul became conscious later" (*Psychological Aspects,* 235). Although it is an ingenious argument, and is certainly more satisfactory than any argument that would use Phil 3:4–6 to prove that Rom 7:7–23 cannot be autobiographical, its very necessity rests upon the unquestioned conclusion that the two passages are incompatible. As we shall see, if one understands "blameless as to righteousness which is by the Law" right in Phil 3:6, there is no incompatibility to explain. Unfortunately, Theissen and others would appear to think that Paul, or anyone who claims to be "blameless as to righteousness under the Law," is claiming sinless perfection. This leads to such statements as "Instead of seeing and addressing in himself repressed incapacity to fulfill the law and anxiety at the demands of the law, he persecutes them in a small group that deviated from the law" (243). But such a solution plays havoc with the rhetorical purpose of Phil 3:6. Paul is claiming in no uncertain terms that he once had just as much right as the Judaizers to take "pride in the flesh," fulfilling the Law blamelessly.

42. W. G. Kümmel, *Römer 7 und die Bekehrung des Paulus* (Leipzig: Hinrichs, 1929).

does not rule out the possibility that Paul was dissatisfied for another reason, and that this other reason is revealed autobiographically even in, or rather especially in, Phil 3, as well as Rom 7 *and* 8.

Far from proving that Paul felt no dissatisfaction, Phil 3 is actually one of the most important texts for properly understanding that dissatisfaction. While Phil 3:6 certainly refutes the interpretation of Rom 7 that Kümmel used it against so effectively, it does not rule out the possibility that Rom 7 is still autobiographical in another sense because *Rom 7 says nothing about an inability to attain "a righteous of my own, based on Law," but about an inability not to sin.*[43] It cannot be too strongly emphasized that these are by no means the same thing. When Paul says that he was "as to righteousness under the Law, blameless," he is certainly not claiming sinless perfection, but rather the meticulous Pharisaic observance he has just mentioned.[44] When he sinned, he surely sacrificed and/or made prayers of repentance. This is what the Law was commonly understood to require for righteousness, not sinless perfection. But Paul was not satisfied with this "righteousness under the Law." *Paul's dissatisfaction with the Law, and hence with Judaism as he had known it, was with its inability to transform* (μεταμορφόω) *and perfect* (τελειόω) *him.*

> For God has done what the Law, weakened by the Flesh, could not do: sending his own Son in the likeness of sinful Flesh and for sin, he condemned Sin in the Flesh, in order that the just requirement of the Law might be fulfilled in us, who walk not according to the Flesh but according to the Spirit (Rom 8:3–4).

He goes on in Phil 3 to say that what "a righteousness from God that depends on faith" offers is the chance that

> I may know him and the power (δύναμις) of his resurrection, and may share his sufferings, becoming conformed (συμμορφιζόμενος) to him in his death, that if possible I may attain the resurrection from the dead. Not that I have already

---

43. Cf. David Wenham, "The Christian Life: A Life of Tension? A Consideration of the Nature of Christian Experience in Paul," in *Pauline Studies: Essays presented to Professor F. F. Bruce on his 70th Birthday* (Grand Rapids: Eerdmans, 1980), 80–94: "If the difference in context and perspective between Romans 7 and Philippians 3 is recognized, then it is possible to consider both as descriptive of Paul's pre-Christian experience even before his confrontation with the gospel. It is possible that, despite his outstanding superficial achievement (referred to in Philippians 3), he did experience inward struggle. And there is no good reason to suppose that he would have failed to recognize that non-Christians (e.g. Jews with a true love of God's law) often can and do experience moral struggle" (84). So far so good, but the plausibility of this scenario is greatly enhanced if Paul's mystical-apocalyptic longings for radical transformation are taken into account. These go far beyond a desire for mere mor(t)al perfection.

44. Cf. Robert H. Gundry, "The Moral Frustration of Paul before his Conversion: Sexual Lust in Romans 7:7–25," in *Pauline Studies: Essays presented to Professor F. F. Bruce on his 70th Birthday* (ed. S. D. A. Hagner and M. J. Harris; Grand Rapids: Eerdmans, 1980), 228–45: "Only by making 'blameless' mean sinlessly perfect could we pit the term against the pre-Christian autobiographical view of Rom 7:7–25. The people at Qumran out-Phariseed the Pharisees; yet among them a deep sense of personal sin co-existed with the conviction that they were the righteous (see esp. 1QH, often written in the 'I'-style)" (234).

attained this or am already perfect (τετελείωμαι); but I press on to make it my own, because Christ Jesus has made me his own" (Phil 3:10–11).

This combination of longing for transformation and perfection is also expressed succinctly in Rom 12:2:

> Do not be conformed to this world, but be transformed (μεταμορφοῦσθε) by the renewing of your minds, so that you may discern what is the will of God — what is good and acceptable and perfect (τέλειον).

What we see here goes far beyond striving for the highest degree of human moral perfection. It is the mystical-apocalyptic desire to transcend a corrupt human nature; to become a Son of God (Rom 8:19ff.); to be a brother of the new Adam (5:12–20), capable of triumphing over sin in one's mortal body (6:1–23), not least because one is freed from the Law (7:1–6).[45] It is a desire to return to an original Edenic perfection before one man sinned and allowed death to reign (5:12; cf. 7:7–12), a desire for *Urzeit* to become *Endzeit*. This apocalyptic longing for ultimate transformation, not an inability to perform works of the Law, is what inspires the frustration expressed in Rom 7:14–25. But if he did not feel such moral frustration and such mystical-apocalyptic longings for radical transformation and perfection before his conversion, then Christ is surely the fulfillment of a desire Paul never had, the answer to a question he never asked.[46] Then we are left with a perfectly contented zealous Pharisee and persecutor of Christians who did an about face for no conceivable reason other than a supernatural epiphany, a notion that is unintelligible not only psychologically, but sociologically and historically as well.

So Paul very likely did feel some dissatisfaction in Judaism. But the overarching concerns, or should we say goals, of Stendahl's hermeneutic discussed above require that he will not find anything significantly critical of the Law, Jews, or Judaism in any Pauline text. Quite the opposite in fact. And so, when he turns to Rom 7 we are not surprised that he so overemphasizes the idea that here Paul is involved in "a defense for the holiness and goodness of the Law" that he reduces the mythological and anthropological observations (i.e., the deceptive activities of Sin and the helplessness of the divided self) to

---

45. See Segal, "Paul's Ecstasy," in *Paul the Convert*, 34–71; Theissen, *Psychological Aspects*, 127–38.

46. Käsemann also thinks the "I" of Rom 7 is not autobiographical. Here it will suffice to reproduce Beker's forceful objections to Käsemann's position: "A deletion of all autobiographical inferences from Romans 7 makes the chapter theologically unintelligible and fruitless for Paul's encounter with Judaism. If the lordship of Christ is simply a totally unexpected revelation that has no experiential antecedents in Paul's Jewish life, it becomes unintelligible how and why Christ supersedes the law. For if Paul was an utterly happy Jew before he met Christ, his Christian hindsight description of Jewish life becomes inauthentic, because there is no trace of a foothold for it in his own experience. How could Paul have affirmed the credal statement 'Christ died for our sins' if the problem of sin vis-à-vis the law was in no way related to his experience?" (Beker, *Paul*, 241).

mere trivialities. Because of this overemphasis and reduction, Stendahl fails to see how what could be construed as an encomium praising the Law and blaming Sin could also have the opposite effect because the Law is made to appear weak, capable of being co-opted at will by the forces of evil. The rhetorical effect of this ambiguity is that Paul can *appear* to champion the Law in order to combat charges that he is an antinomian and Jewish apostate, while simultaneously maintaining his more negative attitude toward the Law through *insinuatio*.

What was that more negative attitude? According to Gal 3:10–14, Paul thinks that those who are "under the Law" are "under a curse." Indeed, there are several reasons why from the perspective of 2 Cor 3 and Galatians Paul would equate being under the Law with being under a curse. According to 2 Cor 3, God never intended the Law to be salvific, but rather to condemn and kill, and according to Gal 3–4, it is synonymous with slavery to the "elements" (στοιχεῖα). Strikingly, Paul does *not* say in Galatians that Israel is under a curse by reason of an inability to fulfill the Law.[47] On the contrary, he states succinctly what the curse of the Law is from his perspective: " ... the Law is not of faith, for 'whoever does them shall live by them.' " (Gal 3:12).[48] And "whatever is not of faith" in his rather black and white, Flesh and Spirit dualistic apocalyptic epistemology, ultimately "is of Sin" (πᾶν δὲ ὃ οὐκ ἐκ πίστεως ἁμαρτία ἐστίν, Rom 14:23c). "Why then the Law? It was added because of transgressions" (Gal 3:10a,b). "But if you are led by the Spirit you are not under the Law" (5:18). To Paul "it is evident that no one is justified before God by the Law; for 'He who through faith is righteous shall live': but the Law does not rest on faith, for 'He who does them shall live by them' " (3:11–12). One might wonder if Paul could have understood the scriptural promise, "he who does them shall live by them" (Lev 18:5), as an intentional deception, a promise the commandment could not keep.[49]

---

47. *Contra* James M. Scott, " 'For as Many as are of Works of the Law are Under a Curse' (Galatians 3:10)," in *Paul and the Scriptures of Israel* (JSNTSup 83; Sheffield: Sheffield Academic Press, 1993), 187–221. Scott ignores much of what Paul actually says about the Law in Galatians in favor of hypothetical reconstructions (1) of how he interpreted the wider scriptural contexts from which he drew his citations, and (2) of his knowledge and espousal of a supposedly widespread historical perspective according to which Israel remains under the curses of Deut 27–32 ever since the exile due to continual disobedience.

48. For strong arguments against the view that Paul considers satisfactory Law observance to be impossible, see Sanders, *Paul, the Law, and the Jewish People*, 20–23. Sanders is right: " ... the whole thrust of the argument [of Galatians 2–3] is that righteousness was never, in God's plan, intended to be by the law" (27).

49. See Martyn's intriguing discussion of "The Textual Contradiction Between Habakkuk 2:4 and Leviticus 18:5," *Galatians,* 328–34. Near the end, Martyn suggests that what Paul is trying to say to the Galatians through the example of the scriptural contradiction set forth in 3:11–12 can be expressed in an emended form of 1 John 4:1: "Beloved [Galatians, in light of the Teachers' work in your midst], do not believe every spirit [or every text], but test the spirits [and the texts] to see whether they are from God" (334). Also, while contemplating an answer to the question asked above, consider Martyn's remarks on 1 Cor 7:19: "In any case, the wording of 1 Cor 7:19 itself suggests that Paul uses the expression 'the commandments *of God*' because

But why does Paul sound so much less negative about the Law in Romans? In chapter three, I suggested that Paul resorted to ambiguity to express his controversial views less offensively. As we have seen, Paul was certainly capable of expressing a less ambiguous attitude toward Judaism and the Law as the situation required. If I were to use the language of 2 Cor 3 to outline the "meaning effect" of Romans 7–8, I would choose the (in)famous 3:6b: "For the script kills [chapter 7], but the Spirit gives life [chapter 8]." In 2 Cor 3, all blame is assigned to "the ministry of death, carved in letters on stone" (3:7). Sin is not even mentioned. But, of course, Paul does not make his point quite so bluntly in Romans.[50] Since he always took the particular audience and rhetorical exigence into account, so must we as we read him.[51] While in Rom 7 he says that it was Sin that deceived him and killed him *through the Law,* in 2 Cor 3, Sin, the scapegoat for the Law we might say, is nowhere to be found.[52] There, *the very purpose of the Law itself is to kill.* It is a ministry/agency of condemnation and death. There, both the "agency" (διακονία) and its "agent" (διάκονος) are not too subtly associated with the deadly deception attributed to Sin in Rom 7.[53] And just as Paul metaphorically found Moses masking the goal/end of the old covenant by veiling his face, so also he found deception in the scripted Moses.[54] The *veil* remains

he presupposes something he does not explicitly state: Not all the commandments come from God!" (519). I would add that, in light of the rhetorical situation set forth at the beginning of the previous chapter, Paul could not explicitly say something like this to the Corinthians without risking rejection. Nor can he speak this way to the Romans. The irony for Paul was that he was frequently faced with Gentile converts who were more positive toward Judaistic Christians, Judaism, and the Law, than he was.

50. While I argued in the previous chapter that Paul's treatment of Moses and the Law is somewhat veiled in 2 Cor 3, it is certainly more openly critical than what we find in Romans. If those scholars are correct who put 2 Cor 10–13 before the writing of 2 Cor 3, then there may be a reason for this. The opening chapters of 2 Cor show that Paul is reconciled with the congregation. Now that he has gotten the upper hand against the super-apostles, he feels he can be more aggressive against aspects of their gospel derived from their Jewish heritage (2 Cor 11:22).

51. Peter Stuhlmacher's Romans commentary is exemplary in this respect.

52. In Rom 7, Paul wants to put the blame on Sin rather than the Law, but he is not convincing. The meaning effect of all Paul's statements on the Law, Sin, and Death is the formation of a "field," a chain of substitutions which all lie on the fleshly side of a Spirit/ Flesh dichotomy: "The major apocalyptic forces are, for him, those ontological powers that determine the human situation within the context of God's created order and comprise the 'field' of death, sin, the Law, and the flesh" (Beker, *Paul,* 145); "The virtual equation of the law with sin and the flesh in some passages (e.g. Rom. 6:14; 7:4–6; Gal. 5:16–18) is not part of a harmonious view of the law which held in balance its destructive and its productive power, depending on human response. . . . It is noteworthy that each step in the series is progressively more negative: from 'the law does not righteous' to 'the law produces transgression' to 'the law itself is one of the powers to which Christians must die, along with sin and the flesh.' Finally, in Rom 7, Paul attempts to pull back; but then, as we have noted, he encounters other problems, either of having the law be used by a power other than God, or of having to separate the law from God" (Sanders, *Paul, the Law, and the Jewish People,* 84–85).

53. The notion that someone might appear to be an "agent of Sin" (ἁμαρτίας διάκονος) is not foreign to Paul (Gal 2:17).

54. On the intimate relation between Moses and text, see above, p. 126, n. 162.

unlifted (3:14). Subtract the Sin scapegoat from Rom 7 and what remains? "The very commandment which was to lead to life proved to be death to me" (Rom 7:10).[55] However holy the Law may be, it produces the exact opposite of what it promises (Lev 18:5). But given the audience at Rome, Paul knows he cannot go this far, *at least not unambiguously and all at once.*

But someone will say, "Granted, Paul appears to attribute the death-dealing effects of the Law to Sin in Rom 7, whereas he attributed them to the Law itself in 2 Cor 3, and even comes close to demonizing the Law in Galatians. But why do you assume that Paul is cunningly and deceptively softening his rhetoric in Rom 7 in order to insinuate his real position? Why not just assume that he changed his mind and that by the time he wrote Romans he realized he had gone too far in his denigration of the Law and now sincerely 'attempts to pull back,' as Sanders puts it?"[56] Due to the very ambiguity of Paul's discourse in Rom 7, this possibility cannot be ruled out absolutely. For three reasons, however, I tend to think otherwise. In the first place, Paul has just echoed controversial aspects of his "earlier" Galatian and Corinthian views of the Law in 7:6 (cf. 6:14). The Law was "what held us captive" and in contrast to "the innovativeness of the Spirit" is set "the obsoleteness of script." The appearance of such potentially offensive language even in Romans is revealing. Paul has not really softened his views on the Law at all. But he realizes at this point that this is precisely the sort of rhetoric that had gotten him into trouble with Christians who had a high view of the Law in the past. So he does, temporarily, "pull back" in 7:7, but only from his scandalous rhetoric, not from his True position on the Law. Secondly, as argued above, Paul's low estimation of the Law is still implicit in his assumption that it is so weak that Sin can co-opt it at will. Consequently, the commandment that was to lead to life, instead leads to death. Thirdly, while Paul piles up a wealth of expressions consistent with an encomium for the Law in Rom 7 ("the Law is *holy,* and the commandment is *holy* and *just* and *good,*" 7:12; "the Law is *spiritual* [!]," 7:14; "the Law *of God,*" 7:22, 25), he also peppers his language from 7:21–8:8 with ambiguous and playful uses of "law" (νομός), often in close connection with "Sin." This is especially surprising since the diatribal question and answer that launched this discussion was "What then shall we say? That the Law is Sin? No way!" (7:7). This is a question that he anticipates his audience will be asking at this point because much of what he has been saying in 6:1–7:6 would seem to point toward just such a blasphemous conclusion (esp. 6:14 and 7:5–6).[57]

---

55. "The phrase [i.e., 'the commandment which was to lead to life'] may also deliberately characterize and echo what Paul regards as the typical Jewish attitude to the law (cf. Lev 18:5, cited to similar polemic effect in [Rom] 10:5)" (James D. G. Dunn, *Romans 1–8* [WBC 38A; Dallas: Word, 1988], 401–2).

56. See above, p. 156, n. 52.

57. Dunn expresses very well this perspective on the relationship of 7:7–13 to what has preceded it (*Romans 1–8,* 399).

And so, in 7:7–20, he is clearly taking pains to show that he means Sin, not the holy and good Law itself, is what kills. But, as we shall see, in 7:21–8:8 he gradually reverts to the sort of language that characterized 6:1–7:6, the sort of language that tends to confuse "the Law of God" with "the Law of Sin (and death)."[58]

What we have here is another example of Paul's tendency to begin, or in this case to begin again, by saying what he knows some of the audience wants and expects, but then later to use ambiguity to introduce his own ideas cunningly and deceptively to those with ears to hear. What we have is True rhetoric. As I suggested above, Paul writes Rom 7:7 not only because he suspects that some think he has gone too far with his controversial redefinition of the Law's origin and purpose in the past, but because he suspects that some of his Roman audience will think he has gone too far in the immediately preceding passages. He must "pull back" now, at first quite decisively (7:7–20), but then less and less so (7:21–8:8). The shift begins to take place when Paul complicates the picture in 7:21 by saying quite ambiguously that "I find then the law, for me who wishes to do the good, that for me the evil lies ready to hand." This very literal translation is offered by Dunn just before he goes against most modern commentators and argues that Paul is talking about *the* Law in verse 21, and not just of some "general rule" or "principle."[59] I agree with Dunn that it is possible to take verse 21 as a summary statement about the Law flowing out of Paul's immediately preceding discussion. But Dunn does not consider the possibility that Paul could have intended to be ambiguous here, leaving the audience wondering whether he is stating some general principle/law about the will's struggle with good and evil, or if he is reverting to a somewhat different and progressively more controversial angle on the relationship between the Law and Sin. The latter possibility is confirmed when Paul introduces an expression he has not used so far, "the law of Sin" (7:23, 25; 8:2), an expression that connects law and Sin in a striking way, a way that tends to unsettle the distinction between the Law and Sin he was so careful to make earlier.[60] The use of this expression in

---

58. Apparently even Stendahl assumes that Paul calls one and the same Law the "Law of God" and the "Law of Sin" in 8:3. In fact, the Law takes on *pharmakon*-like properties in the following passage: "In vv. 7–12 he works out an answer to the semi-rhetorical question: 'Is the Law sin?' The answer reads: 'Thus the Law is holy, just, and good.' This leads to the equally rhetorical question: 'Is it then this good (Law) which brought death to me?,' and the answer is summarized in v. 25b: 'So then, I myself serve the Law of God with my mind, but with my flesh I serve the Law of Sin' (i.e., the Law 'weakened by sin' [8:3] leads to death, just as a medicine which is good in itself can cause death to a patient whose organism [flesh] cannot take it)" ("Introspective Conscience," 92).

59. Dunn, *Romans 1–8*, 392.

60. Notice that Dunn also understands Paul to be reverting to his more negative portrayal of the Law only a little later in v. 23: "In describing the 'other law' as the principal actor, Paul reverts to the portrayal of the law as a power dominating the old epoch (6:14–15): even though the real blame lies with sin (7:7–13), the law can be said to characterize the old epoch, precisely as 'the law of sin' " (*Romans 1–8*, 409).

7:23 and 25 is not that troubling, of course, since in these cases "the Law of God" is being contrasted with "the law of Sin." But by the time one reaches 8:2, the contrast is between "the law of the Spirit of life in Christ Jesus" and "the law of Sin and Death." Somewhat surprisingly, Dunn argues that both expressions must refer to the Torah.[61] Käsemann, on the other hand, rightly insists that Paul could not mean "that the law as such is restored by the Spirit." He suggests that the key to the interpretation of 8:2 is found in 2 Cor 3:6ff.:

> The law of the Spirit is nothing other than the Spirit himself in his ruling function in the sphere of Christ. He creates life and separates not only from sin and death but also from their instrument, the irreparably perverted law of Moses.[62]

I find Käsemann's reading of 8:2 to be far more in keeping with Paul's usual attitude toward the Law, but does that mean that Dunn's reading is wrong? Not at all. Dunn has read this verse precisely the way Paul expected *some* of his audience to take it. That is, we must consider the possibility that Paul intended to express himself in such a way that some readers would discern Paul's *real* position on the Law, that it is antithetical to the Spirit, while others could understand him to be saying again, as in 7:14, that the Law is truly Spiritual and, moreover, can fulfill its life-giving promise among those who are in Christ. The latter readers would see their interpretation confirmed in 8:4 which speaks of the just requirement of the Law being fulfilled among those "who walk not according to the flesh, but according to the Spirit." The former readers would see their interpretation confirmed in 8:14–17 which says that those who are led by the Spirit are sons of God: "For you did not receive the spirit of slavery to fall back into fear, but you have received the spirit of adoption." They would remember that in 7:6 it was the Law that enslaves, but "we serve not under the obsoleteness of the script but in the innovativeness of the Spirit." Paul, through intentional ambiguity, created both the former and the latter readings. One might call the former the "weak" and the latter the "strong" intended reading. And that familiar subject, "the weak" and "the strong," is one to which we now turn.

3. Is "I" I in Rom 9:1–5?

[1]I am speaking the truth in Christ, I am not lying; my conscience bears me witness in the Holy Spirit, [2]that I have great sorrow and unceasing anguish in my heart. [3]For I could wish that I myself were accursed and cut off from Christ for the sake of my brethren, my kinsmen by race. [4]They are Israelites, and to them belong the adoption as sons, the glory, the covenants, the giving

---

61. Ibid., 436.
62. Käsemann, *Romans*, 215–16.

of the Law, the worship, and the promises; ⁵to them belong the patriarchs, and of their race, according to the flesh, is the Christ. God who is over all be blessed for ever. Amen (9:1–5).

In this section, I will try to establish a contextual audience perspective that will make us more aware of the difficulty of the rhetorical situation Paul faced. Why is he expressing his concern for the Jewish people in such hyperbolic terms? Is it not because he feels that many in his audience will have quite an opposite impression of him? Does he not face a crisis of credibility with Jews and Judaeophiles on the subject of the Jewish people and Judaism because of his past rhetoric? Paul would appear to be laboring mightily in vv. 1–3 to establish a new *ethos* for himself, a new "I." In vv. 4–5, he turns from highly emotional *pathos* concerning the Jewish people to certain Jewish "prerogatives" and pillars of Judaism.⁶³ The "proofs" of his attitude in this passage add an element of *logos* to Paul's effort. The fact that Paul freely calls his Jewish brothers and sisters "Israelites" and grants them possession of a long list of theological assets native to Judaism backs up his anguished concern with evidence of profound respect.⁶⁴

Nevertheless, a Judaeophile who had read Romans carefully to this point would probably be very suspicious of Paul's praise (cf. Rom 2:17–24), and if this reader had also heard gossip about Paul's past statements about aspects of Judaism, she would likely find his compliments self-serving at best and, at worst, even ironic. In what follows, I try to read Paul's remarks through such suspicious and unsympathetic eyes, eyes and ears I think would be present in Paul's audience in the form of Judaistic Christians of both Jewish and Gentile ethnicity.⁶⁵ This will serve as a counterpoint to those readings that proceed unproblematically, almost as if Paul were addressing these topics for

---

63. Some interpreters simply trace the historical background of the concepts encountered in vv. 4–5, showing little interest in how Paul has used them elsewhere, even as recently as the preceding chapter in Romans (e.g., Eldon Jay Epp, "Jewish-Gentile Continuity in Paul: Torah and/or Faith [Romans 9:1–5]," *HTR* 79 [1986]: 80–90). Dunn's commentary, however, is exemplary in that he frequently looks back on the way Paul has treated these themes earlier in Romans and elsewhere (*Romans 9–16*, 533–35). The main difference between his reading and mine is that I am making an imaginative reader-response effort to hear Paul's discourse as some of his less sympathetic audience members would have heard it, rather than concentrating almost entirely on what we more "objective" interpreters think Paul "really" intends to say.

64. Romans 10:1–2 is structurally similar to 9:1–5. Paul begins with an emotional declaration of his heart's desire for the Israelites in v. 1, and then gives them some credit — zeal for God — in v. 2.

65. The typical position that the "weak" and "strong" in Rome roughly correspond to Jewish Christians and Gentile Christians (e.g., Fitzmyer, *Romans*, 76–80; 687–88) is too simplistic. F. F. Bruce's position is more attractive: "Among the house-churches of Rome, then, we should probably envisage a broad and continuous spectrum in varieties of thought and practice between the firm Jewish retention of the ancestral customs and Gentile remoteness from these customs, with some Jewish Christians, indeed, found on the liberal side of the halfway mark between the extremes and some Gentile Christians on the 'legalist' side" ("The Romans Debate — Continued," in *The Romans Debate*, 186). Given Paul's enormous expenditure of effort in explaining his position on the Law to a largely Gentile audience, I expect many Gentile Christians were on the " 'legalist' side."

the first time, and as if what he says here would easily be taken at face value by all the Romans, would easily allay all their fears, and would decisively demonstrate to all his essentially positive attitude toward Judaism.

The first thing we must notice is that Paul's highly impassioned oath is primarily about his true attitude toward his Jewish kinsmen (vv. 1–3), and secondarily about his attitude toward important elements of Judaism, several of which are listed in vv. 4–5. As I argued in the previous section, we must always carefully distinguish between what Paul says about Jews and Judaism, and this distinction is especially important in these verses. While I am quite convinced of the sincerity of Paul's expression of sorrow and anguish for his Jewish kin, the problem arises when one examines closely what one might call Paul's mini-encomium of the Israelites, which includes some rather surprising aspects of Judaism. Paul makes several statements in his other letters which Steven Mason has termed "Paul's programmatic statements on Judaism" (1 Thess 2:15–16; Phil 3:2–10; 2 Cor 3; Galatians *passim*).[66] Though calling these statements "programmatic" may be a bit strong, assuming an intentionality for them that is open to debate, we cannot ignore the fact that these statements are uniformly negative, some dreadfully so. Whatever Paul intended by them, their effect on those sympathetic to Judaism would be predictable. When contrasted with these statements, Rom 9:1–5 is rather unique and surprising in the Pauline corpus. It would be naïve to ignore these extremely negative statements while reading a list of Jewish "prerogatives" coming from Paul that includes several fundamental components of Judaism. We should pause to ponder Rom 9:1–5 very carefully before we decide how precisely this "I" is I in vv. 1–3, and how persuasive this Paul's little encomium of Jews and Judaism in vv. 4–5 would sound to a Judaistic Christian.

Paul, the self-styled apostle to the Gentiles, had surely been accused of a lack of concern for his own people and teaching them to abandon Judaism.[67] Indeed, Paul may be countering such accusations by the very way he formulates his "wish." Paul wishes he himself were "accursed" (ἀνάθεμα) for their sake (9:3). This is very likely a term he used on occasion to describe Israel's present state. In Gal 3:10 he says, "For all who rely on works of the Law are under a curse (κατάρα); for it is written, "Cursed be every one who does not abide by all things written in the book of the Law, and do them." Under the influence of the LXX he uses κατάρα, a synonym of ἀνάθεμα, but earlier he refers to those who preach the gospel of circumcision as deserving ἀνάθεμα (1:8–9). The use of such language with respect to Law observance and those who promote it could not fail to make Paul appear as an apostate and enemy of Judaism both to Jews and, very likely, many Christians, Jewish and Gentile alike. But even if a "weak" reader of Paul's letter gave him the

---

66. Mason, "Paul," 195–208.
67. This would seem likely even if we did not have Acts 21:21.

benefit of the doubt in vv. 1–3, just as I would, what would he or she make of vv. 4–5 in light of Paul's letter to this point?

In *Elusive Israel: The Puzzle of Election in Romans,* Charles H. Cosgrove imagines a Roman Christian dialogue between Chariton, Simeon, and Reuben in response to Paul's letter.[68]

> ...I suggest that one associate the gentile name Chariton with a 'charitable' attitude toward Paul, the Jewish name Simeon with a 'suspicious' attitude toward Paul (whom Simeon regards as a radical 'sectarian'), and the Jewish name Reuben with the 'rabbinic' view that 'all Israel has a share in the age to come' — a view that Reuben attributes to Paul.[69]

Since the similarity between Cosgrove's Simeon and my "weak" reader is striking, I have adopted this name for him. And since Simeon did not address Rom 9:1–5 extensively in Cosgrove's Roman dialogue, I offer this speech to the congregation as further thought-provoking "evidence" for why Simeon has a mostly negative and distrustful reaction to Paul's letter. Of course, my Simeon may not absolutely agree with Cosgrove's at some points, but this speech was delivered some time after the dialogue, so Simeon's views may have undergone some further development.

Simeon's "Weak" Reading of Rom 9:4–5

Brothers and sisters,

The first "credit" Paul grants "we Israelites" is the adoption as sons (ἡ υἱοθεσία).[70] But let us not forget that we have already encountered this term twice in the immediately preceding discussion of those "in Christ." Paul declares that "you did not receive the spirit of slavery to fall back into fear, but you have received the spirit of adoption" (υἱοθεσία).[71] I have heard that in the past Paul has explicitly linked Torah observance with slavery,[72] and while he does not come right out and say that Law observance is slavery in his letter to us, I cannot but think that that is what he is implying when he speaks simultaneously of dying to Sin, dying to the Law, and of no longer "serving" under the obsolete "letter."[73] It seems that for Paul, the "adoption as sons" is not at all possible while one observes the Law, but only after one is freed from it.[74] According to Paul's logic, therefore, υἱοθεσία cannot *really* belong to those Israelites who have refused the gospel, and one must wonder what he thinks of those of us who trust in

---

68. Charles H. Cosgrove, *Elusive Israel: The Puzzle of Election in Romans* (Louisville: Westminster John Knox, 1997).

69. Ibid., 4.

70. Simeon deliberately and sarcastically echoes Paul's earlier discussion of how Abraham's faith was "credited" to him as righteousness. He suspects by now that for Paul, faith is the only credit worth having. He also sarcastically echoes Paul's inclusion of himself among the Israelites in 11:1.

71. Rom 8:15.

72. Gal 4:4–5.

73. Rom 6:10–11; 7:4–6.

74. "In Gl. 4.5 reception of sonship is identical with liberation from the Law..." (Schweizer, "υἱοθεσία," *TDNT* 8:399).

Christ but still observe the Law. It may rightly be their inheritance and ours to claim, but can we do so while still observing the Law? One would have to wonder when one hears Paul say "For if those of the Law are the heirs, faith is emptied and the promise disempowered."[75] Sometimes I think that for Paul, doing God's Law is a hindrance to pleasing God! And to make things even more difficult, something Paul seems to enjoy, he seems to think that sonship does not fully belong to anyone in the present when he says that, "We know that the whole creation has been groaning in travail together until now; and not only the creation, but, *we ourselves, who have the first fruits of the Spirit,* groan inwardly as we wait for adoption as sons (υἱοθεσία,) the redemption of our bodies."[76] Moreover, brothers and sisters, one wonders just what Paul really means by this innovative word, υἱοθεσία, anyway. I had already gotten the impression that physical descent plays little if any role in Paul's notion of "sonship," and his remarks shortly after the passage we are discussing confirmed this.[77] Spirit-possession surely plays a bigger role in sonship as he sees it.[78] But God's promises were to Abraham and his descendants. I know he says later that Israel remains beloved because of the patriarchs, and that might suggest that physical descent matters to Paul after all,[79] but when so many of his arguments seem to rule this out, I find it impossible to be sure what he *really* thinks.[80]

The second credit is the glory (δόξα). Just as with υἱοθεσία, we have already encountered this word in the preceding remarks to those "in Christ." Paul confidently proclaims that

> I consider that the sufferings of this present time are not worth comparing with the glory that is about to be revealed to us (τὴν μέλλουσαν δόξαν ἀποκαλυφθῆναι εἰς ἡμᾶς). For the creation waits with eager longing for the revealing of the children of God; for the creation was subjected to futility, not of its own will but by the will of him who subjected it in hope; because the creation itself will be set free from its bondage to decay and obtain the freedom of the glory of the children of God (εἰς τὴν ἐλευθερίαν τῆς δόξης τῶν τέκνων τοῦ θεοῦ).[81]

Glory, like adoption, seems to belong more to the future than the present. This is consistent with Paul's earlier remarks where he speaks of the justified as boasting in the hope of the glory of God.[82] And yet, just as with the adoption as sons, those who are justified appear already to enjoy a taste of glory: "And those whom he justified he also glorified" (ἐδόξασεν).[83] Does Paul think that unrepentant Israelites also enjoy a taste of this glory? I do not think so, oddly enough because the glory to which he refers is intimately related to the third and fourth credits — the covenants (αἱ διαθῆκαι)

---

75. Rom 4:14.
76. Rom 8:28.
77. Rom 9:6–13.
78. Rom 8:14.
79. Rom 11:28.
80. "SIMEON:...Paul is being ironic when he says, 'To the Jew first.' He is mocking the election of Israel'" (Cosgrove, *Elusive Israel*, 5).
81. Rom 8:18–21.
82. Rom 5:2.
83. Rom 8:30.

and the giving of the Law (ἡ νομοθεσία).[84] Brothers and sisters, I have heard gossip that Paul has said some very disturbing things on these subjects in the past. This gossip was so incredible that I did not assume it was true, but it certainly helps to make sense of what Paul says in this letter. I have heard he actually thinks there are two covenants, an old and a new.[85] Paul contrasts the new covenant of which he and his associates are ministers with the old covenant of which Moses was the minister and even goes so far as to hint that Moses tried to hide the fact that his covenant was not salvific and only temporary. In terms of glory, the ministry of justification, the ministry of the new covenant, has so far surpassed the ministry of condemnation, the ministry of the old covenant, that the latter has been totally disempowered. This makes it difficult for me to imagine that Paul really highly regards "the giving of the Law," or that he believes that "the glory" still belongs to the Israelites. Indeed, this gossip also helps make sense of much of Paul's ambiguous words about the Law up to this point. The covenants may belong to the Israelites, but the old one is now worthless, and the benefits of the new one can only be enjoyed if we forsake the old.[86]

The fifth asset is the worship or the cult (ἡ λατρεία). Near the beginning of his letter Paul used the verb λατρεύω: "For God is my witness, whom I worship/serve (λατρεύω) in my spirit in the gospel of his Son, that without ceasing I remember you always in my prayers."[87] This is not surprising since I have heard that Paul calls those "in Christ" God's temple because God's Spirit dwells in them.[88] What does this imply about the temple in Jerusalem? We should not too quickly pass over Paul's connection of worship/service with Spirit. Paul must assume that it is the Spirit which is lacking in the worship/cult of Israel.[89] One must seriously wonder whether Paul really believes that true worship, worship in the Spirit of God, can take place any "place" but "in Christ."[90]

---

84. 2 Cor 3:5–14 is an extensive discussion of precisely these terms and subjects, i.e., glory, covenants, and the giving of the Law. As discussed in chapter three above, much is disputed about this passage, including several aspects of translation, but here I wish only to call attention to what is painfully obvious and relevant to the present discussion. Sandwiched between the two covenants, "old" in v. 6 and "new" in v. 14, is an abundance of "glory" (δόξα occurs 10 times in various forms), but all this glory now belongs to the new covenant.

85. Of course, Simeon knows that Paul might well be thinking only of scriptural covenants here, but with polemical intent he uses this occurrence of the plural where a singular might have been expected — and is found in important manuscripts — to bring up some damaging gossip he has heard.

86. Cf. Acts 21:21.

87. Rom 1:9.

88. "Do you not know that you are God's temple and that God's Spirit dwells in you? If any one destroys God's temple, God will destroy him. For God's temple is holy, and that temple you are" (1 Cor 3:16–17; cf. 6:19). A similar thought is expressed in 2 Cor 6:16, though the authenticity of 6:14–7:1 is doubtful: "We are the temple of the living God." This concept also gets developed in the deuteropauline Eph 2:19–22.

89. Cf. Phil 3:3: "We are the circumcision, who worship in the Spirit of God (οἱ πνεύματι θεοῦ λατρεύοντες), and boast in Christ Jesus, and put no trust in the flesh."

90. Similarly, Simeon does not believe that Paul thinks God's Spirit is found in the synagogue (Cosgrove, *Elusive Israel*, 4). Cf. Hays's remarks (*First Corinthians*, 57) on Paul's "audacity" in "decentering the sacred space of Judaism."

The "promises" (αἱ ἐπαγγελίαι) are the sixth asset on Paul's list. Yet again, Paul has already addressed this subject in his letter.

> The promise to Abraham and his descendants, that they should inherit the world, did not come through the Law but through the righteousness of faith. If it is the adherents of the Law who are to be the heirs, faith is null and the promise is void.[91]

Even at this early point in his letter, Paul states premises that can lead only to the conclusion he will later draw: God has rejected Israel.[92] Yes, my brothers and sisters, I know he vehemently denies this conclusion, but his ensuing explanation reinforces his earlier remarks to the effect that the true Israel has always been a small minority of the Israelites. Since faith cannot be null and the promise void, the adherents of the Law, Israel, cannot be the heirs (κληρονόμοι). They are therefore not true descendants of Abraham, but children of the flesh, just as he says.[93] They cannot be Abraham's children nor God's inheritance (κληρονομία). In fact, it is rumored that in another of Paul's letters he implies that Israelites as a group have *never* been the recipients of the promise, they have *never* been God's inheritance. Instead, the Law "was added because of transgressions, *till the descendant should come to whom the promise had been made.*"[94] We have already seen that Paul separates the promise of inheritance from the Law in our letter.[95] But here Paul goes further and gives another rationale for the existence of the Law. What I want to call attention to is not the rationale itself, a subject on which it seems that Paul is especially confused, but rather his consistent assumption that the Law is a temporary measure until "the descendant should come to whom the promise had been made." We should not pass over this revealing remark too quickly. The dreadful implication is that physical birth has *nothing* to do with determining the true descendants of Abraham. It *never* has. The descendant to whom the promise pertained was Christ. And he is "the *firstborn* within a large family."[96] Those who are "in Christ" are the "heirs," "fellow heirs (συγκληρονόμοι) with Christ."[97] The *many* descendants promised to Abraham *did not exist* until Christ.[98] Does Paul *really* believe that the promises belong to Israel? It would seem they belong to Christ and his fellow heirs, whether Jew or Gentile, in a new Israel.[99] All of this severely complicates his declaration that God has not rejected

---

91. Rom 4:13–14; cf. Gal 3:18.

92. Rom 11:15. Our "weak" reader is not impressed by Paul's proofs in 11:1–6 that God has not rejected Israel. This remnant Israel looks all too much like a mere ingredient in a new Israel made up of Jews and Gentiles he sees Paul setting forth in 9:22–24.

93. Rom 9:8.

94. Gal 3:19. With Rom 4:13–14 cf. Gal 3:18.

95. Rom 4:13–14.

96. Rom 8:29.

97. Rom 8:17.

98. Unlike so many of our weak reader's interpretations, this reading will not be confirmed. It will only be disconfirmed (9:6–12). This is one offense in Paul's past rhetoric on Judaism that he will not risk repeating.

99. This reading would seem to be confirmed in 9:22–24, but then disconfirmed in 11:13–25. Cosgrove's Gentile Christian Chariton understands Paul to be constituting a new Israel made up of believing Jews and Gentiles (*Elusive Israel*, 8–9).

his people.[100] What does he *really* mean? Paul clearly assumes that "the rest" of Israel apart from the "remnant" are rejected at least at the present time.[101] Does he think this situation will change some day so that "all Israel will be saved" can really mean what one might expect it to mean, or is he speaking of this new Israel? Who knows?[102]

But surely "the patriarchs" are a genuine credit in Paul's opinion. Not really. It is *the* patriarch, Abraham, that binds Paul's discussion of several of the preceding matters together.[103] Paul wants to make Abraham the universal father of both the uncircumcised and the circumcised, "the father of us all."[104] Therefore, the promise to Abraham and his descendents is not through the Law, but faith.[105] Indeed, Abraham, the first "believer" in the gospel, was "justified by faith."[106] I have heard that in another of his letters Paul turns the story of Abraham, Hagar, and Sarah into an allegory in which Ishmael was born of Hagar "according to the flesh" while Isaac was born of Sarah "according to the Spirit." Paul has the audacity to say that present day Jerusalem and her children correspond to Hagar the slave who bears children for slavery, while those born "according to the Spirit," those born "through the promise," are like Isaac, "children of promise."[107] It is hard not to suspect that Paul's *real* opinion on Abraham,

---

100. Rom 11:1–2.

101. "SIMEON: Yes, I agree. Paul is one of those fanatical seers who say that the nation will perish but the elect will be saved" (Cosgrove, *Elusive Israel*, 9). But I would hasten to suggest to Simeon that perhaps Paul thinks they are paradoxically rejected and not rejected at the same time. See Mark D. Given, "Restoring Paul's Inheritance in Romans 11:1," *JBL* 118.1 (1999): 95–96.

102. And, consequently, readers will continue to debate this question for twenty centuries. Such irresolvable ambiguity is the crux of Cosgrove's *Elusive Israel*.

103. On early Christian polemical use of Abraham traditions, see Jeffrey S. Siker, *Disinheriting the Jews: Abraham in Early Christian Controversy* (Louisville: Westminster John Knox, 1991).

104. Rom 4:11–12, 16.

105. Rom 4:13.

106. Rom 4:3–5, 9–13, 16, 20–25. Simeon would not be surprised to learn that Paul once wrote that "Just as Abraham 'believed God, and it was reckoned to him as righteousness,' know therefore that they which are of faith, *these* are the children of Abraham. And the Scripture, foreseeing that God would justify the Gentiles by faith, *declared the gospel beforehand* (προευηγγελίσατο) to Abraham, saying, 'All the Gentiles shall be blessed in you.' For this reason, *those who believe* are blessed with Abraham who believed" (Gal 3:6–9).

107. It is intriguing to watch interpreters avoid the implications of this unfortunate allegory. The attempt to limit Paul's apparent excoriation of the old covenant and Judaism *per se* to only the Christian Judaizers who were troubling his Galatian congregation is admirable, of course, but nonetheless apologetically motivated. Betz has stated the situation much more accurately: "in Galatians there is no room or possibility for an eschatological salvation of Judaism as in Rom 11:25–32.... According to Galatians, Judaism is excluded from salvation altogether, so that the Galatians have to choose between Paul and Judaism" (*Galatians*, 251). While arguing strenuously that Paul has Christian Judaizers, not Jews, in mind in this allegory, that "Paul is far from launching a comprehensive attack against Judaism," and that here "it is a grave mistake to speak of a polemic against Judaism itself," even Martyn must still grant that "We may say that Judaism stands somewhere in the *background*, not least because other passages show Paul's firm conviction that the Law is *everywhere* impotent to curb the enslaving power of the Evil Impulse and Sin (e.g. Gal 5:16–18; Rom 3:9; see chapter 15 below)" ("The Covenants of Hagar and Sarah: Two Covenants and Two Gentile Missions," *Theological Issues*, 205, italics his).

true descent, promise, and inheritance is that "... if you belong to Christ, then you are the offspring of Abraham, heirs according to the promise."[108]

Paul saves what would appear to be the greatest asset of all for last. Just as he said at the beginning of his letter, from the Israelites, according to the flesh, comes the Christ.[109] But "according to the flesh" seems to be loaded language in Pauline parlance. Yet again, we have encountered Paul's terminology in the immediately preceding passages. He uses the term "flesh" seventeen times in the preceding discussion.[110] As is well known, Paul likes to contrast spirit with the flesh.[111] Without exception, what falls under the fleshly category is ultimately worthless, often an evil hindrance.[112] In fact, I have heard that Paul has little interest in knowing Christ "according to the flesh."[113] Therefore, to say that the Messiah, according to the flesh, comes from the Israelites, is not exactly a compliment coming from Paul.

Brothers and sisters we must be very cautious about accepting this "apostle" among us. As I have noted, he does eventually say some surprising things about the subjects we have been discussing, the revelation of a "mystery" that makes much of his words and deeds mean virtually the opposite of what they appear to mean! Who would have guessed that Paul thinks the purpose of his largely Gentile ministry is to make Israel jealous and save them? Who would have guessed that Paul thinks "all Israel will be saved" in the end? But if Paul is this ambiguous, how will we know when he is telling us what he *really* thinks? Will he be content to let us continue to observe our "weak" customs, or will he cunningly insinuate his "strong" opinions in his famously cunning ways?

---

108. Gal 3:29.

109. Cf. Rom 1:3.

110. In Rom 7 and 8, that is.

111. But scholars still often fail to recognize just how Greek Paul really is on this subject. In his discussion of spirit and flesh in Paul, Daniel Boyarin comes close to this recognition (Daniel Boyarin, "Paul and the Genealogy of Gender," *Representations* 41 [Winter, 1993]: 1–33). But even though he recognizes the strong inherent devaluation of the body in Paul's anthropology, he is still influenced by traditional Christian views when he says of 2 Cor 5:1–4 that Paul "polemicizes here against those who deny resurrection in the flesh" (5). This reading of 2 Cor 5:1–4 is contradicted by 1 Cor 15:50: "What I am saying, brothers and sisters, is this: flesh and blood cannot inherit the kingdom of God, nor does the perishable inherit the imperishable." For a significant advance in the understanding of the issue see Martin, *The Corinthian Body*, 123–29.

112. For its ultimate worthlessness see Rom 2:28; 1 Cor 5:5; Gal 3:3; Phil 3:3–7; for its aspect as an evil hindrance see Rom 7:18, 25; 8:3–13; 13:14; 1 Cor 3:1–3; 15:50; Gal 5:16–17, 19–21, 24.

113. "From now on, therefore, we regard no one according to the flesh; even though we once knew Christ according to the flesh, we no longer know him that way" (2 Cor 5:16). Obviously this reader understands Paul's denigration of the flesh in this case in such a way as to suggest that Paul's epistemology was not all that different from that of the Corinthian spiritualist enthusiasts. A fleshly/sensory way of knowing is being contrasted with a spiritual/ mystical way of knowing. Martyn believes that while such an interpretation of 2 Cor 5:16 is not totally incorrect, Paul was rather trying to emphasize that "knowing by the Spirit can occur only in the form of knowing by the power of the cross. For until the parousia, the cross is and remains the epistemological crisis, and thus the norm by which one knows that the Spirit is none other than the Spirit of the crucified Christ" ("Epistemology at the Turn of the Ages" in *Theological Issues*, 108).

Reader Response

Because of Paul's views expressed in other situations, and more significantly, earlier within Romans itself, he lacks credibility with Judaistic Christians like Simeon when he tries to give the Israelites, the faithful adherents of historical Judaism, their due. I do not think Paul is insincere in Rom 9:1–3, but the "I" of verses 1–3 both is and is not I. It is an "I" that is being re-constituted, re-defined, and re-presented, a transitional "I," one in transit to Jerusalem we might say. Here, as in so many other ways, Romans is to some extent the re-formation of Paul. Whether Paul was truly reformed, however, would have been, and will probably remain, obscured by Paul's True rhetoric.

4. Is "You" You in Romans 14:1–15:13?

One of the fundamental issues of the Romans debate is whether Romans is decisively different from the other undisputed Pauline epistles with respect to a pastoral purpose. To state the issue in commonly used but overly simplistic terms, is Paul writing mostly for his own benefit and to deal with his own problems, or is he writing mostly for the Romans' benefit and to help them with their problems? The answer is probably both/and. After giving his own statement of this issue at the beginning of the article, "False Presuppositions in the Study of Romans," Karl Donfried takes a strong stand on it with his "Methodological Principle I":

> Any study of Romans should proceed on the initial assumption that this letter was written by Paul to deal with a concrete situation in Rome. The support for such an assumption is the fact that every other authentic Pauline writing, *without exception,* is addressed to the specific situations of the churches or persons involved. To argue that Romans is an exception to this Pauline pattern is certainly possible, but the burden of proof rests with those exegetes who wish to demonstrate that it is impossible, or at least not likely, that Romans addresses a concrete set of problems in the life of Christians in Rome.[114]

Donfried's "Methodological Principle II," which states that we should assume that Romans 16 is an integral part of the letter, would appear to make such a counter-demonstration more difficult. If Paul has many friends and acquaintances in Rome already, surely it is likely that he knows a fair amount about the Roman church's situation.

Donfried's "False Presuppositions" first appeared in the 1977 edition of *The Romans Debate,* and despite Karris's critique of the "history of religions" approach to Rom 14:1–15:3 and of Donfried's principle num-

---

114. Donfried, "False Presuppositions in the Study of Romans," in *The Romans Debate,* 103–4.

ber one,[115] by the time the 1991 edition appeared Donfried could claim confidently that

> Without question a consensus has been reached that Romans is addressed to the Christian community in Rome which finds itself in a particular historical situation. How that historical situation is described varies, but many would point to the polarized house-churches as being a key factor leading to turmoil among the Christians in that metropolis. One major component contributing to this polarization are the varying degrees of Christian attachment to Judaism and the attitudes which such dependence/independence fostered among the various groups toward each other.[116]

I agree that varying degrees of Christian attachment to Judaism in Rome is an important factor of which Paul is well aware while writing Romans, but I remain convinced by Günther Bornkamm's observations concerning the rather generic quality of Paul's parenesis in Romans.[117] If Paul is addressing actual problems between hostile groups in Rome, whatever they may be, he has chosen to do it too subtly.[118] The difficulty in defining the number and character of such groups testifies to the fact. Paul certainly could have been far more explicit about his knowledge of such problems even if he did not want to appear to be asserting his authority too strongly. But Bornkamm's explanation also has problems. He partly explains the generality of Paul's remarks by rejecting chapter 16 as originally a part of Romans, a position that has grown less popular.[119] And while Bornkamm rightly reaffirms the position that Romans is a letter of "self-introduction," he really offers no reason at all for the peculiar qualities of this introduction. True enough, Romans became Paul's last will and testimony, but Bornkamm himself insists that Paul did not intend it this way. Perhaps Bornkamm is still somewhat influenced by the classic "compendium of Christian doctrine" position. The impression I get of Paul from Bornkamm is of a man who might write mostly for the sake of gathering his thoughts, reflecting on past experiences, and reformulating past positions. This image is not to be rejected totally, however, especially when one remembers Paul's upcoming visit to Jerusalem, the hard questions he had faced there in the past, and the controversy his

---

115. Robert J. Karris, "Romans 14:1–15:3 and the Occasion of Romans," in *The Romans Debate*, 65–84; "The Occasion of Romans: A Response to Professor Donfried," in *The Romans Debate*, 125–27.

116. Donfried, *The Romans Debate*, lxix.

117. Bornkamm, "The Letter to the Romans as Paul's Last Will and Testament," in *The Romans Debate*, 16–28, esp. 22–24.

118. And contrary to Donfried's ("False Presuppositions," 104–6) far-reaching claims about what Wolfgang Wiefel's article ("The Jewish Community in Ancient Rome and the Origins of Roman Christianity," in *The Romans Debate*, 85–101) on the origins of Roman Christianity adds to our knowledge of the *Sitz im Leben* of Romans, the fact is that our primary evidence for a church conflict in Rome remains Romans itself.

119. See above, p. 143, n. 5.

reappearance would almost certainly cause.[120] Surely such matters must have occupied his thoughts frequently around the time he wrote Romans and motivated considerable reflection and reformulation. But precisely because Romans was not intended to be Paul's last will and testament, because he does anticipate further missionary efforts and hopes for Roman support, one must suspect that the peculiar contents of Romans are indeed tailored to the audience Paul faces in Rome. But if we have no real evidence of conflict in the Roman churches, why does Paul write passages that warn "you" Gentiles against arrogant Gentile-boasting over Jews (11:13, 18, 25) and that enjoin "we/you" strong, to be patient, accommodating, and non-judgmental toward the weak (14:4, 10; 15:1). In each case, is the "you" *you?* Does Paul mean to address the particular Gentiles and strong in Rome, or do these statements function some other way?

Here again the answer probably lies in Paul's past and his own reputation in such matters. If the audience in Rome is as described earlier in this chapter, *the most important thing rhetorically is that Paul be heard saying these sorts of things.* Through some rather generalized parenesis, a sample of the kinds of things he teaches, Paul wants to re-present his own stance toward the Jewish people and various ritualistic customs practiced by believers whose personal piety is still strongly influenced by Judaism. The reason for this strategy is probably that Paul knows that a significant number of the Gentile Christians in Rome, not to mention a Jewish-Christian minority, are precisely of this type.

Perhaps also a radical minority Pauline faction in the Roman church, radical Paulinists who display a callous attitude toward Judaism and a negative attitude toward the Law, is already arousing suspicions among the less emancipated brothers and sisters. Maybe Paul thinks that some of his own converts and other radicals who would justify their antinomian position by appealing to Paul need to hear what he *now* has to say on these issues, a message that would sound rather different from what they had heard from or about him in the past.[121] But even if this is the case, the function of Paul's remarks remains the same: to make a good impression, if at all possible, on the more Judaistic elements in the Roman congregations, both Jewish and Gentile, through repudiating such attitudes. But one wonders how a "strong" reader might have responded to his efforts.

This strong reader is not to be imagined as sharing his thoughts on Paul's True intentions with the entire congregation. Instead, he speaks to a private

---

120. Adequate treatments of the purpose and occasion of Romans always include a variety of factors. For fine essay-length treatments see F. F. Bruce, "The Romans Debate — Continued," in *The Romans Debate,* and Paul W. Meyer, "Romans," in *Harper's Bible Commentary* (ed. James L. Mays; San Francisco: Harper & Row, 1988). A good book length treatment is A. J. M. Wedderburn, *The Reasons for Romans* (Studies of the New Testament and Its World; Edinburgh: T. & T. Clark, 1988).

121. Cf. the similar suggestion by Mark D. Nanos, *The Mystery of Romans: The Jewish Context of Paul's Letter* (Minneapolis: Fortress, 1996), 128–29, n. 113.

gathering of the more sophisticated members. He does not think that what Paul really means is ever likely to be understood or appreciated by "weaker" Christians which for him include not only Jewish Christians like Simeon and Reuben, but even Gentiles like Chariton as well. Let us call him Marcion.

Marcion's "Strong" Reading of Romans 14:1–15:13

Brothers and sisters,

While I am glad to see that our brother Paul still includes himself among "we strong," his injunctions to us not to pass judgment on the "weak" are quite puzzling.[122] Has Paul changed his mind about the dangers "weak" practices pose? If Paul really feels that Law observance exposes one to possible deception by Sin through the Law,[123] can he really be content to promote a rather Epicurean-sounding moral epistemology in which "nothing is unclean in itself, but it is unclean for anyone who thinks it unclean,"[124] and in which all that matters about considering some days more special than others is that "everyone be fully convinced in his own mind"?[125] This is worlds away from his famous argument with Cephas that "walking straight with the truth of the gospel" requires full commensality of Jew and Gentile,[126] and his horror when he found out that the Galatians were adopting calendrical observance.[127] One might almost suspect that someone had tampered with Paul's letter to us.

Furthermore, these injunctions concerning the "weak" remind me of what he said earlier to "you Gentiles."[128] But who is Paul to warn us against arrogance and conceit where Israel is concerned? Paul himself admits that he "glorifies" his ministry to the Gentiles to make some of his fellow Jews jealous.[129] What can this mean but that he wants Jews to think that many Gentiles and a few Jews are now the true Israel? And even if this is not what he really means, is it not inevitable that many Gentiles will draw this conclusion?

Brothers and sisters, I suspect that Paul is saying these things less to warn "us" about the dangers of such thinking, than to reassure the "weak" that he himself does not mean to encourage it.[130] At first I was quite amazed at how different what Paul writes about the Law and believers who continue to practice it is from what we have heard him say in the past. But let us not forget the veiled way he often expresses his views. This is his way wherever he goes, being "all things to everyone," including the "weak," that he might "by all means save some."[131] It is fascinating to watch Paul carry out this strategy in this letter. For example, we see him make such uncharacteristic

---

122. Rom 15:1; 14:4, 10.
123. Rom 7:7–11.
124. Rom 14:14.
125. Rom 14:5.
126. Gal 2:14.
127. Gal 4:10. See discussion above, pp. 115–16.
128. Rom 11:13–25.
129. Rom 11:13–14.
130. My "strong" reader resembles Cosgrove's Chariton where Law observance is concerned (*Elusive Israel*, 12).
131. 1Cor 9:22.

statements as that it is "the doers of the Law who will be justified," that Jews have great advantages, and that circumcision is valuable in every way, but also make such characteristic statements as that "no one will be justified in his sight by works of the Law," that Jews are not any better off at all, and that circumcision is in spirit, not letter.[132] It seems that Paul has encoded this letter with double meanings that only we "strong" can fully decipher. Take his statement that circumcision is "in spirit, not letter" (ἐν πνεύματι οὐ γράμματι) for example. Some of our less sophisticated members simply think he means that circumcision is metaphorical, not literal. But we can see that he also means that true circumcision exists only in the realm of the Spirit, not the realm of the letter, that is, not where the Law is still observed.[133] As Paul is so fond of saying in his conflicts with Judaizers, "we are the true circumcision, who worship God in Spirit, and glory in Christ Jesus, and put no confidence in the flesh."[134]

If we will only read closely enough, much of what Paul says in this letter is already familiar to us and precisely what we would have expected. No one who knows what Paul *really* thinks about the Law could possibly believe that he would be content to allow the "weak" to stay "weak *in faith*."[135] Their continued observance of the Law makes them not only a danger to themselves but also to others. Even if they have not yet stumbled,[136] as long as they continue to practice it, there is always the danger that they will fall back into pursuing righteousness as if it were by works of the Law,[137] and possibly lead others down the wrong path as well. This is why one must not admit the "weak" into our diacritical dialogues.[138]

I must conclude that Paul simply does not consider us competent to undertake the reform of the "weak." He enjoins us all to tolerate and accept one another so that there will be as little animosity and mistrust as possible when he arrives among us. Then he will, in his incomparably sophisticated way, gently and gradually "save" the weak, at first conforming to their weaknesses as he does in this letter, but then slowly and gently initiating them into the Truth.[139]

---

132. With Rom 2:13 cf. 3:20; with 3:1a cf. 3:9; with 3:1b cf. 3:28–29.

133. Cf. the NASB ("by the Spirit, not by the letter") and NKJV ("in the Spirit, not in the letter").

134. Phil 3:3.

135. Nanos would say this "strong" reader has fallen into "Luther's Trap," the tendency of many commentators to acknowledge Paul's call not to judge the weak, but then do precisely that in the name of Paul (*The Mystery of Romans*, 91–92).

136. The "strong" reader assumes that for Paul to call them "weak *in faith*," they must at least presently understand that the source of their righteousness is faith in Christ, not their observance of customs. In passing, notice that this terminology, "weak in faith," is in itself a devastating blow to Nanos's hypothesis that the "weak" of Rom 14–15 are non-Christian Jews (*The Mystery of Romans*, 85–165). Faith always has an object for Paul and that object is Christ. A Jew who believes in God but not in Christ is not weak in faith but faithless/unbelieving in Paul's terminology (Rom 3:3; 11:20, 23). A second strong reason that could be given for rejecting Nanos's hypothesis is that both "strong" and "weak" are described as observing or not observing, eating or abstaining, "in honor of the Lord" in a context (14:5–9) where "the Lord" is synonymous, as it almost always is in Paul, with "Christ" (14:9). The "weak" are already Christians.

137. Rom 9:30–32a.

138. Rom 14:1.

139. See above, pp. 107–8, 115–16.

Reader Response

Marcion seems rather confident that he truly understands Paul, but Paul's attitude toward the "weak" leaves me with more questions than answers, because if Paul is indeed the sort of cunning rhetor this study has argued, how can we know what he really intends to do in this case when he reaches Rome? Would he have continued his "liberal" policy on these matters after he arrived in Rome "to preach the gospel to you" (Rom 1:15) and "win obedience from the Gentiles" (15:18)? Or is the persistence of Judaistic practices in the Roman congregations precisely why he is so "eager" to preach the gospel to them (οὕτως τὸ κατ' ἐμὲ πρόθυμον καὶ ὑμῖν τοῖς ἐν Ῥώμῃ εὐαγγελίσασθαι) (1:15)? Did Paul do an about face on the issue of reforming the "weak," or is our "Strong" reader on the right track in suspecting that Paul wants both to ingratiate himself with the "weak" and restrain the "Strong" from botching a task for which he does not consider them well suited? In most cases, a Pauline Christian at Rome would be able to read between the lines of Romans and dis-cover "how far Paul was from denying anything that he held deeply, even when he could not maintain all his convictions at once without both anguish and, finally, a lack of logic."[140] Whether that was the True reading is difficult to say. Perhaps we should conclude that on this, as well as several other topics discussed in this chapter, Romans proves to be an ambiguous success, not unlike "Paul's" dialoguing in the Agora, an ambiguous staging of both expected and unexpected arguments that might lead to an invitation to speak not on Mars hill this time, but on the seven hills of Rome.

> This is not to deny that we have made progress in our historical understanding of the Bible. There have, in fact, been enormous advances, especially over the last 150 years. But those advances include not only historical clarification of what the various biblical writings (and traditions) originally meant but also mounting evidence that many questions of exegesis cannot be historically resolved, because the texts themselves are irreducibly ambiguous. This is a momentous learning, and one that is just beginning to receive the attention it deserves.[141]

---

140. Sanders, *Paul, the Law, and the Jewish People*, 199.
141. Cosgrove, *Elusive Israel*, xii.

V

Reel Paul

The sophist is also a master at interweaving for he is constantly entangling two contrary theses. Like Zeno of Elea, who is a true Palamedes, he speaks with such skill that he is able to convince his audience that the same things are now similar to each other and now dissimilar, now single and now multiple. Speeches interwoven like this are traps, *strephómena*, as are the puzzles set by the gods of metis, which the Greeks call *grîphoi* which is also the name given to some types of fishing nets. With their twisting, flexing, interweaving and bending, both athletes and sophists — just like the fox and the octopus — can be seen as living bonds.

— Detienne and Vernant, *Cunning Intelligence*, 42

Circumcision is nothing, and uncircumcision is nothing; but obeying the commandments of God is everything (1 Cor 7:19; NRSV).[1]

---

1. "The degree to which he could change the content of the law, while still saying that it should be kept, is strikingly clear in 1 Cor. 7:19, which I regard as one of the most amazing sentences that he ever wrote..." (Sanders, *Paul, the Law, and the Jewish People*, 103).

1. Peroration

The words *real* and *really* have been used with increasing frequency in the last two chapters. If my thesis has proven at all convincing, the need to resort regularly to this terminology while reading Paul should now be clear. Because of "Paul's sincere conviction that he knew the Truth and had a divine mandate to promote it in an apocalyptic world filled with deception" we can hardly be surprised that "his rhetorical strategies are not always irreproachable when judged by philosophical rhetorical ideals."[2] The real Paul — the *réel* Paul — is the reel Paul, the fisher of ignorant and deceived humanity, who keeps his audience reeling as he enmeshes them in a net woven of ambiguous, cunning, and deceptive words.

> As far back as one can trace it, the terminology of *mētis* associates it with techniques whose relationship to hunting and fishing is obvious. A *mētis* or a *dólos* is woven, plaited or fitted together (*hupháinein, plékein, tektaínesthai*) just as a net is woven, a weel is plaited or a hunting trap is fitted together. All these terms relate to very ancient techniques that use the pliability and torsion of plant fibres to make knots, ropes, meshes and nets to surprise, trap and bind and that exploit the fact that the many pieces can be fitted together to produce a well-articulated whole.[3]

In Paul's case, however, the goal is not to prey on the fish, but to *transfer* them from murky and ultimately deadly waters to living salvific waters where they may see their former habitat for what it was.[4]

To reiterate, in chapter one, after surveying some Pauline scholarship that proves that Paul not only had some rhetorical training but also was aware of the supposed difference between philosophical and sophistical rhetoric,[5] I surveyed some classical scholarship that proves that an absolute distinction between a philosophic rhetoric of truth (ἀλήθεια) and a sophistic rhetoric of fabrication (φαντασία) was already compromised at the source in the rhetoric of Plato's Socrates.[6] The "truth" is that Plato's Socrates and Aristotle, each in their own way, contributed to the development of what could be called a True rhetoric, an ironic rhetoric that quite intentionally conceals and reveals meaning simultaneously.[7] Galvanized by a metaphysically grounded epistemological confidence and a corresponding mistrust of the phenomenal world, True rhetoric freely makes use of ambiguity, cunning, and deception, rhetorical strategies usually associated with sophistry, in order to deceive the deceived and lead them — at least some of them — to the Truth.[8] In

---

2. See
3. Det   *unning Intelligence*, 45–46.
4. The   refully chosen and overdetermined (see Sanders, *Paul, the Law, and the Jew*
5. See
6. See
7. See
8. See

a Platonic-Socratic worldview, the ignorance from which humanity suffers results from the elusive and changing nature of the sphere of becoming, but in Paul's apocalyptic worldview, the deceptive character of existence in "this world" is even more acute because "the god of this world" is himself a diabolically clever sophist.[9] The rhetorical result is a Truly Socratic Paul, one who uses a True rhetoric of ambiguity, cunning, and deception to infiltrate a world of ambiguity, cunning, and deception; a Paul who mimes and models the forms or "elements" of this world, but with a parodic and devious difference.[10]

Chapter two argued that Luke presented Paul as precisely this sort of cunning and deceptive orator through his Socratic exploitation of ambiguity.[11] In the process, I tried to deepen our appreciation of the at once profoundly Hellenistic and Jewish aspects of Luke's "tragic" production of Paul in Athens. The chapter concluded with a brief glance at the difference between Luke's portrayal of Paul and other characters in court.[12] Unlike everyone else in his narrative, Paul is not only like a new Socrates before philosophers, but also like a slippery sophist before the Sanhedrin.

Chapter three shifted the focus to the "real" Paul. After attempting to clarify what to some readers might appear to be a curious combination of historical-critical and deconstructive approaches in my work,[13] I then sought to increase our awareness of Paul's cunning in Corinth by challenging recent readings that have the intended or unintended effect of containing cunning in 1 Cor 1–4,[14] domesticating deception in 1 Cor 9:19–23,[15] and avoiding ambiguity in 2 Cor 2:14–4:6.[16] In my discussion of 1 Cor 9:19–23, I suggested that since Paul considered unconverted Jews, Gentiles, and even the "weak" subject to demonic deception, he felt free to resort to a little divine deception of his own to "gain/save" them.[17] The chapter concluded with a discussion of "apocalyptic logocentrism," an exceptionally strong form of logocentrism that virtually assured that Paul would privilege Spirit and speech over flesh and writing.[18] Thus "faith comes through hearing." I concluded that Paul is often more cunning than many interpreters care to admit, and that apocalyptic logocentrism goes a long way toward explaining Paul's strained, often critical, and sometimes quite negative attitude toward the Law.[19]

1   –37.
1   –77.
1   –81.
1.   –90.
1   –103.
1   3–17.
1   8–26.
        5–17.
        .6–36.
19. See above, pp. 136–37.

Chapter four attempted to bring many of the perspectives of the previous chapters to bear on Paul's rather ambiguous and cunning attempt to address actual and/or potential deception in Rome — Judaistic forms of Christianity. An awareness of Paul's apocalyptic logocentrism adds another dimension to "the Romans debate." If Paul so strongly believes that faith comes through hearing, why does he appear to proclaim his gospel in [a] dead letter? The proposed solution is that he is not proclaiming his gospel in Romans but exploiting writing's deceptive potential to begin the process of deceiving the deceived.[20] Therefore, I concentrated on Rom 7, the NT's premier discussion of deception, and challenged a very influential reading that trivializes Paul's apocalyptic anthropology and, because of insufficient attention to the rhetorical situation of Romans, reads the chapter as an encomium on the Law.[21] I argued that this reading is not so much wrong as incomplete. Paul fully expected some of his readers to hear him this way, but he also expected some readers to detect what he was *really* saying. But, because Paul's ambiguity allowed him to express his controversial views less offensively, even some of the former readers could be subliminally influenced through *insinuatio*.[22] I then turned to Rom 9:1–5, and tried to imagine how a "weak" reader might have responded to Paul's mini-encomium of Judaism, not only in light of the sort of gossip Paul feared had already reached Rome, but also in light of Paul's ambiguous discourse concerning the Law in Romans itself.[23] Finally, I also turned to Rom 14:1–15:13 and imagined a "strong" reader's surprise and confusion over Paul's injunctions to the strong.[24] I concluded that if Romans was a success, we might best describe it as an ambiguous one, somewhat like "Paul's" Areopagus speech: " . . . some mocked, but others said, 'We will hear you again about this' " (Acts 17:32). It indeed could have been "intended for discussion by Jewish and Gentile Christians of Rome," or at least to set the agenda for a discussion that would continue and possibly take some surprising turns after Paul arrived and continued to reveal his apocalyptic "mysteries," turns about which the Romans and we today can only speculate.

2. An Apocalyptic and Rhetorical Theological Reflection

My debt to and respect for historical-critical scholarship that emphasizes the importance of Paul's apocalyptic worldview is obvious in this rhetorical work. With that debt in mind, let us listen once again to Beker, specifically to his thoughts on tensions within Paul's thought.

---

20. See above, pp. 142–47.
21. See above, pp. 147–55.
22. See above, pp. 156–59.
23. See above, pp. 159–68.
24. See above, pp. 168–73.

By "coherence" I mean the stable, constant, cohesive element.... And by "contingency" I mean the variable element....

...what I mean by coherence is the fluid and flexible structure of Paul's thought.[25]

Beker proposes "a coherence-contingency *scheme*" that would provide a *via media* between the extreme of conceiving Paul's gospel as either "a *pure* theological structure of thought"[26] or "a *purely* contingent structure."[27] This formulation is currently very influential in Pauline scholarship. We can begin to recognize why Beker's "scheme" rings so true to Paul by observing what could be considered contradictory descriptions of coherence in the excerpts provided above. Contingency is precisely what we expect — the variable element. But coherence is both stable and fluid, both constant and flexible! This apparent contradiction, however, is far from a weakness in Beker's definition. And, indeed, in a later paper we find him asking the question, "What precisely constitutes the interaction between coherence and contingency? Is it possible or even desirable to draw clear distinctions between the bipolar concepts, coherence and contingency, as if they can be compartmentalized into distinct conceptual units?"[28] The answer is no: "The *fluidity* of this interaction in Paul seems to make a proper delineation of the boundaries of the coherent and the contingent very difficult, if not impossible."[29] It seems that the longer Beker studied Paul, the more fluid he — either antecedent will do — became. *It is hardly fortuitous that such a perspective on Paul emerged from one who took Paul's apocalyptic worldview very seriously.* I hope my study has deepened our understanding of why Paul's rhetorical "fluidity" and apocalyptic worldview go hand in hand. Beker's "scheme" is a faithful reflection of Paul's *schema* as a True philosopher, and a faithful reproduction of his rhetorical net-work composed of "many pieces ... fitted together to produce a well-articulated whole."[30]

---

25. J. C. Beker, "Paul's Theology: Consistent or Inconsistent?" *NTS* 34 (1988): 368, italics mine.

26. Ibid.

27. Ibid., 367.

28. J. Christiaan Beker, "Recasting Pauline Theology: The Coherence-Contingency Scheme as Interpretive Model," in *Thessalonians, Philippians, Galatians, Philemon* (vol. 1 of *Pauline Theology*; ed. Jouette M. Bassler; Minneapolis: Fortress Press, 1991), 16.

29. Ibid., 18.

30. See above, p. 176. However, appreciation of Paul's apocalypticism does not guarantee sensitivity to his True rhetoric. For Martyn, Paul's "rhetoric" is more "revelation" than "persuasion," or, perhaps we should say, revelation than reason (see *Galatians*, 20–23). He even goes so far as to say that "in writing this letter Paul is not at all formulating an argument designed to persuade the Galatians that faith is better than observance of the Law" (23)! This is true, in a certain way, but still the rhetoric ascribed to Paul in this and similar passages sounds more neo-orthodox than Pauline. One also suspects that the false dichotomy between philosophic and sophistic rhetoric discussed above in chap. one is at work here to some extent. It is certainly controlling the distinction between Corinthian "rhetoric" and Pauline "dialectic"

Finally, Paul's True rhetoric of ambiguity, cunning, and deception has a theological dimension lacking in that of Plato.[31] Plato's Socrates teaches in the *Republic* that deception by certain privileged humans is useful and acceptable in a variety of situations, but that no one should say that God ever deceives.[32] The God of Paul, however, is not the impersonal and idealized One of Plato, but the anthropomorphic and active one of his Hebrew heritage, the kind of God who sent a *lying* spirit into the mouths of the prophets (1 Kgs 22:22–23); the kind of God whose Son, "though in the *form* of God ... emptied himself, taking on the *form* of a slave" (Phil 2:6–7); the kind of God who would *seem* to be rejecting his people, but is *really* only hardening their hearts temporarily until the full number of Gentiles come in (Rom 11:25–26).[33] How will this result in "all Israel" being saved? Surely Paul saw his own rhetorical strategy as a mimesis of his God's: "Inasmuch as I am an apostle to the Gentiles, I magnify my ministry in order to make my fellow Jews jealous, and thus save some of them" (Rom 11:13b–14).[34] How Paul would have responded to Socrates' theological question in the *Republic* is not in doubt.

Do you think that God is a wizard (γόητα) and capable of manifesting himself by design, now in one aspect, now in another, at one time himself changing and altering his shape in many transformations (τὸ αὑτοῦ εἶδος εἰς πολλὰς

in the Martyn-influenced piece by Thomas E. Boomershine, "Epistemology at the Turn of the Ages in Paul, Jesus, and Mark: Rhetoric and Dialectic in Apocalyptic and the New Testament," in *Apocalyptic and the New Testament: Essays in Honor of J. Louis Martyn* (ed. Marcus and Soards), 147–68.

31. Since Betz never really comes to terms with the level of intentional ambiguity, cunning, and deception in Paul's rhetorical strategies, his perspective on the relationship between rhetoric and theology in Paul does not include reflection upon these aspects of the God implied by them (see "The Problem of Rhetoric and Theology According to the Apostle Paul," in *L'Apôtre Paul,* ed. Vanhoye, 16–48).

32. *Republic* 382C–383C; 389B–D; 414C–415A; 459D–460A.

33. Note that the God of Paul's Hebrew heritage has far more in common with the gods of popular Greco-Roman mythology, the gods who embody the principles of *mētis* in Detienne and Vernant's *Cunning Intelligence,* than with the God of the philosophers. Cf. Chrysostom's *de laudibus sancti Pauli* 5.5, which provides the following theological precedent for Paul's conduct: "For God appeared also as a human being, when it was necessary to do so. And in ancient times he appeared as fire when times demanded it. One time he appeared in the form of an armed soldier, and at another in the image of an old man; one time in a breath of wind, at another as a traveller, another time as a true human being, one who did not reject even dying" (as translated by Mitchell, "ποικίλος τις καὶ παντοδαπός," 13).

34. Richardson also suggests that Paul may be modeling his adaptation upon a kind of divine accommodation (Peter Richardson, "Pauline Inconsistency: 1 Corinthians 9:19–23 and Galatians 2:11–14," *NTS* 26 [1980]: 347–62, especially 357–58). He does not, however, reflect upon the implications for Paul's image of God. As Mitchell points out, " ... Chrysostom also has one solution which has not as yet found modern (or post-modern) representatives: to celebrate and enjoy the variability of the apostle to the Gentiles, regarding it as yet another instance of a long-standing divine technique of accommodation. But given the current political cynicism, and also contemporary hermeneutical approaches which delight in the implosion and self-deconstruction of language, perhaps this too will be forthcoming" ("ποικίλος τις καὶ παντοδαπός," 17).

μορφάς) and at another deceiving us and causing us to believe such things about him ... ?[35]

Paul would have been banished from Plato's republic along with the poets and sophists, for Paul's apocalyptic God is Truly unsearchable and inscrutable (11:33); a mysterious, ambiguous, and finally *sophistic* God, who cares enough to be cunning and is devoted enough to be deceptive. Of that d, Paul is the True Apostle.

---

35. *Republic*, 380D. Cf. Chrysostom's remarks in n. 33 above. Paul Shorey, the Loeb translator of the *Republic*, footnotes this passage and observes that, "The two methods, (1) self-transformation, and (2) production of illusions in our minds, answer broadly to the two methods of [sophistic] deception distinguished in the *Sophist* 236c."

Bibliography

Alexander, Loveday. "Acts and Ancient Intellectual Biography." Pp. 31–63 in *Ancient Literary Setting*, Vol. 1 of *The Book of Acts in Its First Century Setting*. Edited by Winter and Clarke.

———. *The Preface to Luke's Gospel: Literary Convention and Social Context in Luke 1.1–4 and Acts 1*. Cambridge: Cambridge University Press, 1993.

Amador, J. David Hester. *Academic Constraints in Rhetorical Criticism of the New Testament: An Introduction to a Rhetoric of Power*. JSNTSup 174. Sheffield: Sheffield Academic Press, 1999.

Anderson, R. Dean. *Ancient Rhetorical Theory and Paul*. CBET 18. Kampen: Kok Pharos Publishing House, 1996.

Angus, Ian, and Lenore Langsdorf. *The Critical Turn: Rhetoric and Philosophy in Postmodern Discourse*. Carbondale: Southern Illinois University Press, 1993.

Arieti, James A. *Interpreting Plato: The Dialogues as Drama*. Savage, Md.: Rowman & Littlefield, 1991.

Atherton, Catherine. *The Stoics on Ambiguity*. Cambridge Classical Studies. Cambridge: Cambridge University Press, 1993.

Aune, David. *The New Testament in Its Literary Environment*. Philadelphia: Westminster, 1987.

———. "Romans as a *Logos Protreptikos*." Pp. 278–98 in *The Romans Debate*. Edited by Donfried.

Babcock, William S., ed. *Paul and the Legacies of Paul*. Dallas: Southern Methodist University Press, 1990.

Badenas, Robert. *Christ the End of the Law: Romans 10.4 in Pauline Perspective*. JSNTSup 10. Sheffield: Sheffield Academic Press, 1985.

Balch, David L. "The Areopagus Speech: An Appeal to the Stoic Historian Posidonius Against Later Stoics and the Epicureans." Pp. 52–79 in *Greeks, Romans, and Christians: Essays in Honor of Abraham J. Malherbe*. Edited by David L. Balch, Everett Ferguson, and Wayne Meeks.

Balch, David L., Everett Ferguson, and Wayne A. Meeks, eds. *Greeks, Romans, and Christians: Essays in Honor of Abraham J. Malherbe*. Minneapolis: Fortress, 1990.

Barr, James. *The Semantics of Biblical Language*. London: SCM, 1961.

Barrett, C. K. *The First Epistle to the Corinthians*. BNTC. Peabody, Mass.: Hendrickson, 1973.

———. *The Second Epistle to the Corinthians*. BNTC. Peabody, Mass.: Hendrickson, 1973.

Barthes, Roland. *Image-Music-Text*. New York: Noonday, 1977.

Bartsch, Shadi. *Actors in the Audience: Theatricality and Doublespeak from Nero to Hadrian.* Cambridge: Harvard University Press, 1994.

Bassler, Jouette M., ed. *Thessalonians, Philippians, Galatians, Philemon,* Vol. 1 of *Pauline Theology.* Minneapolis: Fortress Press, 1991.

Beker, J. Christiaan. *Heirs of Paul: Paul's Legacy in the New Testament and in the Church Today.* Minneapolis, Fortress, 1991.

———. *Paul the Apostle. The Triumph of God in Life and Thought.* Philadelphia: Fortress, 1984.

———. "The Faithfulness of God and the Priority of Israel in Paul's Letter to the Romans." *HTR* 79:1–3 (1986): 10–16.

———. "Paul's Theology: Consistent or Inconsistent?" *NTS* 34 (1988): 364–77.

———. "Recasting Pauline Theology: The Coherence-Contingency Scheme as Interpretive Model." Pp. 15–24 in *Thessalonians, Philippians, Galatians, Philemon.* Edited by Jouette M. Bassler.

Belleville, Linda L. *Reflections of Glory: Paul's Polemical Use of the Moses-Doxa Tradition in 2 Corinthians 3.1–18.* JSNTSup 52. Sheffield: JSOT, 1991.

Bender, John, and David E. Wellbery. *The Ends of Rhetoric: History, Theory, Practice.* Stanford, Calif.: Stanford University Press, 1990.

Benstock, Bernard, ed. *James Joyce: The Augmented Ninth. Proceedings of Ninth International James Joyce Symposium.* Syracuse: Syracuse University Press, 1988.

Betz, Hans Dieter. *Der Apostel Paulus und die socratische Tradition: Eine exegetische Untersuchung zu seiner "Apologie" 2 Korinther 10–13.* BHT 45. Tübingen: J. C. B. Mohr, 1972.

———. *Galatians.* Hermeneia. Philadelphia: Fortress, 1979.

———. "The Literary Composition and Function of Paul's Letter to the Galatians." *NTS* 21 (1975): 353–79.

———. "Paul's Apology: II Corinthians 10–13 and the Socratic Tradition." Colloquy 2. Berkeley: Center for Hermeneutical Studies in Hellenistic and Modern Culture, 1975.

———. "The Problem of Rhetoric and Theology according to the Apostle Paul." Pp. 16–48 in *L'Apôtre Paul.* Edited by A. Vanhoye.

The Bible and Culture Collective. *The Postmodern Bible.* New Haven: Yale University Press, 1995.

Bietenhard, Hans. "ὄνομα." *TDNT* 5.242–83.

Blank, David L. "Socratics Versus Sophists on Payment for Teaching." *Classical Antiquity* 4 (1985): 1–49.

Blasi, Anthony J. *Making Charisma: The Social Construction of Paul's Public Image.* New Brunswick and London: Transaction Publishers, 1991.

Bockmuehl, Markus N. A. *Revelation and Mystery in Ancient Judaism and Pauline Christianity.* Grand Rapids: Eerdmans, 1997.

Boers, H. W. "The Foundation of Paul's Thought: A Methodological Investigation: The Problem of a Coherent Center of Paul's Thought." *ST* 42 (1988): 55–68.

————. *The Justification of the Gentiles: Paul's Letters to the Galatians and Romans*. Peabody, Mass.: Hendrickson, 1994.

Bok, Sissela. *Lying: Moral Choice in Public and Private Life*. New York: Pantheon Books, 1978.

Boomershine, Thomas E. "Epistemology at the Turn of the Ages in Paul, Jesus, and Mark: Rhetoric and Dialectic in Apocalyptic and the New Testament." Pp. 147–68 in *Apocalyptic and the New Testament*. Edited by Marcus and Soards.

Bornkamm, Günther. "The Letter to the Romans as Paul's Last Will and Testament." Pp. 16–28 in *The Romans Debate*. Edited by Donfried.

————. "The Missionary Stance of Paul in 1 Corinthians 9 and in Acts." Pp. 194–207 in *Studies in Luke-Acts*. Edited by Leander E. Keck and J. Louis Martyn.

————. *Paul*. Translated by D. M. G. Stalker. New York: Harper & Row, 1971.

Bower, E. W. "'Efodo' and Insinuatio in Greek and Roman Rhetoric." *Classical Quarterly* 8 (1958): 224–30.

Bowersock, G. *Fiction as History: Nero to Julian*. Berkeley: University of California Press, 1994.

————. *Greek Sophists in the Roman Empire*. Oxford: Oxford University Press, 1969.

Boyarin, Daniel. *Intertextuality and the Reading of Midrash*. Bloomington: Indiana University Press, 1990.

————. "Paul and the Genealogy of Gender." *Representations* 41 (Winter, 1993): 1–33.

————. *A Radical Jew: Paul and the Politics of Identity*. Berkeley: University of California Press, 1994.

Brawley, Robert L. *Text to Text Pours Forth Speech: Voices of Scripture in Luke-Acts*. Bloomington and Indianapolis: Indiana University Press, 1995.

Brickhouse, Thomas C., and Nicholas D. Smith. *Plato's Socrates*. New York: Oxford University Press, 1994.

Bruce, F. F. *The Acts of the Apostles: Greek Text with Introduction and Commentary*. 3d rev. and enl. ed. Grand Rapids: Eerdmans, 1990.

————. "Is the Paul of Acts the Real Paul?" *BJRL* 58.2 (Spring 1976): 282–303.

————. "The New Testament and Classical Studies." *NTS* 22 (1976): 229–42.

————. *Paul: Apostle of the Heart Set Free*. Grand Rapids: Eerdmans, 1977.

————. "The Romans Debate — Continued." Pp. 175–94 in *The Romans Debate*. Edited by Donfried.

Bryan, C. "A Further Look at Acts 16:1–3." *JBL* 107 (1988): 292–94.

Bryant, Joseph M. *Moral Codes and Social Structure in Ancient Greece: A Sociology of Greek Ethics from Homer to the Epicureans and Stoics*. New York: State University of New York Press, 1996.

Bullmore, Michael A. *St. Paul's Theology of Rhetorical Style: An Examination of I Corinthians 2.1–5 in Light of First Century Greco-Roman Rhetorical Culture*. San Francisco: International Scholars Publications, 1995.

Bultmann, R. *Der Stil der paulinischen Predigt und die kynisch-stoische Diatribe*. FRLANT 13. Göttingen: Vandenhoeck & Ruprecht, 1910.

————. *New Testament and Mythology and other Basic Writings*. Selected, edited, and translated by Schubert M. Ogden. Philadelphia: Fortress, 1984.

————. *Theology of the New Testament*. One Volume Edition. Translated by Kendrick Grobel. New York: Charles Scribner's Sons, 1955.

Burnett, Fred W. "The Place of 'The Wisdom of God' in Paul's Proclamation of Salvation (1 Cor 2:6–16)." In *Reading Communities Reading Scripture: Essays in Honor of Daniel Patte*. Harrisburg, Pa.: Trinity Press International, forthcoming.

Buxton, R. G. A. *Persuasion in Greek Tragedy: A Study of Peitho*. Cambridge: Cambridge University Press, 1982.

Cadbury, H. J. *The Book of Acts in History*. New York: Harper & Brothers, 1955.

————. "The Greek and Jewish Traditions of Writing History." Pp. 7–29 in *The Beginnings of Christianity*, vol. 2. Edited by Jackson and Lake.

————. *The Making of Luke-Acts*. New York: Macmillan, 1927.

————. "The Speeches in Acts." Pp. 402–27 in *The Beginnings of Christianity*. Vol. 5. Edited by Jackson and Lake.

Calvin, John. *The Acts of the Apostles: 14–28*. London: Oliver and Boyd, 1966.

Cameron, Averil. *Christianity and the Rhetoric of Empire: The Development of Christian Discourse*. Berkeley: University of California Press, 1991.

Caputo, John D. *The Prayers and Tears of Jacques Derrida: Religion without Religion*. Bloomington and Indianapolis: Indiana University Press, 1997.

Cary, Christopher. "Rhetorical Means of Persuasion." Pp. 26–45 in *Persuasion*. Edited by Worthington.

Castelli, Elizabeth A. *Imitating Paul: A Discourse of Power*. Literary Currents in Biblical Interpretation. Louisville: Westminster John Knox, 1991.

Chadwick, Henry. " 'All Things to All Men' (1 Cor. IX.22)." *NTS* 1 (1955): 261–75.

————. *Early Christian Thought and the Classical Tradition*. New York: Oxford University Press, 1966.

Chau, Wai-Shing. *The Letter and the Spirit: A History of Interpretation from Origen to Luther*. American University Studies 7.167. New York: Peter Lang, 1995.

Classen, C. Joachim. "Aristotle's Picture of the Sophists." Pp. 7–24 in *The Sophists and Their Legacy*. Edited by Kerferd.

Cohen, David. "Classical Rhetoric and Modern Theories of Discourse." Pp. 69–84 in *Persuasion*. Edited by Worthington.

Cohen, S. D. "Was Timothy Jewish (Acts 16:1–3)? Patristic Exegesis, Rabbinic Law, and Matrilineal Descent." *JBL* 105 (1986): 251–68.

Cohen, Tom. *Anti-Mimesis from Plato to Hitchcock*. Cambridge: Cambridge University Press, 1994.

Colaclides, P. "Acts 17:28A and Bacchae 506," *VC* 27 (1973): 161–64.

Cole, Thomas. *The Origins of Rhetoric in Ancient Greece*. Baltimore and London: Johns Hopkins, 1991.

Collins, Raymond F. "The Unity of Paul's Paraenesis in 1 Thess. 4.3–8. 1 Cor. 7.1–7, a Significant Parallel." *NTS* 29 (1983): 420–29.

Conzelmann, Hans. "The Address of Paul on the Areopagus." Pp. 217–32 in *Studies in Luke-Acts*. Edited by Keck and Martyn.

Cosgrove, Charles H. *Elusive Israel: The Puzzle of Election in Romans*. Louisville: Westminster John Knox, 1997.

Crafton, Jeffrey A. *The Agency of the Apostle: A Dramatistic Analysis of Paul's Responses to Conflict in 2 Corinthians*. JSNTSup 51. Sheffield: Sheffield Academic Press, 1991.

Cranfield, C. E. B. *A Critical and Exegetical Commentary on The Epistle to the Romans*. 2 vols. ICC. Edinburgh: T. & T. Clark, 1975.

Crenshaw, James L., and Samuel Sandmel. *The Divine Helmsman: Studies on God's Control of Human Events, Presented to Lou H. Silberman*. New York: KTAV, 1980.

Culler, Jonathan. *Framing the Sign: Criticism and Its Institutions*. Norman and London: University of Oklahoma Press, 1988.

———. *On Deconstruction: Theory and Criticism after Structuralism*. Ithaca: Cornell University Press, 1982.

Dahl, N. A. "Paul and the Church at Corinth in 1 Cor. 1:10–4:21." Pp. 313–36 in *Christian History and Interpretation: Studies Presented to John Knox*. Edited by Farmer, Moule, and Niebuhr.

———. *Studies in Paul: Theology for the Early Christian Mission*. Minneapolis: Augsburg, 1977.

Darr, John A. *On Character Building: The Reader and the Rhetoric of Characterization in Luke-Acts*. Louisville: Westminster John Knox, 1992.

Dawsey, James M. "The Literary Unity of Luke-Acts: Questions of Style — a Task for Literary Critics." *NTS* 35 (1989): 48–66.

———. *The Lukan Voice: Confusion and Irony in the Gospel of Luke*. Macon: Mercer University Press, 1986.

Deissmann, Adolf. *Paul. A Study in Social and Religious History*. 2d ed. Translated by William I. Wilson. New York: Harper & Bros., 1957.

De Rijk, L. M. *Plato's Sophist: A Philosophical Commentary*. Amsterdam: North-Holland Publishing Company, 1986.

Derrida, Jacques. *Acts of Literature*. Edited by Derek Attridge. New York: Routledge, 1992.

———. *Dissemination*. Translated with an Introduction and Additional Notes by Barbara Johnson. Chicago: The University of Chicago Press, 1981.

———. "Hear Say Yes in Joyce." Pp. 27–75 in *James Joyce*. Edited by Benstock.

———. *Limited Inc*. Evanston: Northwestern University Press, 1988.

———. *Margins of Philosophy*. Translated with Additional Notes by Alan Bass. Chicago: University of Chicago Press, 1982.

———. *Of Grammatology*. Translated by Gayatri Chakravorty Spivak. Baltimore: The Johns Hopkins University Press, 1974.

———. "Plato's Pharmacy." Pp. 61–172 in *Dissemination*.

———. *Positions*. Translated and Annotated by Alan Bass. Chicago: The University of Chicago Press, 1981.

————. *The Post Card: From Socrates to Freud and Beyond.* Translated with an Introduction and Additional Notes by Alan Bass. Chicago: University of Chicago Press, 1987.

————. *Writing and Difference.* Translated with an Introduction and Additional Notes by Alan Bass. Chicago: University of Chicago Press, 1978.

Detienne, Marcel, and Jean-Pierre Vernant. *Cunning Intelligence in Greek Culture and Society.* Chicago: University of Chicago Press, 1991.

Dewey, Arthur J. "A Matter of Honor: A Social-Historical Analysis of 2 Corinthians 10." *HTR* 78 (1985): 211–17.

————. *Spirit and Letter in Paul.* Studies in the Bible and Early Christianity 33. Lewiston, N.Y.: Mellen, 1996.

DeWitt, Norman Wentworth. *St. Paul and Epicurus.* Minneapolis: University of Minnesota Press, 1954.

Dibelius, Martin. *Paul.* Edited and completed by Werner Georg Kummel. Translated by Frank Clarke. London: Longmans, Green, 1953.

————. *Studies in the Acts of the Apostles.* Edited by Heinrich Greeven. Translated by Mary Ling. London: SCM, 1956.

Dixsaut, Monique, ed. *Contre Platon,* 2 vols. Tradition de la Pensée Classique. Paris: Librairie Philosophique J. Vrin, 1993.

Dodd, C. H. *The Epistle of Paul to the Romans.* London: Fontana, 1959.

Donfried, Karl P. "False Presuppositions in the Study of Romans," Pp. 102–24 in *The Romans Debate.* Edited by Donfried.

————, ed. *The Romans Debate.* Revised and Expanded Edition. Peabody, Mass.: Hendrickson, 1991.

Doty, W. *Letters in Primitive Christianity.* Philadelphia, 1973.

Droge, Arthur J. *Homer or Moses? Early Christian Interpretations of the History of Culture.* HUT 26. Tübingen: J. C. B. Mohr (Paul Siebeck), 1989.

Droge Arthur J., and James D. Tabor. *A Noble Death: Suicide and Martyrdom among Christians and Jews in Antiquity.* San Francisco: HarperCollins, 1992.

Dungan, David L. *The Sayings of Jesus in the Churches of Paul: The Use of the Synoptic Tradition in the Regulation of Early Church Life.* Philadelphia: Fortress, 1971.

Dunn, James D. G. *Jesus and the Spirit.* Philadelphia: Westminster, 1975.

————. "Rom. 7:14–25 in the Theology of Paul," *TZ* 31 (1975): 257–73.

————. *Romans 1–8.* WBC 38A. Dallas: Word, 1988.

Dupont, J. "La structure oratoire du discours d'Étienne (Actes 7)." *Bib* 66 (1985): 153–67.

Eagleton, Terry. *Literary Theory: An Introduction.* Minneapolis: University of Minneapolis Press, 1983.

Easterling, P. E. "Constructing Character in Greek Tragedy." Pp. 83–99 in *Characterization and Individuality in Greek Literature.* Edited by Pelling.

Edlow, Robert Blair. *Galen on Language and Ambiguity: An English Translation of Galen's De Captionibus (On Fallacies) with Introduction, Text, and Commentary.* Philosophia Antiqua 31. Leiden: E. J. Brill, 1977.

Elliott, Neil. *The Rhetoric of Romans: Argumentative Constraint and Strategy and Paul's Dialogue with Judaism*. JSNTSup 45. Sheffield: Sheffield Academic Press, 1990.

Ellis, E. Earle. *Prophecy and Hermeneutic in Early Christianity*. Grand Rapids: Baker, 1993.

Engberg-Pedersen, Troels, ed. *Paul in His Hellenistic Context*. Minneapolis: Fortress, 1995.

———. *Paul and the Stoics*. Edinburgh: T. & T. Clark, 2000.

Epp, Eldon Jay. "Jewish-Gentile Continuity in Paul: Torah and/or Faith (Romans 9:1–5)." *HTR* 79 (1986): 80–90.

Epp, E. J., and G. W. McRae, eds. *The New Testament and its Modern Interpreters*. Atlanta: Scholars, 1989.

Erickson, K. *Plato: True and Sophistic Rhetoric*. Studies in Classical Antiquity 3. Amsterdam: Rodopi, 1979.

Evans, Craig A., and James A. Sanders, eds., *Paul and the Scriptures of Israel*. JSNTSup 83. Sheffield: Sheffield Academic Press, 1993.

Farmer, W. R., C. F. D. Moule, and R. R. Niebuhr. *Christian History and Interpretation: Studies Presented to John Knox*. Cambridge: Cambridge University Press, 1967.

Fee, Gordon D. *The First Epistle to the Corinthians*. NICNT. Grand Rapids: Eerdmans, 1987.

Field, Guy Cromwell. "Sophist." *OCD* 1000.

Fiore, Benjamin. " 'Covert Allusion' in 1 Corinthians 1–4." *CBQ* 47 (1985): 85–104.

———. *The Function of Personal Example in the Socratic and Pastoral Epistles*. AnBib 105. Rome: Biblical Institute Press, 1986.

———. "Passion in Paul and Plutarch: 1 Corinthians 5–6 and the Polemic Against Epicureans." Pp. 135–43 in *Greeks, Romans, and Christians*. Edited by Balch, Ferguson, and Meeks.

Fish, Stanley. *Doing What Comes Naturally*. Durham and London: Duke University Press, 1989.

———. *Is There a Text in This Class: The Authority of Interpretive Communities*. Cambridge: Harvard University Press, 1980.

———. *There's No Such Thing as Free Speech and It's a Good Thing, Too*. New York and Oxford: Oxford University Press, 1994.

Fitzmyer, Joseph A. *The Gospel According to Luke*. AB 28A. New York: Doubleday, 1985.

Forbes, Christopher. "Comparison, Self-Praise and Irony: Paul's Boasting and the Conventions of Hellenistic Rhetoric." *NTS* 32 (1986): 1–30.

Fortna, Robert T., and Beverly R. Gaventa, eds. *The Conversation Continues: Studies in Paul and John In Honor of J. Louis Martyn*. Nashville: Abingdon, 1990.

Foucault, Michel. *Power/Knowledge: Selected Interviews and Other Writings 1972–1979*. New York: Pantheon, 1980.

Franklin, Eric. *Luke: Interpreter of Paul, Critic of Matthew*. JSNTSup 92. Sheffield: JSOT, 1994.

Fudge, E. "Paul's Apostolic Self-Consciousness in Athens." *JETS* 14 (1971): 193–98.

Furnish, V. P. *II Corinthians*. AB 32A. New York: Doubleday, 1984.

———. "Development in Paul's Thought." *JAAR* 48 (1986): 289–303.

———. "Pauline Studies." Pp. 321–50 in *The New Testament and its Modern Interpreters*. Edited by Epp and McRae.

Gagarin, Michael. "Probability and Persuasion: Plato and Early Greek Rhetoric." Pp. 46–68 in *Persuasion: Greek Rhetoric in Action*. Edited by Worthington.

Gagarin, Michael, and Paul Woodruff, eds. *Early Greek Political Thought from Homer to the Sophists*. Cambridge: Cambridge University Press, 1995.

Gamble, Harry. *The Textual History of the Letter to the Romans*. SD 42. Grand Rapids: Eerdmans, 1977.

Garlington, Don B. *The Obedience of Faith: A Pauline Phrase in Historical Context*. WUNT 2.38. Tübingen: J. C. B. Mohr (Paul Siebeck), 1991.

Gärtner, Bertil. *The Areopagus Speech and Natural Revelation*. Translated by Carolyn Hannay King. ASNU 21. Uppsala: Almqvist & Wiksell, 1955.

Gasque, W. Ward. *A History of the Interpretation of the Acts of the Apostles*. 2d ed. Peabody, Mass.: Hendrickson, 1989.

———. "The Speeches of Acts: Dibelius Reconsidered." In *New Dimensions in New Testament Study*, ed. Longenecker and Tenney.

Gasque, W., and Martin, R., eds. *Apostolic History and the Gospel*. Grand Rapids: Eerdmans, 1970.

Gaston, Lloyd. *Paul and the Torah*. Vancouver: University of British Columbia Press, 1987.

Gempf, Conrad. "Public Speaking and Published Accounts." Pp. 259–304 in *The Book of Acts in Its Ancient Literary Setting*. Vol. 1 of *The Book of Acts in Its First Century Setting*. Edited by Winter and Clarke.

Georgi, Dieter. *The Opponents of Paul in Second Corinthians*. Philadelphia: Fortress, 1986.

Gill, Christopher. "The Character-Personality Distinction." Pp. 1–31 in *Characterization and Individuality in Greek Literature*. Edited by Christopher Pelling.

Given, Mark D. "Not Either/Or but Both/And in Paul's Areopagus Speech." *BibInt* 3.3 (1995): 356–72.

———. "Restoring Paul's Inheritance in Romans 11:1." *JBL* 118.1 (1999): 89–96.

———. "The Unknown Paul: Philosophers and Sophists in Acts 17." Pp. 343–51 in SBLSP 35. Atlanta: Scholars Press, 1996.

———. "True Rhetoric: Ambiguity, Cunning, and Deception in Pauline Discourse." Pp. 526–50 in SBLSP 36. Atlanta: Scholars Press, 1997.

Glad, Clarence. *Paul and Philodemus: Adaptability in Epicurean and Early Christian Psychagogy*. NovTSup 81. Leiden: E. J. Brill, 1995.

Gleason, Maud W. *Making Men: Sophists and Self-Presentation in Ancient Rome*. Princeton: Princeton University Press, 1995.

Goldhill, Simon. "Character and Action, Representation and Reading: Greek Tragedy and its Critics." Pp. 100–127 in *Characterization and Individuality in Greek Literature*. Edited by Pelling.

Gooch, Paul W. *Dangerous Food: 1 Corinthians 8–10 in Its Context*. ESCJ 5. Waterloo: Wilfrid Laurier University Press, 1993.

———. *Partial Knowledge: Philosophical Studies in Paul*. Notre Dame: University of Notre Dame Press, 1987.

Gowler, David B. *Host, Guest, Enemy, and Friend: Portraits of the Pharisees in Luke and Acts*. ESEC 1. New York: Peter Lang, 1991.

Grant, F. C. *Roman Hellenism and the New Testament*. Edinburgh: Oliver & Boyd, 1962.

Grässer, Erich, and Otto Merk, eds. *Glaube und Eschatologie*. Tübingen: J. C. B. Mohr, 1985.

Gregory, C. R., et al., eds. *Theologische Studien J. Weis*. Göttingen: Vandenhoeck & Ruprecht, 1897.

Griffiths, J. G. "Was Damaris an Egyptian? (Acts 17:34)." *BZ* 8 (1964): 293–95.

Grundmann, Walter. "ἐγκακέω." *TDNT* 3:486.

Gundry, Robert H. "The Moral Frustration of Paul before his Conversion: Sexual Lust in Romans 7:7–25." Pp. 228–45 in *Pauline Studies*. Edited by Hagner and Harris.

Hadas, Moses, and Morton Smith. *Heroes and Gods: Spiritual Biographies in Antiquity*. Religious Perspectives 13. London: Routledge and Kegan Paul, 1965.

Haenchen, Ernst. *The Acts of the Apostles: A Commentary*. Translated by Hugh Anderson and R. McL. Wilson. Philadelphia: Westminster, 1971.

Hafemann, Scott J. *Paul, Moses, and the History of Israel: The Letter/Spirit Contrast and the Argument from Scripture in 2 Corinthians 3*. Peabody, Mass.: Hendrickson, 1996.

Hägg, Tomas. *The Novel in Antiquity*. Oxford: Basil Blackwell, 1983.

Hagner, Donald A., and Murray J. Harris, eds. *Pauline Studies: Essays presented to Professor F. F. Bruce on his 70th Birthday*. Grand Rapids: Eerdmans, 1980.

Hallett, Judith P., and Thomas Van Nortwick, eds. *Compromising Traditions: The Personal Voice in Classical Scholarship*. New York: Routledge, 1997.

Halliwell, Stephen. "Philosophy and Rhetoric." Pp. 222–43 in *Persuasion*. Edited by Worthington.

———. "Traditional Greek Conceptions of Character." Pp. 32–59 in *Characterization and Individuality in Greek Literature*. Edited by Pelling.

Hanson, Anthony T. *Studies in Paul's Technique and Theology*. Grand Rapids: Eerdmans, 1974.

Harris, R. "Did St. Paul Quote Euripides?" *ExpTim* 31 (1919–20): 31ff.

Harrisville, Roy A., and Walter Sundberg. *The Bible in Modern Culture: Theology and Historical-Critical Method from Spinoza to Käsemann*. Grand Rapids: Eerdmans, 1995.

Hawkin, David J., and Tom Robinson. *Self-Definition and Self-Discovery in Early Christianity: A Study in Changing Horizons: Essays in Appreciation of Ben F.*

Meyer from Former Students. Studies in the Bible and Early Christianity 26. Lewiston, N.Y.: Edwin Mellen, 1990.

Hays, Richard B. *Echoes of Scripture in the Letters of Paul.* New Haven: Yale University Press, 1989.

———. *First Corinthians.* IBC. Louisville: John Knox, 1997.

———. " 'The Righteous One' as Eschatological Deliverer: A Case Study in Paul's Apocalyptic Hermeneutics." Pp. 191–216 in *Apocalyptic and the New Testament.* Edited by Marcus and Soards.

Hemer, C. J. "Luke the Historian." *BJRL* 60.1 (Autumn 1977): 28–51.

Hengel, Martin. *Acts and the History of Earliest Christianity.* London: SCM, 1979.

———. *Between Jesus and Paul.* Philadelphia: Fortress, 1983.

———. *The "Hellenization" of Judaea in the First Century after Christ.* Translated by John Bowden. London and Philadelphia: SCM and Trinity Press International, 1989.

Henry, Matthew. *Acts to Revelation.* Vol. 6 of *Matthew Henry's Commentary on the Whole Bible.* New Modern Edition. Peabody, Mass.: Hendrickson, 1996.

Hock, R. F. *The Social Context of Paul's Ministry.* Philadelphia: Fortress, 1980.

Hommel, Hildebrecht. "Neue Forschungen zur Areopagrede Acta 17." *ZNW* 46 (1955): 145–78.

———. "Herrenworte im Lichte sokratischer Ueberlieferung." *ZNW* 57 (1966): 1–23.

Hooker, Morna D. "Beyond the Things That Are Written? St. Paul's Use of Scripture." *NTS* 27 (1981): 295–309.

Hübner, Hans. "καταργέω." *EDNT* 2:267–68.

Hulse, James W. *The Reputations of Socrates: The Afterlife of a Gadfly.* Revisioning Philosophy 23. New York: Peter Lang, 1995.

Hyatt, J. Philip, ed. *The Bible and Modern Scholarship: Papers Read at the 100th Meeting of the Society of Biblical Literature.* Nashville: Abingdon, 1965.

Ingraffia, Brian D. *Postmodern Theory and Biblical Theology: Vanquishing God's Shadow.* Cambridge: Cambridge University Press, 1995.

Jackson, F. Foakes, and Kirsopp Lake. *The Beginnings of Christianity.* 5 vols. Grand Rapids: Eerdmans, 1966.

Jervis, L. Ann, and Peter Richardson, eds. *Gospel in Paul: Studies on Corinthians, Galatians and Romans for Richard N. Longenecker.* JSNTSup 108. Sheffield: Sheffield Academic Press, 1994.

Jewett, Robert. "Following the Argument of Romans." Pp. 265–77 in *The Romans Debate.* Edited by Donfried.

———. "Romans as an Ambassadorial Letter." *Int* 36 (January 1982): 5–20.

———. *The Thessalonian Correspondence: Pauline Rhetoric and Millenarian Piety.* Philadelphia: Fortress, 1986.

Johnson, Luke Timothy. *The Acts of the Apostles.* SP 5. Collegeville, Minn.: Liturgical Press, 1992.

Judge, Edwin A. "The Early Christians as a Scholastic Community." *JRH* 1 (1961): 4–15.

———. "The Early Christians as a Scholastic Community: Part II." *JRH* 1.3 (1961): 125–37.

———. "Paul's Boasting in Relation to Contemporary Professional Practice." *ABR* 16 (1968): 37–50.

———. *The Social Pattern of Christian Groups in the First Century.* London: Tyndale, 1960.

———. "St. Paul and Classical Society." *JAC* 15 (1972): 19–36.

———. "St. Paul and Socrates." *Interchange* 13 (1973): 106–16.

Karris, Robert J. "The Background and Significance of the Polemic of the Pastoral Epistles." *JBL* 92:4 (1973): 549–64.

———. "The Occasion of Romans: A Response to Professor Donfried." Pp. 125–27 in *The Romans Debate.* Edited by Donfried.

———. "Romans 14:1–15:3 and the Occasion of Romans." Pp. 65–84 in *The Romans Debate.* Edited by Donfried.

Käsemann, Ernst. *An die Römer.* Tübingen: Mohr, 1973.

———. *Commentary on Romans.* Translated and edited by Geoffrey W. Bromiley. Grand Rapids: Eerdmans, 1980.

———. *New Testament Questions of Today.* Translated by W. J. Montague. Philadelphia: Fortress, 1969.

———. *Perspectives on Paul.* Translated by Margaret Kohl. Mifflintown: Sigler Press, 1996.

Keck, Leander, and Martyn, J. Louis, eds. *Studies in Luke-Acts.* Nashville: Abingdon, 1966.

Kee, Howard Clark. "Pauline Eschatology: Relationships with Apocalyptic and Stoic Thought." Pp. 131–58 in *Glaube und Eschatologie.* Edited by Grässer and Merk.

Kennedy, George A. *Aristotle On Rhetoric: A Theory of Civic Discourse.* New York and Oxford: Oxford University Press, 1991.

———. *Classical Rhetoric and Its Christian and Secular Tradition from Ancient to Modern Times.* Chapel Hill: The University of North Carolina Press, 1980.

———. *A New History of Classical Rhetoric.* Princeton: Princeton University Press, 1994.

———. *New Testament Interpretation through Rhetorical Criticism.* Chapel Hill and London: The University of North Carolina Press, 1984.

Kerford, G. B. *The Sophistic Movement.* Cambridge: Cambridge University Press, 1981.

———, ed. *The Sophists and Their Legacy.* Hermes: Zeitschrift für klassische Philologie 44. Wiesbaden: Franz Steiner Verlag, 1981.

Kern, Philip. *Rhetoric and Galatians: Assessing an Approach to Paul's Epistle.* SNTSMS 101. Cambridge: Cambridge University Press, 1998.

Kidd, Ian. "On Socrates' Personal Deity: Introduction." Pp. 294–307 in *Plutarch: Essays.* Translated by Robin Waterfield. London: Penguin, 1992.

Klein, Günther. "Paul's Purpose in Writing the Epistle to the Romans." Pp. 29–43 in *The Romans Debate.* Edited by Donfried.

Knox, John. *Marcion and the New Testament: An Essay in the Early History of the Canon.* Chicago: University of Chicago Press, 1942.

Knox, Wilfred L. *St. Paul and the Church of Jerusalem.* Cambridge: Cambridge University Press, 1925.

Koch, Klaus. *The Rediscovery of Apocalyptic: A Polemical Work on a Neglected Area of Biblical Studies and its Damaging Effects on Theology and Philosophy.* SBT 2.22. Translated by Margaret Kohl. London: SCM Press, 1972.

———. "Paul and Hellenism." Pp. 187–95 in *The Bible and Modern Scholarship: Papers Read at the 100th Meeting of the Society of Biblical Literature.* Edited by J. P. Hyatt.

Kovacs, Judith L. "The Archons, the Spirit, and the Death of Christ: Do We Need the Hypothesis of Gnostic Opponents to Explain 1 Corinthians 2.6–16?" Pp. 217–36 in *Apocalyptic and the New Testament.* Edited by Marcus and Soards.

Kraut, Richard, ed. *The Cambridge Companion to Plato.* Cambridge: Cambridge University Press, 1992.

Kümmel, W. G. *Römer 7 und die Bekehrung des Paulus.* Leipzig: Hinrichs, 1929.

Leitch, Vincent B. *Deconstructive Criticism: An Advanced Introduction.* New York: Columbia University Press, 1983.

Levinskaya, Irina. *The Book of Acts in Its Diaspora Setting.* Vol. 5 of *The Book of Acts in Its First Century Setting.* Edited by Winter.

Levison, John R. "The Angelic Spirit in Early Judaism." Pp 464–93 in *SBLSP* 34. Atlanta: Scholars Press, 1995.

Lévi-Strauss, Claude. *Tristes Tropiques.* Translated by John and Doreen Weightman, New York: Atheneum, 1984.

Litfin, Duane. *St. Paul's Theology of Proclamation: 1 Corinthians 1–4 and Greco-Roman Rhetoric.* SNTSMS 79. Cambridge: Cambridge University Press, 1994.

Long, A. A. *Hellenistic Philosophy: Stoics, Epicureans, Sceptics.* 2d ed. Berkeley: University of California Press, 1986.

Longenecker, Richard N., and Merrill C. Tenney. *New Dimensions in New Testament Study.* Grand Rapids: Zondervan, 1974.

Long, A. A., and D. N. Sedley. *The Hellenistic Philosophers,* 2 vols. Cambridge: Cambridge University Press, 1987.

Lüdemann, Gerd. *Heretics: The Other Side of Early Christianity.* Louisville: Westminster John Knox, 1996.

Lyons, George. *Pauline Autobiography: Toward a New Understanding.* Atlanta: Scholars Press, 1985.

Maccoby, Hyam. *The Mythmaker: Paul and the Invention of Christianity.* London: Weidenfeld & Nicolson, 1986.

———. *Paul and Hellenism.* London and Philadelphia: SCM and Trinity, 1991.

MacDonald, Dennis Ronald. *The Legend and the Apostle: The Battle for Paul in Story and Canon.* Philadelphia: Westminster, 1983.

Mack, Burton. *Rhetoric and the New Testament.* Minneapolis: Fortress, 1990.

Malherbe, Abraham J. "Greco-Roman Religion and Philosophy and the New Testament." Pp. 3–26 in *The New Testament and its Modern Interpreters*. Edited by Epp and McRae.

———. "Hellenistic Moralists and the New Testament." In *ANRW* 2.26.1. Edited by Wolfgang Haase. Berlin and New York: de Gruyter, 1988.

———. *Paul and the Popular Philosophers*. Minneapolis: Augsburg Fortress, 1989.

Malina, Bruce J., and Jerome H. Neyrey. *Portraits of Paul: An Archaeology of Ancient Personality*. Louisville: Westminster John Knox, 1996.

Marcus, Joel. "Paul at the Areopagus: Window on the Hellenistic World." *BTB* 18 (October 1988): 143–48.

Marcus, Joel, and Marion L. Soards. *Apocalyptic and the New Testament: Essays in Honor of J. Louis Martyn*. JSNTSup 24. Sheffield: Sheffield Academic Press, 1989.

Marshall, Peter. *Enmity in Corinth: Social Conventions in Paul's Relations with the Corinthians*. WUNT 2.23. Tübingen: J. C. B. Mohr, 1987.

Martin, Dale B. *The Corinthian Body*. New Haven: Yale University Press, 1995.

———. *Slavery as Salvation: The Metaphor of Slavery in Pauline Christianity*. New Haven: Yale University Press, 1990.

Martyn, J. Louis. *Galatians*. AB 33A. New York: Doubleday, 1997.

———. *Theological Issues in the Letters of Paul*. Nashville: Abingdon, 1997.

Mason, Steven. "Paul, Classical Anti-Jewish Polemic, and the Letter to the Romans." Pp. 181–223 in *Self-Definition and Self-Discovery in Early Christianity: A Study in Changing Horizons*. Edited by Hawkin and Robinson.

Matill, A. J. "The Paul-Jesus Parallels and the Purpose of Luke-Acts: C. H. Evans Reconsidered," *NovT* 17 (1975): 15–45.

May, James M. *Trials of Character: The Eloquence of Ciceronian Ethos*. Chapel Hill: University of North Carolina Press, 1988.

Mays, James L. *Harper's Bible Commentary*. San Francisco: Harper & Row, 1988.

Meeks, Wayne A. "The Christian Proteus." In *The Writings of St. Paul*. Edited by Meeks.

———. *The First Urban Christians: The Social World of the Apostle Paul*. New Haven and London: Yale University Press, 1983.

———, ed. *The Writings of St. Paul*. New York: W. W. Norton, 1972.

Meyer, Paul W. "Romans." Pp. 1130–33 in *Harper's Bible Commentary*. Edited by James L. Mays.

———. "The Worm at the Core of the Apple: Exegetical Reflections on Romans 7." Pp. 62–84 in *The Conversation Continues*. Edited by Fortna and Gaventa.

Middendorf, Michael Paul. *The "I" in the Storm: A Study of Romans 7*. Saint Louis: Concordia Academic Press, 1997.

Mills, Kevin. *Justifying Language: Paul and Contemporary Literary Theory*. New York: St. Martin's, 1995.

Minear, Paul S. *The Obedience of Faith: The Purposes of Paul in the Epistle of the Romans*. SBT 2/19; London: SCM, 1971.

Mitchell, Margaret. *The Heavenly Trumpet: John Chrysostom and the Art of Pauline Interpretation.* HUT 40. Tübingen: J. C. B. Mohr, 2000.

———. *Paul and the Rhetoric of Reconciliation: An Exegetical Investigation of the Language and Composition of 1 Corinthians.* Louisville: Westminster John Knox, 1993.

———. "ποικίλος τις καὶ παντοδαπός ('A Variable and Many-sorted Man'): John Chrysostom's Treatment of Pauline Inconsistency." Paper presented at annual meeting of the AAR/SBL. Philadelphia, November 1995.

Moellering, H. Armin. "Deisidaimonia, a Footnote to Acts 17:22." *Concordia Theological Monthly* 34.8 (August 1963): 466–71.

Montuori, Mario. *The Socratic Problem: The History — The Solutions.* Amsterdam: J. C. Gieben, 1992.

Moore, Stephen D. *God's Gym: Divine Male Bodies of the Bible.* New York: Routledge, 1996.

———. *Mark and Luke in Poststructuralist Perspectives.* New Haven and London: Yale University Press, 1992.

———. *Poststructuralism and the New Testament: Derrida and Foucault at the Foot of the Cross.* Minneapolis: Fortress, 1994.

Moores, John D. *Wrestling with Rationality in Paul: Romans 1–8 in a New Perspective.* SNTSMS 82. Cambridge: Cambridge University Press, 1995.

Morgan, Michael L. "Plato and Greek Religion." Pp. 227–47 in *The Cambridge Companion to Plato.* Edited by Kraut.

Morland, Kjell Arne. *The Rhetoric of Curse in Galatians: Paul Confronts Another Gospel.* ESEC 5. Atlanta: Scholars Press, 1995.

Nanos, Mark D. *The Mystery of Romans: The Jewish Context of Paul's Letter.* Minneapolis: Fortress, 1996.

Nauck, Wolfgang. "Die Tradition und Komposition der Areopagrede." *ZTK* 53 (1956): 11–52.

Neusner, Jacob, ed. *The Social World of Formative Christianity and Judaism: Essays in Tribute to Howard Clark Kee.* Philadelphia: Fortress, 1998.

Neyrey, Jerome. *Paul, In Other Words: A Cultural Reading of his Letters.* Louisville: Westminster John Knox, 1990.

Norden, Eduard. *Agnostos Theos: Untersuchungen zur Formengeschichte religiöser Rede.* Stuttgart: B. G. Teubner Verlagsgesellschaft, 1956.

Ober, Josiah, and Barry Strauss. "Drama, Political Rhetoric, and the Discourse of Athenian Democracy." Pp. 237–70 in *Nothing to Do with Dionysos? Athenian Drama in Its Social Context.* Edited by Winkler and Zeitlin.

Oepke, Albrecht. "ἀνίστημι, ἐξανίστημι." *TDNT* 1:368–72.

Olbricht, Thomas H., and Jerry L. Sumney, eds. *Paul and Pathos.* SBLSS 16. Atlanta: SBL Press, 2001.

Olbricht, Thomas H., Walter Übelacker, and Anders Eriksson. *Rhetorical Argumentation in Biblical Texts.* Harrisburg, Pa.: Trinity Press International, 2001.

Padel, Ruth. "Making Space Speak." Pp. 336–65 in *Nothing to Do with Dionysos? Athenian Drama in Its Social Context.* Edited by Winkler and Zeitlin.

Pagels, Elaine. *The Gnostic Paul.* Philadelphia: Trinity Press International, 1992.

Patte, Daniel. *The Gospel According to Matthew: A Structural Commentary on Matthew's Faith.* Philadelphia: Fortress, 1987.

Patton, J., and Vernon Robbins. "Rhetoric and Biblical Criticism." *Quarterly Journal of Speech* 66 (1980): 327–36.

Pelling, Christopher, ed. *Characterization and Individuality in Greek Literature.* Oxford: Clarendon, 1990.

Penna, Romano. *Paul the Apostle.* 2 vols. Collegeville, Minn.: Liturgical Press, 1996.

Pervo, Richard I. *Profit with Delight: The Literary Genre of the Acts of the Apostles.* Philadelphia: Fortress, 1987.

Pfitzner, Victor C. *Paul and the Agon Motif: Traditional Athletic Imagery in the Pauline Literature.* NovTSup 16. Leiden: Brill, 1967.

Plank, Karl A. *Paul and the Irony of Affliction.* Atlanta: Scholars, 1987.

Plochmann, George Kimball, and Franklin E. Robinson. *A Friendly Companion to Plato's Gorgias.* Carbondale: Southern Illinois University Press, 1988.

Plümacher, Eckhard. *Lukas als hellenistischer Schriftsteller: Studien zur Apostelgeschichte.* SUNT 9. Göttingen: Vandenhoeck & Ruprecht, 1972.

Plutarch. *De genio Socratis.* Translated by Robin Waterfield. Pp. 308–58 in Plutarch, *Essays.* London: Penguin, 1992.

———. *Essays.* Translated by Robin Waterfield. Introduced and annotated by Ian Kidd. London: Penguin, 1992.

Pogoloff, Stephen M. *Logos and Sophia: The Rhetorical Situation of 1 Corinthians.* SBLDS 134. Atlanta: Scholars Press, 1992.

Pohlenz, Max. *Paulus und die Stoa.* Reihe Libelli 101. Darmstadt: Wissenschaftliche Buchgesellschaft, 1964.

Polhill, James B. *Acts.* NAC 26. Nashville: Broadman, 1992.

Porter, Stanley, and David Tombs, eds. *Approaches to New Testament Study.* JSNTSup 120. Sheffield: Sheffield Academic Press, 1995.

Porter, Stanley. "Literary Approaches to the New Testament: From Formalism to Deconstruction and Back." Pp. 77–128 in *Approaches to New Testament Study.* Edited by Porter and Tombs.

Radl, Walter. *Paulus und Jesus im lukanischen Doppelwerk: Untersuchungen zu Parallelmotiven im Lukasevangelium und in der Apostelgeschichte.* Frankfurt: Peter Lang, 1975.

Räisänen, Heikki. "Paul, God and Israel: Romans 9–11 in Recent Research." Pp. 178–206 in *The Social World of Formative Christianity and Judaism.* Edited by Jacob Neusner.

———. *Paul and the Law.* Philadelphia: Fortress, 1983.

Rankin, H. D. *Sophists, Socratics, and Cynics.* Totowa, N.J.: Barnes & Noble Books, 1983.

Rapske, Brian. *Paul in Roman Custody.* Vol. 3 of *The Book of Acts in Its First Century Setting.* Edited by Winter.

Richardson, Peter. *Paul's Ethic of Freedom.* Philadelphia: Westminster, 1979.

————. "Pauline Inconsistency: 1 Corinthians 9:19–23 and Galatians 2:11–14." *NTS* 26 (1980): 347–62.

Rickert, B. "Review of Gregory Vlastos's *Socrates: Ironist and Moral Philosopher.*" *Bryn Mawr Classical Review* 3.3.20 (1992). Cited January 6, 2001. Online: http://ccat.sas.upenn.edu/bmcr/1992/03.03.20.html.

Riddel, Joseph N. "Re-doubling the Commentary." *Contemporary Literature* 20 (Spring, 1979):237–50.

Robbins, Vernon K. *The Tapestry of Early Christian Discourse: Rhetoric, Society, and Ideology.* New York: Routledge, 1996.

————. *Jesus the Teacher: A Socio-Rhetorical Interpretation of Mark.* Minneapolis: Fortress, 1992.

Robertson, A. T. *Word Pictures in the New Testament.* Nashville: Broadman, 1930.

Romilly, Jacqueline de. *The Great Sophists in Periclean Athens.* Translated by Janet Lloyd. Oxford: Clarendon Press, 1992.

Rorty, Amélie Oksenberg, ed. *Essays on Aristotle's* Rhetoric. Berkeley: University of California Press, 1996.

Rose, Martin. "Names of God in the OT." ABD 4:1003.

Rosen, Stanley. *Plato's Sophist: The Drama of Original and Image.* New Haven and London: Yale University Press, 1983.

Rue, Loyal D. *By the Grace of Guile: The Role of Deception in Natural History and Human Affairs.* Oxford: Oxford University Press, 1994.

Russell, D. A. "*Ethos* in Oratory and Rhetoric." Pp. 197–212 in *Characterization and Individuality in Greek Literature.* Edited by Pelling.

Sanders, E. P. *Paul and Palestinian Judaism: A Comparison of Patterns of Religion.* Minneapolis: Fortress, 1977.

————. *Paul, the Law, and the Jewish People.* Minneapolis: Fortress, 1983.

Sanders, Jack T. *The Jews in Luke-Acts.* Philadelphia: Fortress, 1987.

Sandmel, Samuel. *The Genius of Paul. A Study in History.* Philadelphia: Fortress, 1979.

Satterthwaite, Philip E. "Acts Against the Background of Classical Rhetoric." Pp. 337–80 in *The Book of Acts in Its Ancient Literary Setting.* Vol. 1 of *The Book of Acts in Its First Century Setting.* Edited by Winter and Clarke.

Schneider, Bernardin. "The Meaning of St. Paul's Thesis 'The Letter and the Spirit.' " *CBQ* 15 (1953): 163–207.

Schoedel, William R., and Robert L. Wilken, eds. *Early Christian Literature and the Classical Intellectual Tradition.* ThH 53. Paris: Éditions Beauchesne, 1979.

Schrenk, Gottlob. "γράμμα/γραφή." *TDNT* 1:768.

Schüssler-Fiorenza, Elisabeth. "Rhetorical Situation and Historical Reconstruction in 1 Corinthians." *NTS* 33 (1987): 386–403.

Schweitzer, Albert, *Mysticism of Paul the Apostle.* Translated by William Montgomery. London: Adam & Charles Black, 1953.

Schweizer, E. "Concerning the Speeches in Acts." Pp. 208–16 in *Studies in Luke-Acts.* Edited by Keck and Martyn.

Scott, James M. " 'For as Many as Are of Works of the Law Are Under a Curse' (Galatians 3:10)." Pp. 187–221 in *Paul and the Scriptures of Israel*. Edited by Evans and Sanders.

Scroggs, Robin. "Paul: Σοφός and Πνευματικός." *NTS* 14:1 (1967): 33–55.

Seeley, David. *Deconstructing the New Testament*. Biblical Interpretation Series 5. Leiden: Brill, 1994.

Seesemann, Heinrich. "παροξύνω, παροξυσμός." *TDNT* 5:857.

Segal, Alan F. *Paul the Convert: The Apostolate and Apostasy of Saul the Pharisee*. New Haven and London: Yale University Press, 1990.

Seim, Turid Karlsen. *The Double Message: Patterns of Gender in Luke-Acts*. Nashville: Abingdon, 1994.

Shaw, Graham. *The Cost of Authority: Manipulation and Freedom in the New Testament*. Philadelphia: Fortress, 1983.

Siker, Jeffrey S. *Disinheriting the Jews: Abraham in Early Christian Controversy*. Louisville: Westminster John Knox, 1991.

Smith, Robert W. *The Art of Rhetoric in Alexandria: Its Theory and Practice in the Ancient World*. The Hague: Martinus Nijhoff, 1974.

Soards, Marion L. "Seeking (*zētein*) and Sinning (*harmartōlos* and *hamartia*) according to Galatians 2.17." Pp. 237–54 in *Apocalyptic and the New Testament*. Edited by Marcus and Soards.

———. *The Speeches in Acts: Their Content, Context, and Concerns*. Louisville: Westminster John Knox, 1994.

Stamps, Dennis L. "Rhetorical Criticism of the New Testament: Ancient and Modern Evaluation of Argumentation." Pp. 77–128 in *Approaches to New Testament Study*. Edited by Porter and Tombs.

Stanley, Christopher D. *Paul and the Language of Scripture: Citation Technique in the Pauline Epistles and contemporary literature*. Cambridge: Cambridge University Press, 1992.

Stendahl, Krister. *Paul Among Jews and Gentiles and Other Essays*. Philadelphia: Fortress, 1976.

Stockhausen, Carol Kern. "2 Corinthians and the Principles of Pauline Exegesis." Pp. 143–64 in *Paul and the Scriptures of Israel*. Edited by Evans and Sanders.

———. *Moses' Veil and the Glory of the New Covenant: The Exegetical Substructure of II Cor. 3,1–4,6*. AnBib 116. Roma: Editrice Pontificio Istituto Biblico, 1989.

Stone, I. F. *The Trial of Socrates*. Boston and Toronto: Little, Brown and Company, 1988.

Stowers, Stanley Kent. "Comment: What Does *Unpauline* Mean?" Pp. 70–78 in *Paul and the Legacies of Paul*. Edited by Babcock.

———. *The Diatribe and Paul's Letter to the Romans*. SBLDS 57. Chico, Calif.: Scholars Press, 1981.

———. *Letter Writing in Greco-Roman Antiquity*. Chico, Calif.: Scholars, 1986.

———. *A Rereading of Romans: Justice, Jews, and Gentiles*. New Haven: Yale University Press, 1994.

Stuhlmacher, Peter. *Paul's Letter to the Romans: A Commentary.* Translated by Scott J. Hafemann. Louisville: Westminster John Knox, 1994.

Sturm, Richard E. "Defining the Word 'Apocalyptic': A Problem in Biblical Criticism." Pp. 17–48 in *Apocalyptic and the New Testament.* Edited by Marcus and Soards.

Sumney, Jerry L. *Identifying Paul's Opponents: The Question of Method in 2 Corinthians.* Sheffield: Sheffield Academic Press, 1990.

Tabor, James D. *Things Unutterable: Paul's Ascent to Paradise in its Greco-Roman, Judaic, and Early Christian Contexts.* Lanham, Md.: University Press of America, 1986.

Talbert, Charles H. *Literary Patterns, Theological Themes and the Genre of Luke-Acts.* SBLMS 20. Missoula, Mont.: Scholars, 1974.

———. "Luke-Acts." Pp. 297–320 in *The New Testament and its Modern Interpreters.* Edited by Epp and McRae. Atlanta: Scholars, 1989.

———, ed. *Perspectives on Luke-Acts.* Danville and Edinburgh: Association of Baptist Professors of Religion and T. & T. Clark, 1978.

———. *Reading Corinthians: A Literary and Theological Commentary on 1 and 2 Corinthians.* New York: Crossroad, 1987.

Tannehill, Robert C. *The Narrative Unity of Luke-Acts: A Literary Interpretation,* 2 vols. Philadelphia: Fortress, 1986.

———. "Rejection by Jews and Turning to the Gentiles: The Pattern of Paul's Mission in Acts." Pp. 83–101 in *Luke-Acts and the Jewish People.* Edited by Tyson.

Theissen, Gerd. *Psychological Aspects of Pauline Theology.* Translated by John P. Galvin. Philadelphia: Fortress, 1987.

Thielman, Frank. "The Coherence of Paul's View of the Law: The Evidence of First Corinthians." *NTS* 38 (1992): 235–53.

———. *From Plight to Solution: A Jewish Framework for Understanding Paul's View of the Law in Galatians and Romans.* NovTSup 61. Leiden: Brill, 1989.

Thomas, Carol G., and Edward Kent Webb. "From Orality to Rhetoric: An Intellectual Transformation." Pp. 3–25 in *Persuasion.* Edited by Worthington.

Tompkins, Jane P. "The Reader in History: The Changing Shape of the Literary Response." Pp. 201–32 in *Reader-Response Criticism: From Formalism to Post-Structuralism.* Edited by Tompkins.

———, ed. *Reader-Response Criticism: From Formalism to Post-Structuralism.* Baltimore and London: Johns Hopkins University Press, 1980.

Tyson, Joseph B. *Luke-Acts and the Jewish People: Eight Critical Perspectives.* Minneapolis: Augsburg, 1988.

Untersteiner, Mario. *The Sophists.* Translated by Kathleen Freeman. Oxford: Basil Blackwell, 1954.

Vanhoye, A., ed. *L'Apôtre Paul: Personnalité, style et conception du ministère.* BETL 73. Leuven: Leuven University, 1986.

Veltman, Fred. "The Defense Speeches of Paul in Acts." Pp. 243–56 in *Perspectives on Luke-Acts.* Edited by Talbert.

Verdenius, W. J. "Gorgias' Doctrine of Deception." Pp. 116–28 in *The Sophists and Their Legacy*. Edited by Kerferd.

Vernant, Jean-Pierre. "Ambiguity and Reversal: On the Enigmatic Structure of *Oedipus Rex*." Pp. 113–40 in *Myth and Tragedy in Ancient Greece*. Edited by Vernant and Vidal-Naquet.

———. "The Masked Dionysus of Euripides' *Bacchae*." Pp. 381–412 in *Myth and Tragedy in Ancient Greece*. Edited by Vernant and Vidal-Naquet.

———. "Tensions and Ambiguities in Greek Tragedy." Pp. 29–48 in *Myth and Tragedy in Ancient Greece*. Edited by Vernant and Vidal-Naquet.

Vernant, Jean-Pierre, and Pierre Vidal-Naquet. *Myth and Tragedy in Ancient Greece*. Translated by Janet Lloyd. New York: Zone Books, 1988.

Via, Dan. *Self-Deception and Wholeness in Paul and Matthew*. Minneapolis: Fortress, 1990.

Vickers, B. *In Defence of Rhetoric*. Oxford: Clarendon, 1988.

Vielhauer, P. "On the Paulinism of Acts." Pp. 33–50 in *Studies in Luke-Acts*. Edited by Keck and Martyn.

Vlastos, Gregory. *Socrates: Ironist and Moral Philosopher*. Ithaca: Cornell University Press, 1991.

Vogeli, A. "Lukas und Euripides," *TZ* 9 (1953): 415–38.

Vos, Johan S. "To Make the Weaker Argument Defeat the Stronger: Sophistical Argumentation in Paul's Letter to the Romans." In *Rhetorical Argumentation in Biblical Texts*. Edited by Olbricht, Übelacker, and Eriksson.

Wagner, J. Ross. " 'Not Beyond the Things Which are Written': A Call to Boast Only in the Lord (1 Cor 1:4.6)." *NTS* 44 (1998): 279–87.

Walcot, P. "Odysseus and the Art of Lying." *Ancient Society* 8 (1977): 1–19.

Walton, Douglas. *Fallacies Arising from Ambiguity*. Applied Logic Series 1. Dordrecht, Boston, London: Kluwer Academic Publishers, 1996.

Wardy, Robert. "Mighty Is the Truth and It Shall Prevail?" Pp. 56–87 in *Essays on Aristotle's* Rhetoric. Edited by Rorty.

Watson, Duane F. "1 Corinthians 10:23–11:1 in the Light of Greco-Roman Rhetoric: The Role of Rhetorical Questions." *JBL* 108 (1989): 301–18.

———, ed. *Persuasive Artistry: Studies in New Testament Rhetoric in Honor of George A. Kennedy*. JSNTSup 50. Sheffield: JSOT, 1991.

Watson, Francis. *Paul, Judaism, and the Gentiles: A Sociological Approach*. SNTSMS 56. Cambridge: Cambridge University Press, 1986.

Wedderburn, A. M. *The Reasons for Romans*. Studies of the New Testament and Its World. Edinburgh: T. & T. Clark, 1988.

Weiss, J. "Beiträge zur paulinischen Rhetorik." Pp. 165–247 in *Theologische Studien*. Edited by Gregory.

Wenham, David. "Acts and the Pauline Corpus II. The Evidence of Parallels." Pp. 215–58 in *The Book of Acts in Its Ancient Literary Settings*. Vol. 1 of *The Book of Acts in Its First Century Setting*. Edited by Winter and Clarke.

————. "The Christian Life: A Life of Tension? A Consideration of the Nature of Christian Experience in Paul." Pp. 80–94 in *Pauline Studies*. Edited by Hagner and Harris.

————. "The Paulinism of Acts Again: Two Historical Clues in 1 Thessalonians." *Themelios* 13 (January–February 1988): 53–55.

Westerholm, Stephen. *Israel's Law and the Church's Faith: Paul and His Recent Interpreters*. Grand Rapids: Eerdmans, 1988.

White, Hayden. *The Content of the Form: Narrative Discourse and Historical Representation*. Baltimore and London: Johns Hopkins, 1987.

Wiefel, Wolfgang. "The Jewish Community in Ancient Rome and the Origins of Roman Christianity." Pp. 85–101 in *The Romans Debate*. Edited by Donfried.

Wilder, A. *Early Christian Rhetoric*. Cambridge: Cambridge University Press, 1971.

Willis, Wendell. "An Apostolic Apologia? The Form and Function of 1 Corinthians 9." *JSNT* 24 (1985): 33–48.

Winkler, John J., and Froma I. Zeitlin. *Nothing to Do with Dionysos? Athenian Drama in Its Social Context*. Princeton: Princeton University Press, 1990.

Winter, Bruce W. "Official Proceedings and the Forensic Speeches in Acts 24–26." Pp. 305–36 in *The Book of Acts in Its Ancient Literary Setting*. Vol. 1 of *The Book of Acts in Its First Century Setting*. Edited by Winter.

————. *Philo and Paul among the Sophists*. SNTSMS 96. Cambridge: Cambridge University Press, 1997.

Winter, Bruce W., ed. *The Book of Acts in Its First Century Setting*. 6 vols. Grand Rapids: Eerdmans, 1993–.

Winter, Bruce W., and Andrew Clarke, eds. *The Books of Acts in Its Ancient Literary Setting*. Vol. 1 of *The Book of Acts in Its First Century Setting*. Grand Rapids: Eerdmans, 1993.

Wire, Antoinette Clark. *The Corinthian Women Prophets: A Reconstruction through Paul's Rhetoric*. Minneapolis: Fortress, 1990.

Witherington III, Ben. *The Acts of the Apostles: A Socio-Rhetorical Commentary*. Grand Rapids: Eerdmans, 1998.

————. *Conflict and Community in Corinth: A Socio-Rhetorical Commentary on 1 and 2 Corinthians*. Grand Rapids: Eerdmans, 1995.

Wordelman, Amy L. "The Gods Have Come Down: Images of Historical Lycaonia and the Literary Constructions of Acts 14." Ph.D. diss., Princeton University, 1994.

Worthington, Ian. "History and Oratorical Exploitation." Pp. 109–29 in *Persuasion: Greek Rhetoric in Action*. Edited by Worthington.

————, ed. *Persuasion: Greek Rhetoric in Action*. New York: Routledge, 1994.

Wuellner, Wilhelm. "Greek Rhetoric and Pauline Argumentation." Pp. 177–88 in *Early Christian Literature and the Classical Intellectual Tradition*. Edited by Schoedel and Wilken.

————. "Paul as Pastor: The Function of Rhetorical Questions in First Corinthians." Pp. 49–77 in *L'Apôtre Paul*. Edited by A. Vanhoye.

————. "Paul's Rhetoric of Argumentation in Romans: An Alternative to the Donfried-Karris Debate over Romans." In *The Romans Debate*. Edited by Donfried.

————. "Where is Rhetorical Criticism Taking Us?" *CBQ* 49 (1987): 448–63.

Young, Frances, and David F. Ford. *Meaning and Truth in 2 Corinthians*. London: SPCK, 1987.

Zeitlin, Fromma. "Playing the Other: Theater, Theatricality, and the Feminine in Greek Drama." Pp. 63–96 in *Nothing to Do with Dionysos? Athenian Drama in Its Social Context*. Edited by Winkler and Zeitlin.

Zerwick, Max, and Mary Grosvenor. *A Grammatical Analysis of the Greek New Testament*. Unabridged, Revised Edition in One Volume. Rome: Biblical Institute Press, 1981.

Ziesler, John. *Paul's Letter to the Romans*. Philadelphia: Trinity, 1989.

Zweck, Dean. "The *Exordium* of the Areopagus Speech, Acts 17.22,23." *NTS* 35 (1989): 94–103.

Index of
Ancient Sources and Scripture

NEW TESTAMENT

Index of
Authors and Subjects